The American Military
Mission to
China, 1941–1942

The American Military Mission to China, 1941–1942

Lend-Lease Logistics, Politics and the Tangles of Wartime Cooperation

WILLIAM G. GRIEVE

McFarland & Company, Inc., Publishers
Jefferson, North Carolina

LIBRARY OF CONGRESS CATALOGUING-IN-PUBLICATION DATA

Grieve, William G., 1937–
   The American Military Mission to China, 1941–1942 : Lend-Lease logistics, politics and the tangles of wartime cooperation / William G. Grieve.
      p.   cm.
   Includes bibliographical references and index.

   ISBN 978-0-7864-7556-8
   softcover : acid free paper ∞

   1. United States. Military Mission to China—History.
   2. Lend-lease operations (1941–1945) 3. United States—Relations—China.   4. China—Relations—United States.
   5. International cooperation—History—20th century.
   6. Military assistance, American—China—History—20th century.   7. World War, 1939–1945—Diplomatic history.   I. Title.
   D753.2.C6G75 2014
   940.54'25108913—dc23   2013045894

BRITISH LIBRARY CATALOGUING DATA ARE AVAILABLE

© 2014 William G. Grieve. All rights reserved

No part of this book may be reproduced or transmitted in any form or by any means, electronic or mechanical, including photocopying or recording, or by any information storage and retrieval system, without permission in writing from the publisher.

Front cover image: A Chinese soldier guards a line of American P-40 fighter planes (© 2014 Corbis Images)

Manufactured in the United States of America

McFarland & Company, Inc., Publishers
   Box 611, Jefferson, North Carolina 28640
      www.mcfarlandpub.com

To Susan: Everyone who knows Her knows why
and to
Charles F. Romanus: Scholar, Mentor, Friend

Table of Contents

Preface	1
Introduction	7
1. Creation of the Mission: Why AMMISCA Was Established	13
2. America Before the Lend-Lease Program: Isolationism and Anti-War Feelings	26
3. The Commanders: The Leaders of World War II in Asia	35
4. Culture Clash: The Historical Foundation of Sino-Western Relations	52
5. The Antecedents of the Burma-to-China Supply Route	74
6. Early East Asian Advisory Missions	88
7. Maintenance and Repairs on the Burma Road	96
8. The Mission's Involvement at Rangoon	100
9. Logistics Problems on the Burma Road	127
10. The Mission's Role in the American Volunteer Group	158
11. International Strategic Planning	179
12. The Culmination of AMMISCA	201

Epilogue	211
Chapter Notes	217
Bibliography	239
Index	249

Preface

I first became interested in things Chinese when as a small boy I accompanied my family once a year to Chicago's Chinatown for a banquet. The repast was provided by two Chinese-Americans, Oi Hing and his son Oi Hong, friends of my maternal grandparents. The Ois owned a laundry and had run afoul of some nativist Caucasians who in 1943 tried to cheat them out of their business. My grandfather was a physician on whose office walls I recall seeing several posters emphasizing the plight of wartime China. He intervened and the laundry remained in the Ois' hands. The annual dinner was their expression of gratitude. (I must admit, however, that to this day I am unable to eat sharks' fins!)

My undergraduate degree is in history, but it took me some time in the military and business worlds to determine that teaching would be my chosen field; graduate school was my next stop. Ph.D. studies permitted me to make the acquaintance of a wonderful man, Charles F. Romanus, coauthor of the official army history of the China-Burma-India theater. When I explained my quest for a doctoral thesis topic, his comment was, "I know just what you're looking for; you'll be fascinated." He was correct; the subject was the American Military Mission to China (AMMISCA). Their initial task was to order, obtain, and supervise the usage of American Lend-Lease to China. Mr. Romanus became my mentor and, as noted in the dedication, a particular friend.

Mr. Romanus directed me to people at the National Archives and wrote letters of introduction to several military personnel including major generals Haydon Boatner and Edward E. MacMorland. He also shared countless insights into people including Chiang Kai-shek, T.V. Soong, Madame Chiang, Lauchlin Currie, Major General Claire Chennault, Army Chief of Staff General George C. Marshall, and others. On more than one occasion we chatted at his kitchen table consuming the only compensation he would accept from me: Old Granddad 100 proof bourbon.

My original research took place in the 1970s. Thus I was able to make contact with several AMMISCA veterans who generously shared their experiences and personal diaries, and provided additional contacts. Mrs. John E. Ausland graciously provided me a copy of her husband's diary and Mrs. E. E. MacMorland sent me her husband's diary, with several comments about AMMISCA personnel she had known. Nevin Wetzel, with whom I carried on an extended correspondence, generously shared his many insights and also put me in touch with several other AMMISCA participants. AMMISCA medical officer Dr. William Jellison, provided information on the limitless medical problems, logistical and actual, on and around the Burma Road and railway projects. Major General Haydon Boatner warned me in his initial letter that he was not interested in "doing this sort of thing" (he believed he had been greatly maligned in Barbara Tuchman's book on Stilwell), but then proceeded to furnish detailed and candid accounts and assessments of several people and events, especially Lauchlin Currie. Neal Maurer, editor of *Ex-CBI Roundup*, put me in touch with several AMMISCA veterans. A note of thanks goes to Bill Martin, Bob Wildman, Otis Wildy, Richard Reddin and Sterling Wilson. These men, the "Friday Morning Hump Veterans," meet weekly for breakfast and reminiscences at the Decatur, Illinois, airport, and provided several insights.

After the thesis was accepted and I entered the realm of education the AMMISCA text was put aside, except for some limited research on a time-available basis at such places as the National Archives and the British Archives at Kew. The result is a more expanded and specific work than the basic study of several decades past.

The book is intended for those readers who are interested in a close-up account of the experience of the American Military Mission to China and to those who seek to broaden their knowledge of the China-Burma operational area as it evolved into the China-Burma-India (CBI) Theater. It will also appeal to the many people who enjoy delving into World War II military history, especially the less researched areas. The text is not meant to challenge the views of historians whose research covers related areas in depth; rather it is configured to provide a concise regional historical background and an examination of the first American military aid mission with an emphasis on the unique sequence of challenges it faced in a new, totally unfamiliar, sometimes alien cultural environment.

The text also relates the situational judgments, decisions, and actions and reactions of individuals in the unit. In sum, while not a sociological study, it is an overview of men new to war, assigned to a task where they were placed in an "overnight alliance" with people of considerably dissimilar race, ethics

Introduction

> Before Pearl Harbor our folklore about the country [China], our early contact, our aspirations and even our actions in the creation of national policy, had all been a bit unrealistic — that is, we have been rather remarkably vocal about our interests in China, but they had never seemed like vital interests. A curious gap had often emerged ... [which] reflected, no doubt, the gulf between American and Chinese ways and conditions.
>
> — John K. Fairbank,
> *The United States and China*

Soon after the Sino-Japanese conflict began in July 1937 it became apparent that unless China received considerable foreign support it would be unable to conduct anything but feeble, short-duration defensive operations. In the fall of 1937 Japanese intimidation forced the French to cease all arms shipments to China through French Indochina. The German and Italian military advisory missions left Chungking in 1938. Although Russia supplied some weaponry, manpower, and monetary loans, with the advent of war in Europe in September 1939 the Soviets ceased almost all support. China turned to Great Britain and the United States.

Britain was fighting to survive just as much as China. After 1940 the United Kingdom had no allies left. On battlefields in North Africa, Crete, and Europe, in the skies over the home islands, and across its crucial international supply lanes, British forces were stretched to the utmost limit of men and material. London's Asian focus was on preserving Britain's colonial empire. In the fall of 1940, however, the Japanese demanded that London close the main supply route north from Rangoon, the Burma Road, to all shipments of munitions and related materials. The overextended British had little choice but to acquiesce for three months. During that time an American war with Japan moved from possible to probable. But, according to China's President Chiang Kai-shek's American financial advisor, Arthur Young, the decision to

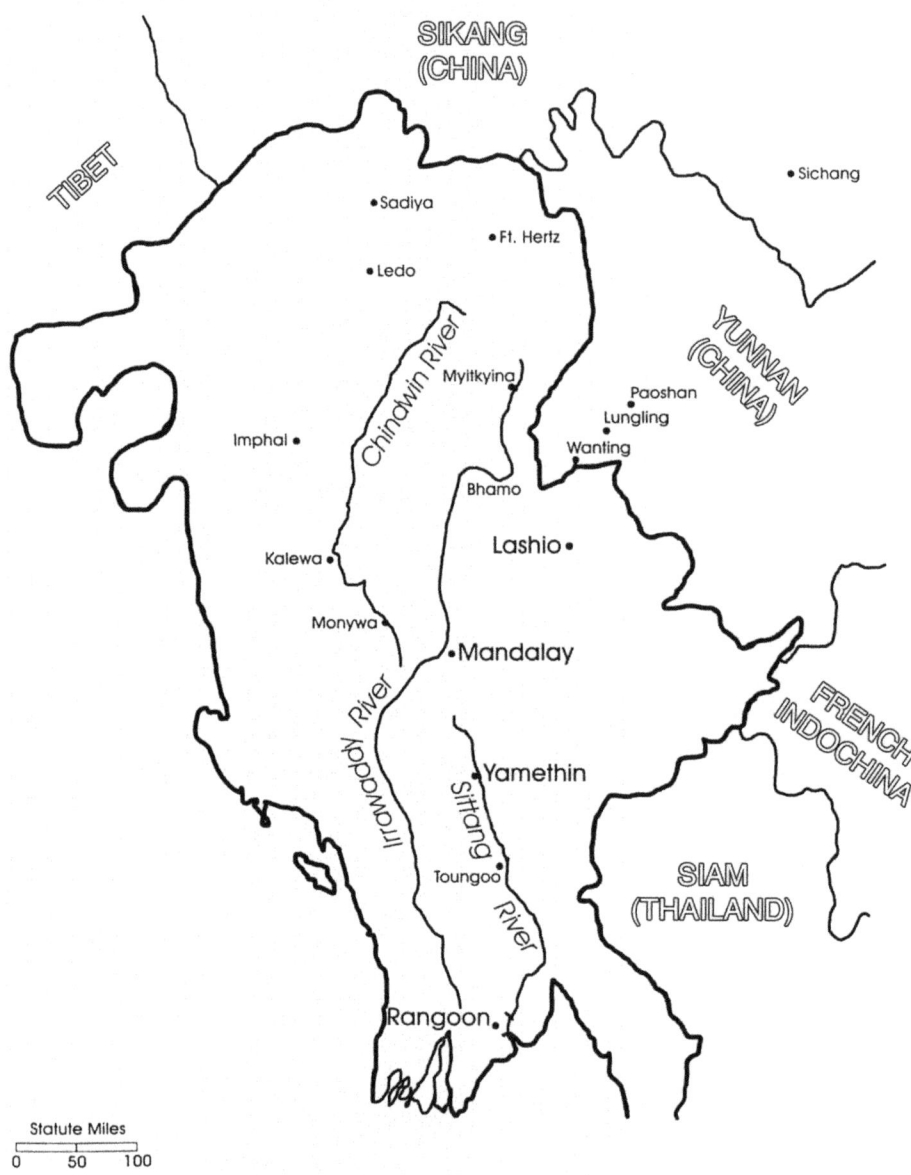

Northern Burma, circa 1938 (Jason Pankoke, 2011).

close the Burma Road, albeit strategically sound, motivated Chiang to declare that the British had done irreparable damage to their prestige in China, and "China would not soon forget."[1]

In America there was always some sympathy for China, usually induced by missionaries back in the States performing lecture and fund-raising activities. But many forces encouraged isolationism: disgust engendered by the failure of the Versailles Treaty to modify Great Power (including British and French) greed, the Great Depression, cultural and social variances, fear of alienating Japan, and the rise of Hitler in Europe. Moreover, in truth, America had never been a great friend to the Middle Kingdom; the United States had just never treated China as unjustly as other nations had.[2]

In the spring of 1941, due primarily to continued German expansion in Europe, a convergence of forces brought congressional passage of the Lend-Lease bill. Compared to Britain, China's needs were regarded as diminutive, but that nation's military opposition to Japan was critical. The Japanese could not be allowed to employ their vast China army of twenty-three divisions and twenty independent brigades, numbering in the neighborhood of one and a half million men.[3] The United States would need a stable basis for future Sino-American military cooperation if war with Japan should come; and there was also a dollop of compassion because of Japanese atrocities at Nanking and elsewhere. These circumstances induced the War Department and others to recommend the dispatch of a military mission to China.[4]

The mission was assigned the responsibility of coordinating Lend-Lease requests, assuring that Lend-Lease supplies were properly ordered and employed, and, along with several other tasks, providing support and coordination for the American Volunteer Group (AVG). On 3 July 1941, Army Chief of Staff General George C. Marshall, gave his approval to the establishment of the American Military Mission to China (AMMISCA).[5] After considering several general officers, including Joseph Stilwell and Hugh Drum (the army's highest ranking unassigned general), Marshall decided the unit would be commanded by Brigadier General John M. Magruder, who in the 1920s had served in China with Marshall.

The dispatch of AMMISCA initiated numerous World War II relationships and logistical and communications policies that reached from Chungking to Rangoon and Calcutta, to London and Washington. The unit quickly became immersed in a unique world condition: powerful military nations with disparate racial, economic, ethical, and ethnic creeds and widely divergent long-term goals became partners overnight. As in all alliances, frequent contentious disputes emerged. One is reminded of Napoleon's adage: "Always give me allies to fight."

After December 7, 1941, AMMISCA's responsibilities were expanded to include the building, improvement, and maintenance of critically needed roads and waterways to relieve a major supply backup at Rangoon. Expediting transit of Lend-Lease supplies north to Kunming in China's Yunnan province was a top priority throughout the AMMISCA era. AMMISCA was also specifically ordered to oversee the construction of a railroad from Burma to China and the construction of a highway(s) to replace the Burma Road; the establishment of an air delivery system of Lend-Lease from India; and the transfer of the American Volunteer Group (AVG, the "Flying Tigers") to the American army air forces. In all of these endeavors AMMISCA personnel were surrounded and pressured by representatives of the three major nations, who consistently sought to achieve their own national objectives. This was especially true of the ruler of China, Chiang Kai-shek, who could summon AMMISCA's commander, Brigadier General John M. Magruder, at a moment's notice.

Magruder had the disadvantages of wearing only one star and being under orders to not participate in Allied planning. Time after time he was called on to represent America at conferences where he was the junior officer. The rank differential also helped instigate backdoor communications and processes within the American State and War departments, and among members of the Roosevelt administration, who frequently circumvented, confused, and even attacked Magruder's efforts to follow proper military chain-of-command channels.

The AMMISCA concept was innovative: no American military advisory unit had ever been assigned to another nation. Because of the domestic economic concerns, cultural differences, and deeply isolationist attitudes of the American public, one might wonder why China was included in Lend-Lease. Even the American military sought common cause with the isolationists in the mid–1930s when the War Department warned that because of Japan's expansionist policies the United States should withdraw army and Marine units carried over from the Boxer Rebellion from the Asian mainland.[6] This posture remained unchanged even after a deliberate Japanese attack that killed several American sailors on the American gunboat *Panay* in late 1937.

World events, however, continued to slowly increase American sympathy for China. Tokyo's retention of a Japanese army in China; a plethora of missionary reports detailing the brutal Japanese campaigns; popular books by China-born Pearl Buck, some adapted to the silver screen by a sympathetic Hollywood, all combined to graphically illustrate the plight of the Chinese. There was also a pro–Chiang Kai-shek "China Lobby," which rapidly attracted influential political support including the Luce media empire, publishers of *Time* and *Life*. The impact of the "China Lobby" on Americans will be examined presently. The United States, with its humanitarian tradition and global economic interest, was led by a president who enjoyed discussing his family's centuries-long commercial relationship with China, but with a profound foreboding of German and Japanese expansion. The president could no longer maintain a policy of withdrawal from international affairs. Hence, AMMISCA was dispatched to Chungking.

The mission was not an effort in altruism. It was a carefully crafted undertaking, primarily designed to help to keep China functioning as a viable anti–Japanese force and, after the war was successfully completed, retain the Middle Kingdom in the postwar era as a political ally and consumer of American agricultural products and manufactured goods. In the AMMISCA era and beyond, in an effort to sustain that strategy, Franklin Roosevelt made many unfulfillable promises of aid to Chiang Kai-shek. The president's priorities were Europe first, Russia second, and then China. Roosevelt also resorted to tactics that cost America nothing to keep China in the war. For example, in early 1943 he requested the Senate ratify a treaty surrendering extraterritorial rights in China. Although Roosevelt always hoped that China would be strong enough to help prevent postwar colonialism in Asia, he never deviated from his Europe first strategy. In addition, his habit of unilateral actions impelled Army Chief of Staff George C. Marshall to comment that in a general sense, Roosevelt "pursued a preposterous course for military operations." Regarding supplies to China, Roosevelt told Chiang, "Even though there be a further setback in Rangoon ... the supply route to China via India can be maintained by air." In point of fact, it was only one of dozens of such "commitments" made to the generalissimo by the president.[7]

AMMISCA thus became not only the first-ever foreign military advisory unit, but a major American diplomatic innovation. For the first time in its history America became involved on the Asian mainland, which meant the Administration accepted the risk of war with Japan. AMMISCA was the beginning of a brand new era of American linkage with China, and as such, established the foundation for the 1942–1944 Stilwell Mission.

1

Creation of the Mission
Why AMMISCA Was Established

> This Division has, from the inception of the Aid to China movement, strongly felt that not only can the War Department be of very great assistance in making really effective the military aid to China, but that it has the definite responsibility of initiating measures to obtain control of the military part of the projected program.
> — Brigadier General Sherman Miles,
> Acting Assistant Chief of Staff,
> War Department Intelligence Division[1]

China's undeclared war with Japan began in July 1937 and within fifteen months Japan overran all of China's seaports, leaving only Rangoon, Burma, as a viable entrepot for supplies. After arriving, supplies still had to be warehoused and then transported by rail, water, and the road link from Rangoon to Lashio and Kunming (Yunnanfu), the Burma Road.

After numerous early victories, while the Japanese paused to consolidate their lines of communication and plan new strategy, Chiang Kai-shek struggled to obtain war materials. His brother-in-law, T.V. Soong was well-connected in Washington and there were many influential people to whom his cause made sense. One of them was the State Department's influential advisor on political relations, and acknowledged Sinophile, Stanley K. Hornbeck. Although regarded by many as holding a job beyond his talents and temperament, Hornbeck's overall role emerges several times in subsequent chapters.[2] A 29 May 1941 memo, written after the passage of Lend-Lease but while the mechanics of distribution were being debated in Washington, clearly reveals Hornbeck's true feelings. "Unlike the situation with regard to the shipment of supplies to Europe, the supply of materials to China has not been subject to loss by belligerent actions while crossing the ocean.... it would seem to be the part of wisdom to proceed as rapidly as possible with the sending of such aid to China as shall insure capacity on China's part to continue to assist itself. The probable adverse consequences — political, military, economic, and moral — of a failure on the part of this Government to live up to the pledges that it has given to China cannot be overestimated."[3]

In early 1943 Roosevelt "struck a blow" that did not cost a single gun or bomber. On February 1 he asked the Senate to ratify a treaty surrendering extra-territorial rights in China. In late 1943, another action designed for show but with little substance was Roosevelt's request that Congress repeal the Chinese exclusion laws.[4] For decades prior to this repeal, Chinese immigrants were unable to become American citizens.

Hornbeck's memo was an attempt to overcome the fact that the Lend-Lease bill heavily emphasized aid to Britain and Russia. China's needs were rarely mentioned and the new law was interpreted by many to mean that aid would go to China only when not needed by Britain or Russia.[5] The memorandum was designed not only to support the Chinese in a humanitarian sense, but to assure the Chinese that they, in the rush by several nations to obtain Lend-Lease materials, would receive enough to continue to be a viable opposition force to Japan. This marked the beginning of the love-hate relationship between Chungking and Washington. Chiang never felt China was receiving as much support as it should have and the Roosevelt administration, especially the War Department, overwhelmingly believed Chungking's requests were based on unrealistic estimates of needs.[6]

To a point, each view was valid. Roosevelt never deviated from the policy of "Europe First" that he made public early in the war. Compared with European adversities, China's were of less urgency. Roosevelt refused to consider suggestions from Marshall and the Joint Chiefs of Staff that the Pacific theater receive more emphasis. When General Magruder was pleading for support for the AVG in early 1942, Roosevelt was concerned with Europe, especially Russia: "I would go out and take the stuff off the shelves of the stores and pay them any price necessary, and put it in a truck and rush it to the boat.... I would rather lose ... anything else than have the Russians collapse."[7] The only category where the Burma-China area had a higher supply priority than Europe was in transport aircraft. In all other categories it was last.[8]

Soong presented his country's first list of Lend-Lease requirements on 31 March 1941. China Defense Supplies (CDS), the primary agency for Chinese Lend-Lease requests and negotiations, became a controversial organization even though customs collectors were notified that CDS had been issued an unlimited (except for munitions) export license.[9] Prior to Lend-Lease, Soong acted as Chiang's "personal representative." On April 30 he was promoted to China's "agent, representative and attorney-in-fact."[10] Harvard historian John

K. Fairbank described the situation: "A realistic equivalent to T. V. Soong's role in China would have been Bobby Kennedy's becoming head of the Bank of America, Chase Manhattan, National Citibank, and the Federal Reserve all at once while JFK was in the White House. The only capital investment possible in China was either through a government agency or an official or under their protection. Law was no safeguard."[11]

Soong requested supplies for three projects: a modern air force; thirty new infantry divisions; and a communication and supply system between China and friendly powers. The projected system included a new railroad from Yunnan to Burma, expansion of the Chinese portion of the Burma Road from Kunming to the Burma border and its maintenance facilities, and aircraft to transport materials into China from the south and west. Soong claimed that if these requests were met, China could assume the offensive in two years. All of these soon involved AMMISCA.

CDS's first president was David M. Corcoran, brother of Roosevelt intimate Tommy "The Cork" Corcoran. His task was encumbered by those he sought to aid, his own failure to recognize how inappropriate the requests were, and his inability to gauge how the reaction to those requests would impact future ones. CDS officials could call on War Department personnel to assist them in the proper, and sensible, preparation of requisitions. But complaints grew that Chinese agents had no idea what was needed and were also unaware of the limitations of the weapons desired.[12] The result was increased entreaties from the War and Treasury departments to "secure more jurisdiction over the whole process of rearming the Chinese Army."[13]

CDS had no competent military advisor. Thus, most of Soong's requests were imprecise, incomplete, unrealistic, and based, to a great degree, on ignorance. One of Soong's early requests, for example, was for a number of four-ton trucks and thirteen-ton tanks that would have torn Chinese and Burmese roads and bridges to pieces. These ill-conceived requisitions increased the negative impression at the War Department. Soong maneuvered to obtain more than the Chinese could even transport to China. These extreme requests, for the biggest and newest equipment regardless of practicality, became repetitive.[14] After presidential economic advisor Lauchlin Currie returned from a fact-finding trip to Chungking in March 1941, the president assigned him the task of administering Lend-Lease for China. Currie, deeply impressed with the generalissimo and Madame Chiang, supported Soong's efforts. They began to bear fruit, and initial shipments of Lend-Lease goods began in late May via Rangoon.[15]

Currie's work as assistant director of the Federal Reserve System's Board of Governors impressed Roosevelt, and that is why he became one of six administrative assistants to the president in July 1939. He quickly made his mark. In early 1941 Roosevelt selected him to represent the White House at Chungking.[16] Harry Hopkins was Roosevelt's top confidant, and although the Canada-born Currie was technically a member of Hopkins' staff, he had direct access to the president and quickly became a zealous advocate of China and Chiang Kai-shek. China-born and Columbia-educated John Paton Davies served at the State Department Far Eastern Desk and in the American Embassy as political advisor to General Stilwell. He knew Currie well and was surprised when Currie confided (incorrectly) "in the tone of one to whom some occult truth had been revealed ... that the Chinese leadership thought just as we did." Davies noted some problems with Currie's unorthodox operating methods, but excused it on the basis that what was happening was typical of the confused style of doing business that Roosevelt employed.[17] Another insight into Currie's thinking is provided by historian Michael Schaller, who states that Currie was ignorant of China's internal economic class and land struggles. He also lacked appreciation of Chinese nationalism, as exemplified by his belief that the Chinese would subordinate themselves to foreign advisors.[18]

Chiang had many other American sympathizers. One of them was Owen Lattimore, former editor of *Pacific Affairs*, former director of the Walter Hines Page School of International Relations, and Roosevelt-selected political advisor to Chiang Kai-shek. In mid–September 1941, he told Currie that he wondered how China was still fighting and was not surprised their thinking was sometimes flawed.[19]

Initial Concept

> On his return from Chungking, Dr. Currie had received from Mr. Harry L. Hopkins, the President's confidential adviser, the task of expediting Chinese lend-lease aid.
> — Charles F. Romanus and Riley Sunderland,
> *Stilwell's Mission to China*

Currie became obsessed with the notion that the United States support China as comprehensively as possible. In his report to the president, he recommended that the United States provide as much consideration in Lend-Lease supplies to China as it was doing for Britain. Currie also advocated "warning" Japan that American naval vessels would convoy supply ships to China even if Japan attempted a blockade. Currie's report emphasized China's need for military support and included the proposal that a military advisory group be assigned there.[20] He pointed out that United States military assistance

1. Creation of the Mission

to China had been almost nil, yet America had been generous in supplying Britain and Greece. He urged that several high-ranking United States naval and army officers be dispatched to China on an "inspection and consultation" trip.[21] This further embedded the concept of military aid and advisors to China.[22] But Currie's integrity and authority were questionable after he was placed in charge of Lend-Lease for China. As will be noted, he recommended to Chiang Kai-shek courses of action that were inimical to the United States and attempted to issue orders to senior army officers.

Roosevelt thought highly of the proposal particularly when the army supported it. The president placed Currie in charge of the organization and administration of all Chinese Lend-Lease, as well as the maintenance and supply of the American Volunteer Group (AVG) program. The AVG pilots, well known as the Flying Tigers, served in the Chinese air force. As became his habit, Currie attempted to garner more aircraft for China than Chiang Kai-shek requested.[23] Currie felt that a larger number of aircraft would not only aid China but also serve as a deterrent to Japanese expansion in Malaya and the Indian Ocean. Any British objections to the rerouting of supplies to China, which otherwise might have gone to England, could be overcome by pointing out that China's active participation in the war in Asia was critical to the well-being of the British empire. His argument was that if Singapore fell, Britain would face much more difficulty in defending the British Isles and winning the war in Asia. Indeed, her very survival would be in doubt.[24] There is no evidence that the British supported Currie's rationale.

When they learned that army personnel would be required to supervise all aspects of supply and distribution of Chinese Lend-Lease goods, the War Department's Supply Division (G-4) prepared its own recommendation. On 16 June 1941, Brigadier General Eugene Reybold, Acting Assistant Chief of Staff, Supply Division, proposed that United States military personnel be placed at Rangoon and along the several Burma supply routes, particularly the Burma Road. Along with Chinese military personnel they would supervise the shipping storage, distribution, and use of Lend-Lease materials. Reybold recommended a program of extensive training of Chinese personnel prior to or concurrent with the arrival of the Lend-Lease material, and the establishment of a priority shipping system designed to reduce congestion at Rangoon and increase the flow of freight over the entire Burma supply route system. Reybold emphasized that the "Soong mission" was incapable of accurately requisitioning the proper material needed by the Chinese armies because there was only one trained soldier on China Defense Supplies' Washington staff. This was a critical point in light of the significance Soong attached to that organization and the expanding low esteem in which CDS was held at the War Department.²⁵

The Supply Division's plan was not unique. Another recommendation came to Marshall the same day as Reybold's. It was submitted by Major Edwin N. Clark, Assistant for Aid to China, to Lieutenant Colonel E. E. MacMorland, Chief of the Defense Aid Division for Lend-Lease aid to all countries. MacMorland was also the War Department Defense Aid Division liaison aide to Currie and CDS. There was frequent contact between Reybold and Clark. Not only were their recommendations issued the same day, they complemented each other quite well in terms of what needed to be done, who should do it (the army), and how it would be accomplished. There was undoubtedly agreement between the two that the army had to do all it could to prevent Japan from moving into Southeast Asia and further into China.²⁶ One might wonder: why were two proposals so similar to each other submitted? Perhaps the thinking was that two would be more persuasive than one.

Clark advocated the establishment of a "China Detail for China Aid" within the War Department. The "Detail" would assign at least 100 officers to Washington and Chungking to insure that Lend-Lease materials of the proper type and quantity were delivered promptly and used effectively.²⁷ The staff in Washington would expedite procurement and submit recommendations for improvements of the program. This would relieve the Supply Division of a great amount of work but would not inhibit the Supply Division or the General Staff's ability to formulate policy. The staff of the "Detail" in Chungking, to be composed of officers from all the army's main branches, would maintain close liaison with the Chinese General Staff, supervise the transportation, delivery, and employment of Lend-Lease supplies, report appropriate information, and submit recommendations to the War Department. Clark warned that a tremendous loss in efficiency and time would result if these suggestions were not followed.²⁸ Currie agreed that some sort of coordinating group would help speed supplies to China, and he used his high-level contacts to support the principles of the Reybold and Clark plans.²⁹

On June 24 the War Department's Personnel Division (G-1) officially approved Reybold's proposal and in less than a week the Intelligence Division (G-2) followed.³⁰ During the first week of July the Planning Division (G-3) concurred. It stated, however, that although it agreed with Reybold's principles, the assistance furnished the Chinese should be in the nature of "advice" rather than "supervision."³¹ Because he was anxious to proceed, Reybold did not oppose the new phrasing. Instead, he maintained that the Planning Division's semantic differences were unimportant distinctions because the officers functioning in China would be "advising," but "supervision" would result from the information they sent the War Department.³²

Another argument that supported creation of a mission and undoubtedly influenced the president and State and War Department officials was a report from the military attaché at Chungking, Lieutenant Colonel William Mayer. He advised the War Department that the British were establishing a military mission under the command of Lieutenant General L. E. Dennys. The naval attaché, Marine Major J. M. McHugh, reported that Dennys' long-range plans included recapturing Canton. Mayer believed the British mission would function only if Britain and Japan went to war. In fact it went into operation on a comprehensive basis months before war began.³³ The British planned to establish guerilla training schools, conduct reconnaissance missions in occupied territory, and bring in transport and air units.³⁴ Implicit in the Attaché's report was a warning that because the port of Rangoon and the transport routes were controlled by the British, they might become Chiang's principal military advisors through their ability to influence the disposition of America's Lend-Lease supplies.³⁵ Mayer noted that the Chinese fear that the Soviet Union might be defeated by the Germans expedited the formation of an American mission to China as a reassuring diplomatic gesture. Russian collapse would release the Japanese troops in Manchuria for use elsewhere.³⁶

In July, after the War Department received intercepted Japanese diplomatic code messages indicating that Tokyo intended to end the war in China and invade Malaya and the Netherlands East Indies, the administration quickly reacted. Roosevelt approved a proposal to equip, man, and maintain a 500-plane Chinese air force and the establishment of an American military mission to China.³⁷

Formation of the Mission

> Whether the Chinese mission would have to be camouflaged under some other title has not yet been decided. In any event, it is going to be very important and will increase in importance as time goes on. When we get into this war actively, the mission will be the liaison for strategic planning and cooperation with our ally, China.
> — Brigadier General Sherman Miles, Acting Assistant Chief of Staff, G-2 (Intelligence)³⁸

For some reason, neither Washington nor Chungking wished to acknowledge initiation of the mission. Although Washington actually originated the concept, Chiang would have accepted a dozen missions if it would have meant more war materials. In any case, each nation attempted to place the responsibility of the mission's inauguration on the other. Roosevelt, for example, told Soong that Chiang had requested the mission, and Secretary of State Stimson wrote Chiang that Magruder would lead the "Military Mission ... created in response to your express request."[39] And, although Soong wanted it known in China that the mission was being sent because the generalissimo had solicited it, Chiang later told Magruder that the mission owed its origin to the American government.[40]

On 11 July 1941, Brigadier General Sherman Miles, Acting Assistant Chief of Staff (G-2), informed Brigadier General John M. Magruder that he was one of three general officers under consideration to head AMMISCA. The others were A. J. Bowley, Joseph Stilwell, and the army's senior officer, Lieutenant General Hugh A. Drum.[41] Bowley's experience was limited, and Stilwell was being groomed for an assignment in North Africa.[42] A minor inter-service obstacle developed when the navy felt its personnel should be included in the mission. Brigadier General L. T. Gerow, Acting Assistant Chief of Staff (WPD) pointed out, to Magruder's later chagrin, that the mission would not be engaged in planning strategy, but would "assist in carrying out certain objectives of the Act of March 11, 1941 [the Lend-Lease Act]." The navy did not pursue the matter further; Magruder was selected.[43]

After combat service in France in World War I, Major (temporary) Magruder served as assistant military attaché at Peking from 1920 to 1924. Just before he left Peking he was commended by the United States Legation for saving the life of an American woman kidnapped by bandits. Magruder's next assignments were advanced artillery school and the prestigious Command and Staff College, where he was a "distinguished graduate."

In 1926 he returned to Peking as the military attaché. He served in China until 1930 before returning to the United States to teach military science at his alma mater, Virginia Military Institute. He then served as military attaché at Berne, Switzerland. Now a full colonel, Magruder became chief of the Intelligence Branch, Military Intelligence Division War Department General Staff, in June 1939. In December 1940, Brigadier General Magruder was assigned the command of Fort Devens, Massachusetts.[44]

Magruder was intelligent and possessed a good understanding of China, gained during his years there observing the nation's people and government. He was regarded highly enough in scholarly circles that *Foreign Affairs* asked him to write an article on the Chinese military. This article, published in April 1931, was comprehensive and included a candid, some might say harsh, analysis of contemporary political and sociological influences on the Chinese military. He could have written the same assessment ten years later upon his return to China and not been far wrong. Some of his most perceptive insights were regarding the docility of the Chinese soldier ("idealism is not sufficient to stir the Chinese soldier up") the contempt that the Chinese people have traditionally had for the military; the fact that Chinese people had no desire to participate in physical games or sports such as fishing or hunting, and how this was reflected in their "distaste for combat"; and the fact that they were rarely allowed to fire their rifles or take target practice.

A principal point: because of their non-aggressive traits, "youthful and unprofessional Chinese generals smile contemptuously at the perfection of western militarism. Their lack of emulation is due to their feelings that it cannot improve the superiority for Chinese racial persistence ... predicated on their belief that the continuance of their race, that sacred and instinctive urge which grips them so strongly, will not be accomplished by the exercise of military qualities. And they have a confident faith in their destiny which seems to lie in their one-mindedness, patience and persistence."[45] We see then how traditional habits and beliefs impacted at all levels of the military. The choice of Magruder to command AMMISCA was a good one. He was constantly frustrated by Chinese corruption, but only at higher levels of political and military command, not by the common soldier.

Regarding the potential growth of a martial spirit in China, Magruder stated, "Given money, equipment and training there is no doubt that a first class fighting machine can be made of, say 20,000 Bulgars or Turks. The same cannot be said of 20,000 Chinese without numerous qualifications. The difference has nothing to do with physical stamina, courage, or intelligence. It is spiritual, or possibly intellectual, and may be loosely summed up in those racial qualities which create a natural antipathy for joining battle with an enemy instead of a relish for combat."[46]

On 20 November 1931, in a private letter to Stanley Hornbeck at the State Department's Far Eastern Section, Magruder revealed some of his personal views regarding China's top leadership. The letter complimented Hornbeck and his section on their response to the Manchurian Crisis in not taking the Chinese claims of Japanese expansion as correct. This was an unusual stance for the notoriously pro–Chiang Sinophile Hornbeck. Magruder believed China was more to blame for Japan's expansion into Manchuria than the former Chinese minister to America, and currently Chinese representative to the League of Nations, was willing to admit:

> After all, the situation in Manchuria, however unfortunate, has been a development of twenty-five years.... The unwholesome treaties and agreements exist, and they did not come into being wholly as a result of coertion [sic] and evil intent on the part of Japan. We all know personally more peddlers of Chinese sovereignty than we do patriots. Japan, rightly or wrongly, has come to depend

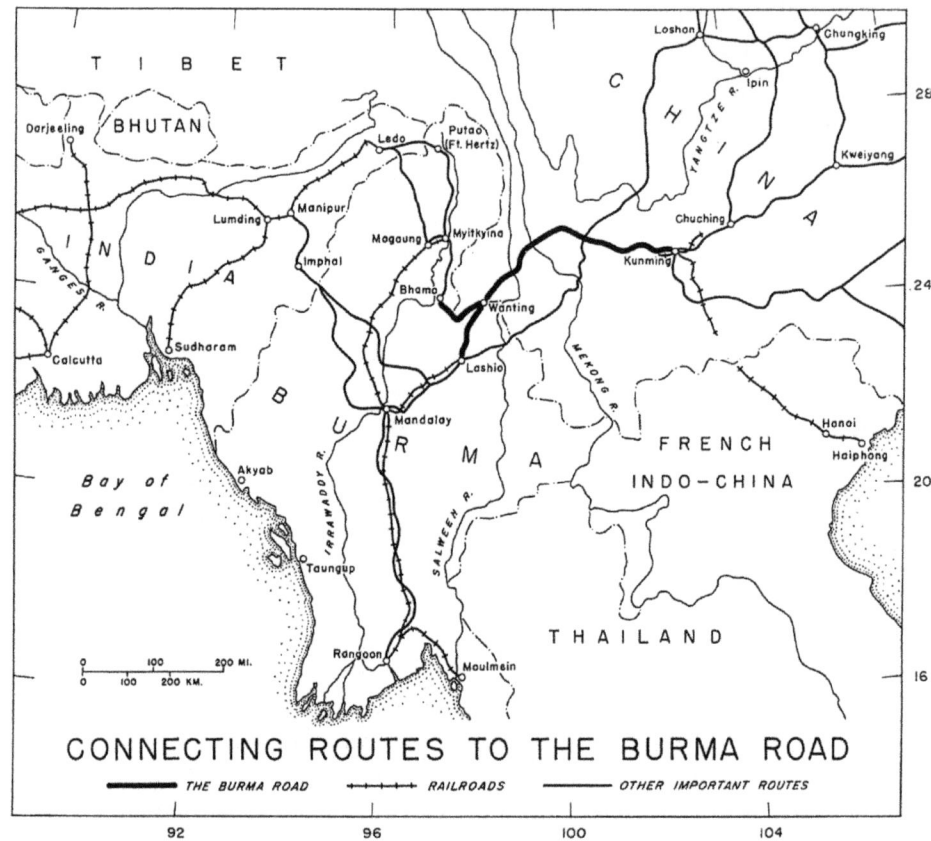

Connecting routes to the Burma Road (University of Illinois Map Library).

on her position in Manchuria as vital to her existence.... China has imperiled that position not by mature, defensible manifestations of strength or proved worth, but by evasion, deceit and destructive measures.... The Chinese being what we know them so well to be, the only way Japan can keep Manchuria from going the way of all China is by the employment of undisguised force at intervals....[47]

It may be argued Magruder was a stereotypical military officer in that he had a strong sense of duty and right and wrong, with very little gray area. He was no more pro–Japanese than he was anti–Chinese; however, throughout his tenure he was frequently driven close to distraction by Chinese obduracy. In light of Magruder's subsequent harsh treatment by Hornbeck, one wonders if he regretted sending him such a candid letter centering on politics.

One of Magruder's subordinates, Major Nevin Wetzel, judged him to be "the most skillful diplomat we sent to China in 1941–1945. He was suave, charming, and tactful, didn't make a lot of waves ... and was the ideal man for the U.S. to have there in China at the backwash of the war.... I would give Magruder top marks regarding knowledge of China and Chinese language [and] in dealing with others, British, Chinese or Americans."[48] His chief of staff, Colonel (later Major General) E. E. MacMorland, "always spoke highly of Magruder, and insisted that the members of the Mission who did not were 'can't take it' men."[49] One of the ranking American embassy diplomats, China-born John Paton Davies, described Magruder as a "thoughtful, urbane China specialist ... [who] took the Chinese way of doing things in his stride. But his staff, some of whom were new to the scene, was shocked by their encounter with incompetence, indifference and corruption...."[50]

In late August Magruder was told that the mission would assist in carrying out the objectives of the Lend-Lease act. This would be accomplished, as Clark and Reybold suggested, by establishing a detail in Washington and another in Chungking. Magruder would command the Chungking Detail and be temporarily attached to the embassy so that he could coordinate with the ambassador and avoid political and administrative complications. He would ultimately be responsible to the War Department, but he was to keep the new ambassador, Clarence E. Gauss, fully informed of all significant matters, especially the types and amounts of material that he believed could be used advantageously in China.

Magruder's orders contained several significant State Department requests formulated during lengthy inter–Department conferences. He was to be "guided" in situations not covered by his original orders, by the interpretation of policy by the ambassador while he waited for directives from the War Department.[51] Later events demonstrated that this was not wise: "For a while it was felt that Magruder should be authorized to staff talks with the Chinese on cooperation between the two Allied powers should war arise in the Pacific between America and Japan ... but it was never authorized. In fact, when the issue came to a head in November [1941], the War Department told Magruder to express no opinions of his own on the employment of U.S. forces in China, and to not discuss any Chinese proposals, but simply to transmit the latter to Washington."[52] This order was inappropriate because the Chinese always overestimated Magruder's influence with the War Department discussions of Lend-Lease arms.[53] And yet, even after the many crises wrought by Pearl Harbor, Marshall's early disenchantment with Magruder, dating from late October, precluded any modification of the order.

Magruder was directed to assist the Chinese in obtaining appropriate military Lend-Lease equipment and ordered to "insure that the most effective use was made thereof."[54] He was cautioned to deal only with Chiang Kai-shek to avoid the morass of the Chinese bureaucracy: "In view of the fact that absolute cooperation was to be sought with individuals of a different race whose mental processes vary widely from our own, it is of primary importance that all possibilities of delay caused by Chinese political maneuvering be eliminated by providing for direct channels of communication between the mission and the heads of the respective military establishments."[55] This was seemingly sensible. But how was Magruder to achieve this when he was restricted by Washington from expressing himself on anything related to policy?

Because he had worked with T.V. Soong and other Chinese while serving as secretary of the Army-Navy Munitions Board, Lieutenant Colonel Edward E. MacMorland was chosen to be Magruder's chief of staff. Magruder also selected some former acquaintances, one of whom was Major Harry Aldrich. In the 1920s Aldrich served with Magruder in China, and upon his return to America in the 1930s, wrote a two-volume Chinese language text that was published by Yale University's Department of Oriental Studies.

Colonel Arcadi Gluckman was particularly well qualified; he was a supply expert and spoke fluent Chinese. One of the unit's medical officers, Dr. Mendlesohn, also spoke excellent Chinese. Most of the officers, however, were simply "picked from a card file." All were asked to volunteer, and when the group was completed it contained reserve as well as regular officers. Although all the personnel were experienced in their military specialties, less than a third were in any way acquainted with China.[56]

The mission, then, was composed primarily of officer specialists. The core group, the "China Detail" rarely numbering more than fifty, was split into several small units. Some were deployed along the line of communications from Rangoon north, some to observe the front at I-chang and on the Indochina border, a few in Calcutta, India, and the rest retained around Chungking. Magruder told his officers their duties would involve work in widely separated areas, often out of touch with Chungking, so that they would have to show initiative and good judgment. However, under no circumstances were AMMISCA officers to exceed their authority by negotiating or making commitments to British or Chinese officials or American agencies until such matters had been approved through diplomatic channels. They were reminded that they could hardly hope to change characteristics that the centuries had implanted in the Chinese, that AMMISCA's "effectiveness will depend not on our efforts to change or reform the Chinese, but upon our ability to put our advice and aid in such forms as to make it practical."[57] Because of the lack of effective communication and on-the-spot oversight, these units often operated autonomously and with the exception of some incidents at Rangoon, their performance was almost always creditable.[58]

The AMMISCA vanguard left San Francisco in mid–September 1941. After a brief stopover in Manila, they arrived in China's capital, Chungking, on October 10, China's "Double Ten Day," comparable to America's Fourth of July. The thirtieth anniversary of the founding of the Chinese republic was also the genesis of AMMISCA. It quickly became apparent that there was a broad difference between Chinese and American aspirations and objectives.

Unfortunately, many of Magruder's assistants were disillusioned by what they found in China.[59] When these officers traveled among Chinese military installations their lack of knowledge of Chinese society became apparent. As professionals, they evaluated their Chinese counterparts in their own environment and based on the manner in which they were resisting the Japanese. The officers reported their negative opinions to their counterparts at the War Department in America. In a November report to Magruder from Lieutenant Colonel Sliney, Sliney related conversations with Chinese officers as well as his own observations. He related that some of the officers thought China could win with little effort because "foreign pressure" (American aid?) would force the Japanese out. He dismissed statements that the Chinese had won big battles and felt they had not "fought Japan to a standstill." Japan in fact was able to push forward any place she wanted to. Sliney acknowledged a strong belief that the Chinese desire for more modern equipment was not "for the purpose of pressing the war against Japan, but was to make the central government safe against insurrection after diplomatic pressure by other nations had forced Japan out of China."[60] He was obviously referring to the Chinese communists.

2

America Before the Lend-Lease Program
Isolationism and Anti-War Feelings

America's Military Unpreparedness Circa 1940

> In the early 1930s ... only about one-fourth of the officers and one-half of the enlisted men of the Regular Army were available for assignment to tactical units in the continental United States. Many units existed only on paper; almost all had only skeletonized strength. Instead of nine infantry divisions, there were actually three.... In the infantry ... in 1932 the 24 regiments available in the United States for field service were spread among 45 posts, with a battalion or less at 34. The United States was not organized or trained for any type of serious international involvement and National Guard and Reserve strength at the time of Pearl Harbor was about 250,000 below the planned end strength of 436,000. In the early 1930s the great depression had the immediate effect of cuts in the appropriations and pay that further reduced the readiness of army units for military service.
> — Maurice Matloff, General Editor, *American Military History*

The 1920s and 30s were a time of widespread negative reaction to World War I. Most of the nations of Europe suffered great losses in treasure and human life, but Great Power self-interest prevailed. There was also the advent and steady growth of the horrors of the Great Depression. The economies of France, Italy, Great Britain, and especially Germany were in dire straits. Russia was in the throes of the Bolshevik Revolution. Americans suffered less, relatively speaking; but a majority believed that American participation in "the war to end all wars" had been a mistake. Americans believed it should never again be sucked into Europe's "old world," corrupt, self-serving machinations.

2. America Before the Lend-Lease Program 27

Most people in the United States also believed President Wilson had been gulled by the British into violating the United States' tradition of neutrality, which contributed to widespread pacifist feeling, especially on university campuses. This was supported by the fallacious, but widely accepted, "Merchants of Death" charge that a post–World War I committee of hard-core conservatives brought against munitions manufacturers. And, as the Depression deepened, Americans became much more attentive to their own economy and less mindful of Germany and Japan's conversion to militarism, Japan's repudiation of the League of Nations, and the Anti-Comintern treaty of 1937. Isolationism made sense; why should the United States become involved in the problems of other nations, thousands of miles away, less than 20 years after the most horrific event in world history: the "failure of World War I"?

Out of this came the Neutrality Acts. In 1935, Congress forbade sales of arms to nations at war. Americans were strongly urged to not sail on ships of these nations to prevent another *Lusitania* incident. In 1936, loans to nations at war were prohibited, and in 1937 the third Neutrality Act required that all trade except munitions must be paid for in cash and carried on other than American ships.

The army was understrength, primarily due to cutbacks induced by the Great Depression, but it began a very slow turnaround in 1936 when some increases in army funding were effected.[1] The turnaround was also reflected in the mobilization of a number of National Guard and Reserve units in 1940–41. This was a relatively smooth process because the Guard and Reserve personnel numbered considerably below the planned 1920 end strength of 436,000 men. The actual number was 180,000m and although it received only 10 percent of the War Department's military budget, the National Guard army was larger than the Regular Army until 1939. Thus, Regular Army units rarely trained in units larger than companies, approximately 250 men, or battalions of about 750 men.[2] In the event of all-out war it would be critical for large units, even divisions of 15,000 men, to have trained as large units to maneuver on large fields of battle.

After war began in Europe in 1939, Roosevelt ordered increases in the army and National Guard to 227,000 and 235,000, respectively. Training at the corps and army level began, although quite slowly. An interesting component of the big picture was the attitude of many American males of draft age. A reporter from the *Nation* claimed he'd spent ten days in August 1941 walking around Times Square talking with hundreds of "Regular soldiers, draftees, [and] National Guardsmen.... But, except for the Regulars, they hated the Army, Roosevelt, General Marshall and Negroes in about equal degree. Few had any idea why they were in the Army or what the Army was for."[3]

Events in Asia and Europe initiated a slow turnaround in American isolationism. They included Hitler's aggression in Spain, Austria, the Sudetenland, Poland, and France. And, through its blatant and atrocity-ridden aggression in China, and seizure of the Dutch East Indies and French Indochina for oil, tin, rubber, and advanced bases in 1940, Japan became an undisputable international threat. The signing of the Tripartite Pact between Japan, Germany and Italy in September 1940 made aggression a worldwide issue for Americans.

In 1940, Congress approved $10 billion for American "military preparedness" along with America's first ever peacetime draft. The passage of the Lend-Lease Act on 11 March 1941 signaled a major American pull-back from neutrality and isolationism as well as a significant projection of the United States into world affairs.

But a year of rearming did not place the United States in a position to carry war to its enemies. When Pearl Harbor was attacked on 7 December 1941, the army numbered some 1,644,000 (including about 120,000 officers) organized into four armies, 37 divisions (30 infantry, five armored, two cavalry), and over 40 combat air groups. Three of the divisions were overseas, two in Hawaii, one in the Philippines; with other garrison forces, they totaled fewer than 200,000.[4]

Seventeen of the divisions in the continental United States were rated as technically ready for combat. But these divisions lacked the supporting units and the training necessary to weld them into corps and armies. A particular weakness was the shortage of all classes of munitions and weapons systems that recent combat in Europe had shown to be indispensable, especially tank and anti-tank guns, anti-aircraft artillery, radios, radar, and aircraft. Some of these shortages were further aggravated by a lack of auxiliary equipment such as fire control mechanisms. Other severe challenges were ship chartering and the construction of shipping point facilities, convoy assembly and a lack of escort vessels. Distance was an issue, especially in the Pacific, where there would be the necessity of constructing military facilities in Australia and a defensive barrier along that continent's northern limits; along with air and refueling bases in the western Pacific.[5]

In terms of material aid to China, perhaps the most significant reality of all was that "ammunition of all kinds was so scarce that the War Department was unwilling to commit more than one division and a single antiaircraft regiment for service in any theater where combat operations seemed imminent. Only one division-size, task force was sent to the far Pacific before April 1942."[6] "Unpreparedness" was an understatement.

Japan's attack highlighted the necessity of an Anglo-American joint

Overhead view of switchbacks on the Burma Road, 1939 or 1940 (Library of Congress Prints and Photographs Division, Washington, D.C., Office of War Information).

weapons and munitions allocation system. The president's and prime minister's military staffs met immediately after Pearl Harbor at the Arcadia Conference. They agreed in principle to the establishment of a "Combined Chiefs of Staff" composed of the military chiefs of both countries, responsible to the president and the prime minister for planning and carrying out grand strategy. In America this included Army Chief of Staff General George Marshall, Chief of Naval Operations Admiral Harold Stark, Air Officer Lieutenant General H. H. Arnold, and the president's chief of staff, Admiral William Leahy. The British deputation, headed by Field Marshall Sir John Dill, met with their American counterparts via bilateral committees.

As will be demonstrated in subsequent chapters, it was critical that the accumulation, allocation and dispersal of Lend-Lease supplies be controlled. Roosevelt and Churchill established the Combined Munitions Assignment Board (MAB) with offices in London and Washington. The board operated under the direct cognizance of the Combined Chiefs of Staff. Other similar boards were established in 1942 for raw materials, production, and shipping. Despite some misgivings in Washington that the British would have an undue influence over the pool of arms while making much smaller contributions, the board worked tolerably well as a means of Anglo-American consultation. When Chiang Kai-Shek put out feelers for membership, he was denied on the grounds that "only nations with disposable surplus should be admitted."[7]

Additional command structures were put in to place: "By February 1942, Joint Chiefs of Staff (JCS) consisting of the American members of the Combined Chiefs of Staff (CCS) emerged as the highest military authority in the U.S. military hierarchy ... and were responsible directly to the President. Like the CCS, the JCS in time developed a machinery of planning and working committees."[8]

In early 1942 it was agreed that the American Joint Chiefs would be responsible for the Pacific war and the British would oversee the Middle East and Indian Ocean areas. Although China requested a much larger area of responsibility, it would control only the terrain within its own national boundaries. Other outcomes of the Arcadia Conference were the decision to "defeat Germany first" and, because there would now be very close relationship with the British General Staff, a revision of the War Department's General Staff. This served to make the department better able to deal with global war. The department's War Plans and Supply Divisions, both of which were influential in AMMISCA's operation, were expanded and modernized.[9]

Lend-Lease: One of History's Most Generous Acts

> In the three years of preparing for and entering World War II, the Army's logistical staffs had both to learn and to apply their craft, unlearning in the process much that they had inherited from their predecessor.... The Army's mobilization and deployment and, even more, the industrial mobilization needed to wage full-scale war, started from low ebb in 1940....
> — Richard M. Leighton and Robert W. Coakley,

2. America Before the Lend-Lease Program

Global Logistics and Strategy: 1940–1943

> We are not seeking to make a loan to Great Britain. We are really seeking to purchase her aid in our own defense. We are buying — not lending. We are buying our own security while we prepare.
> — Edward R. Stettinius, Jr.,
> *Lend-Lease: Weapon for Victory*

War came to Europe in September 1939. American military planners immediately warned of serious manpower and material deficiencies if America went to war with Japan.[10] Such an event if accompanied by a British breakdown in Europe and the Mediterranean could be dire, posing a very real threat to the Western hemisphere.[11] Nevertheless, Britain and France, although in extreme financial and economic straits, were still required to pay gold or dollars for American arms. In mid–December, President Roosevelt returned from a Caribbean holiday with a plea from Prime Minister Churchill asking the president to expand the means by which increased aid of all kinds could be provided to Britain.[12]

The president desired and worked for legislation that would give him the widest discretion in allocating aid, regarding who would receive it, how much and what types of aid there would be, what would be the means of American oversight, and what would be demanded in return. Britain was the top priority; it had to be supported. Conversations between American and British planners, centering on legalities and economics, were held through much of 1940. Topics of discussion included how to legally transfer war materials to the United Kingdom, the British lack of financial resources, and American's own future material needs. The topics were complex and became a never-ending debate between the allies.

From these talks, the concept of Lend-Lease evolved. Perhaps Roosevelt hoped it would permit him to live up to his pledge to not have to "send American boys to fight Europe's wars." This confidence, expressed in a Roosevelt Fireside Chat, also called for America to become the "arsenal of defense," implying that is would be a supplier, not a participant. It was a good selling point, but there is no doubt that the president believed deeply the only way European democracy could be sustained was by American intervention with materials and, ultimately, with military personnel. Congressional debate lasted for months.

There was significant opposition to millions of American dollars going to support other nations, even if most of it would benefit America's economy. The most prominent opponent to Lend-Lease was the America First Committee, which claimed that the United States was not threatened, neutrality was best, and preparedness should only be concerned with continental defense. But, aided by President Roosevelt's famous "garden hose" speech, wherein he referenced loaning his garden hose to a neighbor whose house was on fire, House Bill H. R. 1776, "Lend-Lease," while extensively — and often acrimoniously — debated, passed on 11 March 1941. The immediate problem: who gets what and how much?

Lend-Lease proved to be an unarguable success. America's material wealth and industrial capability gave the allies an enormous advantage. From the time the United States entered the war until the surrender of the Japanese, it produced more than twice as many munitions as Germany and Japan combined.[13] In economic terms it was also a boon for the American manufacturing industries. In fact, the Commerce Department estimated that the United States transferred approximately $48.4 billion in goods and services during the war period.[14] It also benefited America's transportation and communications interests. It must also be recognized that although Lend-Lease was a huge undertaking, the bureaucracy that ran it was efficient. However, as subsequent events will reveal, this assessment would likely be disputed by close observers of Lend-Lease to China. Historian Immanuel C. Y. Hsu states: "From 1942 until the end of the war in 1945, United States' credits to China reached the unprecedented mark of U.S. $500 million. Correspondingly Lend-Lease aid rose to U.S. aid rose to U.S. $1.3 billion, which when combined with the U.S. $26 million in 1941 and the U.S. $210 million in 1946 made a grand total of U.S. $1.54 billion, or 3 per cent of the total Lend-Lease to all countries."[15]

To Roosevelt, and especially Secretary of State Hull, Lend-Lease was also a diplomatic tool. Hull insisted that Britain lift several trade limitations restricting foreign trade with members of the Commonwealth. The matter was not resolved until after the war but was seen by many in Britain as avarice, an inappropriate attempt by the Roosevelt administration to take advantage of its staunchest ally's desperate economic needs to increase its own economic condition.[16] Which, of course, it was.

Another outcome of Lend-Lease was the continuing evolution of the Munitions Assignment Board (MAB). As noted, the board was created in December 1941. General Marshall threatened to resign as army chief of staff if the board was not administered by the Combined Chiefs of Staff: "Although the demand apparently caught Roosevelt off guard, he agreed to establish a munitions assignment board in Washington and another in London both responsible to the CCS (in Washington), for which he obtained Churchill's approval. Roosevelt noted that ... he and Churchill retained the authority to resolve any disagreements that might arise. The Munitions Assignment Boards (MAB) in fact remained in control of the assignment of all military hardware throughout the remainder of the war, and was a factor in the AMMISCA operation."[17]

To Chiang Kai-shek the board was a potential source of large quantities of vital war materials. Although the main thrust behind the Lend-Lease endeavor clearly was to aid Britain, China quickly submitted requests. Roosevelt aide Thomas Corcoran was approached in early 1941 by Lauchlin Currie. Currie stated he was there at Roosevelt's direction to work out a program to assist Chiang Kai-shek. He suggested that Corcoran, as a private individual, charter a Delaware corporation and call it China Defense Supplies (CDS). It would be the sole operating entity for all Lend-Lease materials assigned to China, a civilian operation supported entirely by federal dollars directly from the Treasury Department. Corcoran claims to have had qualms, stating that it would be "dubious" legally, but he complied. CDS was headed by Chiang Kai-shek's brother-in-law and man-in-Washington, T. V. Soong. Although staffed largely by American businessmen, it was formed as a parallel of the British Supply Council to represent China in Lend-Lease transactions.[18]

Before CDS, Soong functioned as an official purchasing agent dealing through the Chinese-owned Universal Trading Corporation (UTC). This corporation used American credits extended to China from December 1938 through December 1940 to buy materials in the United States. With the increase in credit and anticipated Lend-Lease, Soong created CDS, which supplanted UTC, and became China's designated Lend-Lease agent in April 1941: "the many tentacles which Soong used to reach into government agencies prompted [Secretary of State] Morgenthau to remark that when dealing with CDS and its supporters he could not tell who was working for the United States and who for China."[19]

In truth, China was a minor player in Lend-Lease distribution. A primary reason was that Washington had little specific information as to what China's needs really were, because Soong's staff offered only vague generalities. But the War Department wanted Japan to be contained in China, and safeguarding the British Commonwealth's vast Asian holdings was "a major factor in maintaining China as a belligerent."[20] The Department, thus, concluded that China had to be sustained as a fighting force through Lend-Lease and so advised Roosevelt.

The Lend-Lease bill empowered the president to designate aid to "any country whose defense [he] deemed vital to the defense of the United States.... The President could sell, transfer title to, exchange, lease, lend, or otherwise dispose of any defense article." Repayment, if and when, would be in "kind or property, or any other direct or indirect benefit which the President deems satisfactory." The bill did not limit aid to physical materials; technology, training, American repair facilities, and intelligence sharing were included.[21] There was the expectation and hope that the recipients would show their gratitude by reasonable acquiescence to military and non-military American policy proposals. But it soon became evident that the British were reluctant to aid the Chinese, whom they always considered of secondary strategic significance. Chiang Kai-shek knew this and always believed his Caucasian allies deliberately conspired to provide inadequate and promised quantities of Lend-Lease materials to China. Chiang's conviction became a constant source of agitation to AMMISCA, Washington, and London.

China Defense Supplies constantly badgered the War and State departments for additional, and often unreasonable, quantities of Lend-Lease materials. On 11 August 1941, for example, Soong submitted an extraordinary request that would have sent one-third of the American navy's dive bombers to China. The War Department told Soong that all the United States could do was speed the flow of Lend-Lease supplies and facilitate the buildup of the American Volunteer Group (AVG), the fabled Flying Tigers.[22]

Army Chief of Staff General George Marshall's view of Soong's airplane and subsequent weapons requests was expressed in salty terms: "It would be an outrage for me to deny to MacArthur [General Douglas MacArthur, in charge of defending the Philippine islands] something that we send on a roundabout voyage up into China and I can't give any to MacArthur because I've got these regiments with only one [artillery] battery."[23]

3

The Commanders
The Leaders of World War II in Asia

> If we ask, first of all for the object upon which the whole effort of war is to be directed, in order that it may suffice for the attainment of the political object we shall find that it is just as variable as are the political object, and the particular circumstances of the war.
> — Anatol Rapoport, editor, *Clausewitz on War*

    To fully appreciate the events described in this text, a basic knowledge of the character, values, goals and experiences of the primary world leaders of the era is necessary. In the time immediately preceding Pearl Harbor, the prominent international leaders with the greatest interest in East and South Asia were China's President Chiang Kai-shek, Great Britain's Prime Minister Winston Churchill, and President Franklin D. Roosevelt. These men shared comparable traits of nationalism and a desire to shape the postwar world. Each had enough power to believe he could achieve his goals. Their perspectives and methods of implementation of policy were often at odds; especially those of Chiang, whose position was the most precarious, beset as he was by rival war lords, massive corruption, the Japanese invaders, a chaotic economy, and the indigenous Chinese communists. Although he was not a "world leader" it is appropriate to include General George C. Marshall. Marshall was the man at the top of the army's chain of command and it was Marshall to whom AMMISCA was responsible. These men were similar only in their dissimilarity.
    Winston Churchill's primary aspiration was to maintain the British Empire but, after two debilitating years of war with Germany, he was ill prepared to confront the formidable military forces of Japan. Churchill was a "moral grand strategist," but he was also a "traditional if not empire-builder, certainly an empire-maintainer."[1] He was determined to retain Britain's colo-

nial holdings rather than see them fall to the forces of change emerging in Africa, Eastern Europe, and China and Southeast Asia: "Compared with Roosevelt's, his vision was long but narrow; he could see the relation between wartime strategy and post war balances of power in Europe, but he could not imagine the surge of masses of people in Asia or Africa."[2] Roosevelt, however, was aware of the likely postwar upheavals and was, thus, "a devout anti-imperialist" who saw the war as a "crusade to free all oppressed people, including the colonies of America's allies."[3] The president also envisioned the establishment of a pro–Western democracy (and customer) in China.

Franklin D. Roosevelt

> [By 1940,] people were still trying to take the measure of the man. By the end of his second term his bewildering complexity had become his most visible trait. He could be bold or cautious, informal or dignified, cruel or kind, intolerant or longsuffering, urbane or almost rustic, impetuous or temporizing, Machiavellian or moralistic.... The baffling question about Roosevelt was what kind of internal standard, if any, determined which of his qualities would appear in what situation.
> —James M. Burns, *Roosevelt: The Soldier of Freedom 1940–1945*

After Pearl Harbor the principal world leader was President Franklin Roosevelt. He was a consummate politician with years of crisis experience and some deep-seated general ideals, albeit with problem-solving approaches that were unpredictable, pragmatic, and occasionally ill-advised. He also directed the soon-to-be most industrialized and richest nation in the world. According to his biographer James M. Burns, Roosevelt was a deeply divided man of "ideals," "faith" and "vision." But, in the main he was a practitioner of *realpolitik*, short term goals, "protecting his power and authority," and did not discuss his plans with anyone except his close associate Harry Hopkins. Roosevelt seemed to enjoy not sharing or discussing his strategies, perhaps because, ever the politician, he avoided blame if programs or strategies failed. More likely, his experience during the Great Depression had taught him that strategy or policy can never be static, but must be able to be applied flexibly.

Roosevelt had strong "assumptions which came out of the American values he shared with most other members of society." They were linked to his "extraordinary optimism and his public persona of confidence," as well as his "debonair administrative style." Historian Warren Kimball credits Roosevelt's optimism and confidence, which he conveyed to the American people, as major influences in America's energetic willingness to produce massive quantities of war materials.[4]

Roosevelt was a micro-manager and confided only in his top aide, Harry

Hopkins, who served him well in his management of several large New Deal programs. This relationship lasted until late 1943 when a liver ailment forced Hopkins out of the White House. It is worth remarking that Roosevelt was vexed by Hopkins' necessary withdrawal. He demanded loyalty and devoted service even though reciprocity was never his long suit.[5] In the same vein, the president was rarely troubled by modesty or uncertainty. He had tremendous self-confidence, perhaps based on his belief that he had saved capitalism in America.[6]

Many of Roosevelt's decisions as commander in chief of America's military are still criticized, especially by those who claimed the decisions were motivated more by politics than national welfare.[7] He pursued a course of personal close examination of recommendations from his military leaders and frequently ignored or modified them. Even when he accepted his military chiefs' recommendations, they had often been watered down from their original format because the officers knew what they really felt was the best course of action would be rejected out of hand by the president.[8] "The admirals and generals ... had to plan across a longer span of time [than politicians], because the decisions they made at one point — about construction, supplies, equipment, training stations — would affect operational decisions for years. It was part of their doctrine that tactical decisions were feckless and self-defeating unless shaped by broad strategy." The elaborate "war plans" in place for years and designed to defeat any other nation(s) if necessary "were tactically impressive but strategically almost worthless, for they existed in a political void that the Commander in Chief had no interest in filling."[9]

In point of fact, before Pearl Harbor the army and navy leadership submitted several operational plans related to possible U.S. entry into the war. There were also preliminary war discussions with the British from which several proposals emerged, the most noteworthy being "Europe first." But Roosevelt took no immediate position on most of the military's and Anglo-American advisory groups' recommendations. His management system was "fragmentized," and planners found coordination difficult.[10] Roosevelt's exercise of his constitutional power as commander-in chief of the American armed forces "had a marked effect in determining to what uses the military resources of the nation were put."[11] Some historians contend that Roosevelt not only "intended to wield the military power of the United States with his own hands, and not through the Secretaries of War and Navy ... but did not hesitate to ignore or override his military advisors in deciding by what means these ideas should be carried out."[12]

Sometimes Roosevelt's unpredictable behavior confused not only the American military planners but also their Japanese military counterparts: "To Tokyo planners Roosevelt seemed the most baffling of Western leaders. He appeared to shift overnight from conciliation to threats to high-blown preaching to invitations to parley."[13]

Regarding the president's assessments of Chiang Kai-shek and China, there is wide agreement among historians that Roosevelt, although empathetic with the misery of China's massive population and desirous that a postwar democracy be established, was surprisingly unaware of its internal cultural forces, particularly political and social. Thus, to some, the president was "bulldozed" by the Chinese. "The truth was he had contact only with Americanized Chinese like the Soongs, May-ling [Chiang Kai-shek's wife] and T. V. [Chiang's brother-in-law] the kind that other Chinese called 'banana' because they were only yellow on the outside, white on the inside. When the President met Chiang in Cairo in 1943, it was F.D.R.'s first glimpse, he admitted, of a 'real oriental.'"[14] As late as 1945 Roosevelt told historian Edgar Snow that he "was more than ever puzzled by Chiang Kai-shek as a man and a politician." But he also felt it appropriate to tell General Marshall that "the Generalissimo came up the hard way ... an enormously difficult job to attain any kind of unity from a diverse group of all kinds of leaders — the military men, educators, scientists public health people, engineers, all of them struggling for power and mastery ... and to create in a very short time throughout China what it took us a couple of centuries to attain."[15]

Roosevelt was secretive and did not share his plans and strategy. His decisions were often based on personal "gut-feelings" to the frequent consternation of his advisors. He was convinced that he could accomplish things that no one else could. (One is reminded of his naïve statement regarding Joseph Stalin: "I can handle Uncle Joe.") He was as determined to end British colonialism in Asia as he was determined to save British democracy from the Nazis. This study contains numerous examples of how Roosevelt's enigmatic persona negatively influenced numerous proceedings in the China-Burma area of operations during the AMMISCA era.

It is not within the scope of this study to examine Roosevelt's last years, but the question of the president's health in the war years is germane. The incredible stress of his office during the depression years; his devotion to cigarettes; his high blood pressure and congestive heart failure, which restricted the oxygen flow to his brain; certainly affected his intellect and his decision-making capability.

General George C. Marshall

General Marshall's views on strategy have been criticized by some of his former colleagues and subordinates and by a number of his foreign contemporaries. He personally kept silent on these issues, but his atti-

3. The Commanders

tude toward his critics was consistent with his usual readiness to consider all sides of a question. He agreed there had been mistakes, and opportunities missed, but he insisted it was necessary to judge the decision in the light of the knowledge commanders had at the time, and the paucity of their resources.
— Forrest C. Pogue, *George C. Marshall: Ordeal and Hope 1939–1942*

As chief of staff, the top ranking officer of the United States Army, General George Catlett Marshall was instrumental in the approval, establishment, and function of AMMISCA. Marshall, who had been deputy commander of the army's 15th Infantry Regiment in Tientsin, China, in the 1920s, became the army chief of staff in the summer of 1939. He immediately faced limitless challenges. America was still deeply isolationist; the 200,000-man army and army air corps lacked everything including funding, weapons, training facilities, and modern equipment. In the near future he would direct the army through a tremendous expansion to several million men and the construction of a talented officer corps. Fortuitously, Marshall was a "traditional soldier," extremely conscientious and dedicated, a man who did not suffer incompetence, real or perceived. But in all he did and in every decision he made, he put the army and nation first. He was a true man of character. Marshall recognized the necessity of the chief of staff having a close working relationship with Secretary of War Stimson and President Roosevelt. He felt this so strongly that early in his assignment he offered to resign in favor of a younger and more flexible chief of staff.

Because Lend-Lease to China was to consist primarily of munitions and weapons, Marshall insisted on the army's being involved in a supervisory role. Although a reasonable military-political system was created, it was made up of conflicting goals and inefficient

General George C. Marshall (U.S. Signal Corps, Office of War Information, Library of Congress).

chains of command and information. There were incompatible directives from the War Department, the State Department, White House bureaucrats including the president, Chiang Kai-Shek, Churchill, and many others, Americans, British, Burmese, and Chinese.

Marshall was disturbed by what he considered Churchill's ability to overly influence Roosevelt. To sway the president, more than once Marshall allied himself with the chief of naval operations, Admiral Ernest J. King. In the fall of 1942, Marshall and King proposed to Roosevelt that the "Europe" strategy be set aside in favor of a stronger, more aggressive policy towards Japan. It was a bluff, but served to bring about increased pressure on the British by the president. It also demonstrated the chief of staff's diplomatic skills.

Almost from the beginning of the war, Marshall was frustrated by Roosevelt's lack of unified planning for Europe and Asia. He agreed with Secretary of War Stimson that there was a condition of drift and a lack of national purpose, and that the president must bring unity. He was intermittently critical of what he saw as Roosevelt's failure to see the military big picture. Roosevelt tended to make promises, regardless of their impact on established policy. Moreover, he only rarely discussed programs, plans, or policy in a complete sense. Marshall felt that Roosevelt was, in contemporary parlance, a micromanager who believed he could and should deal with individual situations, on a unilateral basis.[16] Historian James Burns describes Marshall as "a planner and an organizer ... trying to apply logic and order to the building of an army ... in a context of unstable domestic politics and unpredictable global turmoil ... [but whose] passion for prudent planning and administrative order ... ran counter Roosevelt's ways."[17] Marshall's view of Roosevelt was shared by numerous high ranking military officers. "Stilwell held a view of Roosevelt shared by many Army officers at the time — that he was a rank amateur in military matters and that he was vacillating, impulsive, and too easily influenced by the last person to see him, especially if that person was British or worse of all Churchill."[18] Stilwell's impression of Washington was one of massive confusion. He wrote Mrs. Stilwell that it was a "rush of clerks in and out of doors, swing doors always swinging, people with papers rushing after other people with papers ... rooms crowded with clerks and banging away at typewriters.... Six months of this and I would be screaming in my sleep."[19]

As relates to the American army, Marshall felt that Roosevelt's personal management of so many issues sometimes restricted AMMISCA's ability to carry out its assigned tasks. The mission followed prescribed military chain-of-command procedures, and was unaccustomed to foreign cultures, Washington civilian insiders and seekers of influence, and people steeped in political manipulations. As will be noted, Marshall believed in the mission and personally selected Magruder to lead it, but he "retained his view formed as a young soldier in Tientsin many years before, of China as a backward and disorganized society."[20] It is not surprising, then, that differences arose between the two generals, and on several occasions Marshall became dissatisfied with Magruder and had no apparent regrets when Magruder departed China.

Winston Churchill

> Winston Churchill's ... thinking was deeply influenced, in the first place, by his memory of what the losses of the First World War had meant to his country and a determination that the defeat of Hitler should not be won at the same cost, and, in the second, by an awareness of the kind of problems that would have to be faced after victory was achieved. In consequence, his strategical ideas had a more emphatically political cast than was true ... in the case of his friend and ally in Washington, Franklin Roosevelt. Of all the political leaders of the major belligerents in the Second World War, Churchill had the greatest experience.
> For the first two years of Churchill's tenure of power, much of the energies of the [military] chiefs of staff had to be directed ... toward trying to maintain a tolerable relationship between him and the commanding generals in the field. For if the Great War had taught Churchill a good deal about the effective organization for the direction of the war effort, it had also left him a low regard of professional soldiers that comported ill with his boundless confidence in his own military judgment and in his talent for strategical and tactical decisions. As the war continued, the concentration of power in the hands of Churchill and the chiefs of staff gradually excluded both the War Cabinet and Parliament from any effective role in the formulation of strategy, a fact that occasioned intermittent protests and complaints, which were, however, rendered ineffective by the system's proven efficiency.
> — Gordon A. Craig, "The Political Leader as Strategist"

After the invasion of Poland in September 1939 and the invasion of Norway in April 1940, the reality of the menace Hitler posed could be denied only by the most ardent pacifists. These invasions, several internal political events and especially Prime Minister Neville Chamberlin's failure to stand up to Hitler at Munich brought the fall of his government. His biographer, Keith Freiling, states that he was not forceful because he was convinced that President Roosevelt could not overcome the "staunchly isolationist" American Congress. Freiling reiterates a Chamberlin statement: "It is always best and safest to count on nothing from America but words."[21] His anticipated successor was Foreign Secretary Lord Halifax, but Halifax was a peer, and no peer or lord had been a prime minister for decades. The Conservatives picked Winston Churchill. As a past member of both the Liberal and Conservative parties over his forty-year membership in the House of Commons, Churchill had also served as first lord of the admiralty, home secretary, secretary of state for war, chancellor of the exchequer, and several other Cabinet posts.

Churchill had not held an office after 1930 except for a short stint as first lord of the admiralty during Chamberlain's last days. He was regarded by many in both parties as an adventurer. But "Churchill, however often he had been wrong in the past on this issue or that, he had been right about Hitler's Germany. He was, moreover, the kind of leader who suited the British people. He was both an aristocrat and a democrat, a combination which the British like and which does not strike them as a paradox." Churchill "possessed, finally, an abundant mental energy. This worked both ways. His habits of work sometimes irritated his advisors who were forced to consider a stream of ideas, some of which were inevitably bad ideas, and to do so at unconventional hours of the day or night. But the gain was great, for with Churchill in command there could never be any doubt whether things were happening or not. Churchill was a leader who had no intention of allowing anybody inferior to give direction, but he was also a respecter of the people and of their principal institution, the House of Commons."[22]

When he linked his "experience" with his — to put it kindly — "high level of self-confidence," he began his gradual assumption of the positions of "head of government and supreme commander of the armed forces." He also assumed leadership over the Ministry of Defense and built "a new high command structure which proved to be the most efficient central system for running a war ever evolved in Great Britain or any other country."[23]

The prime minister and President Roosevelt were not well acquainted prior to World War II; their relationship began via correspondence initiated by Churchill after the advent of war in 1939. It is a fact that the working relationship between the two was a major element in the winning of the war, but it is also true that they were not always of the same mind in strategic thinking and planning. The prime minister always believed his principal responsibility was to maintain the British Empire; the president was equally determined to end colonialism wherever he could. Churchill did not see China as a significant element in the war; Roosevelt intended to reform China and build it into Asia's biggest postwar Western-oriented democracy. "Churchill believed Roosevelt's game was to make China strong enough to 'police' Asia while remaining essentially dependent on the United States. The Prime Minister complained to subordinates that the Americans expected to use China as a 'faggot vote on the side of the United States in an attempt to liquidate the British overseas empire.'"[24] Roosevelt was a strong believer in his own powers of persuasion; he felt he could convince Churchill to do things his way, and if not there was always the manpower and materials supply line emanating from America, "the arsenal of democracy," that could possibly coerce "changes" in British attitude. An early example of this was when Secretary of State Hull sought to gain American trade access to the colonial locations as reciprocity for Lend-Lease. "The concept of using lend-lease as a lever to force Britain to eliminate the imperial preference and extend the Open Door to America throughout the empire was not openly discussed in the State Department before the passage of the Lend-Lease Act, but the Department quickly made up for lost time afterword."[25]

Churchill acknowledged that he never felt he really "knew" Roosevelt. A revealing comment from the prime minister was his belief that "the only thing worse than having allies is not having them." In truth, Churchill was always fearful that materials badly needed in Europe, by far his main area of immediate need, would be sent to the Far East. Given the large quantities of aircraft, munitions, vehicles, petroleum products and other weapons and materials sent to China, he was correct.

The planning of grand strategy featured many Anglo-American differences of opinion, more than a few of which pertained to the China-Burma area of operations. In his account of the early war years in East Asia, John Payton Davies, second secretary of the American Embassy in Chungking, noted not only the different views of Churchill and Roosevelt, but their philosophical differences as to how the war and its outcome should be approached. "For the Americans war was science and technology, the production of weapons and fighting men, assembly and direct application of force." For Churchill, "war was an art. It was making due with scant resources, maneuver, wile, using others, and biding his time."[26] Churchill was responding to his natural instincts but also the immediate reality of the war.

There is no denying that Churchill had a tendency towards impetuosity, even after his authorship of the World War I British debacle at Gallipoli. His eagerness to limit Russia's postwar western expansion, which he always predicted, was reflected in his desire to invade Italy before France. Later in the war, he advocated recapturing Singapore and some of the Dutch and British East Indies rather than a campaign in Burma, which he believed Britain would re-acquire anyway. But he did not want it to happen "through a hemorrhage of British blood in Burmese jungles." Churchill "had no desire to risk an entanglement in the tropical underbrush of Burma delaying British repossession of Singapore, the symbol of Britain's imperial power and authority in Asia."²⁷

Churchill led a besieged and tired United Kingdom at a time when the British people were openly wondering why the Americans were not at their side as they had been, albeit after a similar delay, a quarter of a century earlier? There was widespread resentment and more than a few comments regarding America's letting the British bleed and expend treasure so that the United States at war's end could become the world's dominant military and economic power. Even late in the war Churchill, to a point, shared these sentiments. In a letter to his wife in August 1944, he complained, "We have three armies in the field. The first is fighting under American command in France, the second under General Alexander is relegated to a secondary and frustrated situation by the United States' insistence on this landing on the Riviera. The third on the Burmese frontier is fighting in the unhealthiest country in the world under the worst possible conditions, to guard the American air line over the Himalayas into their very over-rated China. Thus, two-thirds of our forces are being mis-employed for American convenience and the other third is under American command."²⁸

Churchill was quite naturally frustrated with American "dominance": the command structure; the natural irritations that occur in any "alliance"; and frustration that Washington insisted on the west-to-east European strategy as opposed to Churchill's "soft underbelly" strategy. The most trenchant aspect of Churchill for this study is the significant difference between London's and Washington's view of the China-Burma operational area. It demonstrates that the British government (Churchill) placed the Far East "well down the priority list for all manner of war fighting equipment, thus, Burma as an appendage to that theater was so far near the bottom as to be almost out of sight."²⁹ Churchill's famous statement that he "did not become His Majesty's First Minister to preside over the dissolution of the British Empire" should be remembered. His first priority in the Far East was always the preservation of Britain's East Asian colonial holdings.

Chiang Kai-shek

> One day in Singapore, I came upon a curious document entirely by chance. It was a British colonial administration copy of Generalissimo Chiang's old police record in Shanghai, listing assorted murders and indictments for armed robbery. These things were not widely known. There was an unspoken agreement between Americans in particular not to talk about The Soongs — especially the Chiang branch — with any realism; the way people are guarded about some terrible family

3. The Commanders

secret, or about the locked door in the attic where Mrs. Rochester rattles her chains waiting for the big fire. They were part of America's adult fairy tale about China.
— Seagrave Sterling, *Soong Dynasty*

Thinking back through the years, I now freely acknowledge that I myself was not sufficiently cognizant of the almost insuperable problems faced by the Chinese National Government.
— General Albert C. Wedemeyer

Chiang Kai-shek was born in 1887 in south central China's Chekiang province. He participated in the 1911 Revolution. For several years after 1911 he went into and out of society and spent some time establishing ties to the iniquitous criminal Green Gang of Shanghai. He became a prominent military personage in Sun Yat-sen's Tung Meng Hwei ("Sworn Together Society") and later the Kuomintang ("National People's Party" or "Nationalist Party"), hereafter "KMT." When he was sent by Sun to Russia in 1923, he convinced many Russian leaders he was a Marxist.

Chiang was in many ways a traditional Chinese warlord. His military and underworld connections, along with "mutual benefit" arrangements with warlords, served him well in his takeover of the KMT after Sun died in 1925. They were also critical supporters in his subsequent attempt to centralize national control by leading his army, via Shanghai to Peking, in the Northern Expedition of 1927–1928.

Chiang then took a strategic step. He divorced his third wife and married Mei-ling Soong, younger sister of Sun Yat-sen's widow, Ching-ling Soong. The Soongs were one of China's wealthiest Christian (Methodist) families. A third sister, Ai-ling, was married to H. H. Kung, who claimed to be a

General Chiang Kai-shek of China, 1937 (Press Association, Inc., New York, Library of Congress).

75th generation descendent of Confucius. The Soong sisters' brother was T. V. Soong. He and H. H. Kung, both Harvard-trained economists, became advisors to Chiang, although their relationships with the generalissimo were always mercurial, especially Soong's. In spite of almost constant bitter rivalry, the Soongs and Kungs played major roles in Chiang's government.

Kung was Chiang's primary money man, and due to his implementation of several positive fiscal reforms, including the currency reform of 1935, Chiang's regime achieved significant national and international respect in the mid–1930s. A major achievement was the return to a semi-stable economy through the realignment of the national currency in 1935, though this was only temporary:

> The national currency was an important step forward in rationalizing China's financial system and Kung accomplished it with a circular process by which Nanking issued bonds that were deposited in government banks which then used them as security for notes. In effect, Kung was printing money to finance government spending. This fueled inflation. In the beginning that was not a bad thing since it boosted purchasing power and pulled China out of its depression — by the end of 1936, industrial output was rising. But in the longer term Kung's policies undermined the credibility of government finances and created a growing gulf between the vast mass of the Chinese people and a small group of party insiders, personified by the Soong clan.[30]

The chronic budgetary imbalance led to abusive issuance of notes, which later caused severe inflation during the Japanese and civil wars and precipitated the economic collapse of the government in 1949.[31] Since all of this was done with Chiang's approval, he had to share in the ultimate responsibility. But his economic distresses demanded immediate attention, and Chiang judged that temporary solutions, even if flawed, could be addressed later.

Charles Wertenbaker describes Kung and Soong as follows:

> Kung seemed a many-sided character — at once aware of and capable of dealing in terms of the highest western standards of public morality and adept at operating in the Chinese milieu of squeeze, graft, family political considerations, and vendetta tactics against opponents. Soong was more completely western in the style of the American empire builders of the turn of the century, identifying the potential progress of China with the growth of his own fortunes.[32]

Soong was cut very similar to Kung in his value system and methods of operation. But he had a sidekick, Ludwig Rajchman, the Polish former director of the League of Nations Health Organization, who was well known in Washington diplomatic circles. Both "had a highly developed genius for understanding how the disparate parts of a complicated structure like a government bureaucracy fit together. They soon saw that official Washington was a jungle of departments often with overlapping functions and hostility toward

Chinese minister of finance Dr. H.H. Kung (right) visits the White House accompanied by Chinese ambassador Chenting T. Wang on 29 June 1937 (Library of Congress Prints and Photographs Division, Washington, D.C., #LD-DIG-HEC-22949).

one another. The best way to get something done was to collect influential friends who could circumvent or overwhelm opposition."[33]

Rajchman was highly skilled "at collecting influential friends ... particularly ... among the young New Deal reformers." Both men established themselves in the White House by supporting Roosevelt's belief that after the war

China would be a great world power. And, after the creation of China Defense Supplies, Roosevelt suggested that Soong retain William S. Youngman, Jr., as the head of the agency. Following this appointment, "Soong had Youngman staff China Defense Supplies with influential Americans and a few persuasive Chinese."[34] All appointees were preapproved by Chiang Kai-shek.

Using contacts with Harry Hopkins, Secretary of the Treasury Henry Morgenthau, Admiral Harry E. Yarnell, Lauchlin Currie, and Roosevelt relation Joseph Alsop, Soong and his cohorts used back channel means to pursue what they considered a noble purpose. They even bypassed the secretary of state, Cordell Hull. But it paid off; two months to the day after Pearl Harbor, Chiang, "with a keen sense of the new value of his resistance to the Japanese," sought half a billion dollars in loans from Britain and the United States. Although Ambassador Gauss warned of probable "misuse by banking and

On July 1, 1940, Dr. T. V. Soong, governor of the Bank of China (left), was presented to President Roosevelt by China's ambassador, Dr. Hu Shih (Library of Congress Prints and Photographs Division, Washington, D.C., #LD-DIG-hec-28863).

government elements," and even the pro–Chiang State Department's far eastern affairs advisor, Stanley Hornbeck, tried to obtain a clause in the loan agreement specifying how the credit was to be used, the Chinese government basically spent the money as it chose.[35] Secretary of the Treasury Morgenthau inquired of the White House as to "whether Currie was working for the President or T.V. Soong?"[36]

After his marginally successful Northern Expedition, Chiang established his government at Nanking and proceeded to accomplish several notable reforms. Internal improvements in the 1930s included road, railroad, and bridge building, construction of thousands of miles of dikes, the aforementioned reform of bank and financial systems, standardization of the Mandarin dialect (gwo yu) as the national spoken language; and expansion of the national airline (CNAC). He also sponsored the Confucian-based New Life Movement, an effort to emphasize tradition and unify China under the principles of China's greatest philosopher — as interpreted by Chiang. Such movements were not widely respected among foreign observers. American ambassador Nelson Johnson referred to one of them: "It is doubtful whether the personalities interested in the movement are sufficiently pure themselves to give the movement much prestige."[37]

Despite these reforms, Chiang's government was not strong militarily or economically. He was forced to continue to bargain with recalcitrant warlords to gain their support on individual matters, especially fighting the Japanese, which in turn perpetuated the quasi-feudal Chinese society. He was partially kept afloat economically by several significant American loans ($25 million in 1938 for "civilian supplies," and another $145 million in 1940). But the Japanese right-wing mindset, which in the 1930s included a majority of the populace, renewed their focus on China's land and natural resources. This became Chiang's major challenge, although in his mind it was always the communists.

In the 1930s after falling under military domination, Japan was governed by General Tojo Hideki and other totalitarian types. These people engineered an incident at the Marco Polo Bridge outside Peking in July 1937, the beginning of World War II in Asia. Before the end of 1938, Japan overran all of China's major seaports. Tokyo put pressure on Chiang to accede to terms that would have placed China's military and economy under Japanese control. The Generalissimo rejected the peace offer and moved his capital far into the interior up the gorges of the Yangtze River, in some of China's most rugged territory, to Chungking in Szechwan province. Schools, factories, even railroad rolling stock and rails and ties, were hauled or carried on the backs of individuals. This was a truly superhuman effort by gallant and highly motivated people.

By 1941 Chiang's problems had expanded to crisis proportions and the esteem he had gained in the war's early years began to fade. Extremely high inflation, four years of Chinese territorial losses to the Japanese and Japanese atrocities eroded his popularity. Lack of support from China's western associates was disturbing, as was the communist establishment of an armed entity within the nation. Almost none of Chiang's warlord accomplices provided combat support. There was a general reduction in morale among the civilian masses; daily many were being won over by communist cadres. The Generalissimo's army bordered on the pathetic: "On paper the Chinese division included all the arms and services it needed to make it a self-sufficient combat team. Division strength was nominally 9,529, but divisions averaged from six to seven thousand, some of them far under strength. Aside from lacking competent and trained commanders and staff officers and having only the rudiments of a supply system, the [typical] Chinese division had no artillery and was under strength in heavy weapons and rifles."[38] The Generalissimo maintained personal troops, estimated at about 300,000 personnel, whose loyalty to him was reasonably assured. But the loyalties of the rest of China's soldiers lay with their war area commanders, whose commands usually were several divisions. "That the division was its commander's property affected all Chinese tactics and strategy. The division was a political and military asset, not to be expended, for no replacements of men or material would be forthcoming."[39]

Chiang's strategy was simple: trade territory for time and force the Japanese to overextend their supply lines. He aggressively demanded military supplies from America and Britain, even to the point, on several occasions, of threatening to reach a peaceful accommodation with the Japanese. At first there was anxiety in London and Washington because a Chinese withdrawal would free up the Japanese occupation force. There is almost universal agreement among historians that by Western standards the Kuomintang regime was astoundingly corrupt. Chiang portrayed himself as a Bible-reading ascetic, but was in truth ruthless and lusted after power. He saw himself as a military strategist but was actually a micro-manager who frequently flooded frontline commanders with directives that no longer applied to the military situation. "In most cases, war area boundaries conformed to the ancient provincial boundaries. Often the war area commander doubled as provincial governor and exercised both military and political control. In the rear of each war area were a few of the Generalissimo's loyal divisions to guarantee the fidelity of the war area commander." This "wide dispersion of the better troops left the Generalissimo no mass of maneuver."[40] Obsessed with the communists, he stockpiled quantities of Lend-Lease war materials for his planned post–World War II war with the CCP. The corruption, waste, and unreasonable demands

3. The Commanders

for help from Chiang's Kuomintang government provoked many confrontations between Chungking, Washington, and London. It was AMMISCA's fate to become embroiled in many of these encounters, particularly the "quid pro quo" policy, which will be examined presently, that helped bring about the 1944 ejection of General Joseph Stilwell from his post as Chiang Kai-shek's chief of staff.

However, even with all Chiang's flaws, an appropriate question and one perhaps worth examining in a separate study is this: What other options did he have? Almost all the political, economic, and governing methods he employed were traditional in China. Even Madam Kung's order to empty a C-46 cargo plane filled with drums of gasoline and substitute a trousseau for her daughter's wedding was accepted; as was the conversion of a bullet-making factory to one producing cigarettes because it provided a profit that bullets did not.[41] Perhaps Chiang could be seen, without too great a stretch of the imagination, as a throwback to the not-very-long-ago days of China's emperor and warlord rulers' despotic, but very traditional, methods of governing.

4

Culture Clash
The Historical Foundation of Sino-Western Relations

> It might be argued ... that in seeing Chinese foreign relations in historical perspective, we face not a single embarrassing tradition but rather an embarrassment of traditions. A moment of meditation on the China past suggests that if we look back beyond the revolution of the twentieth century, or even past the "middle kingdom" view of the nineteenth, we may find other, older styles of dealing with the world that have also persisted into the modern period.
> — Michael E. Hunt, "Chinese Foreign Relations in Historical Perspective"

When AMMISCA arrived in China in October 1941, most members of the mission were ill prepared to work within the traditions and culture in the Asian nation. Further, the Mission's commanders in Washington and British leaders in London had little understanding of the societies in which the mission was to operate, and what they thought they understood was all too often inaccurate. Mission members faced more than the organizational challenges of distributing Lend-Lease supplies. Without an understanding of the culture and history of China and Burma, they had to cope with whole new ways of looking at the world. Similarly, officials in Chungking had to face their own cultural awakening as they attempted to deal with Western representatives. Throughout the AMMISCA era (October 1941–May 1942), representatives of AMMISCA, Britain, Burma, and China were operating in environments heavily influenced by conflicting presuppositions, differing expectations, and language barriers.

No culture has maintained and lived closer to its ancient ethical underpinning than China. No nation is more aware of its own history and traditions.

Some of China's early historical phenomena that created its "older styles" of dealing with the world that have persisted into the modern period became rock solid traditions early in the nation's existence. This happened for several reasons but primarily because the urban and rural masses accepted and sustained the traditions. Because they were always a society universally tied to the land, "change" invariably meant drought, flood or higher taxes. For this reason, the people always preferred the status quo and were reluctant to accept counsel and establish relationships beyond their borders.[1]

Many Chinese traditions and beliefs date from the ancient time of independent states in northeast China, which through the millennia evolved into the Chinese nation. These traditions were reinforced by China's early accomplishments in science, the humanities, art, and even governmental bureaucracy. These accomplishments led them to feel superior to other nations with whom they interacted. When Western peoples were wearing animal skins, the Chinese elite adorned themselves with silk and jade. Why then, did the Western peoples modernize so much more rapidly in subsequent periods?

For many centuries, in both China and the West, there was little "linkage between science and technology, between the theoretical scholar and the practical artisan."[2] However, when the time came, Europe inherited ways of "thought that made it more ready for scientific thinking." For example, the lack of progress in mathematics from the 1300s to the 1600s among the Chinese can be linked to the use of the abacus. The abacus is sometimes referred to as the earliest calculator, but because it was limited to a few linear digits, it was useless for advanced mathematics.[3]

The Impact of Confucianism

To the Confucianists, utopia lay behind, not ahead. The best has passed; it was not to come. To progress was regression. To advance was to return to the fancied perfection of the ancients.
— Davies, John Paton, Jr., *Dragon by the Tail*

China's beginnings were settlements along the loess banks of the Yellow River in present day northeast China. A socioeconomic dichotomy evolved: the landowning elites and the impoverished peasant masses. Until the end of the twentieth century, 70 to 80 percent of the Chinese people made their living from the land. It was an extremely rigorous life and starvation was commonplace. But the people's main desire was to be left alone so they could work their meager plots of land and avoid starvation. No change was ever a good change.

Confucius, the great sage, helped formulate the philosophy that welded the Chinese people together. With the possible exception of Mao Tse-tung, no man had a greater influence on China than Confucius (Kung Fu-tze). A brief appraisal of this man provides a valuable insight into China's tenacious preoccupation with and adherence to tradition. His legacy, which survives today, includes personal values, morality, education, respect, loyalty — and significantly — obedience.

Confucius did not espouse a religion. A philosopher of the 5th century B.C., he put forth a rather simple program of principles almost none of which he innovated; they were invented before his time. They included an ethical base similar in some ways to modern religions. "He was scrupulous in observing age-old rites to the supernatural but never theorized on its nature."[4] Confucius lived in a violent time and was appalled by man's treatment of his fellow man. He wanted to recreate the moral order on earth he believed existed in

Chinese laborers repairing the Burma Road near Kunming, 1944 (United States Army, Signal Corps, *New York World Telegram*; Library of Congress Prints and Photographs Division, Washington, D.C., LC-USZ62-134787).

ancient times. This could only be done if mankind followed the examples of the ancients.

Confucius affirmed that the sovereign and educated elites were responsible for setting an example and providing education. "It was for them to manifest and inculcate virtues such as righteousness, straightforwardness, and benevolent love of fellow men."[5] The world must live in harmony. Everything must be done in a dignified and decorous manner else there would be excess and conflict. There must also be obedience to the family. This loyalty to family, elders and on up to the emperor was ingrained into everyone born in China, and in this manner authoritarianism came to prevail at all levels. Confucian ideals of imperial benevolence had broad appeal to the masses.

Confucius insisted that China return to the mythological time of the "Sage Kings." They were positive examples of behavior and taught the people how to live in harmony. This was universally accepted by the people. Sadly, this tradition-based concept reinforced China's subsequent inability to react to external aggression from more modern technologically advanced rivals.

Confucius also advocated the superiority of some people and the inferiority of others. It was not difficult for the emperor or high officials to manipulate people's lives. "Each individual and each group had an assigned role in relations to others. Peasants who worked with their hands were much higher in the Confucian hierarchy than merchants who never broke a sweat. No one was to transgress his role and all were to perform in harmony."[6] But there was a caveat. The ruler must care for his subjects, because he ruled through the "Mandate of Heaven."

The Confucian concept of heaven must not be confused with the Western view of heaven. *T'ien* (Heaven) was where cosmic forces resided that impacted every person's daily life. Yang and Yin were the major forces and had the ability to impose severe warnings in the form of drought, flood, and famine on emperors who did not rule benevolently. This deeply ingrained and unshakable emphasis encouraged conformity and along with China's view of its own superiority over all other people, severely inhibited the nation from entering the modern world's comity of nations.

Confucianism evolved along several divergent lines. Schools of Confucian thought ranged from harsh state-controlled legalism with many rules and controls to the humanistic views of the greatest Confucian scholar, Mencius. Mencius believed that all men were born good and remained so until corrupted by the evils of society. The advent of the politically motivated Confucian bureaucracy instituted by the Han emperor Wu-Ti (140–87 B.C.) cemented the future dominance of legalism that haunted China until 1949.

Because Han Wu-Ti's Confucian bureaucracy was portrayed as representing only popular Confucian virtues, it was welcomed by the common people, especially when they were told that government officials were required to pass rigorous examinations based on Mencius' humanistic interpretations of Confucian principles. The emperor and his minions manipulated the Confucian ideals to convince the masses that Confucian altruism was uppermost in government planning and concern for the people was paramount. The opposite was the reality. This system was designed to gain, maintain, and expand power.

The scholar-officials who passed at least two Confucian exams and received a government bureaucratic appointment believed they were the administrators of a universal empire and their emperor (the Son of Heaven) ruled all on earth. Any fragmentation of China via foreign incursion of any sort "was more than a political disaster. It was also a violation of the moral order prescribed by heaven."[7] China regarded itself as the center of the universe and the source of all culture and civilization. As such, the nation believed the Chinese emperor ruled not only the Chinese at the heart of everything, but also the "uncivilized barbarian nations roundabout."[8]

They believed it was Heaven's will that all mankind abide by the natural order of the universe, that is, Confucian harmony. "Just as in heaven the Pole Star remained fixed in the centre and all the other stars revolved around it, so on earth the central ruler, the Emperor ought as the Son of Heaven, to be the immovable pole about which mankind moved. The Emperor stood as link between heaven and earth or between heaven and men."[9]

Early Chinese thought rarely led to aggression. Since China was the center of the world and the sole source of Confucian truth, their concept of empire was not one of colonial dominion but of cultural supremacy, and they believed China should try to civilize the barbarian.[10] Thus, their superiority complex persuaded them to selectively choose among the offerings of the West without betraying their own way of life.[11] This deep-seated belief was one of the primary causes of later Sino-Western hostility, especially when Westerners, ignorant and uncaring of Chinese cultural traditions, tried to impose their own values.

The Tribute System: An Insight into China's Traditional View of Commerce

> That tribute was a cloak for trade has been axiomatic ever since merchants from the Roman Orient reached Cattigora in southern-most China in A.D. 166 claiming to be envoys of Marcus Aurelius.
> —John K. Fairbank, *Trade and Diplomacy on the China Coast*

4. Culture Clash

> So fundamental was this commerce that the [Chinese government] regulations for tribute devote a whole section to it. Tribute missions arriving at the frontier normally included merchants as private individuals or as agents of the tributary ruler who often monopolized the trade. They brought with them commercial goods which they were allowed to sell to China merchants.
> — Fairbank, *Trade and Diplomacy on the China Coast*

The Chinese Tribute System was composed of two elements: Chinese superiority and monetary profit. Historians do not agree on its origin. Few, though, dispute its non–Western antecedents or that it was not administered in a similar fashion from dynasty to dynasty or emperor to emperor. There is no question that commercial profit, influence over the tributary areas, and peacekeeping on the borders were primary motivations. The usually accepted thesis is the system began in the Sung dynasty (A.D. 970–1279) and gained significant impetus and growth during the Ming Dynasty (A.D. 1368–1644). It was a significant factor in the Sino-Western confrontations in the 19th century.

A basic goal of the Sung policy was to reverse the military expansionism of its T'ang Dynasty predecessor. All nations who wanted to trade with China must pay tribute to the government. But because it was less expensive than trying to control uprisings, "gifts" provided by Chinese officials were given to foreign (barbarian) emissaries and commercial operatives to insure peace along their border. In the Confucian political and social hierarchy, merchants were in the lower levels of respectability and they reminded people that Confucius was highly critical of the merchant class, whom he characterized as parasites living off the sweat of others, never getting their own hands dirty.

There were times, aberrations actually, when China was briefly more open to foreign concepts. The major example was in the Ming Dynasty. Emperors Hung Wu (1368–1398) and Yung Lo (1403–1424) sent envoys to surrounding realms including Japan, Korea, Ceylon, Malaya, the Maldive Islands, and Hormuz at the entrance of the Persian Gulf. Profit was not the sole motive; their mission included "showing the flag," exploration, and establishing Chinese "culturalism" as not only the largest and oldest of the world's nations, but also the source of all other civilizations.[12] The voyages were under the command of Admiral Cheng Ho, a Muslim eunuch from western China, and they were a quintessential example of "what might have been" for China — if it had not been so deeply convinced of its own superiority in the world.

The incredible voyages of Cheng Ho are worth mentioning, particularly in their contrast to past and future Chinese practice. These voyages took place a century and a half before the great English sea captain and globe-circling explorer Francis Drake. The first of Cheng's seven voyages reached India with a fleet of 62 ships and 28,000 men. The largest vessel in the fleet measured 444 feet bow to stern and 180 feet at mid-ships and had nine masts. The flagship had four large cannon, twenty smaller ones and numerous rockets and bombs. The fleet could make six knots with a following wind, and the ships with their waterproof compartments were technically far advanced over their European counterparts. The primary navigation aid was the compass, unknown in Europe.

Contracts were made with the subordinate states' rulers primarily to establish a superior-to-inferior relationship. This was achieved in several ways, one of which was the "kowtow." Specifically, the kowtow was kneeling three times and touching the floor with one's head nine times at each kneeling. Asians were willing to perform the kowtow to enhance their commercial profit, so the Chinese saw no reason to modify the practice for the western barbarians. "This [the voyages] was not an aggressive imperialism. Rather, it was a defensive expression of culturalism: foreign rulers if they wished contract with the Middle Kingdom had to accept its terms and acknowledge the universal supremacy of the Son of Heaven. Trade with China might be of great value. Tribute formalities were the price to be paid."[13] The subsequent waves of European traders, however, vehemently disagreed.

Cheng Ho's expeditions greatly expanded China's interaction with the outside world, but tragically they were "suddenly stopped and never resumed or initiated later."[14] There were several reasons for the cessation of the voyages. The first was the great cost. Another reason was that after Emperor Yung Lo, the opponents of exploration were able to overcome the pro-commerce supporters. Diplomatic relations were never of much significance to Chinese bureaucrats due to their outlook on other nations. However, the main reason for the end of the voyages was China's oldest anti-modernization nemesis: Confucianism. The Confucian scholar-official bureaucratic class was so powerful that they quashed future voyages, and most of the log books and charts were destroyed. Cheng Ho's feats were almost totally removed from the historical records.[15] "The Ming [and later] courts unlike that of contemporary Portugal, had no ... grasp of the possibilities of [or threat of] sea power. The Ming voyages were not followed up but remained isolated *tours de force*, mere exploits."[16] The cessation was a lost opportunity that exemplifies China's devotion to the traditional way of doing things.

A legacy of the tribute system was continued opposition to progress in science and commerce, which enhanced the belief that the only acceptable "change" was regression: "a degree of mingled fear and contempt for the outside world and a narrow concentration on the exclusively Chinese way of life produced a growing ethnocentrism. Eventually it dominated Chinese foreign actions and gave an intellectual and psychological immunity to foreign stimuli."[17] This was the frame of reference for China's policy makers until the end of World War II.

Missionaries: The Legacy of Centuries of Efforts to Bring the Christian God to the Chinese

> There is no group of foreigners who have done more harm to China than the modern missionaries, either directly or indirectly. It is in connection with their subversive activities that China has lost the greater part of her dependencies. By their teachings they have denationalized hundreds of thousands of Chinese converts, and have thus been instruments to a great extent, in disintegrating not only the body, but the spirit of the nation.
> — T'ang Liang-li, "Missions: The Cultural Arm of Western Imperialism"

For half a millennium Western religionists endeavored to effect "change," that is modernization, as they defined it, in China. They were not always altruistic, perhaps because to many of them the Chinese were simply heathens. In *To Change China*, Jonathan Spence provides accounts of sixteen such men and their experiences beginning in the 1640s with the Jesuit missionary Adam Schall. The lives of Schall and the others "have a curious continuity.... They bared their own souls and mirrored their own societies in their actions, yet in doing so they highlighted fundamental Chinese values and they speak to us still ... about the ambiguities of superiority and about the indefinable realm where altruism and exploitation meet."[18]

Because of his education in physics, mathematics, and astronomy, Schall became a middle-level office holder in the Chinese bureaucracy. His assignment was "one of those rare moments in time when two streams of history converge..." Sadly, Schall died in Peking under house arrest in 1666. He was a victim of the jealousy of Chinese astronomers whose skills he had surpassed; anti–Christian Chinese who accused him of high treason; and unrelenting anti–Jesuit criticism from Dominican and Franciscan missionaries. Schall's experience foreshadowed many later Western efforts to open China except his was not an aggressive act as was typical of later western missionary zeal.

Before this moment, China secure in its superiority never dreamed that anything of value was to be found in the West. From the seventeenth century onward the Chinese definition of the world was to come under increasing attack. The Westerners were not like earlier barbarians, who could be absorbed by China and learn to accept her values. Instead, their aim was to change China into something acceptable to them, to make China partake of Western values."[19]

In the late 19th century, missionaries often were their own worst enemies. They rode on opium seller's ships into the interior and instilled Christian and other barbarian notions by creating "rice Christians." Rice Christians were converts who were hated by native Chinese for giving up their traditional beliefs for a bowl of rice provided by a barbarian missionary. Chinese were protected from prosecution for transgressions committed as long as they stayed on Mission property.

Wars, Unequal Treaties, and Rebellions

> In retrospect, it is apparent that opium was the immediate, but not the ultimate cause of the [opium] war. Without it, a conflict between China and the West would still have erupted as a result of their differing conceptions of international relations, trade and jurisprudence. Far deeper than the opium question was the incompatibility of the Chinese claim to Universal over lordship with the Western idea of national sovereignty; the conflict between the Chinese system of tributary relationships and the Western system of diplomatic intercourse; and the confrontation between self-sufficient agrarian China and expansive industrial Britain. The power generated from the industrial Revolution and the idea of progress through change propelled the West into overseas expansion. There was no way to stop it.
> — Immanuel C. Y. Hsu, *The Rise of Modern China*

In the 18th and 19th centuries, the British infatuation with tea and the Chinese demand that it be paid for in silver brought a crisis to the British treasury. To offset the outflow of silver, the British began to export opium from India to China. This was not a new phenomenon; Arab traders had introduced it to China in the late seventh century. Recreational smoking by mixing it with tobacco began almost a thousand years later. But with a plentiful supply in the eighteenth century, its use spread quickly and by the 1830s one out of every 165 Chinese was addicted. The vast majority of the product was brought in by the British and, although outlawed, was eagerly purchased by citizens of all socioeconomic levels: royalty, the wealthy, literati, criminal gangs, laborers, even monks and nuns. "In 1838, nine out of ten people in Kwangting and Fukien provinces were addicts and opium shops in towns were as common as gin shops in England. The addict went to any length to acquire the drug."[20]

The only legal importation of any foreign goods was through Canton.

4. Culture Clash

Many areas of the Burma Road, seen here in 1939 or 1940, were subject to weather and damage done by untrained Chinese truck drivers (Library of Congress Prints and Photographs Division, Washington, D.C., Office of War Information, U.S. Farm Security Administration/Office of War Information/Public Health Service Commission, #LC-USW33-043109-ZC).

Known as the Hong system, it was a carryover from tribute days. Foreign traders could not live permanently on shore; could not conduct business transactions with anyone but their Chinese counterparts, the Hong merchants; could bring no weapons or family ashore; and could have no contacts with government officials or communication of any kind with the national government. Corruption in the form of bribery was rampant.

Great Britain, the leading imperialist nation, sought to expand its trade with China through the establishment of formal diplomatic relations. The Macartney Mission was dispatched in 1793. Although Macartney was excused from performing the kowtow, the only tangible result of the interview was a deliberately insulting message to King George III from the Chien Lung emperor; the mission was a total failure. The event stands as an excellent example of the arrogance that permeated both sides and fueled the Sino-Western dissonance. An ill-advised Chinese confiscation of all foreign-owned opium in Canton led to the Opium War, which lasted from 1839 until the signing of the Treaty of Nanking, the first "unequal treaty," in 1842.

This treaty forced a horrendous indemnity of 21 million dollars on the Chinese as well as the cessation of all restrictions on foreign import trade through Canton. Five new ports were open to trade and the importation of opium was not prohibited. It also established *most-favored nation* status, wherein concessions, for example trade rights, granted to any foreign nation would automatically accrue to Britain. In addition, the treaty established *extraterritoriality*, wherein foreign nationals charged under Chinese law would be tried by their own countrymen under their own laws. This Treaty was a set piece of what was to follow. France, America, Russia, Japan and several other nations enacted similar pacts. The Second Opium War, also known as the Arrow War (1856–1860), brought further economic and territorial "lease hold" grants. Ensuing confrontations forced additional concessions and reinforced anti-foreignism among the Chinese.[21]

Concurrent with the international collisions resulting in the Unequal Treaties was China's most serious internal upheaval, the Taiping Rebellion (1840s to 1864). It is estimated that over twenty million Chinese died. The leader of the Taipings was Hung Hsiu-ch'uan, a member of the Hakka minority, whose mental breakdown after repeatedly failing the Confucian examinations caused him to sink into delirium. He claimed to have dreamed he was the son of God, the younger brother of Jesus Christ. In 1847, Hung became acquainted with a Southern Baptist missionary, Isaacher Roberts. The same year he formed the Tai Ping Tien Kuo (Kingdom of Heavenly Peace). His followers were known as God Worshippers. Hung believed the Christian God was the one true God, whose "purity and presence had existed in China until the forces of Confucian belief swayed the Chinese away from the true path of righteousness."[22] Hung devised doctrines he claimed were based on Christian theology, which included concepts of anti-foreignism centering on the expulsion of the ruling Manchu dynasty.

Hung then led a protracted military campaign against the Manchus. Even though his capable military leader was an illiterate charcoal maker and his treasurers were former pawn brokers, he was at first successful.[23] In its initial stage, the movement appealed to many Westerners because of its seeming pro–Christianity, but Hung's interpretation of Christian principles was so distorted that he lost even the support of Issacher Roberts, who left the movement with a scathing condemnation of Hung's doctrines and methodology.

The Taipings were ultimately defeated by an international force of mercenaries known as the Ever Victorious Army, initially led by American Frederick Townsend Ward and including three independent Chinese regional armies that included no Manchu soldiers.²⁴ The rebellion demonstrated the decrepitude of the Manchu dynasty, now a financial ruin, and that the Chinese regarded the Manchus as foreigners. Thus, the Taiping uprising caused an increase in anti–Manchu and anti–Christian fervor that soon encouraged the Boxers and other secret societies. The rebellion also brought opportunity. The chaos provided favorable conditions for men of a democratic turn of mind like Sun Yat-sen, for Confucian reformers such as K'ang Yu-wei, and for regional strong men like future dictator Yuan Shih-kai.

Late 19th Century Events: The Failure of Internal Efforts to Change the Traditional Status Quo

> The period around the turn of the century was characterized by uncertainty and a searching everywhere apparent in the writings of the intellectuals. Historians have significantly failed to give this interim period between China's death and rebirth any specific name. There were few consistent currents. It was a decade and a half of intellectual turmoil.... Famine, suffering, and inept government marked this period. China's future leaders, deep in thought, read voraciously and tried to understand the new concepts and isms the modern world was offering China.
> — Franz Schurmann and Orville Schell,
> *Imperial China: The Decline of the Last Dynasty and the Origins of Modern China*

> In China, winning the acceptance of Chinese officialdom for even minor reforms was a difficult task, for it was the Chinese Scholar-official class which retained the largest vested interest in the old Confucian order. They were not amenable to any alteration of the *status quo* lest their positions be threatened and they clung tenaciously to tradition, vilifying any attempts at reform as a betrayal of the sacred national credo, Confucianism.
> — Schurmann and Schell

A portion of the post–Taiping Rebellion anti-foreign Chinese were intellectuals, mostly nonviolent, who called for reforms that would strengthen China against Western incursions while maintaining Confucian principles. Their dedication was reinforced by China's humiliating loss in the Sino-Japanese war of the mid–1890s. An upper-level Confucian degree holder, K'ang Yu-Wei, was one of the reform leaders. He advocated numerous restructures and felt China must learn of and emulate foreign achievements. He was almost a singular voice, at least in terms of the degree of change he advocated. Most of the reformers, many of them educated abroad, encouraged a "hybrid polity" containing both Chinese and Western rudiments. K'ang, supported by the reform-oriented emperor, Kuang Hsu, formulated the "Hundred-Day" Reforms of 1898. They included a revamping of the top-level ruling bureaus and boards, a revision in the Confucian examination system with the addition of some "Western learning" subjects, and a program to move the nation closer to a constitutional monarchy. It was too much too fast and ended abruptly in disaster.[25]

The reformers had not considered the level of opposition or the power of the ultra-conservatives that Empress Dowager Ts'u-hsi, Kuang Hsu's aunt, and mother of the deceased former emperor Hsien Feng, would muster. She held dictatorial power and when the reforms were announced, summarily removed the emperor from the throne. He was saved from execution only through the intervention of German, Russian, and British diplomats, but was placed in total isolation and died in November 1908. The motivation of the European opposition was their fear that the reversal of the reforms and the emperor's execution would lead to more anti-foreign feeling and the possible loss of the territories they controlled under previous forced leases. There was also concern over Japan's new aggressiveness, naval expansion, and clear desire to increase its influence in China's commerce and distribution of natural resources. Anti-foreignism increased measurably after 1898, as did radical reform movements.

The Boxer Rebellion: Popular Anti-Foreignism Peaks

> The [19th] century ended with the development of the Boxer's association which began as a domestic opposition movement but was diverted by the Empress Dowager against foreign powers in the Boxer Rebellion of 1900.
>
> — Schurmann and Schell, *Imperial China: The Decline of the Last Dynasty and the Origins of Modern China*

In the latter years of the nineteenth century, there were numerous religious and political uprisings. Emotionally stirred and strongly anti-foreign, thousands of young men, especially in the Shantung province, began studying the ancient arts of self-defense, including a type of pugilism. They were motivated by the heavy missionary activity in Shantung, hatred of their "Rice-Christian" countrymen, and the fact that they were controlled by "foreign [Manchu] occupiers." The largest of the several radical groups was the "Society of the Righteous and Harmonious Fist"— the Boxers. At first only a few members of the intellectual class participated. Collectively, they adopted several rites from radical Buddhist and Taoist martial organizations. But, fearful of another Taiping disaster, the empress dowager worked to direct the unrest against the foreigners.

The Empress Ts'u-hsi did very little overtly, but the movement gained large numbers of recruits from among the lowest skilled urban masses and even attracted units of females. In 1900, their numbers in Peking increased and they caused numerous uncontrolled violent eruptions against British missionaries and European businessmen. Western diplomats demanded protection for the Chinese Christians. In mid–June, a multi-national military force began to land near Tientsin to support the foreigners. The force included soldiers from Great Britain (with Indian and Chinese included), America, Japan, Russia, France and others. Two days later in Peking the German minister, who delighted in slashing Chinese with his riding crop, was dragged from his horse and murdered. On June 21, Ts'u-hsi issued a declaration of war against the foreign powers whose diplomats and staffs had taken shelter in their Peking legations, where they were now under siege. The relief force reached Peking in mid–August, lifted the siege, and began taking revenge by looting in the Forbidden City and burning the Summer Palace.

In September 1901 after the rebellion was put down, the greed-driven imperialistic powers — especially the Germans, British and Japanese — levied the Boxer Protocol. All Confucian exams were banned for five years in the five cities where foreigners had been killed, for two years no weapons could be brought into China, and several Boxer leaders were to be put to death. An indemnity totaling 330 million dollars, almost twice as much as the annual Manchu national income, was to be paid in gold to governments who had suffered from the Boxers. The payments would last until 1940. The only positive aspect of the protocol was that America apportioned more than half of its reparation to establish the Boxer Indemnity Fund for the education of Chinese students in America and Americans in China. Nevertheless, this protocol, formulated by seekers of power and profit, was heartless and without common sense and engendered unnecessary rancor, used ever since but especially in the 1920s and 1930s, by anti–Western Chinese to rouse popular feeling.

China's 1911 Revolution: The End of the Manchu Dynasty

> So ... the more than two millennia of China's imperial history were brought to a close and with almost no experience whatsoever in the arts and institutions of self-government, the Chinese people were pre-

sented with the option of devising their own future in a watchful and dangerous world.
— Jonathan Spence, *Search for Modern China*

The post–Boxer Rebellion years brought no respite from the disorder in China. On 10 October 1911, a revolutionary group in Hankow lost their bomb-making factory in an accidental explosion. In the rubble Manchu police found names and addresses of the leaders of other revolutionary groups. Fear of prosecution brought widespread, although uncoordinated, revolutionary uprisings.

Shantung's provincial military strongman Yuan Shih-kai commanded the relatively independent and proficient northern (Beiyang) army. The Manchu leadership approached Yuan and asked him to defeat the rebels. He agreed, overran several rebel groups, and then approached the revolutionary leadership and offered to sell out to them if he became their new commander. Having no choice, they agreed. Several local provincial assemblies ("parliaments") were established. The Peking assembly elected Yuan premier of China and thus the de-facto head of a state badly regionalized between northerners and southerners.

Chinese labrorers forced to work on the road, repairing Japanese bomb damage, 1939 or 1940 (Library of Congress Prints and Photographs Division, Washington, D.C., Office of War Information, U.S. Farm Security Administration/Office of War Information/Public Health Service Commission, #LC-USE6-D-010616).

His primary opponent was the popular southerner Sun Yat-sen. Sun might have created a viable challenge, but unfortunately for his ambitions, he was fund-raising in America at the time of Yuan's ascension to power. Although from a poor family, in the early 1880s Sun attended a religious school in Hawaii. In addition to Christianity, he absorbed the basic principles of democracy. He then went to Hong Kong and became a medical doctor, but he also participated in several revolutionary uprisings. All of them failed and he fled to Japan.

Sun was one of the primary Chinese intellectual reformers who subscribed to Western thought, including economics, philosophy, science, and political systems. After he returned from Japan, Sun formed a revolutionary group and then melded it with a larger group known as the Kuomintang, the National People's Party. In the spring of 1913 the party's leader was assassinated, almost certainly at Yuan's orders, and Sun replaced him. However, by the end of November, Yuan was afraid of their power and he forced parliament to declare the KMT an outlaw organization. Sun again was forced into exile in Japan.

The May 4th Movement: China's Rejection of Itself

> Though Yuan had ambitious plans to revitalize China, he lacked the military power or the organizational skills to hold the center together. Political power, accordingly, flowed out either to the elites in the provinces — both rural and urban — or to the hundreds of military leaders who began to emerge as the dominant power brokers in China's localities....
> The result was a period of political insecurity and unparalleled self-scrutiny and exploration. Many educated Chinese were convinced that their country was about to be destroyed, and they began to study every kind of political and organizational theory, examine the nature of their own social fabric, debate the values of new forms of education and language, and explore the possibilities for progress that seemed to lie at the heart of western science. Known generally as the May Fourth movement, such a concentrated outpouring of intellectual exuberance and doubt had not been seen in China for over two thousand years....
> — Jonathan Spence, *Search for Modern China*

The early twentieth century saw much unrest. The short and chaotic rule of Yuan Shih-kai is a vivid example of the conflicting forces that plagued early 20th century China. Western relations with Yuan's Chinese government continued to create discord both internally and externally. Yuan manipulated the foreigners rather well and succeeded in obtaining diplomatic recognition for his government from America in early 1913 and from Britain in October. He also moved to expand his power internally through restrictive policies regarding education, currency reform, and changes to the recently enacted provisional constitution, especially the reduction in numbers of the members of parliament. This and his later effort to obtain dictatorial powers brought national discord.

Adding to the steadily increasing anti-foreign fervor was the Japanese issuance of the Twenty-One Demands in January 1915. "In these, the Japanese demanded far more extensive economic rights for their subjects in Manchuria and Inner Mongolia; joint Sino-Japanese administration of the huge ... iron and steel works in central China ... the stationing of Japanese police and economic advisors in north China; and extensive new commercial rights in Fujian [Fukien] province."[26] The popular reaction from the Chinese included extended demonstrations and boycotts of Japanese imports. The only genuine sympathy or support for China, and it was only verbal, came from America. Washington advised the Chinese to make the Twenty-One Demands, submitted in secret by the Japanese, known to the world. This did bring a few mild Japanese concessions, but Yuan's popularity steadily declined. In March 1916 he announced he would no longer pursue the throne. Yuan contracted uremia and died three months later.

To moderate at least some of the foreign impositions, Peking, during the war, attempted to obtain a voice at the Versailles post–World War I Peace Treaty negotiations by sending over fifty thousand laborers to France to dig trenches for the allies. They innocently believing their participation would mean their national concerns would be addressed. They were encouraged in this after they, like Germany, presumed that Woodrow Wilson's Fourteen Points program, a lasting world peace agreement, with an end to big power world dominance, would be the agenda at Versailles. But the major world powers, France, Britain, and newly influential Japan, were intent on maintaining and expanding their territories and influence. China's hopes for a reduction of Japanese and Western leaseholds and influence in China were never seriously considered.

On May 4, 1919, student organizations in Peking protested the manner in which China was being treated at Versailles. They had learned that China's Shantung province, Confucius's birthplace, was to become a Japanese holding in return for Japan's support of the European allies in the war. The Japanese had always been held in low regard by the Chinese, who commonly referred to them as "dwarf people." Additionally, at Versailles, the great powers had promised to not oppose Russia's increased influence in Mongolia. For example, Britain's support for Japanese mainland expansion was gained by Japan's agreeing to let the British take over several formerly German-controlled islands in the Pacific.

The students were further enraged by two other events. The first was an agreement between the post–Yuan Shih-kai government in Peking and Tokyo wherein Japan agreed to loan millions of yen to Peking in return for railroad construction and police powers in Shantung. The second incident occurred in Peking when some of the Chinese Versailles delegates, home on leave, were verbally assaulted and threatened by angry student radicals. The home of the minister of communications, who had negotiated the Japanese loans, was burned and a student was killed. The student radicals accused negotiators of surrendering Chinese sovereignty to the Japanese.[27] In addition to Peking students, other universities, overseas Chinese organizations, merchants, and the press provided support. Anti-Japanese boycotts took place for years, even over the opposition of warlord rulers. China did not sign the Versailles treaty.

The primary outcome of the movement was the intellectual ferment manifested in the widespread production of leftist thinking and political activism. Western thought and education materials were translated into Chinese, and Western intellectuals including Bertrand Russell and John Dewey came to China to lecture. Confucianism was openly attacked. "The May Fourth incident served as a catalyst for the intellectual revolution in China.... A split appeared among Chinese intellectuals. Those who were bitterly disappointed by the Versailles Conference began to turn to Marxist socialism under the influence of the Bolshevik Revolution; others who were tradition-bound blamed Western materialism as the cause of the World War I and suggested Chinese spiritualism as an antidote."[28] While it is true that the May 4 Movement was an effective force in destroying the past, it also impacted the future by creating a widespread atmosphere of dissent.

Warlord and Republican Eras: Sun Yat-sen, Chiang, Kai-Shek, and the Kuomintang Ascension to Power

The warlords who dominated much of the geography of 1920s China had a wide range of backgrounds and maintained their power in different ways. A large number had risen through the Beiyang Army and had been protégés of Yuan Shih-kai: many others had served in the provincial armies and had risen to positions of senior officers in late 1911 and 1912. A number were simply local thugs who had seized an opportunity to consolidate a local base. Some dominated whole provinces and financed their armies with local taxes collected by their own

bureaucracies: others controlled only a handful of towns and got their money from "transit taxes" collected at gunpoint or through confiscation. Some warlords were deeply loyal to the idea of a legitimate republic continuing to hope that one day they would be reintegrated into a valid constitutional state; others believed that Sun Yat-sen and the Guomindang [Kuomintang] represented China's legitimate government. Out of choice or necessity, a number worked closely with foreign powers, whether it was the British in Shanghai, the Japanese in Manchuria, or the French in the southwest.
— Jonathan Spence, *Search for Modern China*

Sun Yat-sen was groping for a party organization that could make the transition from a seizure of power to a civil government exercising "political tutelage" over the Chinese masses.
— John K. Fairbank, Edwin Reischauer and Albert Craig,
East Asia: Tradition and Transformation

China's warlord era lasted from 1916 to 1928. The warlords had armies, paramilitary bodies, alliances with each other, in some cases wealth, and no true opponents except each other. The people continued to suffer as foreign influence expanded inexorably and the quality of life reached a new historical low. The period, however, did give rise to some positive occurrences. One of them was economic progress; another was the transition of the KMT into the dominant political entity in China.

Between 1915 and 1920, Sun Yat-sen began to build a military and political base at Canton. Sun's actions reflected the transformation that was 1920s and 1930s China, referred to by many as the Republican Era.

In October 1923, Sun Yat-sen welcomed Michael Borodin and several other Russian communist envoys to Canton. Sun hoped to receive support from the Russians after his pleas for assistance to the Western democracies were ignored. At the Russians' urging, Sun issued a manifesto outlining his reorganization of the KMT. He obtained party approval for reorganization at the first KMT party congress in 1924.

Sun placed a great deal of trust in Borodin, who wrote the first draft of a KMT constitution. It included dual party membership for communists, and a working relationship between the KMT and the Chinese Communist Party (hereafter referred to as CCP) members. It also established a system of local communist cells that sent delegates to upper-level committees but whose main task was organizing mass support and communist membership in the KMT. Sun sent Chiang Kai-shek, his top ranking military subordinate, to Moscow to study Russian military systems and tactics and become imbued with communist ideology.[29]

Upon his return from Russia, Chiang was appointed head of China's

4. Culture Clash

Russian-financed Whampoa Military Academy, where he instituted a heavy curriculum of indoctrination of the officer candidates, the main theme being loyalty to Chiang. The new graduates were initially utilized to support KMT political actions including suppression of uprisings in Hong Kong and the establishment of a KMT government in Canton in July 1925.

Chiang was then appointed commander of the 90,000 man KMT Army. After Sun's death in March 1925, Chiang revived Sun's program to unite China through a "Northern Expedition" to subdue the warlords and capture the national capital at Peking. The next step, he promised, would be implementation of Sun's program of San Min Chu I ("Three People's Principles"), which promoted of nationalism, people's livelihood and democracy.

Two KMT armies, partially equipped by Russia, were sent north. In September of 1926, Wuhan fell and by March 1927, Nanking and Shanghai. At Shanghai, home base for thousands of CCP members, Chiang demonstrated his anti-communist position. Instead of living up to a promise to support a CCP uprising in the city, he rested his army outside the city walls while the communists were slaughtered. Two truths emerged: Chiang had not become enamored with communism while in Russia and, after Shanghai fell, his incarceration of Shanghai businessmen for ransom along with his renewal of ties with Shanghai's infamous criminal Green Gang prompted many to now regard him as a warlord.

Concurrently, Japan was falling under control of militarists. In 1889, Japan implemented a constitutional monarchy with an elected parliament. The Japanese decided to model themselves on the British island's industrial pattern even though they bore much enmity towards what they saw as a greedy Western racist conspiracy to keep them weak industrially. They were being blocked from obtaining the desperately needed natural resources located on the Asian mainland. In addition, the democratic elements were unable to oppose the militarists who assassinated rival generals, high ranking government cabinet members, and even a prime minister or two in the 1920s and 1930s.

In 1928 Japanese militarists acted, fearful that China would be more unified under Chiang. The militarists also lusted after Chinese territory and natural resources. Stationed in Manchuria as a result of the Russo-Japanese war and World War I treaties and not under direct control of Tokyo, the leaders of Japan's Kwantung Army decided to take control of Manchuria.[30]

In mid–September 1931, a small bomb exploded on a Japanese controlled railroad outside Mukden, Manchuria. Within months, Japanese troops overran the rest of the province. The Western-dominated League of Nations sent a commission to investigate, but no sanctions were levied. In late January 1932, the Japanese bombed and shelled Shanghai and occupied part of the city.

A village street along the Burma Road, 1939 or 1940 (Library of Congress Prints and Photographs Division, Washington, D.C., Office of War Information, U.S. Farm Security Administration/Office of War Information/Public Health Service Commission, #LC-USW33-042087-ZC).

Chiang did not concentrate on fighting the Japanese, whom he described as "a disease of the skin." Instead, he conducted a series of so-called bandit suppression campaigns against his "disease of the heart," the Chinese CCP stronghold in Jiangsi province.

After several failures to gain control of the stronghold, Chiang brought in several German general officers. Simultaneously, the communists underwent a power struggle from which Mao Tse-tung emerged as the CCP leader. Because the Germans' tactical advice proved successful, Mao was driven out of Jiangsi and was forced to take his people on the fabled Long March to unite with the last remaining Communist base at Yenan in Shensi province. A hundred thousand soldiers and political leaders began the 6,000 mile trek under almost constant harassment from warlord allies of Chiang. Approximately 8,000 survived, and Mao established a new headquarters at Yenan, near Sian, in 1936. Mao quickly cemented an alliance with the Manchurian army, which had been driven out after the Japanese invasion. Mao's convincing argument was that Chinese should not be killing other Chinese while the

Japanese were cruelly exploiting Manchuria. They should be killing the foreign invaders! Unaware of this coalition, Chiang ordered the Manchurian army, now under Chang Tso lin's son, Chang Hsueh-liang, to put Yenan under siege. But when the young Marshall aligned with Mao's CCP, and Chiang Kai-shek journeyed to Sian to take charge of what he thought would be the final anti–CCP offensive, he was kidnapped.

Chiang's captors forced him to sign an agreement that temporarily ended the war between the KMT and CCP and form a "united front" alliance against Japan. During 1937 several violent confrontations brought all-out war between the two nations. Nanking fell to the Japanese on December 12, and over 100,000 civilians and many thousands of captured Chinese soldiers were butchered, while tens of thousands of women were raped. This event, known as the Rape of Nanking, is surely among the most barbaric atrocities in human history. Before the end of 1938, Japanese forces overran all of coastal east China and almost every area from which nation-sustaining foreign supplies could reach China. The lone exception was Rangoon, in British-controlled Burma. Desperate for foreign assistance of all kinds, China reached out, particularly to the United States.

5

The Antecedents of the Burma-to-China Supply Routes

> [Upon his arrival in China, Magruder's] chief concern ... was the line of communications to Kunming, since all AMMISCA's projects depended on a flow of material from Rangoon up the Burma railway and highway to Lashio, and then over the [Burma] road to China. This problem of the line of communications ... [was] in many ways ... the principal problem of the American effort in China, Burma, and India.
> — Charles Romanus and Riley Sunderland, *Stilwell's Mission to China*

The History of International Trade Through Burma

> For well over five hundred years China exercised some level of control over the political and economic affairs of its smaller neighbors; many of them, including Burma, paid a periodic form of tribute. Trade and profit were the major reasons other peoples were willing to submit to paying these bribes and performing the humbling *kowtow* (kneeling three times and striking the floor with one's forehead three times during each kneeling). Traders in large numbers were always part of the Tribute Missions, and the goods they brought with them were admitted without being taxed.
> — F. S. V. Donnison, *Burma*

The first word of Burma's existence that reached the West probably came from Marco Polo. The first Western trader to reach it was Nicola Diconti, a Venetian merchant, in 1435. The first Europeans to arrive in significant numbers were Portuguese adventurers, missionaries and traders. In the 1600s the government-chartered Dutch, British and French East Indian companies expanded their respective presences. Although there were no measurable rela-

5 The Antecedents of the Burma-to-China Supply Route

tionships established with the Burmese kings, the French and British built shipyards there in the 1700s. The British installed a British Resident post in Rangoon in 1796 although the Burmese were not interested in extending any sort of diplomatic relations. A war between the Burmese and Anglo-Indians took place in the early 1820s primarily over Burmese beliefs that the British were deliberately attempting to subvert their government. Driven by profit and imperialism, the British continued their expansion. An 1826 treaty ceded Assam, Arakan, and Tenasserim to British control and promised to give Britain free rein in Manipur, Cachar, and Jointia. Years of misunderstanding, highlighted by Burmese oppression of traders and enhanced by several mentally deranged kings' imprudent refusals to use diplomacy, brought war again in 1852. Britain annexed the "old kingdom" of Pegu, which when combined with Arakan and Tenasserim, became British Burma, a province of India.[1]

The British emphasis on trade expansion dominated their international planning, and they concocted a scheme to "open a back door to interior China by constructing a railroad trade route from Burma into [China's] Yunnan [province]."[2] In 1875, with Peking's permission, the British vice-counsel, William Margary, led an "exploratory mission" into the Sino-Burma border area. The indigenous people, if they had even been advised of the mission, were not fond of foreigners. Margary ignored warnings from local Chinese officials and was killed near Bhamo. London, of course, held Peking responsible and after lengthy negotiations, the Chefoo Convention was implemented in September 1885.[3] It effectively established Burma as a part of the region's British sphere of influence, the most important element being trade. It also was a classic example of imperialism and created ill-will that lasted until World War II.

Most of the early trade items from Burma were woolen and cotton products. It was the movement of these and other items from Burma to China that led to the establishment and expansion of transit routes between the two realms. British foreign trade in rice and timber became sufficient to cause the expansion of port facilities at Rangoon. The jewel of the British colonial crown was India. It was only natural that in the age of the industrial revolution and imperialism, London's attention would focus across the Indian border on Burma. British capital investment began and trade steadily expanded.[4] Commensurately, their competitors, Russia, France and the United States, also evinced interest in the area. But not until the 1870s was Burma seriously considered an area of potential colonization.

On New Year's Day in 1886 the British government in India, "not without misgivings," made upper Burma a part of British India. Thus, Burma under British dominance was considered an adjunct to its Indian colony, and administered similarly to India's legal and tax systems.⁵ From 1896 to the 1930s a slow progression towards more Burmese involvement in their government took place, although there was no British mention of self-rule. But the traditional British colonialist attitude of aloofness continued to exist vis-à-vis "colonials."

Burma's majority people, the Burmese, were "neither ethnically nor religiously tied to India." The differences were readily seen. "Their language and script had only a distant connection with [India's] Sanskrit."⁶ Indeed there was always resentment regarding the presence of wealthy Indian businessmen in Rangoon and elsewhere in Burma. Ethnic wrath (anti–Indian, anti–Chinese, or anti–British) was frequently instigated by politicians and radicals.

The mechanism for official separation from India was the *1935 Government of India Act* which produced a Burmese constitution. The constitution created an upper and lower house with an elected legislature, and a cabinet of six to nine members appointed by a British governor. The governor had two counselors and a financial advisor, also British. The governor had "responsibility for foreign affairs, defense, currency ... and was empowered to override Parliament in matters gravely affecting peace and tranquility."⁷ As AMMISCA learned, this jury-rigged bureaucratic arrangement caused much confusion and delay: "Even the British Governor's reserve powers were greater in theory than they proved to be in practice."⁸

The Government of Burma (India) Act of 1935 (1937) removed Burma from the India-Burma entity in which it had existed for sixty years. These officials, however, readily became enmeshed in the highly structured old British Raj system of cumbersome and inflexible traditional governmental methodology.⁹

Burma, about the size of Texas, has a unique geography. There are "high jungles, swampy coastal plains, alluvial deltas, a central plain with a dry triangle (Mandalay-Magwe-Toungoo) in the middle, the whole walled in by high mountains which separated it from India in the west, China in the north, and Siam in the East, ... The southwest monsoon blows for five months from mid–May to mid–October, and turns vast areas into swamp and quagmire."¹⁰

The north- and south-running rivers, amidst rugged mountain ranges, dictated that communication routes (read "trade"), until World War II, were limited to water in many locations, although there were some roughed-out land routes. Ferries were required to cross some of the larger rivers, and many of the roads were impassable in the monsoon season. The primary overland route came to be known as the Burma Road, and extended from Lashio to Kunming (Yunnanfu), China. In a generic sense it also came to include the connecting route south to Rangoon.

A railroad to Lashio via Mandalay was also a major route north from Rangoon. This path was a grueling experience: "The major physical bottleneck in the Burma line of communications was the Goktreik gorge between Mandalay and Lashio. There the Burma Railways climb 3,000 feet in twenty-seven miles, about half the distance at a grade of 1 foot in every 25. Trains had to be broken into sections and hauled by hill-climbing locomotives. Because of this ... rail officials could promise no more than 550 tons a day to be laid down at Lashio in November 1941."[11] As a result of British, American, and even Russian shipments of substantial quantities of supplies to Rangoon, especially after the passage of the Lend-Lease Act, a tremendous permanent chokepoint developed at Rangoon.

Pre–Pearl Harbor Japanese Expansion in China

Japan started on her conquest of Manchuria on September 18, 1931, which must be reckoned the most important date in Japan's modern history, not because of the Manchurian invasion itself, but because it marked the beginning of a decade during which Japan has retraced her way to a military barbarism rooted in feudal days while at the same time divorcing herself from her associations with the western democracies which had contributed so much to her progress and advancement in the preceding sixty years.
— Wilfrid Fleisher, "The Manchurian Incident"

Soon after the Portsmouth Treaty ending the Russo-Japanese War was signed in 1905, Japan's semi-autonomous Kwantung army moved into natural-resource-rich Manchuria. Their rationale was that the soldiers were needed to protect the Japanese controlled and operated South Manchurian Railroad. As intended, the soldiers served to provide security for entrepreneurial enterprises such as mining, lumber, and finance, not only in Manchuria, but also in the neighboring Chinese provinces and Korea. Japanese nationalism, a sentiment never far below the surface and inspired by the 1905 victory over Russia, reappeared, as did another durable emotion: militarism based on the samurai tradition.

The League of Nations, deep in the throes of world depression, took no action other than sending a "commission" to investigate. Led by V. A. G. R. Lytton, the son of a well-known British diplomat, the commission was established in December, arrived in April, and did not report its findings until October 1932. The report noted Japan's aggression but also noted Japan's "special financial interests" in Manchuria. It recommended that Chinese sovereignty over Manchuria remain but Japan continue in physical control. No league action was taken and there was no international call for strong measures even after Tokyo announced the creation of the puppet state of Manchukuo ("Land of the Manchus"). The United States' response was unique: Secretary of State Stimson warned Japan that America refused to accept any new border or territorial adjustments resulting from Japan's occupation of Chinese territory. The ultra-right-wing frame of mind of those in control of the Japanese government is clearly demonstrated by their reaction. On 27 May 1933, the Japanese submitted the required two year notice of their withdrawal from the league. Simultaneously they began to exploit Manchuria's natural resources. The territorial takeover and abuse of the land convinced many that Japan intended to expand further into the Asian mainland and western Pacific.

In January 1932 in Shanghai some Chinese street thugs, hired by the Japanese military attaché to Shanghai, attacked five Japanese Buddhist monks, killing one. The contrived incident served its purpose: although the mayor of Shanghai apologized, Japanese marines were landed and careened through the streets of the Chapei District, indiscriminately machine-gunning helpless civilians.

The next morning Japanese naval bombers dropped small bombs on the district. Then "waves of aircraft" indiscriminately bombed targets including a "clearly defined Red Cross refugee camp and the National Oriental Library ... where a priceless collection of ancient books" was destroyed.[12] After a spirited defense of Shanghai, the loss of up to 6,000 men, and a million people dispossessed, the Chinese pulled out of the city. For several years there were no significant occurrences. Then, in July 1937 near Beijing, a company of Japanese infantry on an alleged night exercise near what was known as the Marco Polo Bridge, confronted a similar Chinese unit. In the dark, shots were exchanged, which precipitated other incidents. Tokyo sent five additional army divisions to China and demanded that the two Chinese divisions at Beijing be withdrawn from that area. Japanese bombing and strafing killed hundreds of Chinese. Both sides reinforced, and in December the war that had been pending for six years came to China.

In the first years of the war, China received little foreign support and suffered huge losses of territory and population. In addition, the burgeoning Chinese middle class receded to almost nothing, while the Chinese Communist Party (CCP) expanded in numbers, equipment, and discipline. Chiang lost his economic and political power bases, the cities along the coast, and with them his ability to import adequate war materials and supplies critical to maintaining his nation's basic needs and his own political power.

On 24 July 1941, with the compliance of the Vichy government, the

Japanese took control of French Indochina. Within days President Roosevelt froze all Japanese assets in the United States and placed an embargo on oil exports. Tokyo faced difficult choices: winning the war in China was critical and to gain this victory, oil was essential. Japanese oil stocks at best were at a three-year level and would drain quickly if their China war expanded. Japan imported 90 percent of its petroleum, much of it from America. Tokyo decided the date for victory in China had to be moved up.

In late summer after extensive and bitter debate between Japan's army (who favored war with Russia) and navy leaders (who supported war with America), a plan was agreed upon. They decided the Dutch East Indies, replete with oil, rubber, and other natural riches, would be invaded. To be able to tend to war preparations as well as allay suspicion, negotiations would continue with Washington. If the talks failed, Pearl Harbor and the several resource-rich Asian colonial holdings of Holland and Britain would be attacked. The risk of America, with its industrial and manpower potential, entering the war would be offset by the destruction of the Pacific fleet at Hawaii. The primary target would be the aircraft carriers. Without them the "force projection" capability of the American military would be nil, and Japan could expand into the central Pacific, comforted by the knowledge that they would not be opposed for years and, if American resolve failed, a *fait accompli* might result. This plan became a reality when the pro–Axis but moderate Prince Konoye government was swept out by the army in favor of General Hideki Tojo in the fall. The final decision for war was made on November 25.

Opening the Chinese Portion of the Burma Road

> The road was initially declared open in 1938. Serious slides during the wet season forced its closure, however, and the metalling of the road was far from complete.... It is by no means finished.
> — Major James McHugh, Assistant Naval Attaché,
> to the American ambassador to China,
> Nelson Johnson, 31 December 1938[13]

With Japan's 1937 invasion of China the Western world took much greater notice of events in the Far East, although the British focus was primarily on Singapore. After 1938, China's last seacoast entrepots through which they had obtained critically needed war materials were gone. There remained only rough motor routes across the Mekong and Salween rivers from French Indochina and some caravan roads across northern Burma to Bhamo and on to Kunming. The primary water supply route was from Rangoon up the Irrawaddy River 950 miles to the Chindwin tributary, and then another 300-

China-Burma highway on market day in Chefang, China, 1939 or 1940 (Library of Congress Prints and Photographs Division, Washington, D.C., Office of War Information, U.S. Farm Security Administration/Office of War Information/Public Health Service Commission, #LC-USW33-043109-ZC. Public Health Service Commission).

plus miles to Bhamo. At prime weather periods it was one of the busiest river transport routes in the world. But soon after Pearl Harbor, Japanese air attacks rendered it basically non-functional. This was about 50 miles from where the newly constructed Chinese section of the Burma Road, officially (but far from completely) opened in January 1939, reached the Sino-Burmese border at Wanting. (It is critical that it be understood that the "Burma" Road existed as a road through Burma *and* China, with each nation being responsible for the portion of the road within its territory.) The Port of Rangoon became the point of convergence of the several road, rail, and water routes critical to the sustenance of China. "With the arrival in Rangoon during November 1938 of the British steamer *Stanhall*, bringing Russian arms and munitions destined for transport across Burma to the forces of Chiang Kai-shek, Burma's vital importance in the ... Far Eastern scene came suddenly to the attention of the world."[14] As will be seen, there were many incredible bureaucratic, ethnic, and mechanical challenges.

In late December 1938, just before Chungking declared the road officially

5 The Antecedents of the Burma-to-China Supply Route 81

open, Major James McHugh, USMC, the assistant attaché, traveled over it from Chungking to Lashio by private automobile. He noted,

> It required eight days to get the necessary Chinese passes; there are no stocks of gasoline available; spare parts are not available at points in Central China, except at Kunming, in very limited and uncertain quantity; commercial transportation is not only scarce but mechanically unequal to the strain of such a trip.
>
> The chief point where difficulty will probably occur for heavy trucks seems to be in the elbows of curves at the tops of valleys where the road winds from one mountain to the next. There are a multitude of these in any ascent or descent and in many cases the turn is far too sharp, the culvert or fill not only too narrow, but not squared to the normal approach of the vehicle.... The road needs widening in many places not only to permit the free passage of vehicles, but to strengthen it.... Very strict discipline and schooling of [truck drivers] will be required and thus far no such move has been made ... to any appreciable degree in this respect, not to mention the fact that proper care and servicing of machinery is not an inherent trait of the Chinese. An efficient dispatching system for the control of traffic will also be required especially since the Chinese plan to utilize a large amount of native transport. And finally, "The volume of war material which can be transported over this route and the overhead incident thereto is a matter of simple arithmetic which can easily be computed from the basic statistics of mileage and gasoline consumption of our trip alone—and the result is not encouraging."[15]

Numerous contemporary reports reflect the problems endemic to the China section of the Burma Road. Almost all indicate McHugh's analysis was accurate well into 1941. Hugh Deane in the *China Weekly Review* observed,

> Between Wanting and Kunming 1,000 trucks were available, but many were not running, and owing to this, and the greater distance to be covered by the Chinese trucks, goods were piling up in Wanting. Gasoline, which took up much space, was inefficiently distributed owing to lack of any central organization; consequently many trucks were idle from lack of fuel.... Of the 20,000 registered truck drivers in south-west China only a small percentage was efficient and honest. Most of the government drivers coasted downhill to save gasoline, thereby increasing the wear and tear on the trucks and also risking accidents. The fuel they saved was illicitly sold to the drivers of commercial trucks.... [A further difficulty] was the lack of mechanics for repair work, there being only 2,000 in all.... Very few stations could handle a serious breakdown.... The average life of a truck was about a year.[16]

The British of course were aware of the problems: "By March 1939 British observers had [also] begun to warn that the route had become congested and suffered from poor organization on the Chinese side of the border."[17] Almost all of the Anglo-American reports called attention to defects in the Chinese portion of the road, false Chinese claims of tonnages reaching Kunming, and Chinese inflexibility in their administrative and construction processes.

Corruption at Chungking

> The Kuomintang alone was responsible for the government during the war; it *was* the government. It appointed and directed all government officials. It controlled the national army; all senior officers and over 90% of the men were enrolled at least nominally on the party roster, and political commissars were attached to each unit.... The Kuomintang controlled the censorship; party work was supported by government funds; party functionaries lived on public taxes. And, since all other parties were outlawed, criticism of the Kuomintang became a state offense.
>
> — Theodore White and Anna Lee Jacoby, *Thunder Out of China*

Bribery, in the western sense, is a custom as old as China and survives, indeed flourishes, even under the current communist government's prohibition. Longer referred to by the traditional term "squeeze," it is now known as *kwan his* ("fragrant grease"). One of the most palpable examples of corruption, relating to the Burma-Sino supply line, was the Southwest Transportation Company. Part of the ongoing and accurate western view of China's vast state of corruption sprang from the mismanagement of Southwest Transportation, and, later, China Defense Supplies. AMMISCA officer John Russell reported, "Visible evidence in Rangoon [is] that many Chinese have made large sums out of China traffic."[18]

More than a few contemporary observers emphasized the extensive corruption in Chiang's immediate family:

> Inevitably the Burma Road, although designed primarily for the importation of war materials into China ... offers wonderful opportunities for profitable private business. The Soong-Kung clique [Chiang's brothers-in-law, T. V. Soong and H.H. Kung] were not slow in realizing this, and they now have an enormous carrying organization under their direct control ... that boasts of the name of South-West Transportation Company. This company has every possible facility forcibly placed at its disposal, and is doing a fine trade for its sponsors. It does, of course, carry a considerable amount of war supplies and Government exports, but it also carries a lot of ordinary merchandise, and is understood to be netting the Soongs and Kungs approximately $20,000,000 Chinese per month in profits. But the sponsors are not content with these handsome profits; they want to handle the whole business.[19]

The South-West Transportation Company sought to gain a monopoly of traffic on the Road but most felt it was not in China's best interests to depend on a corrupt South-West.[20]

This condition and problem continued. On 1 October 1941, J. K. Storrs,

Deputy Commissioner, Chinese Maritime Customs, reported, "As regards the charges of corruption and inefficiency of the South-West Transportation Company, these were widespread." Storrs stated that it was a practice of the company to lease out trucks assigned to them under the control of Burma, to Chinese merchants "at rates that allowed the company to pocket a healthy profit. The result was a reduction in the amount of Chinese Government material transported over the road." Storrs also mentioned that Southwest Transportation Company was manipulating truck licensing so there were fewer competing trucks on the Road.[21] A particularly condemnatory assessment of the Southwest Transportation Company is from Sterling Seagrave. "The Director of the Southwest Transportation Company, which provided the six hundred trucks carrying Lend-Lease supplies, was T. L. Soong, the younger brother of T. V. Soong and Madam Chiang Kai-shek. Less than two hours after reaching China, the goods were sometimes for sale on the Chinese black market. At other times they were not seen again. In all, some $3.5 billion U.S. were supposed to have passed through T. V. and T. L's hands during the war." The Soongs diverted billions of U.S. dollars to their own pockets and much never got out of the U.S.[22]

Pre–World War II Disruptive Forces in Burma

> Before the war, the British administration in Burma had been notorious for delays and muddle. When it was put to the test, it perished with the same sense of scandal as the administration in Malaya. The machine of government had been allowed to rust, and its levers broke in the hand when pulled.
> — Peter Calvocoressi, Guy Wint, John Pritchard,
> *The Penguin History of the Second World War*

The immediate pre–World War II history of Burma centers on a combination of internal and international forces including anti–British Burmese independence groups, anti-white racist societies, anti–Indian and pro–Japanese elements, and Japanese subversion. There was considerable anxiety over the Japanese invasion of China, the occupation of French Indochina, and the imminence of war that many felt these phenomena indicated.

The Japanese were encouraged that after British colonial rule in India and Burma, a younger generation was clamoring for independence. The Japanese networks created by the youth formed the core of the Minami Kikan, the Japanese secret subversion organization established to "advance the course of Asian independence from colonialism."[23] One of the most threatening external occurrences was the establishment of a Japanese-sponsored unit fashioned by Colonel Suzuki Keiji. Suzuki's cover was chief of shipping section of the General Staff Headquarters. His real assignment "was to develop an offensive strategy in British Asia and ultimately to close the Burma Road."

Suzuki recruited young nationalistic Burmese students and laborers. The appeal was the 1935 Government of India Act, which was regarded by them as ineffectual and as serving only the wealthy political types, such as prewar premieres U Saw and Ba Maw (later jailed for his ties with Japan). "There was an electric atmosphere among Burmese youth in Rangoon during the last years before the outbreak of war."[24]

There was a broad desire for independence but it was not taken as seriously as the one in India. The most significant of the revolutionary parties was the Thakins. They were a Burmese nationalist society formed in 1930 by Ba Thoung, made up of college students and young intellectuals. The Thakins claimed to be ready to do anything to end British rule.

In addition to the Thakins, many other youthful nationalists were involved in resistance movements of varying character, which led to demonstrations and uprisings in 1938 and 1939. Prominent among the nationalistic youth was Aung San, an admirer of Lincoln, Marx, and Benito Juarez. He became one of Suzuki's Burma Independence Army (BIA) recruits, a member of the famous "Thirty Comrades," created as an anti–British military force, and commanded the BIA after 1942. "The army that Aung San and the Thakins created in those troubled months of 1940 and 1941, fought first with and then against the Japanese invaders of their homeland. The story of Aung San and his Thirty Comrades became in time the founding myth of modern Burma."[25]

Burmese independence leaders attempted to gain concessions from London after Britain's war with Germany began and war with Japan became probable. Among them were Baw Ma and the present prime minister, U Saw. Hoping to build "Burma's fighting spirit," Governor Dorman-Smith acceded to U Saw's request that he be allowed to meet in London with the secretary of state for India and Burma (Leo Avery) and with Churchill. After receiving a warning from Dorman-Smith that he did not want to have to jail him upon his return, U Saw left for Britain in October 1941. Churchill had no use for U Saw. Thus, after unproductive discussions in London, he met clandestinely with Japanese officials in Hawaii and Lisbon. But the British learned of these encounters, and he was arrested and incarcerated in Uganda until the end of the war. Needless to say, "very little came out of his [meetings] ... Burma was so far down the list of political priorities as to be invisible."[26]

The Battle of Britain and Germany's quick victory in France provided Japan the opportunity to further squeeze China's supply lines. On 17 July

1940, after extensive agonizing within the Churchill government, London and Tokyo signed an agreement wherein Britain consented to end the "transit of war materials and certain other articles to China via the Burma Road." An example of the banned items was gasoline over and above that needed to fuel the truck's return to Burma. The British promised to provide "assurance to the government of Japan" of "measures they have taken to effectively stop the transit of the [proscribed] articles." Some of the required "assurances" were timely updates reporting the specific measures the Burmese government was undertaking to stop the transit of prohibited articles to China and official statements providing the value of prohibited goods imported into Burma. The reports were to include the value of prohibited materials that did reach China via routes other than the Burma Road, also where, how, and when they crossed into China, how and where they originally entered Burma, and other information demanded by the Japanese.[27]

The British suspended traffic on the Road indefinitely, then re-opened it after three months, a time period during which (as British diplomats recounted to their colleagues around the world) coincided with the monsoon season during which the Road was impassable anyway. Japanese members of their Rangoon Consulate were given access to inspect locations where they felt prohibited items might be passing to China and judge how the Burmese government handled the problem.[28] After that the aid again flowed, though scarcely more than a trickle.[29]

Even though there was still non-proscribed traffic over the road, the respite could have been used by the Chinese to effect some improvements, especially in the administrative area. They did nothing. The Japanese took advantage of Britain's non-confrontational policy by intimidating the government of non–German-occupied France. And in late September the Japanese occupied northern French Indochina. Most importantly, the closing of the road, however temporary, drove a wedge into Sino-Anglo relations. Chiang declared that the British had lost all their prestige in China.[30]

British Military Unpreparedness

>Wherever they went the English recapitulated England. For every colony with a lowland in its dusty heat, disease, and torpor there was up-country a cool and healthful hill station of graceful bungalows and trim lawns, polo and cricket grounds, and an outpost of the established church. Some families had lived out here over generations in a kind of double exile, dreaming of that moist, green island always known as "home" even to those who had never seen it, and should one of the masters retire and return there — to grow boring and dyspeptic

in a second-rate club on a reduced income — he would always dream of empire: of the vibrant exercise of command, of distant mountains, deserts, and the sea.
— Eric Larrabee, *Commander in Chief: Franklin Delano Roosevelt, His Lieutenants and Their War.*

Although it was accepted that an attack on Burma might now [circa December 1941] be carried out by significant Japanese forces, Far Eastern Command's appreciation was that the likelihood of a major attack was low. It was thought that the Japanese lacked the resources whilst committed in Malaya and the Philippines. Burma continued to take a low priority for reinforcements and equipment. The Burma defense plan continued to be largely based on air defense–surprisingly given there were no bombers in Burma.
— Steve Rothwell, *The Burma Campaign: Preparations for War*[31]

Against Japanese attack Burma was absurdly unprepared. Singapore was the bastion of the East and known to be impregnable protecting the territories to its flank and rear. Thus no one had told anybody to organize the defense of Burma and anyhow there was nothing to defend it with: no antiaircraft, no reserves of rifles or machine guns, and no stocks of other weapons that were better than inadequate. The only British air squadron consisted of 16 obsolete fighter planes; the naval force was a flotilla of five motor launches.
— Eric Larrabee, *Commander in Chief: Franklin Delano Roosevelt, His Lieutenants and Their War.*

A major element in the lack of military readiness to repel Japan's invasion of Burma was the old colonialist policy of excluding Burmese from military service: "In the ... eighteenth century, the Burmese built a reputation as one of the most militaristic people in southern Asia.... After 1886, the British did not recruit ethnic Burmese into their forces as they had the Sikhs of the Punjab when they were conquered generations earlier.... The basic reason ... was that Indians and recruits from the Burmese minorities were cheaper."[32]

In February 1942, when the fall of Britain's major Asian fortress at Singapore became imminent, Churchill sought to divert Australian forces originally intended for Singapore to Burma. He ran into a buzz saw. The Aussies were deeply concerned with their own territorial security and saw Burma as a possible "recurrence ... of the Greek and Malayan defeats." Churchill disagreed and in his memoirs implied that Rangoon might have been saved had the Australian 28th Division been sent to Rangoon instead of Singapore.[33] Australia's Prime Minister John Curtin also rebuffed Churchill's request that Australia's 7th Division be sent to Burma: "The movement of our forces to

5 The Antecedents of the Burma-to-China Supply Route

this theatre ... is not considered a reasonable hazard of war, having regard to what has gone before and its adverse results would have gravest consequences on morale of Australian people."[34]

Part of the British need for imperial troops in Burma was London's mistrust of the local Burmese populations and fear of transferring rural regional security forces to Rangoon. Consequently, only a brigade size force, "including one of only two British regular battalions, the 1st Battalion, Gloucester Regiment, was there to defend the city. In central Burma there were some units of the Burma Frontier Force and the Burma Rifles." The last unit sent to reinforce southern Burma was the under-trained and under-equipped 6th Indian Brigade.[35] There were additional complications; for example, the Hindustani-speaking Indians were unable to understand Burmese and few Burmans spoke Hindi. Many of both ethnicities spoke no English.

As previously stated, Burma's wartime governor, appointed in May 1941, was Sir Reginald Hugh Dorman-Smith. He was born in County Cavan in Ireland and although after Harrow he attended Sandhurst, the British equivalent of West Point, he was classified an "agricultural specialist." He was briefly British minister of agriculture before "falling out" with Churchill. "He was armed with a mordant wit and considerable literary talent, though it is clear that many of his colleagues regarded him as a 'bit of a phony.'" He was inclined to tolerate "pukka, old-style Burmese and Indian politicians."[36] Although clearly loyal and a patriot, he was in a new and unfamiliar environment in a part of the world with which he was not familiar or comfortable. The complications engendered by the exigencies of war further limited his effectiveness and fostered intermittent discord between the governor and the AMMISCA Rangoon personnel.

6

Early East Asian Advisory Missions

> While the Generalissimo has repeatedly indicated his desire to appoint an American managing director, I understand that he considers it impracticable for a foreigner to exercise the full authority contemplated in the Arnstein report.
> The new plan should so operate as to place full responsibility on the Chinese and at the same time afford them the expert American technical and mechanical assistance they require for efficient operation of the road. Centralization of authority over the road, in hands that are willing and able to establish needed police controls and to subordinate provincial and private vested interests to the national welfare, is imperative if American technical assistance is to be effective and if aid to China under Lend-Lease is to materialize as anticipated.
> — Ambassador Gauss to Secretary of State Hull, 24 August 1941[1]

Early Advisory Missions

Several months after the "official" opening of the Burma Road in early 1939 trucks began to roll: 600 of them under the under the auspice of the Southwest Transportation Company,[2] and thus under the control of T. L. Soong, the younger brother of T. V. Soong and Madame Chiang Kai-shek. In August the American commercial attaché, Julean Arnold, alerted Chungking of the situation. However, the Chinese government, aware of the road's defects, had already hired an American automotive expert, D. F. Myers. Myers' report cited numerous serious deficiencies especially the road's all-weather weaknesses, and in July he advised that the road was unsuited as an all-weather route because of bad drainage, constant slides, and poor surfacing.[3]

In September, Chungking's response to Myers' report was to bring in three more American experts led by M. E. Sheahan, a Chicago trucking operator. This team also submitted a list of reforms and improvements. "Their urging brought about some physical improvement of the road, but on other matters had little immediate result."[4] Nevertheless, road traffic significantly expanded in 1939. In addition to the 600 Southwest Transportation Companys trucks, there were numerous independent trucks.

Many problems had been ignored in the effort to open the road, including the material buildup at Rangoon and the poor coordination between the many road regulatory organizations. Drivers were not well-trained and consistently ignored preventative maintenance requirements, and their breakdowns often caused massive congestion. Sheehan's recommendations included resurfacing, better maintenance of vehicles, establishment of inspection and maintenance sites, and better training and pay for drivers and maintenance staff.[5] But as was often the case in China, critical matters were not properly addressed in anything resembling a timely manner, and deterioration continued.

Arnstein Mission

> My first sight of the Burma Road was at Kunming, the Chinese terminus and the last flat spot before this incredible highway begins. We had arrived by plane from Chungking to find awaiting us several American automobiles, a No. 1 boy, a cook, and five Chinese roadmen. From then on for two solid weeks, we saw a road, and road conditions, that would make the toughest U.S. truck driver turn green.... After Kunming we never saw as much as one-eighth of a mile of straight road ahead.
> — Daniel G. Arnstein, "An Ex-Taxi Driver Checks Up on the Burma Road"

In spring 1941, conditions on the road were deplorable; having received several negative reports on road conditions, Chiang Kai-shek employed a private American consulting team to survey the Chinese portion of the road and make recommendations. This was his most serious effort, and there was hope that something positive would come from it. The team was led by Daniel G. Arnstein, a hard-nosed former cab driver and head of the Terminal System (Yellow) Taxi Cab Company in New York City. Arnstein and his assistants evaluated the road in July and August. Their report to Chiang was sixteen pages of candid, often harsh, assessments, beginning with a condemnation of the multiplicity of offices and administrators who had no knowledge of even the rudiments of motor transportation.

The sixteen governmental agencies operating over the Burma Road were overstaffed, incompetent, and concerned only with their local department requirements. Arnstein called for the establishment of a one-person-in-charge system. This administrator would be supported by responsible and knowledgeable executives along the entire route. This would include a strict chain of command system, responsible only to a realigned road commission, in which there would be clear levels of authority vested in several departments: a control office, which was the ultimate authority over all commercial vehicles plying the road; an operations unit that managed all government trucks; a "police organization" that would patrol the road; finance, accounting, and statistics departments; and a communications unit. Throughout the report Arnstein repeatedly emphasized his team's conviction that the managing director should be autonomous, as should be the subordinate departments, to keep them free from political interference.

Accounting and statistical record keeping methods were primitive: "We observed trucks loaded at 8 o'clock in the morning waiting at 5 o'clock in the afternoon for papers to be completed. Throughout, we found that the movements of trucks were delayed to fit into accounting work, rather than the accounting work to fit into the movement of trucks."

Arnstein criticized the current maintenance practices: "It seems beyond belief that the present organizations, which have been operating trucks for several years, have not learned enough and have not taken enough interest in the operations to see that the trucks are lubricated, greased, maintained and dispatched more efficiently. Regardless of how many trucks are put into operation under the present system any increased movement of freight which might be due to these new trucks will be short-lived."[6]

Arnstein's primary recommendation was that "the present [Burma Road] commission should act as a supervisory body rather than attempt to run trucks. One of the most important functions of the commission should be to co-ordinate all the activities on the Burma Road with those on other connecting highways. It should delegate authority to an individual, preferably a foreigner with truck-transportation experience, who might be called the managing director of the Burma Road."

The establishment of a terminal system was strongly advocated. The terminals would be no more than one day's drive apart. The terminal managers would be the most capable men the managing director could find, and would have total authority in their districts, answerable only to the managing director. The report also addressed numerous negative aspects of the present road operation: the selling of trucks in China; sales of illegal cargo in China; and an enforced balance of "commercial" and government cargo on private carriers. Recommendations for solutions included better treatment of Burmese drivers in China; an increase in Chinese truck carrying capacity once the goods crossed into China, and the eradication of most of the tax-collecting and

American GIs were startled to observe rats prepared as food on hibachis on many streets including Chungking (used by permission from the personal collection of Dennis Reinhart).

security check stations and the "deplorable delays" they caused. It suggested implementation of repair and maintenance shops, abolition of the "convoy" system of movement, and institution and enforcement of a schedule system. The revised system included strict maintenance and gasoline consumption records, grease charts, and other vehicle records. To support these maintenance efforts, a large number of mechanics would be trained, and a spare parts inventory control process instituted.

Some segments of the report are quite revealing.

> From our observation, the most serious point of delay was at Wanting, where the roads were lined with waiting traffic and the congestion was such that it was not an easy matter to get through even on foot. Here, both inbound and outbound trucks lined up three abreast across the road completely blocking traffic.... One cause for congestion is due to the number of offices that the driver has to visit, and go through Customs inspection to get clearance papers. Another reason for the delay is due to the limited time that Chinese Customs officials are on the job. They do not open in the morning until between 7 and 8 o'clock, and they close promptly at 6 P.M. regardless of the number of trucks that are waiting and ready to clear. Due to the limited number of hours that the Tax Offices are open, about 200 operating truck-days are delayed daily at this one point. As a contrast to this, the Burma Customs Office is officially closed only between 2 A.M. and 6 A.M. but under strict orders that if any truck reaches the border between these hours, the Customs officer must clear the truck immediately.[7]

In sum, several months before the arrival of AMMISCA it was widely known that scores of improvements were desperately needed before the Burma Road could carry the quantity of backlogged materials so essential to China. The "backlog" and many of the problems cited by Arnstein became problems for AMMISCA.

Arnstein faced his meeting with Chiang, wherein they were to discuss his report, with some trepidation. In a somewhat humorous vein he noted how shocked he was that Chiang was so congenial:

> We were there five hours. Mme Chiang had read the report, and the Generalissimo had a translation, completely indexed in Chinese. He was pleased as punch, so pleased that before dinner he made a long speech, which when translated turned out to be a strange offer that only an Oriental will understand. He asked whether Davis, Hellmon and I would like to take on the Burma Road as a private concession, at so much percentage per truck. It was as characteristically a Chinese offer as an invitation to tea. We were dumbfounded, but in a moment or so found words to decline with thanks. But the Generalissimo was not ruffled. "Now we eat," he announced briskly in Chinese, and sprang to his feet as though he had been thinking about dinner all the time.[8]

Politics played a significant role in the Arnstein–Burma Road saga. Prior to and during Arnstein's project, the Burma Road Commission, made up of representatives of the United Kingdom, China, and the United States, nominally directed the road's affairs. The American representative was John E. Baker.[9] Baker was recruited by Chiang because of his experience as the American Red Cross's expert on Chinese transportation systems. The rest of the commission was made up of two Chinese, one of them Chiang's cousin General Yu Fei-peng, the commission's inspector general (chairman), and one British representative. Baker was the commission's chairman in Yu's absence.[10]

As early as May 1941, the State Department believed Baker was "taking steps to improve both the physical condition of the road and the organization of the transport system."[11] But on August 15, Ambassador Gauss, supported by the naval attaché Major James McHugh, cabled Washington that Baker was unable to handle the situation and should be immediately relieved. Dorman-Smith believed that "Baker has not been given sufficient authority has not got necessary experience and has not enough personal drive. They [Arnstein's group] consider him a failure."[12] Arnstein's report supported the action; Baker was dismissed, and significant time was lost while candidates for his job were put forth and debated by the several governments.

A defender of Baker was Arthur Young, Chiang's American economic advisor. He said Baker "was given neither the power nor the Chinese backing needed, and he was handicapped by red tape. Moreover, he could not hire suitable staff because he was limited to salaries with a top equal to about US $30 per month."[13] Young also notes, "Washington's delay in recruiting and sending the technical staff for which [Baker] had asked — they did not leave the United States until late October — denied him means to work effectively."[14] It must be mentioned that many of Arnstein's recommendations were made months earlier — by Baker.[15] What motivated Gauss and McHugh to speak so harshly of Baker is not known and was out of character for both men. He did not deserve dismissal.

Ambassador Gauss recommended the installation of the Canadian member of the commission as its new inspector general. Chiang opposed the Canadian because he feared "implications of the extension of Burmese [British] authority into Chinese territory," and made it clear he would not accept the Canadian even if Washington supported the appointment. Ironically, Canada-born Lauchlin Currie declared that the Roosevelt administration should not back a foreigner for the job. He suggested that the position be given to Arnstein. Arnstein had also been recommended by Chiang's brother-in-law, H. H. Kung.[16] When it was offered to him, Arnstein declined and expressed support for a proposal from Chiang that a Chinese inspector general and Captain James Wilson, the assistant military attaché, be placed in charge of all operations and maintenance of Lend-Lease vehicles.

Chiang did not want a foreigner directing Burma Road operations even though his cousin Yu Fei-peng had veto power. Gauss believed it was a logical stance for Chiang to adopt because Chiang believed China and the Burma Road were not of significant concern to America, England, France, and Holland, whose primary interests were "Europe First" and their Asian colonial holdings. He declared he did not want such responsibility placed in the hands of an individual whose government "didn't care" about China. Gauss reported, "In a conversation Saturday afternoon the Generalissimo stated that Chinese political commentators are remarking that with the various warnings by the democracies enjoining Japan against aggression toward Thailand, Singapore, Netherlands East Indies, et cetera and no such injunction against an attack on Yunnan and the Burma Road it would almost seem that the democracies had pointed out to Japan what she might make as her military objective."[17]

Currie feared that Wilson, even though recommended by Arnstein, would be subject to the same fate as Baker and did not support him for the position. Also, Currie requested that Washington inform Chiang that Currie's task of expediting Lend-Lease aid to China was being hampered by the lack of a "genuine reorganization" of the Burma Road. He encouraged Chiang to follow the recommendations of the Americans retained in a purely advisory capacity.[18]

In late August Currie did offer to have Wilson serve as an advisor to Yu Fei-peng, the road's most powerful official and administrator of the myriad supervisory control agencies Chiang had established. Wilson would report directly to the military attaché and then to Magruder after AMMISCA's arrival.[19] Chiang never responded to Currie's offer.[20] Thus, when Magruder arrived six weeks later no effective road management system had been created, and the road's physical condition and tonnage capability had not improved.[21] The only change was that the Road Commission was basically defunct and to the surprise of no one, Yu had become the de facto autocratic controller of the Burma Road, a definitely regressive move. Even Currie was upset; he was unusually candid with Chiang: "The failure to bring about a genuine reorganization of the Burma Highway with unified control, sufficient financial backing and police authority has been a decided disappointment to me. My task here has been made very difficult by this failure."[22]

Yu's new role received mixed reviews. Governor Dorman-Smith judged General Yu both capable and energetic, but without the necessary understanding of transport work or the will to devote enough personal attention. The governor also believed the Chinese style of an overabundance of officials would continue: "Introduction of another official probably Chinese between him [Yu] and American assistant also causes misgiving that management scheme will be no better in future than in past."[23] Dorman-Smith was prophetic. Arnstein's report was accurate, and his recommendations sensible, but Chiang ignored it.

On 10 October 1941 the AMMISCA leadership group arrived in China. On the same day, H. H. Craw, Counselor to Governor Dorman-Smith, prepared a statement called "Memorandum on the proposals of General Yu Feipeng for the regulation of traffic on the Yunnan–Burma Highway." It confirmed that Chiang had placed General Yu as chief executive of the Road Commission with financial and administrative control. The appointment was important because Arnstein had warned that American Lease-Lend to China would be regulated in proportion to the flow of traffic along the road. Craw reiterated the British view that the Chinese were their own worst enemy in that they had known of the road's problems "long before" Arnstein's arrival. Additionally, the Road Commission had not had time to progress with the reorganization when Mr. Arnstein came. But with the increase in importation of war materials, although the Burmese government had undertaken responsibility of rail, road, and water routes, the Chinese government would be the primary factor with the most responsibility for the success or failure of the operation. This was an effort to place blame for future problems on the Chinese.[24] The Burmese government, Craw said, was willing to support a single unified organization to control the transportation routes to the border from Lashio and Bhamo only when the Chinese organization was set up and proved itself capable of dealing with the situation. Craw reiterated Arnstein's list of recommendations, remarking that he was disappointed the Chinese had not accepted them "in full." He mentioned several of the more significant proposals and said that they would take years to accomplish. He emphasized that Yu, in a response to Arnstein's proposals, did not mention the indispensable Statistics Department, which would "be essential to supply to the American Government full statistics of arrivals in Rangoon, departures from Lashio or Bhamo, accumulations at various points on the road and deliveries at Kunming." Craw believed that a statistical department would also be of significant value to the Burmese government, and reminded the Chinese that the Burmese portion of the road was built at considerable British and Burmese expense to aid China's war effort.[25] The memorandum essentially echoed Arnstein's observations and the frustrations of those expecting progress on the road. Magruder agreed and worked to augment the road's capacity and other transportation projects to increase the flow of supplies.

7

Maintenance and Repairs on the Burma Road

> The maintenance situation in its entirety is in a deplorable condition. There is no direction as to the specific duties of the maintenance force now employed. No mechanical check is ever made of a truck, and no mechanical work is done until it has experienced a complete breakdown.
>
> — Harry Hopkins Papers, "Chinese Affairs"[1]

Before he left for China, Magruder scrutinized the Arnstein survey and other reports relating to the Burma Road's inadequate vehicle maintenance and repair facilities. He could not hope to fulfill his assignment of moving the mass of materials arriving at Rangoon to China without properly maintained vehicles. He appointed the particularly competent Captain James Wilson to supervise the vehicle service facilities. Wilson was the former assistant military attaché whom Arnstein had supported as Baker's replacement, and who joined AMMISCA when it reached China.[2]

Concurrently, Magruder learned that Chiang also wished to engage Wilson as the assistant director of the well-connected China-Burma Transportation Administration. The War Department recognized that if Wilson were to resign his commission and become an employee of the China-Burma Transportation Administration, his annual salary would increase by thousands of dollars. Magruder opposed the appointment because it would force Wilson to resign his army commission and leave AMMISCA. More importantly, he would be thought to have American sanction, and any failure no matter the cause would be considered an American failure. Wilson would never have sufficient authority, and his technical abilities would be limited in devious ways. Magruder believed ultimate responsibility for all the Lend-Lease should be China's.[3] Wilson was on good terms with Yu Fei-peng, and Magruder believed that Yu would heed Wilson's advice if he remained on the AMMISCA staff.⁴ Magruder was uncommonly impressed by Wilson and tried to have him promoted from captain to lieutenant colonel. The War Department knew that Wilson as a lieutenant colonel would be more respected by the Chinese; typically, they only promoted him to major. Magruder's faith in Wilson proved to be well placed. He served AMMISCA exceedingly well. His initial orders directed him to construct a series of repair shops along the Burma Road, but he also played a significant role later in the evacuation of Rangoon.

On 28 October 1941 Wilson submitted a preliminary study and request for funds to establish a number of what he referred to as ABC Shops. These thirty-four proposed repair facilities would service the anticipated 5,000 trucks that were to operate on the Burma Road between Wanting and Kunming in 1942. The shops would "be closely supervised," presumably by AMMISCA personnel, with rigid inspection, maintenance, and overhaul requirements. The four "A" shops would provide facilities to rebuild engines, transmissions, and other units; the eight "B" shops would do general overhaul and unit replacement; and the twenty-two "C" shops would perform inspection, regular lubrication maintenance, and light repair and replacement work.⁵ There would also be a series of "roadside service shops" placed not more than ten kilometers apart along the entire Burma Road. Their function would be to provide "instant service" such as emergency tune-ups and tire changes. The estimated cost for the shops and related vehicles and equipment was slightly over a half-million dollars.⁶

In mid–November Wilson learned that several thousand trucks originally intended for the Burma Road were to be used on other routes and the number of vehicles hauling cargo on the Burma Road would be much smaller than anticipated. Also, feeder railroads would be incapable of carrying as much freight as hoped. He was forced to alter his agenda.

Within weeks Wilson submitted a revised proposal: the "XYZ Plan," a significant downward revision of equipment and tool needs.⁷ This produced extended discussion and some reverberations in Washington because the War Department and China Defense Supplies feared any revisions would cause delays, reduce movement of supplies, and degrade the output of the XYZ shops.⁸ Wilson also cut many technical items because now, late December, he feared there was not enough time to train the Chinese.⁹ Washington decided to make numerous changes to Wilson's proposals regarding priorities and shipping schedules.¹⁰ In his defense of Wilson's equipment cutbacks, Magruder quoted Arnstein's statement that China Defense Supplies' requests greatly exceeded China's needs and Wilson's revision was a more realistic plan.¹¹

In general the new XYZ plan incorporated existing stations and a small number of new ones into a network of four interlocking "systems" located between Chefang and Kunming. Each system would have one base station and, depending on its size, several overnight stations. The base stations would each contain a headquarters, living facilities, and a main repair facility. Although all runs would originate at a base station, the drivers would spend their nights at satellite terminals that would each accommodate five hundred vehicles. Each terminal would be equipped to provide only those "repair services necessary for continuous operation," but would be capable of housing and feeding five hundred drivers.[12]

The base station would perform preventative maintenance checks on each vehicle every ten days, and each driver would rest the two days it took for his vehicle to be serviced. The facilities that would perform the maintenance would be known as "X" shops, and there would be three at each base station—dispersed to minimize possible bomb damage. Each base station would also have a "base installation" consisting of a machine shop, body shop, and paint, upholstery, and canvas shops. They would be known as "Y" shops. The "Z" shops would be located at each overnight station. Their only mission would be to provide enough maintenance to repair any trucks that came in with minor problems and get them back on the road as quickly as possible.

The XYZ shop plan was not significantly different from the ABC concept, at least as far as service methods were concerned. The principle of having each vehicle assigned to a base was new, as were the ideas of an exactly regulated run for each truck and a more comprehensive maintenance system through the presence of X and Z shops at all stations. The XYZ shops would all be in China with the exception of a base installation at Lashio. A drawback to the XYZ system was that it might not eradicate an obstruction that had also been part of a challenge to the ABC plan: that the freight on the Burmese trucks had to be unloaded at Lashio and reloaded onto Chinese trucks. Wilson was aware of this, and had a solution: tightly controlled border areas. As he cogently observed, Burmese living conditions were so different from Chinese that if Chinese drivers were permitted to enter Burma, "we should be faced by wholesale desertions, not to mention smuggling and other similar evils. For obvious reasons, Burma Immigration Regulations prohibit such wholesale entries of Chinese."[13]

Overall, the XYZ concept was well conceived and would have made good use of existing facilities. It did not require as much new equipment as the ABC proposal, and because a plan of ABC's magnitude was no longer necessary, the XYZ system made good sense and was a tribute to Wilson's skill. But it became caught up in the maelstrom of confusion that permeated the War Department in early 1942. In February, interoffice memoranda in Washington continued to refer to the ABC plan rather than the XYZ. The original

7. Maintenance and Repairs on the Burma Road

ABC shop requisition from China Defense Supplies was still in the pipeline because Wilson's draft of the XYZ plan never reached the "right people" in Washington.[14] In late February, a member of the China Detail hand-carried a copy of Wilson's XYZ proposal to Washington. Little attention was given to it because those members of the War Department who were assigned to deal with the equipment for the road felt the plan "difficult to analyze. [Thus], no attempt to evaluate it has been made."[15] The whole matter of revising and approving Wilson's XYZ plan ultimately fell on Stilwell.[16] He, however, was so engrossed with tactical and political problems that he did not resolve the shop question before the Japanese overran southern Burma and the route to Lashio. The matter then gave way to the much bigger problem of how to supply China from India.

8

The Mission's Involvement at Rangoon

> Lend-lease material was pouring into Burma via Rangoon far faster than it moved up the Burma Road.... In July 1941, of the 79,000 tons of Chinese goods stored in Rangoon, only 22,000 tons were truckable. At that month's rate of moving goods, eight months would have been needed to clear the stockpile, yet more was coming in constantly.
> — Charles Romanus and Riley Sunderland,
> *Stilwell's Mission to China*

On 23 September 1940, the Japanese moved into northern Indochina and severed the Yunnan-to-Indochina railway. This effectively isolated China from its last significant source of foreign supply except through Burma's port of Rangoon. The materials that arrived at Rangoon were verified via invoices, offloaded as quickly as crane assignment could be arranged, and, assigned a dock or storage location depending on the designated shipping destination and priority. As more supplies arrived, modifications, such as storage on the docks, were made.

Prior to Pearl Harbor, one of the world's largest commercial river fleets had plied the Irrawaddy River, which reached from the Bay of Bengal to well north of Bhamo. Traffic was restricted during dry spells by water levels of sometimes less than five feet, and there were places where exceptionally heavy cargoes could not be taken. In the wet season there were floods and often uprooted trees and other floating menaces. Nevertheless, there were as many as 600 vessels of many sizes plying the river — until a few days after Pearl Harbor when the Japanese sank hundreds of them, effectively ending the Irrawaddy supply route. The AMMISCA personnel assigned to Rangoon attempted to build an efficient docking, storage, and distribution system. These men were highly capable and well trained, but had to overcome many bureaucratic challenges. They could have accomplished more if they had not

8. The Mission's Involvement at Rangoon

been hampered by Burmese venality, the regular bickering of the Chinese, British, and Burmese, the presence of a non–AMMISCA American general, and the pro–British bias of several AMMISCA officers.

Employment of the American Volunteer Group

> Despite Chennault's personal accomplishment and the group's initial successes [the AVG] has no staying powers as now supplied and constituted ... its material and maintenance situation is chaotic. Until the receipt of ... replacements of men and material and complete reorganization, its military value will deteriorate further.
> — Magruder to Marshall[1]

The AVG initially went into combat in defense of Rangoon during the third week of December 1941. In mid–December 1941, the AVG's "Hell's Angels" squadron, approximately 25 pilots and 20 airplanes, were moved from the AVG training base at Toungoo to Mingaladon outside Rangoon. Two other AVG squadrons, the "Adam and Eve" and "Panda Bears," were moved from Toungoo to Kunming.[2] In less than a month Chennault's force began to run short of both

Fourteenth Air Force Headquarters, Kunming, China, fall 1942 (photograph donated by Dr. Frederick Hoyt, University of Illinois, to author, 1976; Hoyt was a fellow graduate student).

personnel and equipment. Magruder advised the War Department that Chiang desired assurances that the American government would continue to supply a "steady and increasing flow of planes and men" and additional assurances that the Lend-Lease "supplies previously promised to the Chinese government would continue." These several "assurances" were added to Chiang's demands as a direct result of Currie's incredible December 30 memorandum, wherein he advised and urged Chiang to get everything he could squeeze out of America.[3]

The supply problem was exacerbated by Chennault's habitual backdoor communications with Washington via the generalissimo, Currie, and Harry Hopkins. In one instance, Currie and Chennault, in an effort to maintain their influence with the president regarding China, accused the War Department creators of AMMISCA of trying to undermine the relationship. Chennault went so far as to advise Madame Chiang that Magruder had been directed to end the influence over Lend-Lease enjoyed by Soong and Currie.[4] This and the continuing backchannel messages subverted Magruder, who was attempting — often under significant stress and frustration — to obtain supplies for the AVG through the proper chains of command. Chennault had Roosevelt's approval to bypass Magruder and was strongly encouraged to do so by Currie[5]: "Chennault, even after he re-entered the United States Air Force..., could appeal successfully to the White House against his Air and Army superiors. When his policy was totally at variance with that of the War Department and its representatives in China, chaos reigned."[6]

By the end of January the lack of support prompted Chennault to announce his intention to withdraw the AVG squadron from Rangoon to Kunming. Marshall, well aware of the Chiang-Chennault relationship, immediately ordered Magruder to inform the generalissimo that Washington was aware of the "brilliant piece of work" being done by the AVG. At the same time, however, Magruder was to warn Chiang that if the AVG withdrew, the British would be left in Rangoon with only six fighter aircraft. He was to inform Chiang that the Combined Chiefs of Staff desired the AVG to temporarily continue its operations in Burma until the British could deliver planes, already en route.[7]

Chiang acquiesced by reinforcing the AVG units in Rangoon and ordering them to remain in Burma until February 5.[8] But within a few days, Britain's Washington embassy advised Arnold that the anticipated British reinforcements would not arrive at Rangoon until after February 15, and they wanted the War Department to persuade Chiang to agree to a further postponement.[9] Arnold, with no other option, supported the request, but he warned Marshall that by February 20 few of the P-40s would still be in combat condition.[10]

8. The Mission's Involvement at Rangoon

Nothing changed until Winston Churchill intervened. Through a personal letter to Roosevelt he trenchantly noted that the security of Rangoon was as important to China's security as it was to Britain's. He added that a critical factor was the AVG and its withdrawal could bring a "disaster."[11] Magruder was ordered to contact Chiang and persuade the generalissimo to keep a squadron of the AVG in Rangoon until the British airplane reinforcements arrived.[12] He was successful, but this illustrates another example of Chennault, Currie, Hopkins, the Chiangs, and others confusing the mission's effort.[13] Magruder was only employed at the last minute as a go-between to Chiang, because of his good relation with the generalissimo.

Fifty P-40s were scheduled to arrive in West Africa in late February. But Chennault did not have enough pilots to ferry the planes to Burma, and Pan-American Airline personnel were called into service. But although fifty planes left Takoradi on Africa's Gold Coast, only twenty reached the AVG, a major disappointment. Some were lost through mechanical problems; others were assigned to the Ninth Air Force in Egypt or the Tenth Air Force in India.[14] Worse: no replacement or relief personnel actually reached AVG installations. Worst: in early April a number of additional fighter planes originally allocated to China were attached to the Tenth Air Force and brought the wrath of Madame Chiang down on Currie.[15]

Soon after the AVG learned they would receive only twenty P-40s, Chennault experienced a semi-insurrection by his pilots. Their morale was extremely low due to ongoing fatigue and lack of parts and replacements, which kept their airplanes in poor mechanical condition. There was the necessity of flying in areas of continual forest fires that smoked so heavily the pilots had to fly by instruments anytime they were below ten thousand feet. Another contributing factor to low morale was that some of the combat units received no mail from December 1941 until April 1942.

The confrontation occurred on April 20 when several AVG pilots refused to escort some RAF bombers over an exceptionally well defended target. A group meeting became quite heated, and over twenty pilots wrote out their resignations on the spot. After Chennault declared that anyone not flying would be classified a deserter, six pilots volunteered to support the British bombers. The RAF failed to keep the rendezvous because of bad weather, and the whole matter cooled down. The bulk of the pilots withdrew their resignations, but several did leave.

In light of subsequent events, if Washington had provided replacement and relief personnel and adequate spare parts and supplies, pilot strain, fatigue, and morale would have been of much less consequence. The AVG pilots and ground crews would have regarded service in the American military in a more positive way in the critical weeks immediately preceding induction.[16] Chennault officially took command of the Twenty-Third Pursuit Group on 8 July 1942. Although the Twenty-Third's table of organization and equipment listed four squadrons, the group's total complement of P-40s was only 56; about half of the 100 planes assigned to the original three AVG squadrons. Of these only 30 were operational.[17] Not until 1943 did the Twenty-Third receive substantial resupply. Even then vagaries of the 12,000-mile supply route from the United States prevented the entire Fourteenth Air Force, the Twenty-Third's parent command, from receiving all the planes and parts it required to operate at full strength.[18]

The whole situation, of course, devolved upon personalities and politics, differing priorities (American, British, and Chinese), and the massive confusion along with communication problems then extant; but the AVG suffered most from the shortage of men and replacement parts.[19]

Problems with the British and Chinese

> The British think the Chinese inefficient, incompetent, and subject to squeeze [bribery]. Part of this feeling undoubtedly springs from the mismanagement of Southwest Transportation [Company] affairs in the past and visible evidence in Rangoon that many Chinese have made large sums out of the China traffic. The Chinese think the British are placing obstacles in the way of shipment of goods to China. They constantly complain over lack of good wagons, lorries, etc.
> — Radio, Major John Russell, Rangoon AMMISCA detail, to Magruder[20]

As early as May 1941, the American consul at Rangoon, Austin C. Brady, reported serious transportation congestion in the Rangoon area and noted that the Southwest Transportation Company, the Chinese agency in charge of clearing all goods consigned to China from Rangoon, claimed it was the victim of inflexible Burmese customs procedures. The company's director complained that Burmese customs authorities insisted on treating China, a neighbor and supposed friend as well as a nation at war, more stringently than a "small commercial importer." Formerly, goods invoiced for China had been offloaded directly from ships into barges with only a perfunctory examination. Beginning in June, however, an average of 10 percent of each shipment was examined, which slowed the shipment even more.[21]

In addition, because cargoes were stacked indiscriminately on the wharves rather than in lighters, more delays were created. The Anglo-Burmese authorities also imposed a one-percent transit tax on all goods landed at Rangoon, ordered a second customs examination of all cargo at the Sino-Burma border, restricted the use of Rangoon's only forty-ton crane, and limited Chinese use of the Burmese railroad to Lashio.[22] To Brady and many of the AMMISCA people it appeared that the Anglo-Burmese strategy was to delay goods from reaching China, so as to divert them to British use.

The Anglo-Burmese tax itself was initiated solely to increase revenue. But the Chinese and Americans criticized it and the British and Burmese were not pleased. An editorial in the 22 August 1941 issue of the *Burmese Daily* commented on the unfavorable reaction in Washington and Chungking. According to Brady, the newspaper stated that American assistance to China was little in comparison to what the United States gained during its years in trade with China. The newspaper noted that Burma never gained anything through trade with China, but Japan regarded Burma negatively for permitting the transit of materials to China. If China's thanks would be all that Burma could even expect, why abolish it?

There was a positive reaction. On September 7 the American ambassador to Great Britain, John G. Winant, informed the State Department that after September 9 no Lend-Lease goods for China would be subject to transit duty. Instead the British government, reacting to pressure from Chiang and others, agreed to pay a ten-rupee a-ton fee to the Burmese government.[23]

Brady informed the State Department of another major problem — supplies were arriving faster than they could be moved north. Some of it was "dead cargo," such as 200,000 gas masks, unneeded and unwanted by the Chinese, that occupied valuable warehouse space. This bottleneck at Rangoon had to be eliminated, but Brady warned that little could be achieved until the Burmese and Chinese formed a closer working relationship under British leadership.[24] AMMISCA inherited the dilemma.

Within days of his arrival at Chungking, Magruder dispatched Major John Russell to investigate conditions at Rangoon. In his initial report, Russell advised that the pier, unloading, and warehouse facilities were adequate to handle only "reasonable" quantities of Lend-Lease cargoes and warned that a greater bottleneck would evolve due to the Southwest Transportation Company's inability to expeditiously move the Lend-Lease goods north. Moreover, the warehouse space controlled by the company was not adequate for future Lend-Lease shipments, especially the expected heavy equipment for road and railroad construction. Part of the problem was the thousands of bales of blankets stored in Southwest Transportation Company warehouses. None were being forwarded to China; they were not needed. Yet Chinese officials of the Southwest Transportation Company in Washington were requisitioning thousands more under Lend-Lease.[25]

Lend-Lease shipments to China via Rangoon increased through the fall of 1941, but British cooperation was negligible. AMMISCA personnel repeatedly protested the lack of support to British officials at Rangoon, especially the collector of customs, H. F. Oxbury. Oxbury did not like foreigners and he deliberately provoked Chinese and AMMISCA personnel. A case in point was his complaint about identification of supplies from the cargo ship *Frederick Lykes*. The *Lykes* docked at Rangoon on November 10 with a cargo of munitions, weapons, and asphalt for the Burma Road. The Chinese were naturally anxious to move it north as quickly as possible, but Oxbury refused to accept the supplies as Lend-Lease goods, because the cases were not marked "CDS Rangoon." Only cases with this inscription would be allowed to pass duty-free; others would pay a transit duty.[26] A bureaucrat of the old school, Oxbury was adamant.

The Southwest Transportation Company also suffered at Oxbury's hands. In November the company representative presented bills of lading that Oxbury judged "inadequate," because they did not list the contents of each case. He ordered the goods left on the wharf until he received a packing slip for every case. Both incidents created unnecessary shipping delays and deterioration of Sino-British and Anglo-American relations. Upon receipt of Russell's report, Magruder notified Washington of the delays caused by improper markings on the cargo and lack of bills-of-lading and packing slips.[27] At a meeting with members of the AMMISCA Washington Detail, CDS officials, especially the senior shipping official, John C. Keating, insisted that all shipping papers, including bills of lading and related papers necessary for customs, were included on the carrying vessels and that duplicates were forwarded via air mail to Rangoon as soon as possible. The Washington Detail felt that they could do no more than contact the shippers and manufacturers of all Lend-Lease goods and remind them that the required packing lists had to be endorsed. It is probable that because of worker inefficiency, the press of time, and the lack of trained personnel, American manufacturers were shipping goods without including the paperwork necessary to fulfill the requirements of Oxbury and the other bureaucrats. Also, some of the cartons were marked in a code known only to CDS officials.[28]

Oxbury had numerous other altercations with AMMISCA personnel, especially Major John Ausland, AMMISCA's advisor to the Burma-Yunnan railroad project. Yet Ausland's detailed diary reveals that Oxbury was not unique. He and other AMMISCA officers believed that inefficiency and petty bureaucratic habits permeated every British government office in Rangoon. The diary details the British prohibition on shipments of rice, desperately needed to feed the Yunnan-Burma railway workers, and the

8. The Mission's Involvement at Rangoon

morass of red tape that Ausland was forced to fight to obtain wooden ties for the railway. He notes that frequent delays were due to officials referring to London matters that the local British officials did not want to approve. The following example concerning critically needed trucks is typical. Ausland wrote,

> Fifty-three of our trucks had just been assembled at Rangoon and were ready to come to Lashio with their first load of supplies when Rangoon was bombed on Christmas Day, and the house in which the [transit] papers were kept was hit by an incendiary bomb and burned to the ground, and so for the lack of a few forms, our fifty-three trucks had to stay idle in the woods near Rangoon for several weeks waiting new papers on them during a time when the trucks were much needed to haul things out of Rangoon.[29]

The customs officers were not the only intractable British officials. One of the ranking AMMISCA officers in Rangoon, Major Harry S. Aldrich, was summoned to meet with Governor Sir Reginald Hugh Dorman-Smith, who was attempting to obtain information regarding American supplies for China. Aldrich suspected that Dorman-Smith wished to know what Lend-Lease goods were in Rangoon for purposes of future confiscation, especially after Dorman-Smith openly admitted to him there were supplies in China that the British "would give their eye teeth to get."[30]

AMMISCA personnel sometimes found the Chinese as intractable as the British. Major Russell, now the AMMISCA advisor to the Burma Road Commission, reported additional logistical difficulties. He reiterated his earlier reports that were critical of both Chinese and Americans in Washington who had "no conception of China's real needs." Large duplicate quantities of unsuitable equipment and materials, including more blankets, gas masks, and cotton bales, were still arriving on almost every Lend-Lease ship. Tons of copper and iron communications wire had been stored in Rangoon and Lashio warehouses for months, yet large additional quantities were still arriving under Lend-Lease. There remained the question of whether American 2½-ton trucks, ordered in quantities of thousands, were the best means of transportation in China. In addition, massive quantities of Lend-Lease material continued to be ordered by CDS and American officials in Washington without any regard for the decreasing storage space in Rangoon and Lashio, or the increasing problems in the transportation systems from Rangoon to Kunming.[31]

Russell believed the major cause of the supply buildup in Rangoon was Chinese incompetence and was so irritated with Chinese logistical methods that he recommended all shipments of Lend-Lease cargoes for China be suspended until the Chinese furnished AMMISCA an inventory of supplies stored at dumps at Rangoon and Lashio. He also requested lists of all items purchased prior to Lend-Lease, during Lend-Lease, and currently in transit to China. Finally, Russell urged that no future Lend-Lease purchases be made without the specific approval of AMMISCA's China Detail, and that all goods allocated to China remain under the detail's control until the supplies actually reached Chinese territory. He thought the British would be more cooperative if the Chinese officials were more responsible. China's organization at Rangoon "was not coordinated," "lacked leadership," and "could not make decisions."[32] This was the beginning of Magruder's conviction that limits on Lend-Lease goods should be instituted and used as a means of regulating Chinese reckless ordering and employment methods. It became the "quid pro quo" policy instituted by Stilwell and examined in a later chapter.

Russell's opinion was not unique. Journalist Leland Stowe, a frequent critic of Chiang, excoriated the Chinese leaders and the graft and corruption that permeated all levels of the Chinese government. Stowe claimed, "If the whole story ... is ever written it will make a fat volume stuffed with unsavory facts, but as a racketeering exposé it would deserve to be a best seller."[33] Magruder forwarded Russell's observations and recommendations to Washington, but the War Department gave them no serious consideration. The salient point is that the Asian allies were frequently unable to work together. British dedication to traditional bureaucratic systems, compounded by Chinese graft, favoritism, and traditional government corruption, injected innumerable obstacles and delays into the Rangoon-to-China supply route. In addition, several AMMISCA officers engendered a great deal of Sino-American ill will at Rangoon. Heavily influenced by an American general recently arrived in Asia, one of the major Asian inter-allied crises of the China-Burma-India area took place: the *Tulsa* Incident.

The Tulsa *Incident*

Sino-British relations were strained still more by the incident of the ship *Tulsa* and her cargo of valuable munitions at Rangoon. The British forces in Burma, guarding the last line of communication between China and the outside world, were badly in need of equipment. Space-time factors suggested the Chinese lend-lease stockpiles as the logical means of adding to the defenses of an area in whose safety China was so vitally interested. The War Department was sympathetic to the suggestion that lend-lease be transferred to Burma's garrison, because now it fully appreciated the importance of Burma and feared an emergency might soon develop there. Accordingly, Magruder was asked to persuade the Chinese to the most strategic use of the material. This was the central point, for the Chinese acquired title to lend-

lease goods as they left the United States and so there could be no transfer without their consent.
— Charles Romanus and Riley Sunderland,
Stilwell's Mission to China

Although the Japanese did not invade Burma until mid–January 1942, they began bombing Rangoon in early December. British forces lacked the means of defense, especially airplanes, anti-aircraft guns, and a planned air warning system that had a projected completion date of late 1942.[34] They were deficient in jungle warfare training and relied almost totally on motor transport for mobility and resupply. Moreover, the British anticipated a Japanese attack north of Rangoon rather than the direct east to west assault through Moulmein that forced Rangoon's evacuation in early March. Painfully aware of their own logistical problems, the British coveted the quantities of Chinese Lend-Lease weapons, vehicles, and munitions piling up on the docks and in the warehouses of Rangoon.

A subordinate of Magruder's, Lieutenant Colonel Joseph J. Twitty, was in charge of all Lend-Lease operations in Rangoon. On the night of 11 December 1941, Twitty was summoned to the office of Governor Reginald Dorman-Smith. The governor informed Twitty that the military situation was exceedingly grave and that the British badly needed some of the Lend-Lease supplies stored in Rangoon.[35] Twitty properly advised Magruder and the War Department of the conversation.[36] Although Twitty was later reproached for aligning himself too closely with the British in the events that followed, his message to Magruder outlining the situation indicates that he truly believed the overall Allied effort would benefit by the transfer of supplies to the British.[37] He was confident that the Chinese were unable to move all the supplies out of Rangoon and that the British should make use of the surplus material.

The War Department responded promptly. Twitty was ordered to transfer supplies only as directed by Magruder, and Magruder was ordered to approve transfers of equipment from Chinese to British jurisdiction "only at Chinese request," an unlikely eventuality in view of Chiang's desire to obtain as much American equipment as possible. The orders were transmitted to Magruder on December 14.[38]

On December 15, Magruder warned Twitty that decisions regarding transfers would only be made at "higher levels"— that is, by Chiang— and that the Chinese would "react very coldly" to the diversion of any supplies to the British.[39] Twitty responded by requesting permission to act "in fairness to both parties according to demands of the situation."[40] Magruder, probably to his later regret, replied that high level discussions concerning equipment transfers would soon begin, and he would "obtain early decisions."[41]

Almost simultaneously the Rangoon situation took on a new dimension. Major General George Brett arrived in Rangoon and quickly became a major figure in what was to become the *Tulsa* incident. Brett, an army air forces general, was on his way to Chungking under orders from the War Department to determine if heavy bombers could be based there. Although his presence in East Asia at this time was happenstance, he was the ranking American officer in the China-Burma area, even though he was ignorant of events and conditions there. Thus, the War Department felt it appropriate that he represent the American government at conferences regarding Burma. It must be remembered that Magruder's orders prohibited him from participating in policy making. Brett made several judgmental blunders.

Brett was not familiar with the problems at Rangoon, but he chose to adopt a command posture and conferred unilaterally with the governor. He initiated direct communications with Washington that bypassed Magruder. In sum, Brett projected further into Rangoon affairs than was wise or appropriate. The War Department originally assigned Magruder total control over Lend-Lease affairs, and although Brett outranked Magruder, he was an air officer not authorized to issue orders to AMMISCA personnel. A comment to the author from AMMISCA officer Nevin Wetzel is revealing: "In my opinion if any American officer should have been reprimanded for that mess at Rangoon, it should have been General Brett. He had no business sticking his nose in and of course even a high-ranking Lt. Col. doesn't feel very big around a Major General, even if he's in the Air Corps."[42] But Magruder was over two thousand miles away, and Brett was determined that the British obtain control over some of the Rangoon Lend-Lease stores.[43] Twitty was caught between Magruder, Brett's presence in Rangoon, British pressure, his own Anglophile tendencies, and the Chinese.

On December 18, Dorman-Smith informed Twitty that London ordered him to "seize any lease-lend materials if the worst came."[44] Several hours later, the governor warned Twitty that "enough time had been wasted writing letters and sending cables and [the Governor] was inclined to seize all required articles under the authority he had received from London." Twitty turned to Brett for guidance, a mistake. Twitty was in charge in Rangoon, not in Brett's chain of command. But Brett was there, under War Department orders to engage in policy discussions with the British and Chinese, which Magruder was forbidden to do. So, in spite of Magruder's orders not to place any Chinese Lend-Lease goods in British hands, Brett took it upon himself to pressure Twitty to do just that.[45]

8. The Mission's Involvement at Rangoon 111

Allied leaders in the China-Burma Theater (left to right): British field marshall Sir Archibald Wavell; Lieutenant General Joseph W. Stilwell, commanding all the U.S. Army troops in China, Burma and India; Lieutenant General H.H. Arnold, commanding the entire U.S. Army Forces; Lieutenant General Brehon Somervell, commanding the entire Service of Supply for the U.S. Army; and British field marshall Sir John Dill (Library of Congress Prints and Photographs Division, Washington, D.C., Office of War Information, U.S. Farm Security Administration/Office of War Information/Public Health Service Commission, #LC-USSE6-D-009427).

On December 19, as Twitty later reported, "all items possible were immediately removed to a storage warehouse twelve miles from the docks by British troops working at night in the emergency.... The action was taken as a result of an all–American conference at which Chinese would have been supernumerary due to the secrecy of the general plan at that time."[46] In other words, Twitty permitted the British to secretly impound in their own warehouses Lend-Lease goods consigned, indeed "owned," by the Chinese. The Chinese were not consulted, and the War Department and AMMISCA command level directives were openly violated.

The next morning General Yu F'ei-peng, Chiang's cousin and chief Chinese administrator in Rangoon, summoned Twitty to his office. The general demanded to know why the port authorities would not allow the cargo of the *Tulsa* to be loaded aboard vehicles for shipment to Lashio. Twitty stated that Brett had arrived to make an estimate of the military situation in Burma, and to assess if some of the Lease-Lend supplies in Burma might be needed by American forces. Twitty promised that the *Tulsa* cargo would be held only temporarily, but that "American needs would come first." He assured Yu there was no intent to deceive the Chinese.[47]

Oddly, Yu was not antagonistic. He recognized the fact that all Lend-Lease goods were American property, but wished to know what was going to be done with the *Tulsa* cargo. Twitty reiterated that he had not assigned the cargo to anyone; it would be held temporarily; but its ultimate distribution would be determined by Magruder. Major Russell took notes of the conversation and stated that General Yu appeared to be satisfied with Twitty's explanation and that the Chinese would cooperate. Perhaps the calm reaction of General Yu was due to his awareness of the sensitive situation in Rangoon or because he knew the British could do anything with Lend-Lease material that the Americans approved, regardless of who "owned" them at any particular moment. Also, there is a distinct possibility that Yu was more concerned over the loss of very profitable traffic in Lend-lease materials.[48]

The Chinese authorities in Rangoon were not openly exorcised by the impoundment of the *Tulsa* cargo. Magruder, though, had better insight into the probable consequences of the action. Even before he was aware of the seizure of the *Tulsa* cargo he warned Twitty that nothing could be transferred to the British until the American government received a specific enumeration of items and quantities desired, as well as Chinese approval. The Chinese and British were both aware of this requirement. For unknown reasons the British consistently refused to provide lists of their needs. Magruder urged Twitty to "get behind the British" and have their representative in Chungking present a detailed list of needs to the Chinese. He told Twitty,

> If there is a land invasion of a really threatening nature before the property is turned over to the British, and there is imminent danger of its loss, you are authorized to take such measures as are necessary.... I appreciate the British position of wanting and needing the material but there are other considerations which the War Department has in mind which prevent any precipitate decision on our part. The Chinese have a case as well. Certainly the British should indicate their real needs.[49]

On December 21 Magruder received a memorandum from Brett stating that he had advised Twitty to impound "everything" until further plans could be made—and that Twitty had done so. The use of the word "everything" is important; Magruder did not immediately realize that it included the entire

Tulsa cargo.⁵⁰ He responded only by radioing Twitty that "the impounding or retransfer of Lease-Lend materials to the British is not, repeat, not authorized by me."⁵¹

Magruder may have somewhat sympathized with Twitty, feeling his actions had been forced on him by Brett and the intense British pressure. He expressed this in a memorandum submitted for the record, probably on December 21 or 22: "The whole transaction smacks of British high-powered tactics to obtain blanket authority to get all of the Chinese Lend-Lease material by stampeding me into a decision ... to let them have all they ask for."⁵² Magruder also regarded Wavell's refusal of Chinese troops to be "inconsistent with the picture of Burma's defensive state, presented to justify requests for the transfer of China's lend-lease."⁵³ His chief of staff Colonel E. E. MacMorland expressed it cogently in his diary: "I am becoming almost anti–British when I consider their stupidity in handling Asiatics. They invariably antagonize them." And regarding Twitty, on 21 January 1942 MacMorland's diary states, "Long talk with Twitty. He had his troubles in Rangoon, not the least of which was unsound advice from Gen. Brett."⁵⁴ In defense of Brett, Romanus and Sunderland point out, "While in Burma Brett had observed Chinese methods of operating the line of communications from Rangoon northward and had received a very bad impression of Chinese ability and integrity, an impression he believed Wavell shared."⁵⁵

Magruder was temperate. In his next communication with Twitty, on December 23, he said he had discussed the situation at Rangoon with Brett, who arrived in Chungking on December 22, and they had decided it was a matter for the British and Chinese to settle between themselves. Magruder repeated that nothing should be permanently transferred to the British until specific requests were made, and reiterated his feelings regarding the British. He recalled how Washington had "implored the British for driblets of .30 caliber and .50 caliber ammunitions for the AVG." But the British "refused to disgorge a round." If only the British would make up their minds and submit a list of specific needs, the whole matter could be resolved.⁵⁶ At no point did Magruder censure Twitty for allowing the British to impound the *Tulsa*'s cargo, although he was now undoubtedly aware of the seizure. The impoundment of the *Tulsa*'s cargo caused extended dissension between the allies.

Meanwhile, in Rangoon, Anglo-Chinese-American relations were tranquil. On December 20 another joint meeting was held to discuss the disposition of the *Tulsa*'s cargo. A list of all materials on the ship was reviewed to determine if the American or British representatives objected to their release to the Chinese. They agreed to release the entire cargo to the Chinese with the exception of airplane parts and aviation gasoline. Twitty, chaired the meeting and insisted these items still had to be "controlled." The gasoline and parts were consigned to the Chinese National Airline and the AVG. Both organizations were playing important roles in the war against Japan, and American personnel staffed each of them. This raises the question of why were they singled out for delay, since the parts and fuel before being loaded on board the *Tulsa* were consigned to CNAC and the AVG, both vital elements of the anti–Japanese effort and staffed by Americans. Whatever the case, Twitty and the committee approved the delay.[57]

Yu hastily called a second conference that day, including General Brett, to obtain an explanation of the seizure several hours earlier by British soldiers of 150 Lend-Lease trucks from a Southwest Transportation Company storage area. Yu claimed the soldiers had no written authorization to take the vehicles. Twitty and Brett responded that at the first meeting the decision had been made to turn the trucks over to the British. When General Yu asked why he had not been notified, Brett declared that it was the responsibility of R. C. Chen (the Chinese representative to the conference) to inform Yu.[58]

The truth was that the appropriation had taken place just prior to the earlier meeting and, that while Chen had been aware that a transfer of trucks was discussed, he did not know of the British seizure. Brett deliberately distorted the facts and attempted to mislead General Yu. Yu certainly recognized

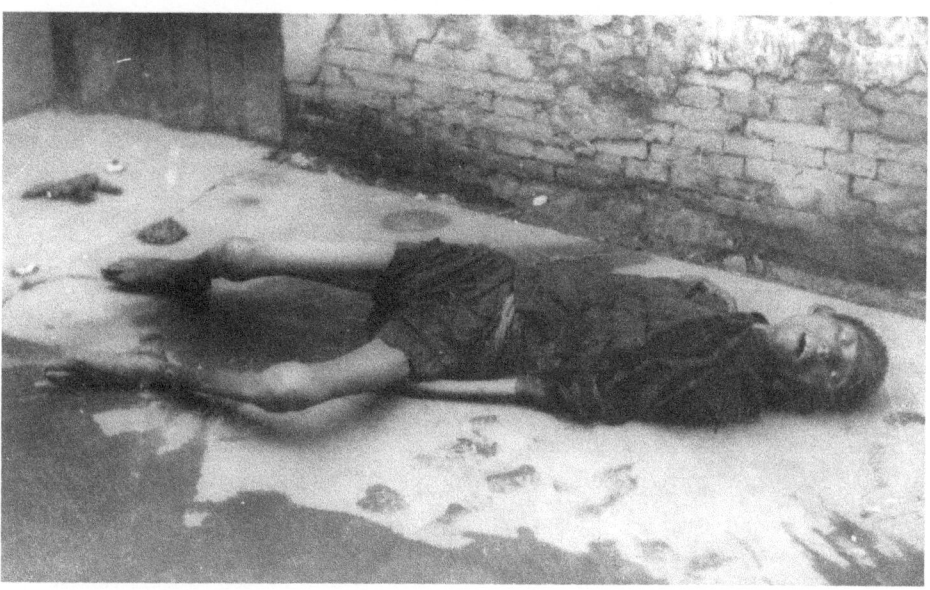

A man starving to death in the street, Chungking, China, circa 1942 (used by permission from the personal collection of Dennis Reinhart).

8. The Mission's Involvement at Rangoon

the seizure was an Anglo-American scheme to circumvent the Chinese, yet his reaction was moderate, particularly for a man of Yu's aggressive reputation. He stated that in the future, proper procedures would have to be established for transferring goods from Chinese to British jurisdiction, and final allocation of the *Tulsa* cargo would have to be made in Chungking, where Wavell, Brett, and Chiang were to meet. In the meantime any further cargo urgently needed by the British would conceivably be turned over to them, but only after their requests were forwarded to the Chinese government and the final decision made at Chungking. Fortunately for Sino-American relations, Yu and Chen agreed to release the trucks to the British.[59]

Again, the lack of British action is difficult to comprehend. Magruder was still committed to support their petition for the transfer of supplies if they would submit specific lists of needs. Yu implied he would not refuse to transfer materials the British truly needed, and his approval of the truck transfer seemed to bear this out. Yet perhaps because they were unable to break the old colonialist operating method, or because they felt the Chinese would refuse to transfer what they really needed, or both, the British refused to go through channels. In fact, when they learned that all requests would have to be submitted through Chungking, they hardened their stance. Only after exerting tremendous pressure was General Yu able to learn the whereabouts of the *Tulsa*'s cargo and granted the right inspect it. Even then the British agreed to supply the information to Yu only by confidential letter.[60] In fairness to the British, they desperately needed significant amounts of the materials being held by the Chinese, and were convinced, correctly as subsequent events proved, that the Chinese would not use it.

On December 22, AMMISCA officer Major Frank D. Merrill (later the leader of Merrill's Marauders) met with General Yu. Merrill, acting as Twitty's subordinate, had been summoned by Yu. Merrill opened their discussion with the statement that he had "no power to settle anything."[61] The general was, uncharacteristically, openly angry. He had just been informed that trucks were being taken from the Rangoon General Motors Lend-Lease assembly plant without Chinese approval or notification. He demanded to know why and how long it would continue. Yu asked under whose authority the action was taken — British or American. Merrill stated that the Lend-Lease supplies were in the custody of American army officers in Rangoon "acting under competent authority" and stored in a secure place. Yu asked if this method of appropriation would continue. Merrill responded affirmatively, although he said every effort would be made to release as much as possible to the Chinese. Yu terminated the meeting by stating that he wanted Merrill to understand that although responsible to the Chinese government, within the limits of his power he wanted to cooperate. Merrill knew that AMMISCA understood Yu's position but had to consider the British effort as well as China's.[62] Neutral observers of this era must at least somewhat empathize with Chiang's constant frustration and mistrust of his allies.

Merrill's statement disclosed the at least tacit American approval of the *Tulsa* cargo's impoundment. Plainly Brett and the AMMISCA personnel in Rangoon were disillusioned with the Chinese, especially over their failure to move the Lend-Lease supplies out of Rangoon. Twitty believed that the British would employ the supplies more efficaciously, and, under Brett's influence, decided to ignore Magruder's directives ordering him not to transfer materials to the British. In a December 22 memorandum to Secretary of War Stimson, Brett admitted that he had "advised" Twitty to insist on Anglo-American control of the Lend-Lease supplies because the British needed immediate resupply of materials in almost every category.[63]

The *Tulsa* incident entered its most bitter phase at a Christmas day conference held at the Ministry of Foreign Affairs in Chungking. Present were General Ho Ying-ch'in, the Chinese minister of war, Magruder, and the British military attaché Major General Dennys. Chiang ordered Ho to convene the meeting to discuss the transfer of Lend-Lease supplies to the British. Ho noted that Chiang, although he had previously authorized the release of supplies to the British and planned to release additional quantities, now had changed his mind. He had just received a memorandum from Chiang referring to the events in Rangoon, and the generalissimo was outraged. He (Chiang) took serious objection to the retention of the *Tulsa*'s cargo, considered it an unfriendly act, and told General Ho to inform generals Magruder and Dennys that all Lend-Lease material at Rangoon could be given to the British in its entirety or returned to the American sources from which it had been received, and that all Chinese personnel would be forthwith returned from Burma to China. All cooperation between Britain and China would end, and the Chinese would no longer fight the Japanese along with the British.[64] Magruder faced a potential disaster. Chiang was probably bluffing, but Washington would not be happy if this three-power incident became a major crisis. With a straight face, General Dennys disclaimed knowledge of the entire affair. Magruder, attempting to be a peacemaker, stated the matter was a great misunderstanding and asked for an appointment with Chiang to assure him that Twitty had acted without orders. He reminded Ho that it was not American policy to transfer Lend-Lease material without consent of the Chinese government. Ho promised to arrange the meeting.[65]

Magruder met with Chiang on the day after Christmas and on December 27 radioed a report to the War Department including his assessment of the

Tulsa incident. Although he claimed he had first learned of the seizure at the meeting on Christmas Day, this is questionable because Twitty and Brett sent Magruder several communications outlining the impoundment prior to Christmas. Magruder must have discussed the situation with Brett when the latter arrived in Chungking on December 22. Whatever the timing, Magruder believed he knew the Chinese very well, but in this case he misjudged their reaction, probably because of Yu's initial moderate response to the seizures. Magruder certainly knew of the events surrounding the *Tulsa* incident before he met with Ho on Christmas Day.[66] He assured General Ho that the policy of the American government was to not retransfer Chinese Lend-Lease material without Chinese consent, and said that Twitty must have misinterpreted the policy.[67] Magruder assured the generalissimo that American policy vis-à-vis retransfer of Lend-Lease goods had not changed, and whatever had happened in Rangoon was not approved by the American government.

He reported that his comments were well received by the generalissimo, who although wrathful at the beginning of the meeting became "visibly pleased" when Magruder assured him there was no change in American policy. Chiang's anger was directed primarily at the British, and he asked Magruder to warn them if they interfered again a grave situation would result. Magruder stated in conclusion of the report that he was going to recall Twitty, because even if he had just used bad judgment he had to be disavowed.[68]

The British offered several arguments in defense of the seizure. Although he had claimed no prior knowledge of the event, Dennys chose to lamely defend it. He claimed the cargo had been sequestered because air raids were imminent and there was no time to warn anyone. He scapegoated Twitty by claiming that he had approved the seizure and no cargo was kept except some guns approved by Chiang at a post–*Tulsa* incident meeting with Wavell and Brett. He stated only "a few" lorries had been borrowed, a reference to the over one hundred trucks permanently appropriated on December 20. He then implied that Twitty had instigated the whole affair. Dorman-Smith sided with Dennys. He maintained that supplies from the *Tulsa* were congesting the docks and interfering with the movement of British military stores and asserted that the Chinese could have had anything they asked for from the sequestered cargo. The British were not totally forthright: the Chinese in fact had submitted several requests for the airplane parts and gasoline before even a portion was released, and the Chinese transport capability was further reduced by the British appropriation of the Lend-Lease trucks.[69]

The British overplayed their hand, as Twitty was in no way guilty of or responsible for the British seizure of the *Tulsa* cargo. At worst, he was an abettor and under Brett's influence. The *Tulsa* seizure was followed by a similar high jacking of General Motors trucks that no American had preapproved. Dennys' claims of no knowledge were obviously false as was, seemingly, his claim that Chiang had approved the appropriation. Dorman-Smith's contention that the materials were seized to alleviate congestion at the docks was just as flimsy as his excuse for denying the Chinese requests for the gasoline and airplane parts in the seized goods inventory. The British knew the Japanese were preparing to expand the war in Burma.

The most significant political effect of the *Tulsa* incident was the State Department's affirmation of Chungking's right to control the Lend-Lease goods consigned to China. In a memorable message to Consul General Brady at Rangoon, Hull told him to inform the British that without Chiang's approval the American government would not consign to the British Lend-Lease material originally invoiced to China.[70] Hull also ordered Ambassador Gauss to convey a message to Chiang stating the president had given his personal attention to reports of the *Tulsa* incident and desired to further assure the generalissimo that the action was contrary to American policy. Material invoiced to China could be transferred only after prior conference and consultation with, and by inference the approval of, the Chinese government.[71]

The War Department followed suit. Marshall sent messages to Magruder at Chungking and to Lieutenant Colonel Adrian St. John, Twitty's designated relief, at Rangoon. Magruder was instructed to see that no personnel in the mission displayed hostility or lack of patience with any official of the Chinese government. St. John was ordered to allow no nation other than China to be the recipient, even temporarily, of Lend-Lease materials consigned to China "unless this material or equipment is in imminent danger of loss or destruction" or unless authorized by Chiang.[72] Washington correctly believed these reassurances would reinstate Chiang's faith in America. As for the British, however, Chiang was unforgiving.

Even after the *Tulsa* incident early in 1942, the British pressed the Chinese for large quantities of supplies they needed to oppose the new Japanese advance into Burma. Magruder supported the transfer if the Chinese approved. Having foreseen such an eventuality, and to help institute a workable transfer procedure policy, Magruder in late December asked the generalissimo to assign a Chinese official at Rangoon with authority to arrange transfers of supplies to the British. But Magruder was realistic and doubted the request would be met. In a message to the secretary of war on January 4, he noted that the British had a habit of irritating the Chinese, and it was highly unlikely that the generalissimo would consent to anyone but himself approving the transfer of supplies.[73] He was correct: in January Chiang ordered all British supply requests forwarded to Chungking for final approval.[74] This procedure saved no time but did engender additional mistrust.

Few people at the several *Tulsa* meetings felt the British actions were proper, nor were the AMMISCA officers convinced that Twitty was to blame. The AMMISCA chief of staff's diary maintains that Twitty "was evidently the scapegoat for some sculduggery [*sic*] between the Chinese and the British. We have recommended that he be reassigned outside China."[75] MacMorland also noted, after talking with Twitty, that he felt Twitty had received "unsound advice from Brett."[76]

Twitty submitted a memo "for the record" on December 31. His statements were defensive and emphasized that in his meeting with the governor on December 18, Dorman-Smith had told Twitty Churchill had directed him, "if the worst came," to seize Lend-Lease goods. He stated that Brett himself had not only approved the appropriation of the *Tulsa*'s cargo but had recommended the seizure of all other Lend-Lease materials in Burma. He maintained that the seizure did not delay or prevent shipments of cargo to Lashio. In fact, "once the goods, including the trucks, were returned to the Chinese ... they [the Chinese] stated that more stuff was moved out of Rangoon at that time than any other similar period." Twitty pointed out Major General Brett had been in Rangoon (thus, in de facto command) for the duration of the "incident," and had kept War Department aware of what was happening. In addition, the fall of Rangoon seemed inevitable, and there was no "suitable code" with which he could communicate with Magruder to obtain his approval. Why not put the Lend-Lease materials to some good use by giving them to the Chinese? Twitty also claimed the Chinese demanded his attention with too many time-wasting meetings and R.C. Chen, the Chinese representative, did not keep General Yu apprised of the decisions made during meetings.

Throughout the memo there is an undertone of condescension towards the Chinese. He concluded that because a condition of "extreme emergency" existed, he felt that he "had opened an avenue for helping the British defend the line of communications so vital to China." Twitty believed Brett agreed and approved. If so, it is clear that Brett's ignorance of conditions in Rangoon and Burma was apparent to everyone but him. An excellent example was his mid–December statement, "Burma is the place from which to strike the Japanese." In fact, there were no bombers in Burma, none were expected, there few facilities to support them, no supply lines to provide fuel and materials, and they would have been sent to Singapore if they had become available.[77]

To help smooth Sino-American relations and improve the retransfer program, Magruder relieved Twitty. Surprisingly, Twitty did not leave China under a cloud as far as the War Department was concerned. When Lieutenant

Colonel Adrian St. John arrived at Rangoon in early January, he radioed Magruder that Twitty had acted with "excellent judgment and initiative."[78] Marshall stated that the War Department "placed no credence" in unconfirmed reports critical of Twitty.[79] Twitty was simply ordered to a new post in Australia with no apparent blot on his record.[80]

Even after the conclusion of the *Tulsa* incident the disposition of Lend-Lease goods in Rangoon continued in disarray. On December 28, Brett radioed Secretary of War Stimson that the situation in Rangoon was acute. He claimed that communications with Chungking were almost nonexistent and there were no directives from the Chinese leadership as to disposal of goods. He said that Twitty, still in charge at Rangoon, was under pressure from ship captains anxious to unload and quickly leave the threatened harbor. Brett therefore "strongly" recommended "that Twitty in collaboration with British Governor and General Yu Fei-peng, be given full authority to act for the U.S. government" on all matters related to Lend-Lease supplies and equipment, "action to take form of military control."[81] In other words, Brett was not only end-running Magruder, he was calling for action that would undoubtedly have led to another Anglo-Chinese-American jurisdictional confrontation.

Magruder perceived the danger in Brett's proposal and told St. John to disregard Brett's recommendations when he took over at Rangoon. Moreover, St. John was to restrict himself to carrying out only the mission's primary responsibility of advising and assisting the Chinese, and scrupulously avoid having AMMISCA become regarded as the enemy in Chinese eyes.[82] Magruder's caution was wise. MacMorland's diary refers to Brett's "throat-cutting" of Magruder in Brett's direct contacts with the War Department.[83]

On 20 January 1942, the Japanese invaded Burma. Two divisions moved west from Thailand into southeastern Burma near Moulmein. Their goal was to quickly traverse the less than two hundred miles to Rangoon and sever the Burma supply line to China.[84] Throughout January and February, the British struggled to build up their defenses around Rangoon, which after the fall of Singapore they regarded as their most valuable Asian possession.[85] Their frustration grew as they watched additional tons of Chinese Lend-Lease goods flow into Rangoon's warehouses. St. John, another Anglophile, sought Magruder's assistance to convince Chiang to part with some of the supplies that were unlikely to move north before Rangoon fell.[86] Magruder responded that Chiang had refused to give anyone in Rangoon authority to transfer Chinese Lend-Lease materials, on several occasions, and it was now up to the British to convince Chiang to act. He again ordered St. John to do nothing more than witness transfers and report them to the War Department through Magruder.[87]

St. John was not happy. He believed Magruder was not aware of the delays caused by the Chinese insistence that all decisions regarding supply transfers be made only at Chungking; the age-old "man on the ground versus the home office" syndrome. It was true that as a result of Chiang's obdurance large quantities of supplies were still in Rangoon. St. John became as frustrated as Twitty had been; but his entreaties evoked no change in Magruder's orders.[88] The general was a firm believer in the chain of command and did his best to ensure that directives from his office and Washington were followed as written.

Another example of Magruder's concern that orders be obeyed was his warning to his subordinate in Calcutta, Major Paul L. Freeman, Jr., to remain aloof from all Chinese-British debates over supplies. Freeman was ordered to avoid the mistake made at Rangoon of considering the Lend-Lease materials subject to local Anglo-American disposal. Freeman was reminded of the policy regarding transfer of supplies and that even if the Japanese pushed toward Calcutta he was not to allow British pressure to force him to turn Chinese-consigned Lend-Lease material over to the Indian government.[89]

As the threat to Rangoon increased in mid–January the British finally began to provide the Chinese with lists of requested Lend-Lease articles. The lists were presented to a committee of the Chinese National Military Council, chaired by General Shang Chen, where they were discussed and then sent to the generalissimo for his approval.[90] The usual time for deliberation in Chungking was relatively short, usually less than two weeks, but supply inventories at Rangoon continued to build up as air raids and other obstacles, mostly bureaucratic, increased. Magruder, in accord with his orders, did not become involved in any way except to once more direct St. John not to make any transfers without Chinese approval.[91]

The Evacuation of Rangoon

> The Chinese blamed the British for "defeatism" and there was a great deal of truth in this. Some troops did arrive from India in the days before the fall of Rangoon. But the home authorities were already determined not to waste more reserves in fruitless attempts to hold Burma.
> — Christopher Bayly and Tim Harper,
> *Fall of British Asia, 1941–1945*

At their meeting with Chiang on 23 December 1941, Brett and Magruder, in addition to discussing the crisis at Rangoon caused by the *Tulsa* incident, attempted to gain more of the stockpiled material support for the British. In his report to the War Department Brett noted that too much time was devoted to irrelevancies instead of the ever-expanding material overstocks at Rangoon; the growing Japanese threat to that city; and the need for the AMMISCA representative in Rangoon to have the authority to make immediate decisions regarding Lend-Lease transfers to the British. Brett and Magruder both reported to Chiang, but he remained unmoved and continued, in Brett's words, to assign every bullet and gallon of gasoline that went to the British. Brett also observed that until Washington was ready to put greater pressure on the generalissimo, this condition would continue.[92]

Moulmein fell to the Japanese on January 30 and Yu Fei-peng instituted an emergency Rangoon evacuation plan of Lend-Lease goods north from Rangoon. A truck shuttle would then be established between Mandalay and Lashio. Magruder recommended to Chiang that he approve the diversion of supply ships to Calcutta and, in the event that Singapore fell, to Bombay.[93]

The Chinese responded immediately. Two supply ships docked at Rangoon were ordered to cease unloading and to transport the remaining cargo to Calcutta. In addition, the Chinese broached the idea of moving supplies then being held in Rangoon to Calcutta, much to the disgust of St. John, who correctly predicted that shipping them to India would be assigning them to oblivion. St. John believed the British authorities in Calcutta would appropriate the Chinese-owned supplies and probably forward them to Malaya, which was in dire straits. Magruder was still concerned St John's Anglophile tendencies might allow some of the Rangoon Chinese-owned Lend-Lease materials to fall under British control. Magruder informed St. John that in Washington there was a "subsidiary to [the] Chinese government," which in essence was working around AMMISCA and "obtaining decisions" without consulting members of the mission. He advised St. John to not impede the removal of supplies bound for Calcutta from Rangoon and reminded him that orders to move cargo to India came from Washington and Chungking.[94]

On January 28 Chiang ordered the diversion of Lend-Lease ships to Calcutta and Bombay.[95] Malaya, with the exception of Singapore, was overrun before the end of January. Singapore itself surrendered its garrison of seventy thousand and to General Yamashita's army of thirty thousand in mid-February.[96] Within days St. John advised Magruder that, contrary to Magruder's directive, he had retained four ships at Rangoon that the Chinese had ordered sent to India. He defended his action by claiming the Chinese had overemphasized the Japanese threat and "panicked." All four vessels had been successfully unloaded, but he also confirmed that no more cargo ships should be sent to Rangoon.[97]

St. John's accomplishment was the last good fortune the allies experienced at Rangoon. When Moulmein, directly across the Gulf of Martaban from Rangoon, fell, Rangoon was subjected to heavier bombing and submarine raids.[98] On January 29 St. John advised the War Department that he, General Yu, and the American consul agreed that shipments of all cargo to Rangoon should cease for six months. The ships could not be protected and eight months' tonnage had already accumulated at Rangoon. Moreover, railroad coal was in short supply and the British withdrawal north required almost all the railroad cars. In addition, because the British planned to use Mandalay as their main evacuation center, AMMISCA could only move the Chinese Lend-Lease supplies as far north as Yamethin, one hundred and thirty miles south of Mandalay.[99]

With the support of AMMISCA Rangoon Detail officers the evacuation went into full operation on February 3 when over one hundred trucks left for Yamethin.[100] The same day a small reversal of fortune took place. Word was received that the fuel shortage had eased and more coal was now available for the railroad. Thirty railroad cars a day were assigned to AMMISCA, and a week later this allocation increased to sixty.[101] Despite a brief altercation with truck drivers concerning wages, by February 5 the evacuation was going smoothly. Major James Wilson, who supervised the AMMISCA portion of the evacuation, estimated that a thousand tons a day were being moved from Rangoon to Yamethin. On February 10 Wilson informed Magruder that as soon as all supplies were removed from Rangoon the AMMISCA operation would be relocated to Yamethin and from there would be moved to China. He also reported the Chinese were relying on AMMISCA to move the Lend-Lease materials to China.[102]

The cooperation between the Chinese and British in Rangoon was born of desperation and did not solve the Sino-British controversy over the allocation of Lend-Lease material. Magruder was still very concerned with extraneous and unneeded materials being ordered by China Defense Supplies. On January 31, he radioed Washington that all future materials shipped to India should be placed in a common pool even though originally earmarked for a particular nation; the decision for their final allocation would be made when the goods arrived in India.[103] But on February 14, St. John complained to the War Department that goods such as lead were still being received in Rangoon even though a great quantity of it was produced in Burma. He referred to this as an "inexcusable waste of shipping space."[104] As a result, of the 1,700 railroad cars of Chinese Lend-Lease supplies at Newport News in mid–February, 700 were returned to War Department warehouses and the remaining 1,000 were rescheduled to leave in late February.[105] This did not help. By April 25 the backlog amounted to 1,800 freight cars, over 100,000 tons of material waiting for shipment to India. Lend-Lease allocations to China were sharply reduced.¹⁰⁶

In Washington, Soong increased his efforts to get the materials shipped from Newport News. In a letter to Assistant Secretary McCloy, Soong complained of being caught in a vicious circle. He noted that no ships had been designated for Chinese Lend-Lease use from December 8 to mid–January, and because of this, the United States government refused to allocate additional supplies for China. Soong disingenuously claimed that a depot for Chinese supplies was being established in India, an air transport system was being organized, and improvements were being made on roads in north Burma. In reality, none of the projects had proceeded beyond the initial planning phase.¹⁰⁷

By the second week of February, nine hundred trucks were operating between Rangoon and Yamethin, and the General Motors assembly plant was producing fifty trucks daily. But the fall of Singapore, the largest surrender in British history, was a psychological blow. Although Claire Chennault's American Volunteer Group temporarily maintained allied air superiority there was a definite lack of British leadership, offensive spirit, and resupply. In Burma, the Japanese soon outnumbered the allies four to one in aircraft, and by mid–February they crossed the Salween and Bilin rivers and destroyed two British brigades at the Sittang River.¹⁰⁸ These rivers were the last natural barriers to an assault on Rangoon.

As the Japanese forces closed in on Rangoon, Magruder arrived in the city. He learned that the Japanese had crossed the Sittang, and although he tried to coordinate with the British authorities there was no organized defense of Rangoon. He inspected the AMMISCA-administered warehouses, decided to destroy the unrepairable vehicles, and on February 24 ordered St. John to evacuate. Everything that was left was either burned or blown up, including 972 trucks, approximately 500 tires, and 1,000 bales of blankets.¹⁰⁹ Major Nevin Wetzel and other AMMISCA officers used gasoline from fifty-five gallon drums to destroy vehicles and buildings. They also went from truck to truck firing .45-caliber slugs into the vehicle's cylinder heads, rendering them useless.¹¹⁰

A newly arrived British soldier's account of Rangoon's final hours graphically described the chaotic conditions:

> Tutt [the soldier] saw numerous bodies in the Rangoon streets — looters shot down by troops, and victims of the bombing and strafing attacks. When he returned to the city to participate in unloading the battery's [artillery unit's] gear, he noticed kites [vultures] gorging themselves on the corpses. They rose with slow laborious wing flaps as we passed. They were so sated that they could

hardly get off the ground, and as they moved off, the dogs came in. Rangoon sank into anarchy. According to Tutt, "The Burmese started to settle old scores with the wealthy Indians and Chinese who had grown rich in their country."[111]

A contradictory perspective comes from British historians Christopher Bayly and Tim Harper who note, at Rangoon, "British honor suffered" because "while a large part of the Anglo-Burmese population was able to join the British retreat, many Anglo-Burmese and Anglo-Indians stayed on. They continued to man the essential services in Rangoon and elsewhere until the very last minute."[112]

The secretary of war requested an after-action report on the final events at Rangoon dating from the first of January. St. John was tasked to compile it, but the confusion, misplacement of records and breakup of the Rangoon AMMISCA team delayed its completion until April 12. The report reveals that there was mistrust and prejudice aplenty. The major problems in pre-evacuation Rangoon were the commandeering of the *Tulsa*'s cargo, the inability of the Chinese to transport the *Tulsa*'s goods once they were returned by the British, and the deliberate attempt by the British to prevent the transfer to the Chinese of those parts of the *Tulsa* cargo they wanted to keep. There was the continued influx of supplies, many unneeded, requiring offloading. There were ongoing problems with the incredibly inept bureaucratic civil government (Anglo-Burmese), who, even as the bombs were falling and the British resistance to the Japanese invaders was crumbling, insisted on spending not hours, but days, double-scrutinizing licenses and bills of lading. On March 6 Magruder reported to the War Department that Rangoon had been evacuated and all AMMISCA personnel had left the city. Under Wilson's direction they were organizing the movement of the supplies dumped at Yamethin up to Lashio.[113] Although Rangoon was successfully evacuated, the loss of the city was a devastating blow; it was China's last sea link with its allies east of India.

In summary, when AMMISCA personnel arrived at Rangoon in October 1941, the military-economic-political situation was far beyond their ability to meaningfully influence. Traditional Burmese-Chinese-British antagonism manifested itself daily through the Anglo-Burmese bureaucracy's insistence on atypical customs duties, unnecessary inspections, and numerous trivial forms of harassment. The Chinese contributed to their own problems through imperfect ordering, inventory, warehouse, and transport methods, and their failure to convince the British to provide them better dockside and transportation equipment. Moreover, the inability of the Chinese to plan and submit their needs on a priority basis and lack of responsible leadership in Rangoon reinforced the British belief that the Chinese were incompetent.

British political and military leadership at Rangoon was weak and hampered by bureaucratic red tape; the British failed to implement an air defense system for the city; and they failed to provide sufficient aircraft, jungle-trained troops, mechanized and motorized equipment, and logistical support. From their arrival AMMISCA reported the Anglo-Chinese problems to the War Department, but Washington ordered Magruder not to intervene. This cautious attitude prevailed until Brett and Twitty acted in their ill-advised manner regarding the *Tulsa* supplies.

St. John's report contained curious information regarding the General Motors plant. He acknowledged no contracts had ever been affected, and until close to the end management insisted on using only one working shift and closing down on Sundays. But largely through the efforts of the AMMISCA Rangoon unit, although much too late, several changes were made that briefly improved conditions. Licensing and bill of lading time was shortened, a second shift was added at the GM plant, and some of the *Tulsa*'s seized materials were returned to the Chinese. Nine hundred seventy-two trucks in the General Motors plant were destroyed, but "not one pound of usable American or Chinese government property was left in Rangoon on our Departure."[114] But Rangoon was lost, and China's only hope for sustenance, desperately needed if it was to remain in the war, was in using air and road routes from India that were not yet established.

9

Logistics Problems on the Burma Road

> In translating the funds from the First Lend-Lease Appropriation into actual contacts and deliveries, primary emphasis has been placed on improving China's long lines and means of communication with us and with the world. Having materials to resurface the Burma Road, earth-moving equipment for grading and repairing the road, insecticides for the malarial marshes along the highway, trucks, spare parts, spare tires, gasoline lubricants, wreckers, service station equipment and the services of a number of experienced American loaders, dispatchers, mechanics are being provided in this phase of the program.
> — Edward R. Stettinius, Director of Lend-Lease, to James Roosevelt, Captain USMC[1]

When AMMISCA arrived in Chungking monthly shipments over the northern portion of the Burma Road (Lashio to Kunming) were approximately 15,000 tons. The Chinese hoped to double this amount in 1942.[2] They also planned to facilitate transportation of the goods by constructing a railroad from Kunming to Lashio to connect with the Burmese railroad that ran from Rangoon to Lashio via Mandalay. The mission's task was to move supplies over the entire route, of which the key portion was the Burma Road. The road itself was in no better condition than what Major McHugh reported in December 1938.[3] And, in early 1940 the American military attaché, Major David D. Barrett, reported that the "general condition of the road can be rated only as fair, with many stretches in bad condition."[4] He warned that the trucks and drivers underwent "terrific punishment"; the drivers were invariably careless; and claims of tonnage shipped were exaggerated.[5]

As China's seaports continued to fall to the Japanese, cargo ships were rerouted to Rangoon, forcing the storage facilities at Rangoon to become even more overloaded. The allocation of limited dock space, the overuse, and subsequent frequent breakdown of cranes and other equipment, and poor logistics planning forced the establishment of "dumps" north along the line of the Burma Road, especially near Lashio. Thus, the Road became heavily congested well before Pearl Harbor.[6]

American Civilians Employed on the Burma Road

> Each American hired to work on the Burma Road became a member of the Burma Road Technical Group and was advised that "Your country will be judged by your efforts and conduct."
> — Adj. General Eglin (Washington AMMISCA detail) to each member of the Burma Technical Group[7]

The employment of United States technical experts in China was a pioneer venture. Never before had there been a situation wherein American civilians officially served in their government's employ in a foreign country under wartime conditions. Two civilian technical groups were financed by Lend-Lease dollars to work on the Burma Road: motor-vehicle maintenance engineers and technicians, and traffic and transportation experts. Known collectively as the Burma Road Technical Group, all of them later served under AMMISCA's cognizance. Although there were less than fifty of them prior to Pearl Harbor, by early 1942 their ranks numbered several hundred.[8] The War Department retained final approval on all individuals hired for the technical group. Magruder requested a total of 274 employees ranging from propeller mechanics to medical doctors. Even after Stilwell's arrival and the upgrading of the area to a theater of operations, the War Department hierarchy retained final approval on the hiring of even lower echelon Burma Road personnel, another element of the bureaucratic misunderstandings and delays detrimental to AMMISCA's mission.[9]

Of the several civilian businesses engaged in Burma Road enterprises, General Motors participated most heavily and employed the largest number of technicians. General Motors' history in China and Burma began with their pre–AMMISCA era sales of trucks to the Burmese and Chinese governments and the construction of an assembly plant at Rangoon in 1939–1940. It was natural, then, that General Motors would be involved in the Lend-Lease vehicle assembly project administered by AMMISCA.[10] Most of the General Motors people were located in Rangoon and were supervised by the plant manager, C. F. Ladin. Several of these people worked at no cost to Lend-Lease; General Motors paid their salaries and provided their services to AMMISCA gratis. Magruder planned that they and those yet to be hired would be the cornerstone of a China-Burma parts system composed of a truck assembly plant, a single base depot located at Rangoon, and multiple sub-depots.

The War Department could not begin contractual negotiations for the sale and distribution of completed trucks and parts to China until a customs problem was solved. It centered on the previously mentioned Burmese government's attempt to levy a one percent import tariff on Lend-Lease goods, including parts for Burma Road vehicles. Burma's well-being was contingent on China's successful opposition to Japan, but the Burmese authorities chose to see it as an additional source of revenue that would expand in the months ahead.[11] Magruder was ordered to "expedite settlement" of the problem and to submit recommendations on locations for parts depots.[12] Before he could respond, he learned of a Chinese plan to take fiscal advantage of American Lend-Lease. In mid–November he warned the War Department that China intended to levy charges on the unloading, handling, and shipping of spare parts. He added, "This gradual tendency on the part of the Chinese to place financial burdens on lend lease also places heavy administrative burdens on the Mission which we are unable to handle without addition of personnel. Also Chinese must be made to realize that any funds expended here diminish material obtainable by them in United States."[13]

The Chinese then demanded control over the main parts depot and objected to locating it in Rangoon.[14] General Motors executives and Daniel Arnstein argued that the main depot should be at Rangoon, where its primary responsibility would be record keeping. Several sub-depots on the Burma Road and other highways "will carry a greater part of the stock and facilitate easy distribution." Magruder supported them because he desired the "least interference by Chinese officials."[15] In addition Magruder was advised that over a thousand tons of spare parts would be shipped by early December, even though Washington had told him there would be no negotiation of the General Motors contracts and, thus, no place to locate the parts until Magruder made his formal location recommendations.

Magruder was in a difficult position; his traffic expert, Captain James Wilson, favored the placement of the depot at Kunming so that it would more conveniently serve all of the Burma Road and Yunnan. Because of the high pilferage rate on the Burma Road, Wilson believed full truckloads of parts would have a better chance of reaching Kunming for distribution to the northern sub-depots and repair shops than would trucks carrying mixed loads of small items. On the other hand, "the shipment of large quantities of spare parts initially would place another serious burden on the already overloaded Burma Road itself." And, "whichever system ... is adopted the difficulties will be very great ... due to a dearth of efficient and trained assistants."[16] In early January Magruder recommended Rangoon as the site for the main depot. It was approved, contracts were completed, and leases were signed for depots, warehouses, and an additional truck assembly plant.[17]

Magruder believed that China should not have jurisdiction over the depots and assembly plants even though he knew that under the terms of the Lend-Lease Act it was informally agreed that materials requisitioned by China Defense Supplies automatically became the property of the Chinese government when they were put aboard ship in the United States.[18] However, Magruder had witnessed so much mismanagement and venality in Chinese operations that he solicited a major policy change from Army Chief of Staff General Marshall. He recommended that the United States, presumably AMMISCA, retain complete control over all parts, plants, and distribution centers. Magruder was aware that news had reached the upper echelons of the War Department of the disputes between his subordinates at Rangoon and Chinese officials. He warned Marshall that if America did not retain control over Lend-Lease materials, there would be increased loss, misuse, and improper allocation of materials, as well as further "friction" between British, American, and Chinese officials in Rangoon.[19] Although the War Department did not directly respond to Magruder's suggestions, his recommendations did influence departmental policymakers to institute a major policy change later in 1942. This "quid pro quo" supply policy, described below, limited Lend-Lease shipments to China.[20]

By the end of January 1942 the military situation was ominous and Rangoon's future as a port worse than tenuous.[21] Still, Ladin insisted that expansion of the Rangoon facilities go forward.[22] When it became clear that the fall of Rangoon was imminent Marshall overruled Ladin. He then contacted St. John and ordered him to accelerate truck assembly and move as many trucks as possible to northern Burma. St. John was also ordered, "in collaboration with proper Chinese and British authorities," to prepare to destroy the military hardware in Rangoon to prevent its capture by the Japanese.[23] Magruder shared Marshall's concern. On February 10 he recommended that the main parts depot and vehicle assembly operation be shifted to the west coast of India, and sent his chief of staff, Colonel E. E. MacMorland, to Rangoon on an inspection tour.[24]

MacMorland's report supported the transfer of the operation to India and also revealed serious weaknesses in the General Motors operation. He noted the Rangoon assembly plant was working just one shift and assembling an average of only forty-two trucks a day, eighteen below its capacity. The low assembly rate was not due to lack of material; there were fourteen hundred trucks in packing cases in the storage yard. MacMorland believed that Ladin, although experienced, did not appreciate the gravity of the military situation and reported that St. John had been forced to order Ladin in writing to add a second shift.[25]

The report prompted Magruder to reiterate his recommendation for a supply base in India. He also submitted an additional recommendation for the opening of a ground supply route from India to a series of parts sub-depots in China.[26] Washington responded that there were eleven hundred tons of vehicle parts at sea and since there were no plans to build any sub-depots in China the War Department intended to construct a massive depot in Bombay. The new depot would have "sufficient capacity for needs of Chinese, British in India, and the Russians and British in Iran"; what was Magruder's opinion?[27] Magruder knew there would be tremendous transportation problems from India to China, but he felt that Bombay was safe from Japanese attacks. He concurred with the department's proposal.[28]

After the fall of Rangoon in early March the responsibility for parts storage and vehicle assembly passed out of Magruder's jurisdiction, but in a message to the quartermaster general he emphasized the problems created when civilian technicians became involved in foreign countries under wartime conditions. The General Motors people "planned more for the future than for the exigencies of the moment"; they "lacked energy" and could have assembled and shipped over one thousand more trucks than they did. He was never comfortable in his relationship with General Motors and believed that since AMMISCA people regularly worked around the clock, civilians could too. War needs, he said, were poorly served by the "peacetime methods" used by Ladin and his subordinates. The Chinese were antagonized by the lack of respect for their customs displayed by the General Motors personnel, and the whole effort was put together haphazardly because General Motors had pulled together whatever people happened to be available in the Far East regardless of their type and level of training.[29]

AMMISCA functioned in a pioneer supervisory role in this initial American effort to provide militarily supervised technicians and advisors to a foreign power in war time. Misunderstandings and delays were not unexpected and for many reasons mistakes and errors in judgment were made by everyone. But as the Japanese moved further into Burma it was obvious that China could not survive without American assistance via new supply routes to China. It was painfully clear that new systems would be extremely difficult to establish and sustain.

The Yunnan-Burma Railroad

> Unfortunately the deficiencies of the Burma Road are likely to be felt more keenly if China tries to avail herself of the opportunities offered by the Lend Lease Bill. When all is said and done, the fact remains that the Burma Road was never intended for very heavy traffic. According to the original idea, the Yunnan-Burma railroad was to serve as the main artery between Lashio and Kunming.
> — Bruce Bliven, "Burma Road Bottlenecks"

In the years preceding Pearl Harbor the Chinese several times proposed the construction of a railroad from Kunming, China, to the railhead at Lashio, Burma. As the Japanese steadily sealed off China's ports, the requests for aid increased. London, ever fearful of alienating the Japanese, was concerned that a railroad might permit an influx of non–Burmese into the country. In addition, they were aware that the French might object because of their own rail line into Yunnan and a 1914 treaty with China giving the French the right to build a railroad from Indochina into Szechuan. "However it was revealed that [during] talks [regarding] the on-going [China] loan discussions, official British involvement in the [Burma-Yunnan Railroad] project was rejected but the Chinese were told that there would be no objections from government circles if private investors agreed to sponsor the plan."[30]

In the summer of 1938,

> a group of British companies did express interest in the Burma-Yunnan Railway Project and applied to the Export Guarantees Department for financial aid towards $2 million worth of railway materials. Of some interest is Chiang Kai-shek's advice to Sir Stafford Cripps that the railway would be useful as a means of providing Chinese manpower to help protect British interests in the Far East. The War Office conducted a study on the impact the railroad would have on Burmese security and concluded that because of the "strategical" negatives the project should be rejected, which it was.[31]

As early as May 1940, reports from American military attachés and other observers alerted the War Department to the inadequacies of the road supply route north of Rangoon and to the fact that a narrow gauge railway from Lashio to Kunming would be a valuable supplement to the Burma Road, as there was an eight-month backup of shippable materials at Rangoon.[32] In December, the British secretary of state for Burma sent the governor the summary of a proposal from Chiang Kai-shek stating that railway communications were "absolutely indispensable," emphasizing "the desirability of construction in Burma simultaneously with construction in China," and stating that America would be involved. He sought the governor's input.[33]

The list of equipment needs submitted by T.V. Soong in March 1941 included materials for a railroad, among them 30,000 tons of rails but with no specifications as to type.[34] Nevertheless, Currie, almost always ready to overlook such Chinese discrepancies, submitted a plan for a Burma-Yunnan railroad to FDR, and Chiang presented it to British authorities. London and Washington approved the idea and the Chinese began their section in April 1941.

Because American Lend-Lease funds would be used, the American military (AMMISCA) was automatically involved. The War Department assigned Major John Ausland, a former executive of the Chicago, Burlington and Quincy Railroad, soon to become a member of AMMISCA, to oversee American interests on the proposed railway. The government of Burma assigned Sir John Rowland, director of construction, and the Chinese provided the services of Brigadier General Tseng Yang-fu, vice-commissioner of communications. The British appeared to be sincerely interested in the project but it was evident that London's primary goal was to obtain American participation in the railroad to help sustain the British colonial presence in Burma and to moderate Japanese pressure on Britain to again close the Burma Road.

In February 1941, even before final passage of the Lend-Lease bill, the British embassy contacted the State Department's advisor on political relations, Stanley Hornbeck, to see if the United States would permit the Chinese to use Lend-Lease dollars for a Yunnan-Burma railroad, and share in any other way in the project.[35] State's reaction was guarded because the department did not know if American dollars might legally be used, or if participation might be perceived as supporting Britain's current border dispute with China.[36]

The State Department's legal advisor replied that unless the president declared that American lives were endangered or United States security threatened, federal funds could be used to purchase railroad equipment, which American ships could then transport to Rangoon. Therefore, American participation in the Yunnan-Burma railroad enterprise would not violate the 1939 Neutrality Act.[37] Fortuitously, the day after the legal opinion was rendered the State Department received word from the American embassy that Britain and China had reached a partial agreement on the sensitive Sino-Burma border question.[38]

In 1940–41, American popular opinion was opposed to any viable participation in China that involved United States personnel, but there was some popular sentiment for the plight of the Chinese people.[39] There were also people in the government including the president, several of his chief advisors, and Secretary of the Treasury Morgenthau, who believed it necessary to render aid to the Chinese. In late April, undoubtedly under pressure from the White House, the State and Treasury departments agreed that the United States could participate in the railroad project. Secretary Morgenthau advised Under Secretary Welles that he supported the project and it should be completed as soon as possible. He added that there was prohibition regarding China's using Lend-Lease dollars to purchase rails and railway materials. The War Department formulated plans for active American involvement.[40]

There was not unanimity in the War Department. A notable example was Major Hayden Boatner, Secretary of the War Department Lend Lease Aid Committee to China. (He was later a major general and famous for his rescue of American officers kidnapped by North Korean and Chinese prisoners of war on Koje-Do Island.) Boatner, who ultimately became Stilwell's chief of staff, had been a Boxer Indemnity Scholar in China, spoke fluent Chinese, and maintained a lifelong correspondence with his classmate, the dean of America-China scholars, John K. Fairbank. He wrote the author, "I got myself reassigned [from the Aid Committee] because I thought or had a hunch it [certain aspects of Lend Lease] were crooked."[41] Lauchlin Currie, "an administrative aide to the president of the U.S. handled the matter [Lend-Lease to China] for the U.S. On several occasions I pointed out to him how impractical it was for us to try to build a railway connecting Lashio, Burma with Kunming, China. It had been approved in a very ... White House 'back door' manner. Finally he got quite provoked with me and told me he thought a soldier was supposed to follow or take orders — that the President of the U.S. had approved it and he directed me to refrain from objecting to it."[42]

Boatner compiled a study that "cited the number of [equipment requisitions] and that contrary to regulations had never even passed thru the War Dept, but had emanated in the White House. The study reported the port of Rangoon did not have the cranes or facilities to unload locomotives for the [Burma-Yunnan] railway."[43] Boatner contended that the railway materials and equipment would have required the "total tonnage of the Rangoon to Lashio railway for 3 to 5 years."[44]

The War Department solicited a railroad cost estimate from the Railway Section of the Corps of Engineers; it totaled $28,000,000. This amount covered all materials, locomotives, workshops, rails, and related items. But the rails and accessories would not be available for eighteen months, and the repair and maintenance equipment would not be available for two years.[45] Nevertheless, the Chinese began construction.

The Chinese portion of the railway was to run from Kunming to the Sino-Burma border near Lashio. It was 335 miles in length and divided into three districts. The project's director general was Dr. Tseng Yang-fu, a University of Pittsburgh graduate. Tseng was intelligent, efficient, and a taskmaster. But he was continually short of materials and his labor force was constantly beset with serious medical problems, especially malaria.[46] His task was further compounded by extreme distance from supply points to work sites and mountainous terrain, but worst of all was the necessary acquisition and distribution of food and pay for the laborers. By March 1942 over 150,000 laborers were employed on the railroad. Many were fifty to one hundred miles away from the Burma Road supply line. Their rice requirement alone totaled over 150 tons each day.[47]

The remote work areas and the vagaries of the Chinese government's finances frequently resulted in delayed or missed paydays. At one point Tseng had to borrow Chinese $180 million from bankers when the payroll failed to arrive. Major Ausland, the AMMISCA project advisor, attributed the payroll shortages to friction within the various government bureaus caused by "the finance men in Chungking."[48]

Another impediment to completion of the railway was the physical breakdown of many of the Chinese workers. The railway was truly a *manpower* operation; there was "no machinery larger than a wheelbarrow along the Chinese line of construction."[49] In the summer of 1941 work slowed because of malaria, especially in the jungle regions of Yunnan. In June, with the advent of the rainy season, a thousand men labored so that supplies and additional workers could be brought in as soon as the dry season arrived. By December 100,000 men labored on just the middle section of the railroad.[50] Many not native to the area were unaccustomed to the climate and highly susceptible to malaria and typhoid. Throughout the subsequent months they died in droves, or, in some cases, deserted to die later in the jungle.[51] *Life* magazine reporter George Rodger described the labor conditions: "As for the coolies ... I saw them sick and dying in the squalor of their camps, and I smelt their dead where they had thrown them aside to rot or be eaten by the jungle rats and jackals."[52] In one eighteen-mile stretch over 1,000 of the 2,600 laborers died of malaria.[53] Sometimes in order to get new laborers it was necessary to resort to subterfuge. Ausland related that at least one town, "known far and wide as for its malarial mortality," had its name changed by the railway officers so that laborers would go there willingly to work.[54]

Even before Pearl Harbor, the United States Public Health Services sent to Burma one of its most prominent senior surgeons, Dr. (Lt. Colonel) Victor H. Haas, who was tasked to combat the disease. In July 1942 he sent a caustic letter to the director of the National Institute of Health excoriating the Chinese for their lack of support and cooperation regarding the health of their workers on the Burma Road and Burma-Yunnan railroad. He documented numerous specific instances, but emphasized the major problem was that the managers, "resent any time, labor or effort spent on public health work because it takes men off the construction.... They hope to get as much labor as possible from workers before disease strikes them down. They worry about disease only when convenient and disregard orders when it suits them." Because of the health issues, he felt it unwise to continue the Yunnan-Burma railway or the China-Burma-India Highway.[55]

But malaria was not the only affliction among Chinese workers. Dr. M. C. Balfour, head of the Rockefeller Foundation in the Far East and chief advisor to the Public Health Service Medical Commission, determined that opium was even more debilitating. He estimated that 50 percent of the laborers smoked opium, primarily because it relieved the rigors of their toil. And it was contagious. As Balfour explained, "The non-smoker sees smokers who are not complaining about their lot and another addict is made."[56] The Public Health Service units attempted, with some success, to reduce the use of opium and to teach hygiene to the laborers. But as George Rodger informed his editor,

> Where sickness was concerned, fevers, cholera, typhoid and festering surface wounds, the coolie's suspicious nature proved to be his own worst enemy. In their ignorance they fought the white man's methods; they mistrusted him; suspected him of dealing with the devil. Their only method of treating internal troubles was to be out in the sun; a method that had sufficed them for over a thousand years. Still, the remaining workers, many of them ill, displayed tenacity and courage as they continued to work.[57]

A medical missionary for thirty years reported his amazement at the amount of work that the anemic, underfed, emaciated men could do. He thought that some fat and protein added to their rice would increase their labor and provide a reserve to fight malaria when attacked. This would "allow more men to stay on the job."[58] Ausland made requests for foods of more nutritional value than the two-pound daily ration of rice furnished to the laborers. Although he believed the requests "fell on deaf ears," they were in fact noted. Currie initiated a plan to ship wheat and "certain concentrated foodstuffs" as early as November 1941.[59] Magruder recommended against importing food because he believed that any shipments would not be enough to alleviate the problem and would be expensive to move over routes already overburdened. He felt rigorous foreign supervision would be required to assure the food shipments actually reached the work force.[60]

Major Ausland, who was overseeing the project, was brilliant according to his AMMISCA subordinate, Captain Nevin Wetzel. "He could think up solutions to problems a mile a minute."[61] Because of the scarcity of rails in China, one of the initial problems was to obtain War Department approval for the purchase of a branch line of the Mandalay-Myitkyina railroad. Only one train a day was passing over the line, and if it were torn up and used as the core of the Burma-Yunnan line usage could be increased tenfold. War Department approval was prompt but the British, for unstated reasons, refused to permit the line to be removed even though the remaining rail bed could have been used as a truck road. This meant that all the track material would have to come from America.[62] The War Department purchased a 125-mile segment of the Denver and Rio Grande Western. They planned to ship these rails to China to reduce the shortage but the rails never left America because of the attack on Pearl Harbor.[63] The resultant delay, combined with Ausland's belief that some of the necessary materials would be lost en route or transferred to Europe, led him to advise Tseng to complete the roadbed with no track laid and then use it as a truck road until all the rails and rolling stock arrived. Tseng offered no objections, and work continued.[64]

Other challenge to AMMISCA included a shortage of cut wood. Strangely enough, although Burma was half-covered with teak, ironwood, and palm trees, there was a shortage of railroad ties. Ausland notified Washington of the shortage and received orders to cut from the local supply.[65] The problem, however, was not lack of wood; it was lack of cutting tools, ordered through Lend-Lease. Ausland's estimated need for the Yunnan-Burma railway was 900,000 ties. The early acquisition of enough tools was unlikely, so, after consultation, Washington agreed that over half of the needed ties could come from the United States, specifically from the Memphis, Dallas and Gulf railroad.[66] Ultimately a total of only 92,000 ties were manufactured in the Burma-China areas, and no ties were ever shipped from the United States because of cargo priorities.[67]

When the railway project was approved the War Department believed that sophisticated construction tools could be shipped to China by the end of 1941.[68] Yet problems of bureaucratic coordination and differing priorities arose. One particular example was the acquisition of air compressors and rock drills to be used in hewing railroad tunnels through Yunnan's mountains. Apparently unaware of the needs of the Yunnan-Burma railroad or that the highly specialized equipment was not available from any manufacturer's inventory, the Army and Navy Munitions Board's Priorities Committee assigned it a relatively low priority of A-1-i.[69] This priority meant that the railroad's needs were placed below the needs of many other projects and that the equipment could not be manufactured and shipped to China before early 1942.

Hoping to obtain and ship the compressors and drills before the end of 1941, the War Department's Defense Aid Division's quartermaster (supply) office requested a higher priority of A-1-a.[70] The Munitions Board's Priorities Committee rejected the request by claiming that its present rating of A-1-i would "obtain a substantial amount of the items needed."[71] This was true, but time was of great importance. The Priorities Committee assured the Defense Aid Division that when "choke points" arose the committee would reconsider higher priorities, a meaningless commitment.[72] Even if the committee considered an appeal for a higher priority during a time of great need, or "choke point," and approved a higher priority, months would pass before the equipment could be shipped. The tunnel equipment project was only the first of several vain attempts to expedite deliveries to China.[73] Even the myriad delays in construction and the Japanese advance had not prevented the railroad's completion, but the difference in brakes on the British-built Burmese locomotives and the American-built Chinese locomotives prohibited the direct transfer of freight cars from one line to another. All the supplies from Rangoon would have to have been offloaded at Lashio and reloaded onto the Chinese freight cars for shipment to Kunming.[74]

In mid-October Ausland completed a five-week inspection tour of the railroad route. He found that the British were making very little effort to complete a vital Salween River bridge, and would not complete the railway from Lashio to the Chinese border until well into 1942, months behind schedule.[75] Ausland suggested to Magruder that the British and Burmese be pressured to allow Chinese laborers to begin work immediately on the section from the Salween to Yunnan. Under Ausland's plan the Burmese government would pay the laborers. The British were reluctant to have thousands of Chinese cross into Burma, and as a result Ausland's proposal was never given real consideration. Although it is unlikely that full British participation would have significantly speeded completion, the lack of British cooperation, evident throughout the project, appeared to be deliberate and provoked irritation in Washington and Chungking. For example, even before Ausland's inspection additional questions emerged in Washington regarding the sincerity of Britain's pledge to help build the railway. On July 17, Stanley Hornbeck told the British minister, Noel Hall, "There [have] come to us rumors to the effect that activities at the Burma [British] end toward construction of this railway seemed to be slow in getting under way."[76] He told Hall that although the railway project was officially a British-Chinese enterprise, the United States, under Lend-Lease retained a substantial interest in it and would observe with "rightful concern" the manner in which the British and Chinese worked towards an early completion of the project.[77]

A three-man railroad leadership group evolved. The British representative was Sir John Rowland. General Tseng Yang-fu was the Chinese representative and Ausland represented America. Rowland, the former Burmese commissioner of railways, had retired to Australia but was called back to head the project. He was directed to "connect" the existing Burma railways with the proposed Yunnan-Burma railway in China.

The three appeared to be compatible and work began on the Chinese section in April. Unfortunately, as Ausland's diary notes, Rowland "did not like the Chinese in general, and in particular, Dr. Tseng." His view of Tseng was widely shared. However, Colonel MacMorland held Tseng in high esteem: "Tseng is a real organizer and an enthusiastic advocate of the completion of the railroad, come what may. He is one of China's ablest men."[78]

Rowland also carried a reputation for irascibility: "The man knows railway and construction, but is hot-tempered, and it is better to keep him and the Chinese separated, which I plan to do." Even Ausland came under fire when his necessary proximity to Rowland brought them into a procedural disagreement over the British effort.[79]

Ausland was aware that his orders from Washington placed him in a subordinate position. He was directed to assist and expedite the Chinese construction of the railway, oversee the employment of Lend-Lease material, and coordinate Chinese relations with the British railway authorities in Burma. He felt he could not advise Sir John on the construction of his railway, but he could communicate with Dr. Tseng and share that info with Sir John. Clearly, since the Chinese planned to complete their part of the line months before the British, "coordination was needed."[80]

On September 29, Ausland wrote Tseng, with a copy to Rowland, and used phraseology that angered Rowland for weeks. The letter warned Tseng that if he finished his

> program as planned it will be of limited value unless the British section is done also. Therefore, it will probably be necessary for you to survey and construct that part of the line in Burma from the Chinese border south to the Salween River, and I recommend that you take this up with your government and the British at the earliest possible moment, so that no time is lost. By the British I mean Sir John Rowland. If he assures you that he plans to be done with the grading on his section by May 1942, then you need not do anything in Burma. If he does not do so, then I think you should have blanket authority from your government, from him and his government, to proceed south of the Chinese border as far as necessary.[81]

This was a remarkable communication. By proposing a policy that was tantamount to an intervention in the relations between China and Great Britain, Ausland directly violated his orders to only "assist." A stormy meeting followed. Sir John correctly demanded to know who appointed Ausland liaison officer between him (Rowland) and the Chinese; after all, Ausland was just a "watchdog for lend lease." On October 22, Major General Dennys told Magruder that "Burma" had queried him as to Ausland's official status. Dennys knew nothing of Ausland's being designated a liaison officer, although he was acting in that capacity. Magruder responded that he had not appointed Ausland to such a position but he had no objection, if the Chinese desired it, for him to be a "liaison agent for purely technical matters." He included a copy of a memorandum he sent to all AMMISCA officers instructing them not to exceed their authority.[82] Dennys and the Burmese government also complained to Washington. However, two days prior, Magruder, upon receipt of a Washington query and directive to put a leash on Ausland had sent the Major the following: "The [radio from Washington] message is unsatisfactory in that it doesn't say who got the impression [that Ausland was acting inappropriately] or where he got it. I frankly don't know what it means. However I want to quote it for your information and guidance." This was followed by several warnings from Magruder. For example, "You must not undertake, independently, for example, to negotiate with Burmese officials undertakings involving either the United States or the Chinese without my specific authority." The last paragraph of the message, however, was the truth-teller: "I was much amused at your taming of the Australian lion. Keep the flag flying but don't hope to modify British character and traditional colonial practices."[83]

Ausland's diary relates that the relationship improved when it became clear that Rowland was not familiar with the Chinese route or the construction's progress. Rowland claimed he would soon have 35,000 men at work on the Burma portion and would ask the Chinese for men. Ausland felt Rowland had an anti-Chinese attitude, but included his high opinion of Rowland's abilities, and the two became "the best of friends." In his summary of this conversation with Rowland, Ausland included this:

> He is of the fast disappearing type that built the British Empire, and I respect him for his courage and energy, but I could not let the job continue with the Chinese working on a fifteen month and the British on a two year schedule or longer. Sir John had to change his program, not only for the sake of his own reputation as an engineer, but for the sake of white supremacy, which I assume he believes in just like the rest of the British, but some of his own men and some of the British government officials in Burma are so certain that the railway will take years to finish that they refuse to alter the even tenor of their ways enough to see that he gets what he wants.[84]

On 16 January 1942, Tseng, Ausland, Rowland, and one of Rowland's officers, Captain Whitehouse, discussed construction schedules. "Dr. Tseng mentioned that he expected to finish the grading on his 335 miles before the end of 1942. Whitehouse, who doesn't believe we can, said very deliberately, 'Well, our part ought to be complete in 1943 or 1944.'"

"I thought Dr. Tseng was going to explode. I saw his eyes snap as he looked wildly around the room as if hunting a corner in which to gnash his teeth." Ausland said Rowland was "mad" because he was embarrassed, but quickly gave the impression of being genuinely desirous of completing the total railway. He "asked Dr. Tseng if he would take over the construction of that part of the railway in Burma, which is north of the Salween."[85] Rowland promised to get London's approval. Even if he applied for the approval, it never came.

Ausland believed that higher British authority ("Rangoon") deliberately tied Rowland up with red tape to delay progress on the railway. Ausland claimed to have certain knowledge that "Rangoon ... provided Sir John with two separate letters. One for public consumption which told him to push the construction of his 115 miles with all possible speed; the other told him to disregard that and make a lot of dust so as to befog the Chinese and make them think he was going to finish on time, but to do as little as possible and spend as little money as he could."[86]

In the fall Ausland and the Chinese again approached the British and proposed that Chinese laborers complete the British section from Lashio to the Yunnan border. The British refused to allow Chinese to enter Burma.[87] The contrast between the British and Chinese efforts is unmistakable. On the Chinese side of the border the employment of massive labor forces brought relative success. By January 1942 the workers in some sections had completed all but the laying of the rails. One section, Junming to Chuching, was in operation and all sections were expected to be fully operational by the end of 1942. The British, however, had not even completed the survey of the relatively short Lashio-to-Yunnan portion of the railroad. Wetzel observed, "The British brought in a small handful of Indian labor, constructed a few miles of sub-grade [foundation] and laid track on it north of Lashio. It was a token demonstration signifying nothing."[88] Ausland was convinced that the British government did not want the Chinese strengthened and alleged Rowland was being restrained by his government. After Rowland had been appointed to direct construction only "8 miles had been pegged out; the rains had stopped the survey."[89]

There was little knowledge among the non–British allies as to the lack of progress of the Burma section of the railway. But there was a common Sino-American belief, based on both countries' anti-colonial convictions, that the British hedged on the railway financing and admitted a prior right of the French (although it had expired). The British were now negotiating a joint enterprise for further railroad development in Yunnan that would be an extension of the present French line to Chungking and Chengtu with a vague idea of building a branch down to Burma later. McHugh exclaimed, "If I know the French, the latter will never transpire. The British really are too naïve for words sometimes!"[90]

Not all the slowdowns were of British origin, however. The Chinese had agreed to 130 kilometers of rails being transferred from Rangoon, but not to release fishplates or bolts. Negotiations were in progress for 15,000 Chinese laborers to be sent to Burma to supplement the Indian labor that was available in Burma.[91] The British were not enthusiastic about a rail line to China and wished to utilize all available resources to build up Burma's defenses against the Japanese concerns that a Burma-Yunnan rail link might open the country to increased Chinese influences. A safer supply route, further north, was part of London's strategic thinking.[92] From a British perspective, this is a defensible thesis.

In what might be termed the "realistic view," Governor Dorman-Smith asked the War Office to permit him to remove Rowland from the Burma-Yunnan railway project and involve him in Burma defense work, stating that while he appreciated the political importance of the railway, he'd never regarded it as a major war-winning factor. He clearly felt continuation of the railway construction would be wasting Rowland, trained engineers, men, and material on something that would take too long to meet the present needs. He added that British General Headquarters in India put land links between Burma and India as their first priority. The War Office responded negatively, stating it was politically inadvisable to abandon the railway project completely since Japanese successes in British territory had demoralized the Chinese. Thus, although defense of Burma was the first priority, they agreed to keep up at "least a semblance of work on the railway."[93]

In a matter of a few days Dorman-Smith's plan was also opposed by the commander in chief of India, who was also concerned about "appearances," but felt the rail link to be a long-term project that absorbed 250 tons a day of the Mandalay-Lashio railway. He suggested slowing the construction to a token rate and diverting resources to other areas.[94]

With the fall of Rangoon imminent allied emphasis did change. Several northern supply routes through Assam, a route from Sadiya to Myitkyina and another from Siberia through Tibet were considered. Because of the rapid Japanese advance, none of them were considered viable.

On 11 February 1942, one of General Marshall's assistant chiefs of staff warned him of the probability that the Japanese would soon overrun Rangoon and cut the supply route to China.[95] To counteract this, the Chinese planned to build a different truck road from Ledo, India, to Lungling, China. This "Ledo Road" would not necessarily replace the Yunnan-Burma railway. But the lack of railway equipment and the potential Japanese threat to southern Burma was forcing a change in emphasis from railroads to roadways.

A week after the Ledo Road project was announced, Magruder requested that the "Yunnan-Burma RR bed be converted into [a] one way motor road ... [albeit] without prejudice to [railroad] construction when materials [become] available."[96] In March Currie informed the president that General Stilwell, who had just arrived in China, recommended that the "shipments of material for the Yunnan-Burma railroad ... might temporarily be suspended" because of the lack of transportation.[97] Work on the line ceased in April, and the laborers were transferred to the truck road projects linking China and India.[98]

The Chinese achieved commendable construction goals through the use of immense labor forces. Their sections of the railroad would probably have been employed at peak capacity by the summer of 1942 if they had received rails and rolling stock from the United States (or other sources in the case of the rails) in a timely manner and if Japan had not captured Burma. There are several "ifs" here, but the contrast with the lack of British participation is clear and dramatic, and glaringly exemplified by the fact that while the Chinese completed 90 percent of their portion, the British completed only five percent of theirs.[99] In fairness to the British, they were beset by multiple crises. They were never sure to what degree America would support them on any given issue, and Japan was a constant threat. There were numerous forces at work in their planning realm including the man-on-the-spot Dorman-Smith; factions within the War, Colonial and Foreign offices; Churchill, always at odds with American aims in the China-Burma area of operations; and numerous opinions engendered by the "experts" in all these offices and related special interest groups.

The Pipeline

> Another important problem to be met is the scarcity of gasoline. One of the present difficulties is that a truck fully loaded with a cargo of petrol consumes 20 percent to 25 percent of its cargo between Lashio and Kunming (35 percent if the journey is extended to Chungking). When it is considered that these figures are doubled for the round trip, the surplus can scarcely be regarded as impressive. Moreover, the cost of transporting gasoline, as well as all other commodities, is enormous.
> — Bruce Bliven, "Burma Road Bottlenecks"

For most of the duration of World War II, United States participation in China and Burma focused on supply and training rather than commitment of American troops. Washington's policy that available United States aid go principally to Europe meant that the best America could do for China was to support its air defenses and army. This strategy, however, required massive quantities of petroleum for the vehicles on the Burma Road, the AVG, and the army air forces units that were to follow. Means of transporting petroleum products had to be found, and the most appealing solution was a pipeline. The new China-Burma area leadership, including Stilwell, apparently felt that sufficient petroleum products could be supplied from Assam without a pipeline. This was the view even though Burmese stocks would soon be "seriously affected" by Japanese bombing. It was unarguably the case that while "the Burma road was open, gasoline was like liquid gold.... Trucks were wrecked for it. Convoys were hi-jacked to get it. They would have had to put a 4" pipeline miles in the air, and even then someone would have found ways to tap it."[100]

On September 18 before he left for China, Magruder proposed the construction of a portable pipeline to be financed with Lend-Lease dollars. The line would be used primarily to supply gasoline to the Burma Road vehicles and would cost approximately $5 million. The single most expensive item was sixteen thousand tons of steel pipeline.[101] In October when Magruder reached Chungking, he discovered that the Lend-Lease funds allocated to purchase oil were approximately three times China's needs because more was coming in than could be distributed. He recommended a pipeline to equitably apportion the gasoline stored at Rangoon and other locations, which would provide its own storage facility and carry only the needed quantities of gasoline.[102]

The War Department's chief of engineers supported Magruder's proposal, and the department sent a Shell Oil expert, Allen Hall, to China to make a feasibility study.[103] But because it took him two months to arrive in the area, no further action on the pipeline was taken until after Pearl Harbor.[104]

In February 1942 the War Department announced its support for a pipeline from Assam to the Burma Road, but this route conflicted with other proposals. Hall advocated building a pipeline only along the Burma Road, and Magruder suggested a pipeline from Ledo, India, to Hsiakwan, China.[105] These proposals caused further delay. China Defense Supplies officials supported all the proposals, hoping to get at least one approved, and they filed a request for Lend-Lease funds to pay for a pipeline and storage tanks.[106] In March, however, the pipeline project was required to submit to additional War Department research and observation.[107] The chief of engineers constructed a test pipeline in Chicago, and the tests were judged successful. The results were then submitted to a joint meeting of China Defense Supplies and

War Department engineer personnel, and Hall's proposal was approved unanimously.[108] Shipments of pipeline material could have begun as early as June, at the rate of three thousand tons per month.[109] But too much time had been wasted by the bureaucrats, and after March 1941 when the tactical situation in Burma began to rapidly deteriorate, the pipeline suddenly became a project of low priority and was discontinued "temporarily."[110]

After the fall of Burma the Chinese attempted to exploit their domestic petroleum resources in Kansu. The effort was unproductive, and it was almost two years before the "hump" air route over the Himalaya Mountains was able to begin transporting worthwhile quantities of petroleum from India.[111] Still, the concept of a pipeline did not die. Construction of a pipeline on Magruder's proposed route parallel to the Ledo Road, finally began in the spring and summer of 1943.[112] In terms of its long-range success, "there were 3,192 miles of pipe in the CBI [China-Burma-India] system of pipelines, 1,642 being six-inch pipe, and 1,550 four inch.... More than 150 million gallons of fuel was pumped through the system from the time it began until the end of the war in Europe."[113]

Alternate Routes of Supply

> With the severing of the Burma Road, which has been China's chief channel of communication and supply with the outside world, the importance to China and to the cause of the United Nations as a whole of maintaining a continuous flow of essential military supplies to China by all possible available means cannot be too strongly emphasized.
>
> — Secretary of State Hull to the U.S. ambassador to Russia (Standley)[114]

A month and a half before the Japanese invaded Burma in 1942, China Defense Supplies sent a memorandum to Edward R. Stettinius, director of the Lend-Lease Administration, asking for Lend-Lease funds to build a thousand mile road from the rail center at Sadiya, Assam, to the terminal point of several trade roads at Sichang in China's Sikang province. Although the overall cost was estimated at $9,000,000, Washington felt the route would be more secure than the Burma Road because the rugged terrain south of it would inhibit the Japanese advance.[115] Construction could begin almost immediately, but millions of dollars of road building equipment would be needed before substantial progress could be made. Even if it arrived as scheduled the road would not be completed until spring 1944. Stettinius asked the War Department to obtain more information.[116]

The War Department ordered Magruder to examine the project. He did, and encountered a substantial Anglo-Chinese divergence over potential road routes. The British favored a southern route from Assam through Ledo to Sichang that would be administered by the Burmese. Chungking supported a road north through Tibet, a route that was longer, over more difficult terrain, and closed by snow four months a year. The Tibetan-Chinese border was undefined, and the Tibetans refused Chinese survey teams access to Tibetan territory. Although Magruder felt the Tibetans would probably cooperate, he believed the northern route would take longer than the two years predicted by the Chinese to complete the project and warned the War Department that the total cost would run almost four times the $9,000,000 estimated by the Chinese.[117]

Magruder reported a conversation with officials in the Chinese Ministry of Communications who confided to him that the southern route would be more practical, even though the northern route was better for China. But he felt primary emphasis should still be given to the Burma Road, and he recommended that Washington give "urgent priority" to improving the road and its feeders. The Chinese route, he asserted, would be of dubious value "in this war."[118] The southern route was apparently acceptable if the Burma Road were lost.

T. V. Soong was also skeptical of the northern route. In early January he asked the Rangoon office of China Defense Supplies for recommendations on transporting supplies from Sadiya to Myitkyina by air via the Chinese National Aviation Corporation.[119] From Myitkyina the cargos could be distributed over the existing land routes to Mandalay, Lashio, Bhamo, and other critical supply centers for shipment to China. The China Defense Supplies office approved the concept and when queried, so did Magruder.[120]

In late January, buoyed by this support, Soong launched a campaign to enlist War Department and presidential support for the Sadiya-Myitkyina-China air route. In communicating with American authorities he argued that because China was no longer receiving substantial aid from Russia, it was now more dependent on America.[121] He appealed for 100 Douglas C-53 aircraft to fly cargos from Sadiya to Kunming or Suifu. Soong emphasized that Magruder, experts from Pan American Airlines, and the Douglas Aircraft Company had all pronounced the project feasible. The C-53s were capable of carrying anything then being transported over the Burma Road. Soong said if one hundred could be put into use, "the loss of the Burma Road would be offset."[122] As an incentive, Soong promised Roosevelt that the planes would not return to India empty, but would carry strategic materials such as tin, tungsten, and wood oil (such as tung tree oil used for the preservation of wood products). These items, when shipped to America would help offset China's financial debt. Roosevelt replied promptly in the affirmative, but cautioned that "only some new planes may be available."[123] The key words were "some" and "may," and Soong must have known that Roosevelt would do no more; he did not press the issue and the project faded into obscurity.

Soong's was not the only proposal. War Department planners led by Brigadier General L. T. Gerow, the assistant chief of staff, War Plans Division, were attempting, undoubtedly with Marshall's approval, to streamline the China supply system. On February 2, Gerow learned that Chungking, apparently without advising Soong, now planned to construct a road south of the Sichang-Sadiya route, and another from the railhead at Ledo, Assam, to Myitkyina to Lungling, Szechuan, a one-year project. Gerow endorsed the Ledo Road concept, but only if the Burma communication route could be held until the Ledo Road was completed. Gerow recommended that in the interim the United States support a British proposal that included a road and water route from Imphal in Manipur province, India, through Kalewa, Burma, Monywa, Mandalay, and then northeast to China.[124]

This route called for a great deal more international coordination than had been demonstrated to date. The cargos would go by rail in India to Imphal, then by truck to Kalewa, then via the Chindwin River to Monywa. There they would be shipped via the Irrawaddy River to Bhamo, and finally trucked to China. Or, they would be put aboard trucks at Monywa and hauled, via Mandalay, to Lashio. The plan was heavily encumbered by a lack of resources and trained personnel, and the fact that it required total Sino-British cooperation and coordination.

Gerow then contacted the British to confirm specifically the several routes they favored.[125] The British reconfirmed they would build and control the Imphal-Monywa route. They emphasized this would mean an absence of the international political difficulties that theretofore had beset almost every joint Anglo-Sino-American project. They warned that although the British were in favor of the project, India would probably oppose construction of road communications between itself and China or Tibet because of potential security problems. They also made it clear that they opposed the Sichang-Sadiya route, "in the strongest terms," because of its inability to stay open year-round and because the Chinese would control it. But they did approve the Chinese Ledo Road proposal.[126] The Sichang-Sadiya route was abandoned and the Ledo Road became preeminent.

Never an Anglophile, Magruder doubted the sincerity of the British and feared they would not fulfill their promise to build the Imphal-Monywa road. He asked Marshall to maintain pressure on the British to live up to their com-

Chinese laborers offloading drums of gasoline from a C-46 having just flown the hump to Kunming (used by permission from the personal collection of Dr. William Martin).

mitment and requested all assistance possible for the Chinese Ledo Road project.[127] Marshall responded by ordering Magruder to impress upon the Chungking Military Council, composed of the chiefs of the British and American missions and General Ho Ying-ch'in, the importance the United States attached to the rapid completion of the Ledo and Imphal routes. The British reiterated their commitment to construct the Imphal-Monywa road.[128]

By mid-March a condition reminiscent of the stockpiling at Rangoon was evolving at several Indian ports. Stilwell, in China only a week, was advised by AMMISCA's Major John Russell that the Burmese (British) government was not working on the Imphal Road and supplies were piling up.[129] Stilwell ordered a cutback in shipments of Lend-Lease materials, including a temporary embargo on trucks.[130] China Defense Supplies protested and initiated a campaign for more vehicles, their rationale being that there had to be trucks available or there would be a similar truck shortage on the new roads as had existed on the Burma Road.[131]

9. Logistics Problems on the Burma Road 149

Trucks were available in America. The Lend-Lease Administration had previously allocated three thousand 2½-ton trucks for China and stored them in American warehouses. China Defense Supplies asked that they be shipped at the rate of one thousand a month beginning in April. They said this schedule was necessary to provide an adequate number of vehicles for road construction and cargo haulage on the two new roads.[132] The War Department refused to approve the request without first obtaining Stilwell's recommendation. Stilwell was contacted on March 27, and in turn solicited the advice of Magruder, whom he had relegated to commanding general of the newly created Division of General Affairs.[133] Magruder urged that no trucks be shipped until June 1 and, because he believed the Chinese were still submitting unrealistic requests, he ordered Major John Russell to conduct a survey of the road areas. This was significant in that it was the beginning of Stilwell's direct involvement in developing the "quid pro quo" policy explained in a later chapter.

Russell's basically negative survey report, compiled at the same time Chiang raised his request from three to six thousand trucks, convinced Stilwell that Magruder's advice was sound. Magruder then requested that Marshall restrict all truck shipments until June.[134] Russell also reported that the British planned to restrict the Imphal-to-Monywa route to almost exclusive British military use. He warned that when it was completed, only a token amount of traffic would be allocated to the Chinese. Moreover, the British now planned to limit the route north of Monywa at Kalewa. But even in the Kalewa area work was progressing so slowly that Russell could not provide even a tentative completion date.[135] He warned that the Imphal Road would be impractical for Chinese use, and none of the three thousand trucks Chiang had requested, and then doubled, were necessary.[136]

Russell also inspected the Ledo-Lungling project; a route he believed would be useful only if the Japanese did not gain control of the Lashio airfield. He estimated the earliest possible completion date would be 1 November, 1942, which would be met only if work continued through the summer monsoons. Russell hesitated to estimate daily tonnage, because work had just begun, but 200 trucks a day would be the maximum. Referring to Chiang's attempt to obtain three thousand trucks for the Ledo Road, Russell recommended thirteen hundred. "If 3,000 trucks were used on this road with three stages to the journey, it would necessitate dispatching 21 vehicles an hour for every hour of the 24, an obvious impossibility under Chinese management."[137] But within a week of Russell's report, Lashio fell to the Japanese. And as Russell had warned, the airfield provided a base from which the Japanese were able to bomb and strafe the Ledo Road route. Within months the supplies originally stockpiled for Ledo Road laborers were being consumed by the remnants of the Chinese 22nd Division and civilian refugees fleeing the Japanese.[138]

Installation of an India-China Air Supply System

> When the traffic over the Burma Road is no longer possible an airline into China will become a necessity. Advance agents for our ferry service are already working on this and when facilities become available we will take airplanes off the main line for the China branch line. Total number of airplanes to be used in China may be anywhere from fifty to seventy five. That also depends upon facilities and personnel available. Planes taken off the main line will be replaced from production in the United States.
> — Lieutenant General H. H. Arnold, Army Air Corps Commander, to Colonel Chaney, Military Attaché, American Embassy at London[139]

General Arnold's statement exemplifies the strategy employed by allied planners after all the functional land and water supply routes through Burma had fallen. Air transport appeared to be the best recourse. However, the few planes available could carry only a small tonnage, and weather conditions often prohibited flying. Even when fighter and maintenance support was available, the amount of supplies brought in by air proved to be much less than planned.

Roosevelt approved the establishment of an India-China air supply route on 30 January 1942. The president was reacting to a Magruder request for the gradual shipment of one hundred cargo planes that could transport 12,000 tons a month to China.[140] Stilwell was ordered to establish an airline supply system when he reached China, even if the Burma Road was held.[141] On February 9, the president sent another illusory "keep the faith" message to Chiang Kai-shek. "I can now give you definite assurances that even though there should be a further setback in Rangoon, which now seems improbable [the opposite condition prevailed], the supply route to China via India can be maintained by air."[142] Responsibility for the air supply system was assigned to Major General Lewis H. Brereton, commander of Stilwell's small-air arm.[143] Brereton's pilots were destined to fly supplies over the Himalayas, one of the world's most treacherous areas, known to the men who flew their multi-engine cargo planes over it as "the hump."

There have been many books and articles written by and about "the men who flew the hump." A number of them shared similar experiences, but every pilot and crew had several unique incidents in their flights. They flew in

9. Logistics Problems on the Burma Road

intense below-freezing temperatures, 20,000 feet above the earth, harassed by Japanese fighter aircraft, and had frequent delays as their planes, on some occasions, ran out of gas necessitating forced landings on extremely rugged terrain.

The common tribulations were the heat and stench of their billeting and flight line areas; a short, 2–3 hour, turnaround time in Kunming; the rigors of a flight one thousand miles plus each way; and landing on Kunming's two crushed-stone landing strips, which often caused tire blowouts. Other problems included newly assigned copilots, many of whom had never flown in the type of aircraft they encountered in India. Often they required training from their pilots on such basic functions as raising the landing gear and lowering the airplane's flaps.[144]

The return flights from China were more hazardous. Badly needed "surplus" fuel, if any, was drained off at Kunming, leaving only a thirty-minute reserve. The westbound route was over higher mountains, and opposing winds often slowed the planes to much lower speeds than their air speed indicators showed. There were also massive thunderstorms that could not be avoided. Other common experiences were the anguish over friends lost to weather, fuel shortages, and Japanese planes[145]

The first air logistical units were shipped less than a week after Roosevelt's message to Chiang. Concurrently, the fall of Rangoon became inevitable, and the need for supplies by air significantly increased. Chiang Kai-shek, desperate for aid, went to India and established an agreement with the British wherein India and Britain would construct port facilities, railheads, airfields, and an airplane assembly plant at Karachi, all dedicated to expediting shipments to China.[146]

In late February, Air Force Brigadier General Sari Naiden was ordered to Calcutta by General Arnold to work with Stilwell on a Calcutta-to-Kunming air transport line.[147] After Naiden arrived, one of Stilwell's first directives was that he and Magruder were to estimate requirements on the airfields in India that might possibly be used for air freight traffic.[148] They, along with representatives of India, Burma, and China, visited all the airfields in India and decided which could best be used as terminals for air traffic to China.[149]

But inspections and planning did not provide airplanes. Roosevelt's commitment to supply China with one hundred transport planes, primarily two-engine DC-3s, seventy-five for the military and twenty-five to the China National Aviation Corporation (CNAC) proved to be another failed promise.[150] There were no DC-3 transport aircraft available in the United States in early 1942 but in an effort to provide a part of what Roosevelt had promised the War Department successfully negotiated with several American commercial airlines to acquire twenty-five DC-3s then in use on domestic routes. The planes and their crews, some of them former civilian crews, were scheduled to depart from the United States on April 1.[151]

There was an almost immediate jurisdictional problem: were the planes to join the government-controlled CNAC, which was down to two operable transport aircraft, or were they to come under direct military control?[152] Magruder was notified that all crews and aircraft would be under purely military command; their role was to "supplement" the Chinese airline. But the transition would be slow. The aircraft were to be employed first on a ferry basis between Africa and Calcutta and then "fed into the Calcutta-Chungking operation as rapidly as local facilities would permit."[153] The limited supply of aircraft also provoked other issues.

On February 16 Magruder informed the War Department that the lack of airplanes and parts had reduced CNAC to only a few aircraft. The airline was losing many key personnel because it could not provide them with sound aircraft. This situation impacted the planned airlift, as the airline's pilots and navigators were the only flyers in the China-Burma area familiar with the vagaries of the Himalayan Mountains' terrain and weather. These pilots had to be retained so their expertise would be available when new planes and their inexperienced crews arrived. Magruder considered it essential that at least five DC-3s and numerous personnel be provided immediately if air supply routes were to be preserved and CNAC personnel prevented from leaving. Meanwhile Magruder planned to sustain the air line with the smaller C-39 airplanes that he had been told were en route to China.[154]

The War Department informed Magruder that there were not enough military personnel to quickly remedy CNAC's deficiencies in pilots, ground crew, and supervisory staff, but sufficient trained personnel would "soon" be available; the department reiterated these people would come under "strict military control." Magruder assumed Washington was referring to the additional personnel and C-53 aircraft, not the C-39s.[155] This good news was followed by more. Magruder was advised on February 21 that four DC-3s were en route directly from the Douglas aircraft factory to Calcutta, a fifth would be available in March, and General Stilwell's group would arrive aboard the C-39s in early March.[156]

The era of limited prosperity was short-lived, though; within a month events took a negative turn. In mid–March General Stilwell, now in command of all United States operations in China including Lend-Lease supply distribution, determined that the C-39s were inadequate for China because of their poor performance at high altitudes. Consequently he requested they be replaced with C-53s from the army's ferry command.[157] He also requested two C-53s "for my movements to exercise effective command."[158] Neither request was approved. In addition, Stilwell was advised that the DC-3s promised for the Chinese National Aviation Corporation in February were to be delayed. Stilwell replied that even though the airline had repaired two aircraft, its total complement was still only four transports, which would remain serviceable for only a matter of weeks due to a severe lack of spare parts.[159]

As previously noted, Sino-American relations had become more strained in December and January because of the dispute over supplies stored in Rangoon, which were expanding daily in quantity. In May, relations deteriorated further because of Washington's effort to reduce the Rangoon inventory by decreasing supply tonnage from the United States to China. T. V. Soong continued to regularly submit lists of material needs to the War Department's Defense Aid Division for equipment the Chinese army would not use. The War Department estimated that long-term Chinese needs would approximate 7,500 tons per month. Soong's major problem lay in his inability to obtain transport to India for what supplies were made available. Another problem was the department's Defense Aid Division's belief that this quantity of supplies could not be flown from India to China. In fact, by the end of April there were 1790 carloads of material at the China Defense Supplies' pier at Newport News with no prospect of being moved.

A rough calculation of material available at factories, depots, and ports and railroad cars revealed a total of 150,000 tons–500,000 tons if materials for the Yunnan-Burma Railway were included.[160] Therefore, the Munitions Assignment Board cut Soong's request in half.[161] They emphasized their belief that the India-China air transport system was not capable of handling even this reduced tonnage. The board also noted the severe scarcity of the types of supplies requested by Soong. Their judgment was sensible, but Chiang regarded it as wrong and arbitrary. This was Chiang's second major rebuff dating from Stilwell's arrival, but not as significant as his rejection by the Combined Chiefs of Staff in April.

On April 19, the generalissimo requested membership on the Combined Chiefs of Staff (CCS), made up of the United States and Britain. He was told that China's participation in the war was vital, but his petition was turned down. A major reason behind the refusal lay in the fact that CCS membership would have entailed membership in the Munitions Assignment Board, probably Chiang's primary goal. The board's function was to allocate the pooled Anglo-American munitions production. The American and British board members believed China could contribute nothing to such a pool and would only make demands for a greater share in it.¹⁶² The decision was sensible to the western allies but not to Chiang.

Concurrently, Roosevelt pressured his air forces commander, General Arnold, to come up with planes and new supply routes to China. Arnold's only suggestion was to convert some B-24 bombers until he "discovered" they could not be spared. Roosevelt and Arnold agreed the only way to keep the India-China route open was to use whatever commercial planes that might be found. Roosevelt was probably influenced by the War Department's Operations Division, who believed that the air route to China would be only "a token operation." If Chiang ever doubted that Washington was placing a much lower priority on China than Europe (despite Roosevelt's promises), it was certainly made clear to him by the American failure to deliver the promised aircraft. Less than a week after the Munitions Assignment Board's action, Chiang was told that the fifty four-engine cargo planes, one of Roosevelt's earlier commitments to him, were not to be made available for the India-China supply route. A blunt summary: there was nothing of even token value to help the air lift project.¹⁶³ Chiang warned Stilwell that this would have a "most serious effect on China's future prosecution of the war."¹⁶⁴

The Generalissimo telegraphed Roosevelt claiming that two-motor transport planes were "entirely inadequate for the India-China route" and asked the president for fifteen four-motor DC-4s that he had been advised were due off the production line that same day.¹⁶⁵ The request provoked considerable dialogue between the White House and the War Department. Major General Lewis H. Brereton, commander of the Tenth Air Force and in charge of air supply from India to China, was consulted and stated that the two-engine transports then in use in China were "sufficient."¹⁶⁶ Roosevelt questioned this, and asked Arnold's opinion as to whether the two-engine planes could and should continue on the India-China run.¹⁶⁷ Arnold agreed with Roosevelt that two-engine planes were inadequate. However, he told the president that the four-engine C-54 aircraft to which Chiang referred were few in number, could not be shipped in June, and were all destined for Europe. In addition the airfields in India were being so heavily used by British and American fighter and bomber groups that they were "saturated" with overuse. Additional four-engine aircraft, even if available, could not have been effectively employed.¹⁶⁸

Almost simultaneously, Sino-American discord expanded when the Tenth Air Force was temporarily put under British control without Chiang's approval. Chiang, who was the supreme commander of all Allied efforts in China, was also advised that his request for 300 additional AVG aircraft would be limited to eighty. The decision regarding the eighty planes was reached unilaterally, and in Chiang's view directly contradicted the American promise to supply him with fighter aircraft.

The Munitions Assignment Board acted in accord with what they believed actual conditions were in China. Reports, such as one from Magruder on February 8, warning that the potential for operation of American aviation in China was extremely limited because of numerous logistical considerations, undoubtedly influenced the board's decision.[169] In mid–June Chiang learned that the five DC-3s, earmarked in February for the India-China supply line, had been diverted to Africa — again without his approval.[170] And almost as if calculated to further drive a stake into Sino-American relations, a handful of heavy bombers in India were diverted to help defend the critical supply route through the Suez Canal.

Simultaneously, thirty A-29 light bombers en route to China were diverted to Africa.[171] Thus with no warning, major air elements that Chiang and Stilwell had been promised and counted upon heavily for logistical and tactical support were being snatched away. This ramped up the initiative for a quid pro quo system.

In an exchange of communications between Washington and Chungking, Chiang reiterated, among other threats, his inclination to seek a separate peace with Japan.[172] As will be noted, Chiang's frustration and anger, especially his reiteration of his separate peace threat based primarily on America's failure to deliver the airplanes, was a significant element in the formulation of the quid-pro-quo policy. But at this time, his anger, however justified, did not overcome his common sense; he did not follow up on his threat.

Like Magruder, Stilwell was concerned with jurisdiction over aircraft assigned to the Chinese National Aviation Corporation. In June he notified Washington that CNAC's airplanes were not being employed effectively due to unspecified "commercial and political considerations."[173] Marshall confirmed Stilwell's assessment through other sources and ordered all American equipment used by the airline put under military control. This was not as arbitrary as it might appear; the Lend-Lease administration had contracted for China National Airlines Corporation's entire capacity.[174] However, military control did not improve airlift deliveries, and Chungking regarded it as another deliberate affront. Even though the number of national airline and military airplanes increased to almost fifty by July 1, only 259 tons of Lend-Lease supplies were shipped from India by air during May, June, and July 1942.[175] For well over a year there was ill will between Chungking and Washington over the air supply route from India. It did not abate until the American change of command from Stilwell to Lieutenant General Albert Wedemeyer in 1944.

Land Supply Routes from Russia and Iran

> The dominating circumstance conditioning all plans from May 1942 onward was the sheer difficulty of getting supplies to the Chinese armies.
>
> — Richard M. Leighton and Robert W. Coakley, *Global Logistics and Strategy: 1940–1943*

After Burma fell, and when it became apparent that air transport would not suffice, the Chinese had only two remaining supply route alternatives: by truck, from Iranian or Russian seaports. The Iranian route would be overland from ports on the Persian Gulf. The Russian route would be from Siberian ports and then to China via steamers and trucks. Wellington Koo, the Chinese ambassador to Britain, informed Harry Hopkins that the Chinese were actively pursuing both routes but would be happy with either. The proponents of the Siberian route, although acknowledging the brief season of navigability of the northern waterways, emphasized that Russian railways would be needed for only eight hundred miles; the Iranian route would tie up two thousand miles of railroads. Time was vital; if quick Russian approval could be obtained and America persuaded to assist, 30,000 to 40,000 tons of supplies could reach China in the summer of 1942.[176] There was strong American support for the project, but because of seasonal restrictions and diplomatic ramifications, particularly Russia's hesitancy to provoke Japan, Soviet approval did not come until the fall of 1942.

The route agreed upon in September 1942 was a compromise. It would run from Bandar Shapur, Iran, northeast to Sargiopol, Russia, then southeast to Lanchow and into China along the old pre–1941 Russo-Chinese supply route. This western route appealed primarily because it could be used to move 80,000 tons of Lend-Lease supplies from Indian warehouses to China. These supplies would be freighted north from Karachi on the Turkestan-Siberian railroad facilities and fed into the main supply route at Ashkhabad, Russia.[177] The Russians consented to allow the Chinese to ship nineteen thousand tons annually by rail from Ashkhabad to Alma Ata, and then by truck to Sinkiang. The Russians also promised to furnish four thousand tons of gasoline and one thousand tons of lubricants each year for truck maintenance. In return, the Chinese would provide the Russians with four thousand tons of assorted merchandise including tung oil, tungsten, tin, wool, and silk.[178] The Russians and British agreed that if the Russians moved all supplies from Meshed, Iran, to Ashkabad, and then to Lanchow, the Chinese would receive 60 percent of the goods, while the Russians could retain 40 percent for themselves.[179]

The American government took no direct part in the negotiations and

AMMISCA was no longer involved, but there was an AMMISCA legacy. As noted above, the AMMISCA logistic and supply systems were constantly haunted by problems of cooperation, coordination and changes in priority. Regarding the Iran-Russian-China supply route, this condition did not change. In October the Russians and Chinese notified the Washington that if the route were to function, they would need 1,100 and 2,400 trucks, respectively, plus spare parts and maintenance equipment — all from America.[180] Trucks were not shipped during 1942, the Chinese were unable to ship any raw materials to the Russians, and no supplies were shipped from Iran to China.[181]

10

The Mission's Role in the American Volunteer Group

The Charge to Support and Assist the AVG

> The Generalissimo and Madame Chiang Kai-Shek welcomed Magruder at a Chungking conference on October 27, 1941 The Chinese leader was satisfied with Magruder's approach to the [major] issues but singled out aviation for the top priority, for he was expecting early arrival of the Lend Lease aircraft. The Generalissimo proposed that AMMISCA assume control of and develop the [American Volunteer Group] AVG, even at the cost of separating it from the Chinese Air Force.
> — Charles F. Romanus and Riley Sunderland,
> *Stilwell's Mission to China*

Of all the American air units serving during World War II, the Flying Tigers is probably the unit with the most enduring reputation. Their P-40 planes painted with the tooth-filled open mouth below the nose remain an iconic image almost 70 years after their active role in Burma, India, and China. Stories of the AVG and their pilots have been told many times. In this chapter, there is information usually omitted in stories of the AVG.

AMMISCA's involvement in the establishment of the (AVG) as a viable fighting force has been given minimal attention. Historical texts typically center on Chennault, Stilwell, and the transition of the Flying Tigers into the Fourteenth Air Force. But the AMMISCA mission did play a noteworthy role, beginning with its being assigned the initial responsibility for personnel and material resupply for the AVG. It was also the unit tasked to supervise and assist the induction of the AVG into the army air force.

The AVG came into being at the instance of numerous "interested parties." In 1940, retired U.S. Army Air Corps Captain Claire L. Chennault was a colonel in the Chinese air force. He was a soon-to-be favorite of Madame

10. The Mission's Role in the American Volunteer Group 159

Chiang Kai-shek and a student of Japanese air strategy. He proposed a program of tactics designed to take advantage of Japanese weaknesses and overcome their greatly superior numbers. For years the Chinese attempted to build a viable air force, purchasing airplanes and employing instructors from several nations including the Jouett Mission from America. None were successful. In November 1940, Chiang sent the director of the Chinese air force's Operations Division, Major General Mao Pang-tzo, to Washington. He was accompanied by Chennault. A scheme was concocted involving William D. Pawley, long a proponent of unofficially establishing American air elements in China.

Chiang's brother-in-law H. H. Kung and Pawley formed the Central Aircraft Manufacturing Corporation (CAMCO). Funding was provided by Lend-Lease via China Defense Supplies. With presidential approval, CAMCO recruited pilots and crews at American military bases. Chennault and Pawley accepted fliers who would agree to resign their commissions and sign on with CAMCO.[1] The group of volunteers was named the American Volunteer Group (AVG) and was commanded by Colonel Chennault. Their honorary commander was Madame Chiang and their de facto commander was the generalissimo. The choice of the Curtiss-Wright P-40 Tomahawk IIB was Chennault's.[2]

Within two weeks of his arrival in China, Magruder met with Chennault at the latter's headquarters at Toungoo, Burma. Magruder quickly became convinced that the AVG had the potential to perform an important role in maintaining Chinese morale in the struggle with Japan and soon became one of the AVG's staunchest advocates. When President Roosevelt officially approved the formulation of the AVG in April 1941, no provision was made for material or personnel replacement. So, throughout AMMISCA's involvement with the AVG, Magruder's foremost challenge was obtaining sufficient aircraft, spare parts and personnel.

And, of course, there was politics. Chennault, a compulsive careerist, demanded much. He had the strong support of the generalissimo and Madame Chiang, both of whom regarded the AVG as vital to China's survival. Chennault had many Chinese and American supporters in Washington, especially White House Economic Advisor Lauchlin Currie. The AMMISCA–AVG relationship was never close although Magruder did his best to obtain men and materials for Chennault and may have jeopardized his career by his ceaseless insistence on War Department support. Among the reasons for this was that Chennault resented the fact that Washington provided AMMISCA with staff officers whom he felt he could have put to better use, and he was fearful the mission would hamper his operation. Another cause was confusion: "Nobody quite knew how the AVG, the War Department, and AMMISCA fitted together."[3]

When it became apparent that Washington would not provide all it promised, Magruder was often bypassed by Chiang and Chennault in favor of direct contacts with Currie, Army Chief of Staff George C. Marshall, Secretary of War Henry L. Stimson, the president, and others. This happened even though the War Department had stipulated that Magruder would be the top American officer in the China-Burma area and had assigned him the extremely difficult and frustrating task of initiating and supervising the transfer of the AVG from Chinese control to the American army air forces.

Magruder spent an inordinate amount of effort providing Washington with detailed situation reports, continually emphasizing the critical need for AVG materials and personnel, and informing Washington of the many ever-expanding problems created by the lack of spare parts, ammunition, and tools. Beginning with his initial reports to Washington, Magruder insisted that the AVG receive only the "highest performance" materials, because the group's success was of "vital importance" to the Chinese.[4]

In late October Magruder reported that Chennault planned to retain the AVG in Burma near its Rangoon supply source because it was not ready for combat. Although morale was high the unit still lacked administrative personnel and essential supplies. And, until these arrived, China would have to wait for the AVG to enter combat.[5] Chiang naturally wanted the AVG relocated to China, especially to support his armies in the Kunming area, where he feared an imminent Japanese attack on his vital Burma Road supply link. The Generalissimo asked Magruder what American policy was regarding reinforcement and resupply for the AVG. Magruder forwarded Chiang's questions and comments to Marshall. In an effort to provoke action, he included his own list of six possible methods of employing the AVG.

All six were dependent on one unknown: to what degree the United States would support the AVG logistically and provide trained personnel. Magruder believed Washington's options ranged from "breaking faith" with China by withdrawing all support for the AVG to the opposite extreme of employing substantial American forces in China. Magruder conceded the latter option could lead to war with Japan.

In the original message Magruder prepared for the War Department, he included one other alternative: if there was an emergency, the Chinese government should turn over complete control of the Burma Road operation to the British military in order to assure effective operation. He believed the British were experienced with this kind of problem and also had the Burmese base, which they essentially controlled. This was deleted from the alternatives in the message actually sent to the War Department, but it is essential to the

10. The Mission's Role in the American Volunteer Group 161

narrative because it emphasizes Magruder's belief that the Chinese were usually inefficient. But no decisive action was taken, and the AVG went into combat the week preceding Christmas 1941.[6]

Before the AVG became part of the American air forces in July 1942, they flew hundreds of combat and attack missions over China and Indochina as well as hundreds more in defense of Rangoon and Chungking. Their record, although disputed, especially by Japanese accounts, is generally conceded to be around 300 Japanese planes destroyed, 75 percent in the air, with AVG pilot losses at less than 25. Magruder's depth of feeling regarding support for the AVG was demonstrated by the fact that, after this message, almost every Magruder contact with Washington regarding the AVG contained an urgent reminder of the AVG's material and personnel needs.

In the message Magruder was careful to acknowledge he was not privy to top level policy, so he could not specifically recommend any of his six suggestions. He estimated the AVG would not be ready for combat until at least early 1942, and even then would not last long unless the volume of supply was substantially increased. He suggested that some kind of unified American and British "support for China" might convince Japan to act less belligerently, and he warned that an AVG defeat would be severely disheartening to the Chinese people and there would be repercussions in America.[7] Surprising no one, the message urged the War Department to support the AVG, but with a new argument: the British, wary of an increased American presence in Burma, would be more willing to supply significant air support.[8]

But Chiang, fearful of the AVG's future and always eager to expand his military base via allied contributions, decided to try to expand and strengthen the anemic Chinese air force, which in 1941 had only a few trained personnel flying a handful of outdated Russian and Italian aircraft. In late October Chiang conferred with Magruder and acknowledged that he was "afraid" of the lack of combat efficiency of the Chinese air force, and urged AMMISCA to reorganize and retrain it. He also requested that an American army air force officer of "high rank" be sent to Chungking to command the air force; his obvious strategy being the acquisition of additional aircraft and materials.[9] Chiang promised there would be no interference in any American effort to restructure his air force. Magruder believed the Chinese air force to be "wholly ineffective," so he recommended the War Department send an army air force general with a staff of at least five officers to China to assume immediate command of the AVG and then reorganize the Chinese air corps. Magruder's support was based on his belief that the AVG could never be an effective force due to its piecemeal replacement of personnel and equipment. It would always be an organization without a solid foundation or close ties to America or China.[10] He felt that the AVG could play an essential interim role while the Chinese air force was being built only if properly supported, and that his assessment in no way was a criticism of Chennault.

In mid-November, a frustrated Magruder intensified his campaign for more material support. He pointed out that seven P-40s had been lost in training, one had arrived in need of a complete overhaul due to rust, numerous AVG pilots had never trained in the P-40s, and no replacement aircraft had been received. He again warned the War Department that if the United States did not keep even the initial allocation of aircraft in good condition, American prestige would fall tremendously in both China and Japan. In addition, spare parts and assemblies were needed so desperately that they should no longer be shipped via sea, even from the Philippines, but must be shipped by air immediately from wherever they could be obtained.[11]

Weeks passed with no response. Magruder continued to appeal to the War Department, this time pressing for at least a minimal task force to train American and Chinese maintenance personnel.[12] There is little doubt that his constant petitions were annoying, perhaps even to the chief of staff. At the end of November he received a temporary spark of hope. A message from Air Force Chief of Staff Henry H. Arnold stated that Brigadier General H. B. Claggett, who had headed an earlier air mission to China, was available. Magruder was ordered to "coordinate with proper authorities." In other words, Magruder was to determine if Chiang would accept Claggett.[13]

Before Chiang could make a decision, the spark was extinguished: Magruder was advised that the Claggett mission was cancelled and no personnel would be released for an air mission or command group.[14] Thus, even though America was not yet in the war and was not yet allocating large quantities of supplies for its own use, the War Department, in contravention of Roosevelt's assurances, decided that no army air force personnel would be sent to China. Equally significant, the department would not even provide enough planes, pilots, and parts to maintain the AVG at its original strength. This was due to General Arnold's belief that his first duty was "building the air forces of the United States itself." He thought Chennault was a "crackpot" and was not about to accept the concept of the AVG as the forerunner of the U.S. air forces in Asia.[15] Arnold miscalculated. This and similar decisions complicated Magruder's task of creating a major anti-Japanese fighting force out of the AVG. It also negatively impacted his next assignment of transferring the AVG into the American air force.

Induction of the AVG into the American Army Air Forces

> If after discussion with General Brett and Chiang Kai-shek you recommend absorption of the AVG in United States Army the following authority is granted you:
>
> 1. Constitute a board of officers under your command to commission all American pilots and appropriate administrative personnel of the AVG in the army of the United States, ...
> 2. Restore Claire L. Chennault to active duty in the Army of the United States and promote him to appropriate rank.
> 3. Enlist all Americans now employed by the AVG for the duration of the war.
>
> The above personnel will be used to activate the Twenty-Third Pursuit Group.
>
> — Brigadier General L. T. Gerow, Acting Assistant Chief of Staff, Intelligence[16]

Pearl Harbor significantly altered America's China policy. On 8 December 1941 Lauchlin Currie, China's staunchest and most outspoken supporter in the Roosevelt administration, sent a memorandum to Roosevelt suggesting that because the United States was now in the war the AVG should be made into a regular American military unit. Under Currie's plan all AVG personnel would resume service in the American military through the return of the commissions or ratings they had given when they joined Chennault's unit.[17] But although Roosevelt concurred, Chennault and Chiang had to be convinced. Moreover, because both men were extraordinarily ambitious — as well as closely linked politically — they had to be approached as delicately as possible.

Tasked by the War Department to play a key role by negotiating with both Chennault and Chiang, Magruder felt it best to query the generalissimo only after he had discussed the subject with Chennault and the War Department had initiated the question officially with Chiang. On December 12, Magruder asked Chennault if he would accept a commission in the American army air forces and, if so, at what rank. He also asked Chennault's opinion regarding re-commissioning the rest of the AVG personnel and establishing them as an American military unit in China.[18]

Chennault vigorously opposed the whole concept. Chiang, when informed of the proposal, was initially willing to bargain.[19] The Generalissimo's willingness to discuss induction overrode Chennault's objections, but Chiang wanted to negotiate, particularly regarding Chennault's future rank and authority. Clearly the generalissimo appreciated Chennault's talent and total loyalty and desired that he obtain a prominent and influential — and helpful to Chiang — position in the new unit.

Through the above directive from Brigadier General L. T. Gerow, the AVG would be the nucleus for a new East Asian American interceptor unit, the Twenty-Third Pursuit Group. The Chinese were to be paid for all airplanes and materials taken over by the group. Significantly for AMMISCA, it appeared to some people that Magruder was to become the commanding general of all American forces in Burma and China, including the former AVG flyers.[20] This was probably due to the post–Pearl Harbor expansion of his original orders. Magruder was now expected to administrate responsibilities, for example the AVG, which fell beyond the normal responsibilities of a one-star general. No mention was made, however, of an alteration to Magruder's original orders that prohibited him from participating in allied planning, again revealing the confusion of orders for those operating in the area.

After Christmas, Magruder began extensive negotiations with Chiang regarding AVG induction into the army. He notified the War Department that Chiang was considering the proposal — and took the opportunity to once again appeal for men and materials. He also requested that former naval flyers be given the option of renewing their commissions in the navy but with the provision that they could be attached to the army while they flew in the Twenty-Third Pursuit Group. This was the first in a long series of requests by Magruder, and later Stilwell, to offer the AVG personnel as many inducements as possible to stay with the group.[21]

Currie supported induction and told the generalissimo that making the AVG an American unit would mean a "steady and increased flow of planes, supplies and men" to China. He urged Chiang to exact as much as he could from the negotiations, and get American assurances of continued air support for China, and army air force units in China to operate under the general command of the generalissimo.[22] This was an incredible statement for an American Presidential aide to make: Currie was actually encouraging a foreign head of state to act in a manner beneficial to him and to his nation, with total disregard for America's interests.

Currie's urging stiffened Chiang's demands. On December 31, Magruder submitted his first official induction progress report. He said Chiang had tentatively agreed, under the condition that the commanding general of U.S. forces in China and Burma (in this case it appeared it would be Magruder) operated under Chiang's command in all joint operations in China. Chiang stated his decisions would be "governed by directives from appropriate U.S. military authorities."[23] Chiang indicated he was willing to assist American

10. The Mission's Role in the American Volunteer Group 165

operations by furnishing additional military facilities, and arranging for CAMCO to cancel its contracts with each AVG employee on the date they entered Chinese service. But then Chiang insisted on adding some demands which he euphemistically termed "recommendations."

Chiang's demands were undoubtedly supported by Currie's exhortations to him to get whatever he could from America, as well as requests from several unnamed officials close to Chiang who were reluctant to give up the profits they derived from their supply contracts with CAMCO.[24] Although Chiang stated that the "recommendations" were negotiable, he was adamant that he serve as supreme commander of all American forces in China. Magruder recognized that such a policy would prohibit movement of American forces into and out of Burma and give Chiang control over all air forces located there. He urged the War Department to not approve Chiang's proposals, even though it would slow the transfer of the AVG into the American army air forces.[25]

Magruder's role was diminishing at the War Department. He was shocked to learn that while he had been preparing and submitting required induction situation reports, the War Department, at the president's direction, had already suggested to Chiang that he (Chiang) become the supreme commander in the Chinese theater. Magruder was not made aware of the War Department's recommendation, because Roosevelt's message was submitted to Chiang through the naval attaché, Marine Major James McHugh, significantly junior to Magruder. A bit of irony: whoever ordered the routing of the message must not have known that Magruder and McHugh were brothers-in-law! Nevertheless, it is clear that the commander on the ground was deliberately ignored by the War Department.

Magruder's anger over the McHugh incident was justified, especially in light of the message two weeks previously that implied that he would command all American troops in Burma and China when induction was completed.[26] The message stated that the British would be advised of the arrangement and that the AVG forces might be withdrawn from Burma if Magruder chose to do so. Britain's General Wavell, the non–Chinese Far East commander, was informed within days of the new arrangement.[27]

Magruder's heated reaction to the delivery of Roosevelt's message by a junior officer was amply demonstrated in a New Year's Day message to the chief of staff: "My status was compromised ... by the incident which resulted from the forwarding to Chiang through the Naval Attaché instead of through me of the President's December 30th suggestion that the Generalissimo accept the supreme command of the Chinese Theater. In inviting me to accompany him to present the message, the Naval Attaché was generous."[28]

There were other indicators of the erosion of Magruder's standing.

AMMISCA functioned without benefit of information known in Washington that should have been passed on to Magruder; an unusual situation for a commanding general, even one of such a diminutive force as AMMISCA. A possible explanation is that Marshall began to lose confidence in Magruder as early as a month after AMMISCA arrived in China. The issue was Magruder's misguided threat report, pressured by Chiang, of the likelihood of an attack on Kunming in 1941. There were other factors. One was the pure confusion that existed at the War Department for months after Pearl Harbor and General Marshall's tendency to not provide his officers second chances. There was undoubted frustration in the War Department due to Magruder's unrelenting communications seeking additional support for the AVG. These, combined with plans in Washington to send a higher ranking officer (Major General Joseph Stilwell) to China to coordinate the Sino-American war efforts, all created an attitude at the War Department that Magruder no longer had a "need to know."

Another portent to Magruder regarding his diminishing status was a response to his query seeking clarification of his and AMMISCA's future role in the AVG induction process. On January 5, he radioed the War Department that he was "in doubt as to American plans and objectives in regard to Burma."[29] On January 9, Assistant Chief of Staff (Intelligence) Brigadier General L. T. Gerow asked Magruder if he required "clarification of your authority" in light of the president's support of Chiang as supreme commander in the CBI. Gerow thus notified Magruder that Chiang would tell him whatever he needed to know. Until the new general officer arrived, Magruder would be directly under Chiang's control, which created a quandary since Magruder's role in AVG induction did not come under Chiang's cognizance.[30]

Magruder was a good soldier and was not deterred from his effort to effect the AVG induction, so when contradictory War Department induction directives caused further confusion, he queried the department: was he still expected to lead the induction process?[31] On January 15, Marshall clarified the War Department's stand by ordering Magruder to proceed.[32] Somewhat mollified, Magruder carried on with induction.

Those who hoped for an early induction did not anticipate the difficulties they were to face, although we will only examine those pertaining to AMMISCA. Magruder believed it would be unfair to re-induct any AVG personnel at ranks they had held when they signed on with Chennault. He told Washington this would create an injustice to the AVG people who might have advanced in rank, and he requested authority to appoint personnel to whatever grade he felt appropriate.[33]

In late January, the transfer program received several setbacks. Magruder, still the official negotiator, was warned by Chennault that the Japanese threat to southern Burma prevented further progress towards induction. Chiang indicated that he favored induction, but became "non-committal" and "evasive." Magruder was told by several of his field officers that only a few of the AVG personnel showed any interest in becoming members of the American military.[34] Magruder felt this lack of interest was due to their present high pay, bonuses of $500 for every Japanese plane they shot down, and other "attractive perquisites," along with the absence of formal military discipline. He was critical of the AVG personnel for a lack of patriotism. He added — probably through gritted teeth — that Chennault was doing nothing to assist the induction effort.[35] Magruder's assessment of the AVG personnel is indirectly supported by historian Jonathan Spence, who notes, "The Chinese loved those tall round-eyed wild men.... They loved them in spite of their flair for driving their jeeps into the sidewalk shops of Kunming and running over pushcarts and rickshas, and they even loved them when they laughingly upset the coolies carrying honey buckets balanced on gin poles." The pilots were "great American adventurers who would have fought just as hard for peanuts or Confederate money — as long as they were flying for ... Chennault and flying their beloved P-40s." Of Chennault as leader, Spence comments, "There was a minimum of red tape — he was a tactician, coordinator, commander. It all seemed so simple. With a few planes and a few pilots he had wrought great havoc."[36]

Chennault avoided openly supporting induction from the moment it was suggested, and it became a significant obstacle. Frequently, with Chiang's covert but discernible assistance, Chennault articulated numerous reasons for not immediately accepting the command of the Twenty-Third Pursuit Group. An examination of the events of the first several months of 1942 demonstrates that Chennault was not truly opposed to commanding the Group; his goal was apparently to achieve as influential a rank and role as possible.

His next ploy in mid-January was to suggest to Magruder that induction would destroy the AVG's present combat effectiveness because many members would terminate their service. He felt any new operation would be dependent on facilities and services currently provided by the Chinese, which would require months and great expense for America to match. Magruder believed Chennault's opposition was due to being subordinate to another air officer, and to the fact that Chiang desired to retain him, Chennault, as his top air commander.[37] A conference was scheduled for 29 January 1942 with Chennault and Chiang present to discuss the matter.

Although Magruder recognized the political forces at play he was a pragmatist. He believed in Chennault and continued to praise him as an "extraordinary" leader and probably the only man with the qualities and experience who could take effective command of American and Chinese air forces. Therefore, he recommended Chennault's appointment to command the Twenty-Third Pursuit Group and any additional American air components sent to China.[38] But Magruder's credibility at the War Department continued to ebb; there was no response to his recommendation.

In early February, Currie commandeered a more prominent induction role. He said to Chennault that it was in China's best interest that he accept command of the Twenty-Third Pursuit Group. Currie knew that Chennault's ambition was a barrier to successful induction, but he assured him that in addition to the Twenty-Third Pursuit Group, he would command additional pursuit and bomber elements including Chinese units. But the War Department and Stilwell wanted one of their men to be Chiang's chief air officer, and their choice, Colonel Clayton L. Bissell, was assigned the billet. In his message to Chennault, Currie attempted to placate him and Chiang by pointing out that Bissell's appointment was a political necessity to "secure Army [War Department] cooperation for really large scale efforts."[39]

Chennault, as usual placing self ahead of induction, replied that he appreciated Currie's interest. Claiming to have China's interests paramount in his mind, he said he felt Bissell could not handle the situation. He thought Bissell very headstrong and one who always pursued "different ideas of pursuit tactics."[40] One of the "differences" to which Chennault referred was Bissell's infamous statement in 1931 that the best way to destroy bombers was by dropping chains into their propellers. Chennault truly disliked Bissell.

Another example of deliberate foot-dragging came when the scheduled January 29 meeting between Chiang, Magruder, and Chennault was cancelled. Although the generalissimo's desires regarding Chennault's promotion to brigadier general were met, Chiang did not order Chennault to Chungking for the meeting to clear the way for induction.[41] Thus, induction was further delayed.

Currie then advised Chiang that he had urged Chennault to take the pursuit command, and asked Chiang to help by pressuring Chennault to accept. Currie reassured the generalissimo by saying this would gain planes and supplies for China, and Chennault would become a brigadier general in the American army air force. Currie stated emphatically that it was imperative that Bissell remain in overall air command because he had contacts, could "get equipment," and would still be under Chiang's ultimate control.[42]

Madame Chiang responded. She cabled Currie that Chennault had told her he would resign if he had to work under Bissell. She hoped to ease the situation by talking to him personally.[43] This was another move to gain con-

10. The Mission's Role in the American Volunteer Group 169

cessions from the War Department. A week later, she notified Currie that Chennault would "consider" taking the pursuit group command if Bissell would be his "advisor" and "supply facilitator." But a week after that, she told Currie that Chennault still felt it best to resign because he was discouraged that promised men and planes had not arrived.[44] The Chiangs, deeply involved in countless complex political schemes, could still play a tough game of bluff and stall.

Currie's response was a warning that indecision was damaging the induction effort in Washington.[45] He was referring to the reality that supplies were hard enough to obtain under normal conditions and Commander of the army air forces, Lieutenant General Arnold, himself a stubborn man, would not provide any more logistical support for the AVG until the situation was stabilized. Currie urged Chiang to again remind Chennault that his command would be much larger than the AVG.[46] He was correct: in addition to the Twenty-Third Pursuit Group, Chennault eventually commanded two squadrons of B-25 medium bombers and the 308th Heavy Bombardment Group, which flew B-24 heavy bombers, which ultimately constituted the Fourteenth Air Force.[47] But "the reluctance of the Chinese to allow the AVG to become the 23rd Pursuit Group until China had gained every possible diplomatic advantage from the situation kept the most effective Allied air unit in Southeast Asia from the control of the potential U.S. theater headquarters, AMMISCA."[48]

In late March 1942, Chennault decided he could gain nothing more through Magruder; he would wait until Stilwell arrived. There were no more Magruder-Chennault meetings of substance. Stilwell arrived in Chungking in early March with orders from the War Department placing all AMMISCA personnel under his command. Magruder, as noted, was not formally assigned a particular task; he was appointed commanding general, General Affairs Division, with only administrative duties. He was, however, ordered to continue his involvement with the AVG induction process.

Almost immediately upon his arrival Stilwell met with Chennault. Chennault indicated a willingness to serve under Stilwell and support induction, but made no commitment. Stilwell's diary notes that Chennault's initial positive response was "a big relief" because he knew that he was dealing with an extremely strong personal relationship between the Chiangs and Chennault.[49]

Stilwell attempted to win a commitment from Chennault by appealing to his ego. He requested Secretary of War Stimson to send a personal note of appreciation to Chennault for his "excellent work." Stilwell told Stimson this would assist in achieving induction.[50] Three days later, Stimson sent a memorandum to "Colonel" Chennault which stressed the admiration the American public held for the AVG's "fighting record and gallantry," and emphasized "your leadership."[51]

On March 24, Stilwell notified General Arnold that Chennault now seemed willing to cooperate but the chaotic military situation in Burma, where the allies were in full retreat, now made induction impossible.[52] Stilwell also reported, "Chennault is requesting a 3 month loan of thirty pilots and fifty mechanics from American Army crews stationed in India." Always suspicious of Chennault's motives, Stilwell recommended that nothing be done until the induction situation was "clarified."[53] Despite Stilwell's suspicions, there is good reason — in this case — to believe that Chennault's requests were appropriate because they were an attempt to remediate the long-term problem of badly needed replacement personnel and material support. Due to the many missions flown, the crews were exhausted and the airplanes were in great need of extensive maintenance. Support from America continued to be almost nil; Chennault's petition was justified.

Chiang and Chennault notified Currie that talks between Chennault and Stilwell were unsatisfactory. They warned Currie that destruction of the AVG would result if the American government insisted on induction. In a confidential portion of the message, Chiang promised Currie he would do everything he could to persuade Chennault to accept induction, but stated that the result was uncertain.[54] Chiang remained determined to get all the Lend-Lease he could, and to place "his man" (Chennault) into the highest possible position in the American military.

Until Stilwell was recalled in October 1944, his relationship with Chennault was rancorous and created such a toxic environment that his replacement, Lieutenant General Albert C. Wedemeyer, later described it as "rife with dissension and disorganization."[55] Stilwell was determined that the AVG receive minimal assistance until an acceptable induction program was completed.

The War Department, certainly aware of the collusive forces at work in the Chiang-Chennault strategy, became even more anxious to consummate induction. Perhaps if more airplanes were sent to China, Chiang would become more amenable. What did Stilwell think? Stilwell called Magruder in for consultation. Magruder stated that Chennault's request for men and materials was valid, but his statement was ignored. Stilwell advised Marshall he would not recommend airplane resupply until a final decision was made on induction.[56] It was an additional step towards the quid pro quo policy supported originally by Magruder and taken up by Stilwell, but was it wise? Was Stilwell's personal dislike for Chennault affecting his ability to comprehend the contribution the AVG had made and would continue to make as the 29th

10. The Mission's Role in the American Volunteer Group 171

Pursuit Group? Chennault regarded it as blackmail, and his relationship with Stilwell thereafter was one of barely mutual tolerance. In defense of Chennault, he was also trying to help his men, China (his employer) and, it could be argued, his country. None of these would be achieved without American support, and Chennault held Stilwell responsible for obtaining them. Both men placed their beliefs and egos above the common good.

Chennault was particularly angered because he saw the AVG deteriorating through what he believed was Stilwell's stubbornness. The AVG, in almost daily combat and single-handedly carrying on the air war in Burma and China, was gradually being reduced through irreplaceable losses of men and supplies. His anger increased through the spring of 1942, when lack of material forced extensive improvisation and cannibalization to keep the equipment useable, although dangerous to fly. The level of animosity went several notches higher when Stilwell's staff air officer, Colonel Clayton L. Bissell, told the AVG that there would be no reinforcements in planes or personnel until induction. If Bissell was sincere, and if he truly spoke for Stilwell, Chennault's resentment was well-founded.[57]

Another blatant Currie intervention came in early February when some P-40s become available and created a sharp disagreement between the War Department and Currie. Currie contacted Magruder directly and, in terminology that can only be characterized as an "order," directed him to "ask Chennault to send ... twenty pilots immediately to Calcutta and twenty-two more by February twentieth to be flown to Takoradi [Africa] ... to ferry back P-40s." (Why Currie chose in this one case to work through Magruder, rather than through Chiang, as was his habit, is unknown.) His message, emanating from the White House rather than the War Department, prompted Colonel Eglin, from the Adjutant General's Office, to send a memorandum to the secretary of the General Staff asking, "Who's running the forces in China?" AMMISCA was a military operation; why was a presidential assistant giving it orders?[58] Magruder was not the only one confused by the back-door processes of Chiang, Chennault, and Currie.

As early as mid–January Chennault developed the well-founded suspicion that supply requests forwarded through normal channels (AMMISCA and the War Department), would not prove fruitful because of high level War Department disapproval of the AVG. So he increased his back-door communications. On January 16, in a private message to Currie, Chennault requested airplane parts and additional staff officers for the AVG.[59] On the same day, Magruder queried the War Department regarding the department's personnel and supply plans for the AVG. The irony was that Magruder was attempting to gain this information so that he could meet with Chennault as he had been ordered to do and mutually determine solutions to AVG supply needs.⁶⁰ But Chennault's avoidance of Magruder become habitual, not only regarding supply requests, but in communicating directly with Currie on policy formulation.⁶¹

In early May, Bissell notified Marshall that with induction less than two months away numerous vital areas still lacked "key personnel."⁶² Bissell requested specialists ranging from carpenters and mechanics to technicians and administrators.⁶³ Marshall promised only a partial shipment of personnel to fill Bissell's needs, but the majority of them did not reach the AVG before induction. Moreover, many personnel, like the P-40s, were siphoned off to the Middle East or India.⁶⁴ In a mid–May directive to Stilwell that indicated great ignorance if (or great unconcern for) the true situation, and surely enraged Stilwell, Marshall advised, "We anticipate that the means available to you as Commander of all American Army forces in India, Burma and China will permit you to supply the AVG, effect transfer of replacements to the AVG, and maintain it as a an effective combat unit."⁶⁵ Only two days before Marshall's radio message, Stilwell forwarded to the chief of staff a message from Bissell: "There is a dangerous rumor within and outside the AVG that U.S. air corps is sabotaging [attempts] to deliver to us any personnel whatsoever to replace its combat losses of the last few months.... Chennault and others have done wonders with very little. They cannot do the impossible. The whole effect of promises of help by the President and the W. D. [War Department] is wearing off due to our failure to deliver a single man to replace steady combat losses. AVG must receive trained personnel, both pilots and enlisted men quickly."⁶⁶

Havoc wrought by the internecine warfare that occurred at various levels of intensity between Chennault, Bissell, Stilwell, Arnold, AMMISCA, the War Department, Currie, the president, and the Chiangs exacerbated the process, as did numerous civilian employers who had learned of the possible availability of a number of highly trained flying and ground personnel. There was dissonance and disagreement among the pilots. Most were unwilling to leave highly paid employment with handsome bonuses and a relatively undisciplined existence for the rigors of a wartime military establishment.

The degree to which any one individual or group's negative actions and attitudes impaired or delayed the transfer of personnel and supply shipments cannot be determined. But that they existed, were numerous, and often detrimental cannot be denied. Marshall's biographer Forrest C. Pogue notes, "Magruder's group, with its very extensive control over Lend-Lease shipments was only one entry in the field." Currie was able "to appeal [directly] to President Roosevelt against the War Department and its representatives. He [was]

10. The Mission's Role in the American Volunteer Group   173

a strong supporter of Chiang's plans and the channel through which Chennault funneled his proposals to the White House."[67]

After the arrival of Stilwell, AMMISCA's role in the induction process diminished. Yet Magruder was still used by Stilwell as a consultant and, because of his good relationship with Chiang, as an emissary regarding induction, and several other sensitive matters. Magruder and Bissell conferred with Madame Chiang on March 30. They warned that a quick decision by the generalissimo regarding induction was necessary if the present gradual loss of effectiveness of AVG is to be counteracted. Madame Chiang told them that Chennault claimed he could hold the majority of the men until the end of their contracts but no longer. Some of the men were already breaking their contracts and leaving China; Chennault estimated that 90 percent would terminate their contracts rather than accept induction into the American army.[68]

As late as the end of March, Stilwell believed Chennault was still the "key to the entire situation," even though "the conclusion that he is playing personal politics is inescapable." He decided the only way to bring about induction was for Chiang to make a rapid decision to support it. He hoped this would force Chennault to accept the command. Stilwell accordingly effected a significant change in strategy. He asked the War Department to promptly supply considerable parts, materials and personnel to the AVG.[69] Supply leverage was to be secondary to induction.

Chiang responded by agreeing to establish a firm induction date. At a meeting on April 1, Stilwell, Bissell, Chennault, and Magruder agreed that induction would take place formally on July 4. They also agreed that in the interim every effort would be put forth to maintain the strength of the unit.[70] The agreement received Chiang's immediate approval, but he insisted that the War Department place the acquisition of personnel and equipment, enough to bring the Twenty-Third Pursuit Group to full strength, in the highest priority.[71] Chiang's agreement ensured that Chennault would accept command of the Group.

Establishing a fixed date for induction did not solve the controversy of how Chennault would fit into the American air force hierarchy in China. There is no doubt that Stilwell always preferred Bissell, as did Marshall and the War Department.[72] Marshall wanted to promote Bissell, now acting as Stilwell's top air officer, to brigadier general, a more appropriate rank for that position. He held the promotion in abeyance while awaiting Stilwell's input. Stilwell's solution was that Bissell and Chennault receive their stars at the same time. On April 4, with Chiang's concurrence, Stilwell recommended Bissell's promotion to brigadier general — one day before Chennault's promotion to the same rank.[73] Thus, part of the problem was solved, although

Chennault later accused Stilwell, Arnold, and Bissell of conniving against him.[74]

Even though Chennault appeared to be safely in the pro-induction fold, he continued to do little to win over the pilots and ground crews to the cause. Part of this was due to the ongoing Stilwell-Chennault feud. The depth of the feud is shown by their actions when Stilwell was directed to promote Chennault and administer the oath of office for his active duty with the army air force. Stilwell simply forwarded the promotion order to Chennault. Standard War Department procedure required Chennault to acknowledge acceptance of the orders. Stilwell sent Chennault three separate notifications, and Chennault responded to none of them. Stilwell finally elicited a response by sending a message through Madame Chiang, but irritated by Chennault's attitude, Stilwell simply told him to "stop by the next time you are in Chungking."[75]

As each day brought the AVG closer to the formal induction date, it became clear to Stilwell that very few of the personnel planned to transfer to the American air force. He and the War Department embarked on a selling campaign; every possible inducement was offered. On April 10, Stilwell was ordered to recognize "previous meritorious service" by inducting personnel into the Twenty-Third Pursuit Group at higher ranks than they had held before joining the AVG. Stilwell was allowed to offer the rank of full colonel to people he felt worthy of that recognition, regardless of the number of vacancies in that rank called for in the pursuit group's table of organization.[76] In addition, the War Department reiterated its policy that navy and Marine personnel could elect induction in either the army, navy, or marines, although the navy restricted induction to the grade held previously in that service. The navy secretary, under pressure from the army, did agree in February to allow former navy and Marine AVG pilots to receive regular navy and Marine commissions and serve in the Twenty-Third Pursuit Group temporarily.[77] Stilwell was authorized to convey to the AVG personnel the personal request of President Roosevelt that they remain in their present assignments until conditions permitted them to leave.

As a further inducement, Stilwell was authorized to improve the living conditions of officers and enlisted personnel through the purchase of American food and sundry items at army expense. This measure was particularly important because the salaries of the men that underwent induction would be significantly lowered.[78] The War Department also gave its approval to carrying an excess of enlisted grades over and above the table of organization. It was agreed that to get the experience and maintain overall morale, overages in grade would be carried as an excess until normal attrition reduced the numbers in any job specialty to the desired quantity.⁷⁹ Thus there were numerous carrots in the bunch, but the stick was not ignored. Stilwell was ordered to inform those who chose not to be inducted that they would be subject to the draft upon their return to America. Stilwell protested that the rules laid down by the Navy Department discriminated against former navy and Marine officers. If they chose to be reinstated into the navy or Marine Corps and only serve on a temporary basis with the Twenty-Third Pursuit Group, they would not be eligible for the rank they deserved–the former army flyers with whom they had flown would outrank them. Moreover, their former naval contemporaries who had not joined the AVG would also outrank them. The War Department after receiving a similar recommendation from naval attaché modified the policy. The Navy Department agreed that while former navy and Marine Corps pilots would be inducted at the grade previously held as reserve officers, once they were inducted they would be promoted to grades held by their contemporaries who had remained in the American military.⁸⁰

From a traditional military perspective the War Department's concessions were generous. But a new challenge to induction was added in the form of civilian agencies and businesses anxious to hire the experienced and highly employable AVG flyers and ground staff. They offered much higher income and much lower risk. On April 20 Chennault advised Stilwell that the Chinese National Airline Corporation and Pan American Airlines were offering jobs to AVG personnel. He said that many men were quitting the AVG to take better jobs with the airlines, and he requested the War Department to restrain the would-be employers. He also asked Stilwell to prohibit American army transports from carrying discharged AVG personnel from China to America. Stilwell replied coercion would not be used to hold personnel because of the desire to enlist as many AVG personnel as possible on July 4. He did agree to contact China National Airline Corporation and seek its cooperation.⁸¹

The American navy also contributed to the induction problems. In early May, contrary to its previous policy, one of the AVG ground crew received an offer from the Department of the Navy that he would be granted a rating one grade higher than the one he held prior to joining the AVG. He would also receive full credit towards retirement for the time spent in the AVG, and a $400 enlistment bonus. Stilwell immediately asked Naval Attaché McHugh to notify the navy department that such offers posed a threat to the successful formation of the Twenty-Third Pursuit Group. An indication of the severity of the situation was the notation in the attaché's message that such actions, if continued, would hamper serious efforts to induce the volunteer group since there was already widespread opposition among members of the group.⁸² No further offers were made by the navy department.

In mid-April the lack of AVG volunteers convinced Bissell and Stilwell that an undesired but necessary action had to be taken. They forwarded a request to the War Department for the temporary assignment to Chennault of a complete pursuit squadron, less aircraft, so that the Twenty-Third would be at fighting strength personnel-wise when induction took place. The squadron would come from the Tenth Air Force in India.[83] Washington's reaction was unexpected. Instead of expressing an awareness of the AVG's personnel difficulties, Arnold ignored the request and told Stilwell that it was desirable for AVG experience to be utilized in America to train new units. He requested Stilwell to submit the names of individuals suitable to act as squadron commanders or as group staff members.[84] In sum, there would be no assistance from the Tenth Air Force. For some reason Washington assumed there would be a surplus of AVG personnel available after induction. This illustrates the War Department's ignorance of the realities of the induction situation and perhaps was reflective of the Arnold-Stilwell relationship.

In late April the induction situation became so serious that Roosevelt and Chiang were asked to make personal appeals to the AVG. Even though Roosevelt lauded the "gallantry and daring" of the men and told them, again, that large numbers of new planes and personnel were on their way, and that leaves of absence would be granted as soon as replacements were available, the effect was minimal.[85] Chiang's appeal was equally unsuccessful.[86] Additional inducements were offered: the application date for transfer was extended; civilians under contract to Pawley and CAMCO were permitted to apply; mechanics and other vital ground crew personnel were approved for induction at "suitable" ranks (regardless of previous rank) and a hospital unit attached to the AVG was approved for induction. Stilwell and the Naval Attaché made inquiries of their respective services to determine whether service in the AVG would count towards retirement. There is no record of a reply to their queries but the issue was revived after the war by AVG veterans. The War Department searched its adjutant general files but failed to turn up any commitments to give retirement credit for service in the AVG.[87]

By the end of May Stilwell was so concerned about the lack of applications that he requested the War Department to call the AVG pilots to active duty. All of them had previously held army or navy reserve commissions, and Stilwell believed they could be legally conscripted without their consent.[88] Marshall replied that the AVG pilots had all resigned their commissions prior to entrance into the AVG and that no provision existed to authorize Stilwell to call these pilots to active duty without their consent. In a mild rebuke, Marshall also reminded Stilwell that he, Stilwell, had previously told Chennault that coercion was not to be used to hold AVG personnel.[89] Stilwell's inclination to be forceful is understandable. Less than a week before, Chennault had informed him that only three AVG pilots had applied for induction. Chennault and Bissell were each convinced that this was because no replacement pilots and few spare parts had been received by the AVG for almost six months.[90] Nor could Stilwell's demeanor have been improved by the continued efforts of outside employers to lure AVG personnel. In early June, he'd learned that Pan American Airlines had made an attractive offer to the AVG's only meteorologist.[91]

At the end of June, with induction imminent, only four pilots, twenty other officers, and a handful of enlisted personnel had volunteered to stay.[92] Stilwell asked Chennault to prevail upon the remaining AVG pilots and ground crews to serve two extra weeks with the Twenty-Third Pursuit Group. This was undoubtedly galling to Stilwell because it was an admission that the induction would be more ceremony than substance and that it would be some time before the group could be a viable fighting unit. Stilwell's attitude is exemplified in his reaction to a War Department query regarding publicity for the induction. Stilwell replied that he desired no publicity whatsoever; the group would be devoid of combat capability and he feared Japanese reaction. "Fact is AVG is quitting under fire and walking out on United States in an emergency. They are placing personal interests before those of their country. This won't stand publicity."[93]

Responsibility for the failure of AVG personnel to transfer to the Twenty-Third Pursuit Group lay in Washington as well as China. Chaos existed in the War Department, and the president made promises that he knew could not be fulfilled. Magruder, a by-the-book soldier but unskilled in politics, was naive enough to believe that his "work through designated channels" approach would be respected by the other players.

Chennault's and Chiang's intransigence and the low esteem in which they were each held at the War Department made matters difficult, especially due to the attitudes of Marshall and Arnold. There were also inappropriate interventions, with presidential approval, by Currie and others, and the unofficial, but actual relegation of the China air effort to a priority lower than that of the Ninth and Tenth Air Forces. Chennault's arrogance and self-serving actions (partially based, it must be admitted, on talent and success) and the animosity between Chennault and Stilwell make it amazing that induction ever happened. Threats and other bizarre induction tactics, such as Bissell's widely publicized remark to the pilots at Kunming that "those who do not volunteer will be drafted the minute they step ashore in America," did not win many converts.[94] Other barriers included the often strikingly obtuse policies established by civilian Washington, Stilwell and Chennault's adamancy, and the War Department's neglect of the AVG.

Chennault's self-seeking role in the induction process was a primary factor. In its initial stages he opposed the induction strongly and did not speak out in support. He held back to see how he could best obtain higher rank and position; he wanted to become the ranking air officer in the China-Burma area of operations. Only when it appeared that the transfer of the AVG to American command might fail did he act. The AVG chaplain, Paul S. Frillman, speaking later in Chennault's behalf, stated, "Chennault toured all the fields with Army and Navy induction officers, offering a last chance to sign up, indeed insisting on it."[95]

At Chennault's request, some of the pilots agreed to stay on temporarily when it became plain that there would be no Twenty-Third Pursuit Group if they did not. One of the forty-four men who volunteered to serve two extra weeks was John E. Petach. He was killed on July 10 when his plane exploded in mid-air after his rack of bombs was hit by ground fire. In January he had married one of the two AVG nurses, Emma Foster, and signed up for extended duty to try to make some extra money for the baby that was already on the way.[96] Cupidity doubtless contributed to the exodus of some of the AVG people, but not all were motivated solely by material concerns.

The most potent factor contributing to the small number of AVG applications for transfer was that many of the AVG personnel were disgusted by the lack of support that the AVG had received from the United States government. A letter to the author from a senior sergeant in Chennault's ground echelon, E. J. Harris, emphasizes Bissell's verbal blunders and threats; it notes that Chennault in public opposed induction, and although he did travel to AVG bases, he did not openly encourage personnel to transfer to the American military. As one of those who resigned, Harris says, "I believe lack of logistic and personnel support did play some part in decisions to leave China, but I believe this was one among many reasons. Homesickness, physical tiredness, mental fatigue, Bissell's threat — these and others affected decisions."[97]

11

International Strategic Planning

The mission, in brief, of the Military Mission to China is as follows: "...assist the Chinese government in obtaining appropriate military defense aid as contemplated in the Lend-Lease Act, and in insuring that the most effective use is made thereof."
— Magruder to Marshall[1]

As I look back upon the period to which I now turn, my memory (perhaps an unfair or incomplete one) is of a department without direction, composed of a lot of busy people working hard and usefully but as a whole not functioning as a foreign office. It did not chart a course to be furthered by the success of our arms, or to aid or guide our arms. Rather it seems to have been adrift, carried hither and yon by the currents of war or pushed about by collisions with more purposeful craft.
— Dean Acheson, *Present at the Creation: My Years in the State Department*[2]

In its original orders to Magruder the War Department directed him to work with the Chinese in only two areas: training and logistics. Because AMMISCA officers were often the only eyes and ears located "on the ground" in India, Burma and China, after Pearl Harbor the War Department, White House, and to a lesser degree the State Department usually gave some credence to their situation reports. As chief of the mission and the only American general officer in China, Magruder frequently was asked to attend high level allied planning meetings.

However, "the Generalissimo was not told that Magruder was forbidden to engage in staff talks; undoubtedly he assumed that was a major reason for Magruder's presence in Chungking."[3] Apparently Magruder felt his relationship with Chiang would be stronger if the generalissimo was not aware of his lack of authority. Since this policy never emerged in communications between China and the War Department and White House, it must be surmised that

Washington shared this strategy. Even given the fact that Magruder was military, not State Department, restricting his authority was a mistake.[4]

"For a while it was felt that Magruder should be authorized to conduct staff talks with the Chinese on cooperation between the two Allied Powers should war arise in the Pacific between America and Japan. If adopted, this provision would have helped fill one of the gaps in prewar planning, but it was never authorized."[5]

As previously noted, within days of his October arrival, Chiang summoned Magruder to discuss his concern that the Japanese were preparing to assault Kunming. There was also discussion of a proposal by Chiang that AMMISCA take control of the American Volunteer Group. "Thus, despite the precautions of those who had drawn up Magruder's directives, the Chinese had immediately involved him in a discussion of major points of U.S. Pacific policy."[6] Despite some accusations by his critics, Magruder never sought to unilaterally influence policy formulation except through his formal reports and recommendations to Washington. Magruder saw himself as an informational conduit between Washington and Chungking and faithfully reported his activities to his superiors. But Chiang, because he saw Magruder as another means of focusing American attention on China's material needs, was eager to include Magruder in several aspects of Allied planning.

Magruder, especially after Pearl Harbor, felt it would damage his relationship with Chiang to ever refuse an invitation from the generalissimo, regardless of topic to be discussed. Washington admonished him for his "diplomatic efforts" as early as mid–November 1941. But since Magruder was led to believe he would become the commander of all United States troops in China and Burma, a position that would have meant his promotion to major general, he felt he would certainly become involved in high-level planning at Chungking. But from the beginning of the mission and throughout its tenure, Magruder's directives from Washington were often vague, incomplete, and contradictory, including those he interpreted as indicating a greater future role for him. Thus, even before the advent of the war, he became caught up in the numerous misunderstandings that haunted AMMISCA-Washington relations throughout Magruder's tenure.

There is no doubt that Magruder was restricted by his one-star rank. This was an error by Marshall, who sometimes let his private feelings regarding subordinates influence his otherwise first-rate judgment. Others understood there was a need for Magruder to be promoted. An example is the 31 December 1941 radio message to Marshall from the army military attaché, Lieutenant Colonel William Mayer. Mayer observed, "Because of increased responsibilities and to preserve U.S. prestige again urge Magruder be given appropriate rank. Russian Military Mission Chief is LT General. British is Major General."[7] The matter resurfaced in May, but was dealt with by the bureaucratic War Department method of sending it from one department to another and then back to Stilwell, where there was no hope of approval.[8]

Washington-Chungking Discord Involving AMMISCA: Kunming

> We have had for some time very much in the mind the situation created by the menace of a Japanese attack against Kunming from Indo-China to which you call special attention. When I received the first of your messages under reference, [30 October 1940] officers of this Government, including high officers of the Department of State, the Army and the Navy, entered immediately into consultations in order to give renewed and urgent consideration to all aspects of the problems underlying that situation. It soon became our conclusion that, while it should be a grave error to underestimate the gravity of that situation, it did not appear that preparations by Japan for a land campaign against Kunming had advanced to a point which would indicate probable immediate imminence of an attack. Given the difficult character of the terrain and the formidable resistance which your land forces would offer in Yunnan, an invasion of that province from Indochina by land forces calls for substantial preparation and extensive operations. At the same time we fully realize it is important that your forces be adequately prepared, and equipped and disposed in all branches. Under existing circumstances, taking into consideration the world situation in its political, military and economic aspects, we feel that the most effective contribution we can make at this moment is along the line of speeding up the flow to China of our Lend Lease materials and facilitating the building up of our American volunteer air force, both in personnel and in equipment.... I shall do my utmost toward achieving expedition of increasing amounts of materials for your use.
> — Message to Chiang Kai-shek from President Roosevelt handed to the Chinese ambassador to the United States on 14 November 1941[9]

The reduction of Magruder's credibility at the War Department continued. On October 27 he met with Chiang Kai-shek to discuss improving Lend-Lease services to China. This was their first extended meeting, and Magruder had a lengthy agenda presented to Chiang with a list of five AMMISCA proposals. They dealt with communication, aviation, reorganization of the Chinese quartermaster corps, raw material supply, and training of Chinese personnel. Chiang agreed, in principle, especially with those proposals dealing with aviation.

But the generalissimo refused to discuss the proposals in detail and shifted the topic of conversation to a more immediate personal concern. He was convinced that Japanese forces in Indochina were maneuvering to sever the Burma Road through an attack on Kunming, in Yunnan province, "sometime in late November," and if Kunming were lost, "China might be out of the war."[10] This of course was a ruse, employed numerous times in different forms by Chiang to obtain American aid. Magruder had two choices: to maintain his close relationship with Chiang or tell the generalissimo that he was not authorized to become involved in policy matters. Magruder believed that Allied unity demanded that he follow the former course.

Chiang then startled Magruder by pressuring him to obtain airplanes and crews from the British, claiming that only air support could stop an attack on Kunming. The AVG would not be combat ready for several months; additional Lend-Lease air supplies would not arrive until too late; and the only hope for Kunming was support by British units from Singapore. He asked Magruder to prevail upon Roosevelt to provide immediate assistance.[11]

Chiang urged Magruder to make direct contact with the British commanding general at Singapore to ask for air units. He also wanted Magruder to ask Roosevelt to warn the Japanese that a move southward would be detrimental to American interests and if Kunming were attacked, whether the American government would interpret the attack as raw Japanese aggression. Chiang was asking a great deal, but he was unaware Magruder's influence was not what he thought it to be. He hoped that noticeable Anglo-American public support, with the added possibility of air support, would deter Japan from attacking Kunming. Even if it did not discourage the Japanese, Chiang would gain two strong allies.

Magruder reported Chiang's remarks and requests to the War Department, adding that the Chinese air force was of "no combat value" and the AVG quite weak. But the "alleged" threat to Kunming became a major factor in Magruder's credibility at the War Department. This was the beginning of his persistent — some would later say incessant — campaign for expanded air support for the AVG. In this case he suggested, at Chiang's insistence, that British air reinforcements from Singapore or American forces from Manila be dispatched to China in the near future.[12]

Romanus and Sunderland state that Chiang's warnings seem to have originated before Magruder's arrival in Chungking. They imply that this may have been a ploy by the generalissimo "to obtain an emergency issue of arms."[13] Soong had made two such requests in late September, both of which were in addition to, but not related to, his earlier request submitted in March 1941. "The first [Soong] request may have been a testing of the American position, for he [Chiang] promptly followed it by sounding the alarm in the strongest manner."[14] Magruder, being quite new to Chungking, was, of course anxious to build a good relationship with Chiang. Under the generalissimo's persuasive powers, he may have misunderstood the total tactical picture, which was somewhat confused because there actually was a Japanese gathering of forces to attack somewhere else; they hoped create a diversion, apparently successful, by appearing to have Kunming as the main objective. In addition, on November 8, Soong confused things further by asking for the release to China of one-third of the American navy's dive bombers. Soong claimed that without them "China could not resist an attack on Kunming."[15] It is certainly possible that Chiang was using all these events to try to create an illusion of China's situation being much worse than it was. Any war materials that might result, or hopefully war between Japan and America, would be welcome.

Although Magruder did not specifically advocate the use of uniformed Americans in combat, Marshall felt the implication was there. Magruder was supporting a potentially dangerous course of action if Japan, as was likely, chose to construe such action as an act of war. But Magruder was anxious to build a relationship with the generalissimo, and he genuinely — and mistakenly — believed a Japanese attack on Kunming was more than just a possibility. His concern was not well received by the chief of staff or General Arnold. Romanus and Sunderland contend that Magruder's influence at the War Department was much less than Chiang believed it was. They note, "Magruder sent [Chiang's] warning ... to Washington." In this manner, "despite the precautions of those who drew up Magruder's directive, the Chinese had immediately involved him in a discussion of major points of U.S. Pacific policy."[16] Marshall regarded this as misguided thinking as well as unsuitable temerity on Magruder's part.

Concurrently, Madame Chiang cabled Lauchlin Currie a summary of her husband's discussion with Magruder. She sought Currie's support by warning that if the Japanese occupied Yunnan, Kunming's home province, their next step would be an attack on the British holdings in East Asia. Quick action was vital: if Britain took a firm stand and reinforced its holdings immediately, the Japanese air force could be destroyed in Indochina and the threat to East Asia removed.[17]

In defense of Magruder's assessment of the Japanese threat, his concern was shared by Owen Lattimore, Chiang's American political advisor.[18] Lattimore was one of the most knowledgeable China specialists in America. He spoke impeccable Chinese and had just returned to Chungking from a tour through Yunnan. He warned Currie that a concerted Japanese offensive would probably be successful. Lattimore advocated "an immediate American [air] initiative" for the defense of Kunming and Yunnan, because without American aid the Burma Road would fall since Britain would not unilaterally defend it. Lattimore related conversations with British and Australian officials in Yunnan that demonstrated British "lack of determination" regarding Burma's defense.[19] There was also a modicum of support for Magruder from the British ambassador to China, Sir Archibald Clark Kerr. The ambassador consulted with his staff and stated, "We agree that Chiang Kai-shek has not overestimated the potentialities to Kunming or overestimated the effects in the Far East of its capture." He warned that "a Chinese collapse [would ensue] if Kunming fell."[20]

Upon receipt of Lattimore and Magruder's messages, Currie solicited the advice of the War Department. Marshall was angered by his subordinate's recommendations and was openly critical. He said that Magruder was probably overly sympathetic with the Chinese and had a "tendency to overreact." Marshall stated that he knew Magruder well and blamed himself for not cautioning Magruder before he left about his weaknesses. He had served with Magruder in China and felt he could properly interpret Magruder's messages. He thought, in addition, that Magruder had a tendency to become "stampeded."[21] Given these harsh criticisms of Magruder within two weeks of his arrival in China, one wonders why the chief of staff selected him to be the AMMISCA commander. The "threat to Kunming" message, however, was the beginning of Magruder's fall from grace.

Although the War Department regarded Chinese needs sympathetically, there would be no reinforcements available for East Asia until early December, and these were scheduled for the Philippines, not China. In an obvious reference to Magruder and Lattimore's recommendations regarding American air intervention, Marshall stated firmly that the United States should not become involved in the Sino-Japanese hostilities.[22] He consulted with the chief of naval operations, Admiral Harold R. Stark, who agreed with him. They advised Roosevelt that the course of action recommended by Magruder "would lead to war" with Japan.[23]

Here the situation became muddled. Marshall and the War Department plainly opposed intervention in China, but the State Department and the White House vacillated. The chief of staff's conviction that Magruder was overly pessimistic was related to Currie by two of Marshall's aides. The War Department believed that reinforcement of the Philippines would be the most effective means of aiding China, and, although aid to China was important, it was more essential to avoid war with Japan. Currie replied that he believed the State Department wished to aid China in every way short of war with Japan and agreed that uniformed Americans should not fight in China; he hoped to bring about diplomatic pressure on Japan.[24]

Magruder's message was further evaluated at the State Department by Secretary Cordell Hull, Under Secretary Sumner Welles, Hornbeck, and several other department officials. They compared it to a separate navy department memorandum stating only combined American and British air support could block a Japanese invasion of Kunming's home province of Yunnan. The group was apparently influenced by the navy memorandum and accepted as credible the Magruder-Chiang warning that a Japanese attack was imminent and could only be defeated through Anglo-American air intervention.[25]

The War Department's official response was non-acceptance of Magruder's analysis. The department stated that an attack on Kunming could not possibly take place for at least two months, and that the terrain in Yunnan was so rugged that Chinese troops could defeat a ground attack without extensive air support. The memorandum also contained an evaluation of the army air forces in the Philippine Islands that revealed that the transfer of a considerable portion of the air garrison would seriously risk the islands' security.[26] When the British Military Mission in Washington was informally consulted by intelligence officers, the response was that British air resources at Singapore were inadequate even for the defense of that city and, even if planes became available, no units of the Royal Air Force would be sent to Yunnan for fear of alienating Japan.[27] This is a classic example of the forces at work in the executive wing of the government: uncertainty of alliances; too little in the way of almost all military assets; and confusion in Washington, especially in terms of the actions and reactions, especially Japan's, that might result from almost any decision.

The matter was finalized when Marshall and Stark told the president that if Kunming fell and the Burma Road was lost, China could fall. But they warned Roosevelt and Hull that any American operation undertaken to prevent loss of that supply route, no matter how well disguised, would lead to war with Japan, for which America was not prepared. It was also their opinion that if war came soon, China was not economically or strategically important enough to be of primary concern. Marshall and Stark felt American efforts should center on defense of the Philippines and the British and Dutch holdings.[28] Thus, the War Department leadership decided that Magruder's recommendations regarding increased American participation in China were flawed and if followed could lead to serious consequences. Further, the "Europe first" policy was, of course, always in the minds of the decision-makers. With respect to the AMMISCA's and Chiang's communications, Marshall and Stark recommended that no U.S. armed forces be sent to China but that aid to China be increased and that no ultimatum be sent to Japan. The State Department agreed.[29]

Owen Lattimore, no stranger to Chiang Kai-Shek's rages, told Currie that he had never seen the generalissimo as angry as when he was told of the War Department's decision. Chiang communicated his feelings directly to Roosevelt and Churchill, warning them again of the potential collapse of Chinese resistance. After an Anglo-American exchange of messages, they repledged their "continued support" for China. The two leaders emphasized their own military problems, and promised to do what they could, diplomatically, to forestall further Japanese expansion. Neither indicated he would send military support since they agreed it was absolutely necessary to avoid war with Japan.[30]

Their course was the proper one: Japanese operations in Yunnan during the AMMISCA era were never of the magnitude predicted by Chiang and Magruder. In fairness to Magruder, he was undoubtedly under a great deal of pressure from Chiang, who thought Magruder could be persuaded to support him in Washington. Magruder was anxious to build a rapport with Chiang so he may have overstated his recommendations, and did not realize he was out of tune with current War Department thinking. Had they been followed through, it might well have brought war with Japan. Thus, he lost significant prestige at the War Department and with Currie.[31]

Magruder also provoked Hull, who was always sensitive regarding State Department prerogatives, and accused Magruder of engaging in diplomacy. Although the Kunming-Yunnan situation involved international relations, it was certainly of military significance, and Magruder made no political recommendations. Hull's criticism was inappropriate and was based solely on an October 28 Japanese radio broadcast that accused Magruder of pressuring Chiang to allow the construction of United States air force installations in China. Hull had "no opinion" regarding the basis of this particular broadcast, and admitted that the State Department had no information that differed from Magruder's report of the Yunnan-Kunming situation. Clearly, Hull saw the matter as more political than military and reiterated that Magruder should not be involved in "political" matters.[32]

In truth, Magruder's information was the only material regarding the threat to Kunming received in Washington, and Hull was upset that Ambassador Gauss had not provided this information before it came from the War Department. This was an obvious effort to prod Gauss into gathering and forwarding more timely intelligence. Hull was also noticeably displeased over the "roundabout methods of sending messages and use of several different channels in each of which the messages are reported in different words."[33] This was unacceptable, and the ambassador was ordered to so inform Chiang, Magruder, and the Naval Attaché McHugh. When Gauss met with Magruder

11. International Strategic Planning

to discuss it, Magruder pointed out he had made no recommendations concerning political policy and had submitted recommendations only on military matters.[34] Nevertheless, the confusion led to a rebuke from the War Department.

On November 15, Assistant Chief of Staff Brigadier General L. T. Gerow advised Magruder that in all future dealings with the Chinese he was to limit himself to matters concerning the United States military forces already in China, which included AMMISCA, the AVG, several small support groups, and Lend-Lease. Henceforth he would have "no latitude" for entering discussions concerning the use of any other American military forces. He was not to engage in discussions with anyone. "Anyone" presumably referred to Chiang. This was extremely unrealistic and, given Magruder's excellent relationship with Chiang, unwise. Magruder was ordered to render no opinions regarding employment of other American military units and was ordered to confine himself to relaying Chinese points of view and his own impressions of the "general situation."[35] This was more than a reprimand; it was the end of Magruder's relationship with Marshall. With only a few exceptions, subsequent AMMISCA recommendations and situation estimates were regarded with much less credibility. Gerow's messages, directed by Marshall, were based on AMMISCA's original orders not to become involved in any kind of Allied policy planning. But why then did the War Department and Marshall allow Magruder to attend top level meetings with Brett, Wavell, and Chiang (examined below), others with Chiang, and still others that included British and other international high-rankers? Some of the discussions in which he was directly involved employment of the AVG, the *Tulsa* incident and, particularly, policies regarding distribution of Lend-Lease. Also, at nearly all of them various methods of "halting the Japanese" were sought. In sum, it was acceptable for Magruder to participate, but only if the War Department (Marshall) was happy with the outcome. Magruder was the man on the spot, but Marshall, by undercutting him, surely lowered his prestige in the eyes of Chiang, foreign military officers, his own subordinates, and people such as Currie, Chennault, Hornbeck, Hull and others. Moreover, there is no doubt that Marshall's treatment of Magruder contributed even further to confusion in Washington and Chungking regarding AMMISCA's actual day to day mission.

Chiang may have manipulated Magruder by taking advantage of their early positive relationship to try to obtain overt American support, and carrying it a step further, perhaps even draw America into war with Japan. Did Marshall, an even more experienced "China hand" than Magruder, perhaps have the same suspicion and thus regard Magruder as a dupe of Chiang?

Post-Pearl Harbor Allied Policy Formulation at Chungking

> There was, however, one gap in the [American aid to China] program. There was no planning to meet the effect of war in the Pacific by a combined Sino-American effort. Such staff talks had been held between British and Americans, but there had been none between Chinese and Americans. Partly as a result of this, Magruder had no directive as to what his mission would be were war to result from the current Japanese-American crisis in the Pacific.
> — Charles F. Romanus and Riley Sunderland, *Stilwell's Mission to China*

> Stilwell is granted complete freedom of action to make use of personnel of China Mission [AMMISCA] as he may deem appropriate in accomplishment of his mission due to changed military situation since issue of Magruder directive. Without reference to War Department, personnel of Mission may accordingly be transferred....
> — Stimson to Magruder[36]

While offering his sympathies to the United States for the Pearl Harbor losses, Chiang expressed the hope to Magruder and the British ambassador that their countries, with the Dutch, would mount a united offensive against Japan. Chiang promised that all of China's resources would be mobilized to support a general offensive. He also offered to support Hong Kong with nine divisions, proposed to attack Canton, and planned to mount an offensive in Burma. He had two goals: the establishment of an Allied force in China and Burma under his command, and an increase in Lend-Lease shipments to China. The British, undoubtedly skeptical of Chiang's willingness to fulfill his promises, did not desire Chinese troops in Burma. Retention of colonial Burma would be more difficult if a significant number of non–British Asian troops remained there at war's end. This vision prevented the British government from recognizing the significance of the growing indigenous social and economic forces throughout the European colonial world.[37]

British skepticism regarding China's willingness to support the war effort was strengthened on December 22 when Chiang withdrew his troops from Hong Kong because of a Japanese threat to Changsha. Chinese uncertainties regarding British support increased, especially after the loss of the battleships *Prince of Wales* and *Repulse* and the fall of Hong Kong on Christmas Day.[38] At Washington's request, and persuaded by Magruder's rational arguments, Chiang allowed the AVG to be used in Burma. Magruder was also able to induce Chiang to extend the time the AVG unit could stay to defend Rangoon.

But when the British refused to employ Chinese troops in Burma and Rangoon, and confiscated a quantity of the *Tulsa*'s cargo with American compliance, Magruder was unable to ameliorate the Sino-British enmity, especially after Chiang learned that Magruder had supported Britain's policy of limited Chinese participation in Burma.[39]

Three days after Pearl Harbor, Magruder was summoned to Chiang's office and informed of the generalissimo's extreme disappointment that there was so little "allied cooperation." He suggested the formulation of an "East Asian" allied leadership group headquartered, of course, in Chungking. Chiang would be the group's ranking member but, obviously for political reasons, he proposed that America take the lead in its creation.[40] This was one of several times Magruder was propelled into the kind of discussion of international significance that he had been told to avoid. But the long-term military and political opportunities for such a group were formidable, and because Magruder believed China should be included in high-level Allied strategy planning conferences he endorsed Chiang's proposal. Apparently the War Department did not object to this sort of "involvement" on Magruder's part, at least not yet.

Magruder's advice was heeded, due more to Roosevelt's desire to forestall Japanese peace overtures to Chiang than to a reversal in Magruder's status at the War Department. On December 14 Roosevelt officially asked Chiang to head a group of Allied planners headquartered at Chungking. Major General Brett, soon to arrive on an army air forces assignment, would be the American representative and Magruder his deputy. The president requested that a permanent organization be established by December 20 to plan and guide "our direct effort."[41] Chiang undoubtedly hoped that Roosevelt's request would provide the opportunity to influence policy, gain additional material support, and strengthen his position vis-à-vis the British. But, for reasons already cited and despite Roosevelt's encouragement, allied cooperation failed to evolve.

The day after Roosevelt's message to Chiang, the British again rejected the Chinese offer of the use of 75,000 men, accepting less than 10,000. The British military attaché, Major General L. E. Dennys, acknowledged the Burma garrison was undermanned and that vehicles were available to transport the Chinese soldiers to Burma; but he insisted that the main Chinese effort be to pin down Japanese troops in China to prevent their transfer to Burma. He also requested the transfer of some Lend-Lease materials in Burma to the British.[42] Dennys' words confirmed Chinese suspicions that the British were willing to sacrifice Chinese lives to save their own and were interested solely in obtaining Lend-Lease supplies intended for China. Concurrently, Magruder advised the War Department that the generalissimo was further upset with the British because promised reinforcements for the Royal Air Force had not arrived, and the three Asian allies seemed unable to agree on a tactical plan for East Asia, due primarily to British intransigence.[43]

Temporarily overcoming his antipathy for the British, because he realized the formulation of an Allied planning group was vital to China's interests, Chiang continued to push for it. On December 17 he publicly announced that Roosevelt had asked him to establish by December 20, an Allied military council in Chungking that would submit a general plan of action for the Far East. The Generalissimo said he would like the group, called the Joint Military Council, to quickly create a "grand strategy" for the Far East. The main elements would be operations, planning, and the establishment of supply routes from India to China. In this manner Chiang hoped the council would obtain a voice in the distribution of all Lend-Lease supplies before they were allocated to Britain and Russia.[44]

A series of confrontations began just before Christmas. Chiang's anger with the British re-erupted when London waited until after December 20 to send permission for Dennys and General Archibald Wavell, the British Far East commander, to participate in the Joint Military Council.[45] Chiang had given the British less than a week to approve Wavell's participation, but the generalissimo stuck by his belief that London was deliberately slighting him and did little to hide his feelings from the council. At its initial meeting, on December 22, which included Magruder, Chiang let it be known that he saw himself as the only force standing against Japan. He did not intimidate Wavell or the Americans.

Wavell took immediate exception to Chiang's opening announcement that the primary item of consideration should be Allied grand strategy. He contended that the council was not authorized to arrive at a settlement on such a high-level issue as grand strategy. It should instead discuss more practical matters such as air strategy, pooling of Lend-Lease supplies, and the defense of Burma. Brett maintained his pro–British mindset and sided with Wavell. An impasse quickly developed, and the council adjourned before it could even agree on an agenda.[46]

Hoping to rejuvenate the council, the top British and United States representatives met bilaterally on December 23. But Brett and Magruder found the British difficult to deal with; Wavell was wholly preoccupied with Britain's needs. He was gravely concerned with the developing Japanese threat to Burma. In addition, the thousands of tons of Lend-Lease supplies stored in Rangoon warehouses, urgently needed by British troops but consigned to Kunming, were a constant frustration to him. He knew that if Rangoon became the objective of a determined Japanese offensive the Chinese would

11. International Strategic Planning 191

not be able to remove the weapons, munitions, petroleum, and vehicles he desperately needed. His line of thought was understandable; from the beginning of Lend-Lease the British had presented organized and realistic requests. Soong was vague and confusing. The British could have put to use the materials sitting in the warehouses.[47] But Wavell was tactless and bullheaded, one of the Britons in East Asia who were unaware that the war would end colonialism. Stilwell prophetically characterized them and their future in his diary: "It's just the superior race complex for which they will pay dearly."[48] Wavell was determined to improve the grim British logistical situation in Burma and, like Chiang, saw the Joint Military Council as a means of obtaining Lend-Lease materials.

At their next meeting, although Brett attempted to establish a list of priorities for discussion, Wavell ignored him and turned the conversation to a determination of what Lend-Lease supplies were available for British use. Magruder told Wavell that the British would have to submit specific lists of desired materials before a transfer could be approved. Wavell disregarded him and requested the transfer of radio equipment. Magruder repeated the transfer conditions; Wavell responded by asking for the transfer of some Bren guns.

This pattern continued until Brett's patience wore thin. When Wavell requested 4,000 trucks; Brett abruptly reminded him that Britain had recently shipped a large number of trucks to Burma. Wavell quickly backpedaled by lowering his request to 2,000, asserting that the other trucks were needed "in India." Magruder warned Wavell that the Chinese would be disinclined to transfer so many vehicles and, even if they did agree, he would not approve the transfer until he received the War Department's endorsement. He also reminded Wavell that there were several people at the War Department not favorably inclined towards England because of a recent British refusal to supply ammunition to the AVG.[49] On this discordant note the conference ended. No unified plan had been formulated on how to react to Chiang's grand strategy concept, and Wavell's dogged concentration on British needs did not increase optimism regarding future meetings.

That same day, December 23, Wavell told General Ho Ying-ch'in that Burma was short of supplies and equipment and had to be defended for China's sake as well as its own; thus it was to China's advantage to provide Britain some of its Lend-Lease goods. Magruder supported Wavell and informed Ho that the British had now, per policy, provided a partial list of needs, which AMMISCA personnel were checking against their inventory. If the Chinese agreed to transfer the supplies it could be done without approval from Washington since the nature of the materials was "not critical." Ho warned that China had limited industrial capacity to produce munitions and weapons, no raw materials, and no capacity to produce trucks or airplanes. If London would accept the additional Chinese troops offered by Chiang, these troops would draw their supplies from stocks of Lend-Lease materials in Burma. In his usual indelicate manner, Wavell replied that the British did not intend to use additional Chinese troops; all they needed to defend Rangoon and Burma was part of the Chinese stockpile of Lend-Lease supplies. Ho promised to confer with Chiang.[50]

Although Ho was willing to discuss supply transfers, he insisted on pursuing the employment of Chinese troops. He told Wavell that China was prepared to launch two armies against Indochina in an effort to take the pressure off Singapore. Wavell acknowledged the offer but claimed he could not provide supplies for the Chinese troops, and therefore he did not want them. If help were needed, imperial soldiers could be brought in from India. Ho tactfully did not ask how the imperial troops would be supplied if Chinese troops could not be, nor did he give evidence of taking offense at the manner in which his offer was rejected. He simply reminded Wavell that the armies were there if he wanted them. In truth the Chinese bitterly resented the continuing British refusal of Chinese troops.[51]

At a Christmas Day meeting with Chiang, another dispute widened the Sino-British breach. Chiang restated Roosevelt's desire for a permanent Chungking planning organization by resurrecting the issue of the council's becoming the primary strategy planner in East Asia. Wavell reminded the group that a grand strategy had to be prepared at Washington, a reference to the Anglo-American Combined Chiefs of Staff. Brett supported Wavell by asserting that only recommendations for "all of East Asia" should be discussed by the Chungking Council. Fully aware that Chiang's strategy-planning proposal was a ploy to increase Lend-Lease to China, Brett also reminded Chiang that only the Combined Chiefs could decide which war zones would get men and equipment. Chiang reasonably enough replied that the council could establish "reasons and facts" regarding East Asia's situation and submit them. If the Combined Chiefs decided they were of high priority, the Council's time would have been well spent. Brett did not think this was possible because "only a few persons in the United States government had more than a dim understanding of the needs of the Far East." This comment played into Chiang's hands; he replied that this was why the council had to initiate its own concept of strategy — so the Combined Chiefs would have more knowledge of East Asian conditions. Brett argued that coordination would be done at a much higher level; there was no way the council could plan even its own theater operations without knowing, for example, what supplies were to be made available to them. Obviously irritated, Chiang asked Brett to prepare a memorandum to Roosevelt containing Brett's ideas of what the council should do.⁵²

Brett's memorandum draft was criticized by both Wavell and Chiang. His proposals were "too long-range" and "the next two months would be vital to Burma and China." Moreover, he called for extensive air attacks when there were no aircraft available. Chiang properly told Brett his plan was not adequate. He would send his own ideas to Roosevelt.⁵³

At the same meeting it was agreed that Magruder would head the American delegation to the Joint Military Council when Brett left. Although this would seem to be an elevation to a more responsible position, Magruder was selected only because he was the highest-ranking American officer in China. Because of the diverse objectives sought by each of its member nations, the council did not convene regularly and Chiang eventually abandoned it. Magruder, with the exception of muting additional demands from Wavell, was able to claim no council successes.

The Christmas meeting convinced Chiang that the Joint Military Council would not function as he desired, and he decided to not deal further through Wavell, Brett, or Magruder. His first step was to advise Roosevelt that he had designated T. V. Soong the "Chief Delegate of China to such conference or supreme War Council as you contemplate to set up in the immediate future."⁵⁴ He hoped this would place Soong on the recently planned Supreme Allied War Council and other similar groups. But it was over a year before China gained a seat on a prominent Allied planning council: the Combined Chiefs of Staff.

Allied confrontations did not abate after Brett left China. As discussed in the chapter on Rangoon, the seizure of the *Tulsa*'s cargo was the most noteworthy. Because he thought it the right thing to do, Magruder supported Wavell's attempts to obtain Chinese Lend-Lease supplies even though he was still bitter over the *Tulsa* seizure. He was critical of British high-handedness at Rangoon and Wavell's failure for weeks to submit specific lists of needs. Wavell refused to use Chinese troops, even when the British used Burma's "defenselessness" as a reason for seeking increased material support.⁵⁵ The *Tulsa* incident hardened Magruder's view of the British because he was forced to defend the ineptness of Twitty and, especially, Brett, for an action he believed the British had instigated.

At a December 27 meeting, Magruder and Chiang discussed the seizure of the *Tulsa*'s cargo. Magruder felt it proper to state that Twitty and Brett had taken action without orders because "they had to act." Significantly, Magruder linked Brett's name to Twitty's because he believed Brett was more involved in the incident than was recognized. When Chiang asked him if he and Brett had discussed the matter, Magruder replied affirmatively, but added that his information from Brett claimed no significant action at Rangoon. Magruder maintained he was still not certain exactly what had transpired and revealed that Wavell had urged him to act unilaterally and that he had refused to do so without the generalissimo's permission.[56]

Magruder's explanation did not improve Chiang's opinion of Brett, whom the generalissimo believed was in league with the British. The most recent evidence was a week before the Chiang-Magruder meeting when Brett told the governor of Burma that because the United States, Britain, and China were operating against a common enemy, the individual needs of the various countries had to be disregarded and Lend-Lease materials pooled "for the common interest." Magruder replied that Brett had made the statement with incomplete knowledge of American policy. But Magruder agreed that even mitigating circumstances did not justify the removal of the supplies. After all, the British had stalled the construction of their Burma defenses and still had nothing more than a haphazard and piecemeal arrangement. Warming to his subject, he insisted that America and China should not let the British interfere in their heretofore excellent relationship. The Generalissimo agreed and promised to send an additional AVG squadron to Burma, even though the action was a great sacrifice and England had refused to help him even though they had "hundreds of planes at Singapore."[57] Magruder's efforts and acumen in this incident were some of his finest moments as AMMISCA's commander. Although Magruder left China under unusual circumstances, he always had a good relationship with Chiang and a successful negotiating record.

The Evolution of the American Policy of "Quid Pro Quo"

> I have consistently advocated loans and supply of lend-lease materials to China as a national policy hoping for long-range benefits.... But I am now convinced that the expenditure cannot be measured in terms of appreciable increments to China's offensive strength.
> Some straight talking ultimately will be necessary in our military relations with the Chinese Government. Chiang Kai-shek is a great man ... but ... his recurrent coercive forays should be met with rational resistance.
>
> — Magruder to Marshall[58]

AMMISCA was in China during the most critical era in the history of Sino-American relations. After Pearl Harbor there was turmoil in every world capital. In Washington, for example, confusion was the order of the day, and many decisions were made based on expedience dictated by immediate international and domestic considerations with little attention allocated to long-term consequences. Ignorance of other cultures and inappropriate priorities frequently predominated; indecision was common.

Amidst this unsettled environment, AMMISCA was tasked to implement procedures Washington felt vital to Sino-American affinity and to maintain China as a viable opponent of Japan. Despite the usually congenial working relationship between Chiang and Magruder the task was never easy; misunderstandings were frequent, frustrations constant, and decisions made in some areas that ignored "past practice." One of the most notable was Lend-Lease acquisition and distribution, where Magruder helped initiate a course of action that was to bear bitter fruit during Stilwell's time in China.

In this case Magruder's analysis and recommendations emphasizing the lack of proper utilization of Lend-Lease supplies reflected Marshall's own feelings and were regarded by the War Department as accurate, particularly when he was supported by Gauss, Lattimore, and the naval attaché. The reports, phrased in forceful terms, convinced the War Department and Stilwell that a harder stance on Lend-Lease supplies was necessary. They realized coercion was the only way the Chinese would accede to American policy imperatives, and this brought about the concept of quid pro quo.

Magruder liked the Chinese people, but as his assignment extended into 1942, he was forced to regard the national leadership in a more strategic manner than a humanistic one. Throughout his tenure, Magruder steadfastly maintained that Lend-Lease materials were more useful politically than militarily because they were not great enough in quantity to significantly affect strategic planning and outcomes.[59] He believed Lend-Lease would not do much more than help keep Chiang in power because the materials ordered by China Defense Supplies were consistently not needed, improperly employed, or senselessly stockpiled. Magruder's observations and recommendations were supplemented and verified by reports from War Department officers working with China Defense Supplies; the War Department officials reported that China Defense Supplies officials in Washington often altered AMMISCA requisitions.[60]

In early February 1942, Magruder advised Marshall that the Chinese army was so deteriorated that it lacked any offensive spirit and Chinese commanders hoarded troops and supplies and refused to fight. Magruder was convinced that the Chinese propaganda organization in the United States, sponsored by eminent persons including "missionaries, liberals, and radicals," was so influential that it was falsely convincing even conservative Americans that China was achieving a large number of military successes. The truth was that the Chinese were expending relatively little in the way of human or material energy, and it was "almost impossible" to deal with Chinese officials rationally. "They demand extravagant amounts in unusable kinds of military equipment with utter disregard for practical considerations" and persist "in seeking aid for new and often nonessential projects." Magruder warned that while he supported Chiang, the War Department should "be ready to oppose and temper his [Chiang's] frequently exorbitant demands with prudence and intelligence."[61]

Marshall reacted by asking for Ambassador Gauss's comments. Gauss enthusiastically agreed with almost everything in Magruder's report, adding that China was in danger of becoming convinced that it need not participate heavily in the war effort.[62] Magruder's proposal that Lend-Lease supplies be used as a lever to force Chiang to accept American policy and strategy[63] struck a chord with Marshall, who as early as July 1941 unsuccessfully advocated a similar approach to Currie and the State Department.[64]

Marshall told Magruder the AMMISCA observations matched his own estimates of the situation. Meaningfully, he said that Stilwell's orders would grant him power to initiate appropriate action regarding unrealistic Chinese demands for supplies and allow him to speak with candor and authority when dealing with Chiang. In this manner, the Soong-Stimson Accord that established the Stilwell Mission gave Stilwell a great deal of latitude over the allocation of Lend-Lease goods.[65]

This was the actual beginning of what evolved into the Marshall-Stilwell hardline policy of "quid pro quo" regarding Chinese requests for and employment of Lend-Lease goods. It included a warning to Chiang that Stilwell had authority and control over Lend-Lease materials and could restrict their importation and usage.[66] Thus, when Stilwell arrived in China the stage was well prepared for confrontation over supplies between the strong-willed Generalissimo and his new, and equally stubborn, American chief of staff.[67]

On March 15 the War Department advised Magruder that one of Stilwell's functions would be to supervise and control all United States Lend-Lease affairs for China. Less than two weeks later Marshall pulled back; he told Stilwell that no Lend-Lease goods were to be transferred or loaned without the generalissimo's endorsement. But he also ordered General Wheeler, chief of the Service of Supply, to divert or loan Lend-Lease supplies consigned to China only upon Stilwell's orders. In other words, Stilwell could effectively veto the delivery of Lend-Lease goods if he chose to do so.[68]

At this point a closer look at Stilwell is appropriate. Stilwell soon had the opportunity to demonstrate his power. On April 1 he became outraged over what he described as "craven actions" by some Chinese division and army commanders, nominally under his command. Because they did not participate as he ordered in a joint Sino-British attack, Stilwell felt he had lost a great deal of credibility with the British.[69] Two weeks later Stilwell (in retaliation?) asked Marshall to reduce Chinese-requested Lend-Lease supplies from 6,000 tons a month to 2,000. Stilwell as the Munitions Assignments Board's designated "agent" could not officially regulate how much Lend-Lease China could receive, but he could propose quantities to the board that would be given serious consideration. And because his authority came from Marshall, Stilwell's recommendations were almost certain to be approved.[70] The cutback in Lend-Lease supplies was not done solely to spite or intimidate the Chinese, as there were also transportation problems from India to China. However, given subsequent events and Stilwell's irascible nature, there is little doubt that he was somewhat motivated by the desire to warn Chiang regarding his ability to influence supply allocation.[71]

"At the end of April, the War Department suggested that Stilwell and the Generalissimo agree on China's lend-lease, and then forward a series of periodic agreed-on requisitions. Magruder [holding down the Headquarters at Chungking] answered for Stilwell, who was at that moment on the ox roads toward Myitkyina," leading the withdrawal from Burma. Magruder dismissed the suggestion as "nothing but a treatment for symptoms and proposed [a more specific] quid-pro-quo policy which dominated the War Department's view for months to come."[72]

Marshall and Stilwell's position regarding Lend-Lease supplies as policy tools was reinforced by a strong follow-up message from Magruder in early May. Magruder urged a doctrinaire approach and said the United States should state unequivocally that Lend-Lease materials were granted for the purpose of defeating the Japanese. He advised the release of excess Chinese Lend-Lease stocks being held in American staging areas to other theaters. In a rare assault on Chiang, Magruder said that the generalissimo was guilty of dispersing supplies "willy-nilly" or placing them in depots for future "selective use" against the Communists. Magruder recommended that Chiang be forced to agree to a definite planned use of all raw materials and manufactured goods.[73]

In late June and July, there was an exchange of strongly worded messages between Chiang and Roosevelt. On June 22 the War Department's Munitions Assignment Committee recommended that no consignment be made to China for July because the lack of transportation prevented its delivery. T. V. Soong somehow learned of this before it became public, and in a letter to Harry Hopkins, Soong repeated Chiang's time-worn ploy that China might "abolish the China Theater."[74] In late June, Major General Lewis Brereton's heavy bomber and transport wing was ordered from India to Egypt and almost simultaneously the A-29 light bomber squadron scheduled for China was retained at Khartoum. Chiang was outraged and demanded to know if "the Allies want the China theater maintained." Roosevelt assured Chiang of the "urgent necessity" of maintaining the China theater.[75] In response to Roosevelt's attempt to placate him, Chiang issued what came to be known as his Three Demands. Essentially they were an ultimatum for three divisions of American soldiers and a Chinese air force of 500 airplanes provided and maintained by the United States. The third demand was for 5,000 tons of supplies per month.[76] Chiang might be excused for making additional demands on his benefactor. After all, for months he had received false promises and disappointments. And with Roosevelt's renewed interest in the Soviet Union, it became more necessary for the generalissimo to obtain the Lend-Lease supplies.[77]

The White House took the Three Demands under consideration, along with a request made several weeks earlier asking that Harry Hopkins come to Chungking to discuss Lend-Lease and other topics.[78] The proposals were debated within the administration for weeks — much to the disgust of T. V. Soong, who told Chiang the Americans were stalling. Ultimately, in a strongly worded message, Roosevelt responded to both matters. He advised the generalissimo he would send Currie, not Hopkins, and was "greatly disturbed and upset" over Chiang's intimation that the China theater was not important to America. Roosevelt said the Middle East supply route had to be kept open or China would receive no supplies whatsoever. Therefore it was proper to divert aircraft and supplies originally intended for China to that theater. But then the president dropped a bomb. Referring to the fact that all war materials to China came from America, Roosevelt stated by virtue of the American "position," he intended to fill the role of Allied commander.[79]

Roosevelt's patience was obviously wearing very thin. He directed Currie to meet with Chiang and tell him that too many statements, behaviors, and requests emanating from Chungking were unjustifiable and unreasonable. It was the president's belief that Stilwell was in a better position to make "effective" requests for Lend-Lease requirements than any of the Chinese in Washington. Currie was to make it clear that even though the president wanted to hear the generalissimo's complaints, he was to "dissuade Chiang from making such requests (for additional supplies) as appear to be unreasonable or impractical."[80] Soong told Currie it was "too late"; nothing could be achieved, the situation was hopeless and beyond mere talking. Soong, who undoubtedly reflected Chiang's views, said he would deal directly with Roosevelt.[81]

Chiang persisted and complained that he was being forced to go to Stilwell and "beg for lend-lease supplies already delivered to China." Marshal, with the president's approval, informed the generalissimo that even if Stilwell were replaced, "any successor would have exactly the same powers over lend-lease ... and the same primary responsibility to the United States."[77] These messages to Chiang demonstrate that Roosevelt, during the summer of 1942, supported the "quid pro quo" policy.

That Lend-Lease supplies had become a substantial bargaining tool was demonstrated vividly on July 18. Undoubtedly with Roosevelt's approval, Marshall advised Stilwell that he could now officially use Lend-Lease goods as a political lever. From this time forward Lend-Lease shipments would no longer be made on an unorganized basis, and the shipment schedule would be reassessed monthly. The War Department could stop shipments whenever they would satisfy no further useful purpose.[83] This effectively strengthened Stilwell's hand as the commander. This revised policy received support from an old China hand, the second secretary of the Chungking Embassy, John P. Davies, Jr., and from Ambassador Gauss. Davies believed the Chinese government was overly interested in its own postwar perpetuation and domestic supremacy. It was therefore husbanding its military strength to come to the peace table as militarily powerful as possible. "It follows that the transfer of lend-lease supplies to China without any *quid pro quo* demand will result in the supplies being hoarded and not used against the Japanese, as is the intent of lend-lease legislation."[84] Gauss's views were similar: the main American effort should continue to be in Europe, and China should receive only such aid as was necessary to continue its resistance to Japan and "contain the Japanese forces now in China."[85] In late July Stilwell's hand was further strengthened when Marshall informed him that the War Department supported him beyond regulation of Lend-Lease supplies. If he chose, he could institute program recommendations, opposed by Chiang, that were designed to prepare Chinese ground and air forces to take the offensive.[86]

In summary, in early 1942 the Roosevelt administration initiated policies based upon Magruder's repeated warnings of Chinese improprieties in the ordering and employment of Lend-Lease goods. Following Magruder's initial recommendations, the War Department decided to use Lend-Lease as a means of pressuring Chiang to accept Stilwell's five programs. Roosevelt's support for this policy was repeated in his message to Chiang on China's national holiday, 10 October 1942. The portion of the message that dealt with Lend-Lease was clear: China had to do more in the fight against Japan; American warplanes, even those in the Chinese air force, would remain under American command; the United States would send no additional troop reinforcements; and Chiang should follow Stilwell's tactical and logistic recommendations.[87]

Chiang did not reply for over a month and then was equally brusque. He informed Roosevelt that he would organize the Lend-Lease aircraft in the way he felt most proper and if America could not send troops then he expected an increase in aircraft and prompt delivery of China's supplies.[88]

The Stilwell-Chiang relationship was never amicable, and its ultimate dissolution was at least partially caused by Stilwell's prejudicial allocation of Lend-Lease supplies. Conversely, the War Department believed that Chiang had too many times demonstrated an almost obsessive desire to obtain and stockpile materials, and not use them effectively. From the beginning, the members of AMMISCA were critical of Chinese methods and demands. Magruder agreed with many of their insights and recommended to Washington that a severe policy vis-à-vis Lend-Lease supplies be implemented. Historian Tang Tsou notes there were many American officials "in Washington and familiar with China" who seconded Magruder's perspective. "They were familiar with the high-pressure tactics practiced by the Nationalist government and the evasion and delay indulged in by Chinese officials." These American officials "were convinced ... that the only way to implement American policy ... was to use lend-lease ... as a lever."[89] Ultimately the War Department and Roosevelt concurred. The initiation of the "quid pro quo" policy, although it contributed to the deterioration of Sino-American relations in 1943 and Stilwell's recall in 1944, was an essentially successful AMMISCA-sponsored event.

12

The Culmination of AMMISCA

> General Eisenhower [assistant chief of staff] indicated that Gen. Magruder first went to China with the primary mission of administering lend-lease affairs but that the picture has undergone material change since December 7.
> — From the minutes of a conference held in the office of the Assistant Chief of Staff, War Planning Division, 20 January 1942[1]

Stilwell Takes Command

Prior to Pearl Harbor there had been no planning of possible strategic action regarding China except in a staff study. No comprehensive plans stated what the United States would propose as assistance to the Chinese if war came with Japan.[2] There was no well-planned program established for the China-Burma region until the end of 1942. Instead, President Roosevelt took over supervision of military operations. He did not earn rave reviews; for example army Chief of Staff Marshall at one point claimed that the president pursued a "preposterous course for military operations."[3]

Immediately after Pearl Harbor, the War Department initiated interdepartment discussions regarding the advisability of sending a high-ranking American officer to China to serve directly under Chiang. Magruder was possibly one of those initially considered.[4] On December 28, Roosevelt ordered that something be done to help the generalissimo's morale.[5] The next day, without consulting Chiang or the Joint Military Council, the Combined Chiefs of Staff recommended the creation of a China theater.

On December 30 Roosevelt sent a message to Chiang suggesting that he take over as supreme commander of the China Theater, subordinate to no one. The theater would include China and whatever portions of Thailand and Indochina that would be occupied by Allied troops.[6] High-ranking officers from the United States, China, and Britain would support Chiang as planners at Chungking. Magruder's name was not mentioned in Roosevelt's communication. If indeed Magruder was ever considered for the position later assigned to Stilwell, he held scant chance of being selected given that Marshall's confidence in him was slight compared to the esteem Marshall held for Stilwell.[7]

Chiang accepted Roosevelt's proposal and asked that an American officer be sent to serve as head of his Allied staff. General Ho Ying-chin would remain chief of staff of the Chinese army. Secretary of War Stimson's first choice for the billet was Lieutenant General Hugh A. Drum. Because some of Drum's views differed from Marshall's and Stimson's, and because he vacillated, he was rejected in favor of Stilwell.

Marshall held Stilwell in high regard as a tactician and a trainer of troops. He knew Stilwell was not a diplomat, but "as military attaché in China [Stilwell] ... had examined the mechanism of the Chinese Army and meticulously studied every Sino-Japanese battle of the 1937–38 period."[8] When Stilwell agreed to take command, albeit unenthusiastically, he was designated chief of staff to Chiang and commanding general of all the United States forces in China, Burma, and India.[9]

Stilwell was ordered to increase the effectiveness of United States assistance to the Chinese government and support the improvement of the Chinese army's combat efficiency.[10] He would also supervise and control United States defense-aid affairs.[11] Stilwell knew in January he would also assume Magruder's responsibilities.[12] Although this meant that Stilwell would administer Lend-Lease, it was some time before Magruder was informed, another deliberate slight by Marshall.

Upon his appointment, Stilwell reviewed the staff studies on China and conferred with Chinese officials and members of China Defense Supplies. He also reviewed Magruder's correspondence with the Washington Detail, especially the requests for specialists and equipment to train and outfit Chinese frontline divisions. After he completed his study, Stilwell asked Marshall to approve the following: that his contingent and all personnel who subsequently joined it would be called a "task force" to distinguish it from the smaller AMMISCA "mission." As it became available, enough material would be shipped to him to equip thirty divisions; and, if Rangoon were lost, supplies would continue to flow to India and then on to China on airplanes supplied by America. These requests were approved, but another proposal was not. He requested at least one corps of United States soldiers, approximately 35,000 men, armor, and artillery, to be assigned to him as they became available. He was advised that there was no objection to supplying China, but the personnel did not yet exist.[13] Nevertheless, Stilwell organized his staff on the basis of a corps headquarters.

12. The Culmination of AMMISCA

Before departing for China, Stilwell asked the War Department to allocate a "minimum" amount of machine guns, rifles, artillery pieces, and ammunition to his command. He was assured that the greater portion of what he had requested would be provided. With these assurances, Stilwell and his staff left for China and arrived the first week of March 1942.

He soon became embroiled in strategy planning with Chiang and a few weeks later went into Burma as commander of the Chinese Expeditionary Force, "where Chiang treated him exactly as he did his other commanders."[14] In Burma he was involved with but not responsible for the defeats suffered by the Chinese armies who were driven back to China. His plan was to go to Chungking and brief Chiang on the situation and request to be relieved and given an independent command. He left Burma on the last day of March. After his overland "walkout" to China, Stilwell's well-known comment was, "We took a hell of a beating."

From this time until he left China, Magruder was never sure what role he and the mission were supposed to be filling. He was furious and complained to the War Department over their failure to have him carry Roosevelt's message. Since Chiang would now be the supreme commander, and his own position would thereby be "modified," he needed further instructions regarding his authority over American units in Burma and China.[15] Magruder was told only that an army officer of "very high rank and prestige" would be sent to China if the generalissimo would accept him. He was informed that this did not imply any open lack of confidence in him, and he would retain control over Lend-Lease, although this was untrue.[16] What Magruder had no way of knowing was that Washington was still not certain who would command the new unit. There was a great deal of confusion engendered by General Drum's vacillation after being offered the command.[17]

After two weeks elapsed with no further information, Magruder requested further clarification. Until he knew what the United States' commitments to China and Burma were he could not formulate intelligent responses on questions "being posed almost daily" by the War Department and Chiang. He emphasized that he was the designated troop commander for the China-Burma area, but did not know what his responsibilities were.[18] The War Department did not directly respond. On January 25, however, he was informed that he was still slated to command all American troops and air units in China and Burma.[19] The War Department was probably not deliberately misleading Magruder, but playing a waiting game to Stilwell to determine AMMISCA's and Magruder's future roles.[20] There is no logical reason why he would have been told, a second time, on January 25, that he would be the regional troop commander since it had already been decided earlier that he would not become Chiang's chief of Staff.

On February 3 Magruder radioed the War Department with tactical recommendations regarding the importance of southern Burma. He warned that AMMISCA personnel in Calcutta reported a serious lack of preparedness there and that British officialdom was in a state of "somnolence" despite the Japanese threat to Rangoon. Thus, with the future of Rangoon in doubt it became imperative, if he were to act intelligently, that he be informed of the plans envisaged for American operations in this area. He also asked what the long-range command situation would be regarding American forces in Burma and China, and whether that area was to be a separate and subordinate command — presumably under his jurisdiction.[21]

In three days Magruder received Marshall's response. All American forces in China and Burma would be under "Stilwell's direction" even though Stilwell would be under the command of the generalissimo. And in an extremely trite manner, Marshall thanked Magruder for his various messages and suggestions. He did not provide any hint regarding Magruder's future.[22] Since Marshall disliked Chennault immensely, part of his animosity towards Magruder undoubtedly resulted from Magruder's constant advocacy of support for the AVG.

Upon his arrival in China Stilwell did not immediately assign Magruder to a specific billet, even though the secretary of war advised Chiang that Magruder would become one of Stilwell's "principal assistants."[23] In mid-March Magruder again contacted the War Department seeking knowledge of the future status of the AMMISCA group. Was the mission to continue under Stilwell's command and carry out the original directives of the secretary of war? If not, what was to be done with the AMMISCA personnel?[24] On April 9 Marshall ordered Stilwell to reassign the AMMISCA personnel throughout the China-Burma-India theater.[25] This message effectively terminated the January 4 War Department commitment that Magruder continue to supervise Lend-Lease.[26]

Soon after his arrival, Stilwell removed Magruder from all Lend-Lease responsibilities and ordered him to command the newly created Division of General Affairs, an inconsequential position that failed to take advantage of Magruder's experience and good relations with Chiang Kai-shek.[27] Despite his assignment to oblivion, in Stilwell's absence and several times at his direction Magruder was called upon for significant participation.

His responsibilities were not specified and he was given no real authority. This, of course, had a negative effect on Magruder, and several incidents followed that deepened his frustration. In early April, he inopportunely told

12. The Culmination of AMMISCA

some people at a cocktail party that he favored an end to America's "Oriental endeavor," an opinion reflected later in his early May recommendation to Marshall that the War Department harden its stance on Lend-Lease. Unfortunately he expressed it publicly, in an inappropriate environment, and in front of the wrong people. In addition, on May 8 when a Japanese column mildly threatened Kunming, Magruder recommended the formulation of contingency plans for an American evacuation of Chungking. This plan was so reminiscent of his October 1941 message regarding Kunming's security that it was strongly criticized by Gauss, Hull, Hornbeck, and Marshall.[28]

The events followed an earlier controversy centering on Magruder and the State Department. On February 10 he sent the War Department a detailed memo extremely critical of Chinese "symbolism" as expressed in China's "national escape-psychology." (Note the difference in this expression of Magruder's honest assessment of the Chinese "character" compared to the way Marshall had described him "as overly sympathetic to the Chinese people.") Magruder was perhaps subconsciously blaming Chiang's concern over Kunming, his lust for Lend-Lease goods, and his willingness to go around Magruder with Currie and others. He also denounced the biased and inaccurate manner in which the generalissimo was being portrayed in the American media.

The message contained comments supporting this contention: "She [China] has consciously given free rein to her native penchant for alluring fiction in Chinese propaganda abroad. People in other countries swallow glib untruths whole without realizing they are being deceived." And reports "emanating from Chinese diplomatic sources abroad, referring to the marvelous achievements and abilities of the Chinese Army ... are without foundation." Magruder reported, "Chinese officials demand such impossible quantities and such impractical varieties of arms and munitions that they are fast becoming a headache to deal with. Over and over again they recommend that air activity be carried on with Chinese landing-fields as bases. When they are politely told that no adequate transportation facilities are available for handling even a slight fraction of the tonnage needed for such air activity, they refuse to change their minds ... they continually demand aid for projects that are unnecessary and chimerical."[29]

Magruder related that there was little anti–Japanese activity, but areas evacuated by the Japanese were widely hailed as "a smashing victory for China. The American press has given absolutely disproportionate prominence to trivial engagements between Chinese and Nipponese forces." Although acknowledging that China could not "inaugurate a large scale offensive," because "she lacked the proper weapons," Magruder noted, "She herself is to blame for her failure to carry on a successful program of annoyance and attrition. The reasons for this failure are found in her own lack of aggressiveness and initiative, and in the age-long practice of Chinese commanding officers of regarding soldiers as static assets, to be conserved for assistance in fighting against their fellow-countrymen for economic and political supremacy." In this Magruder was prescient; Chiang Kai-Shek knew that after the war there would be difficulties in bringing the numerous rogue warlords under his control, and a considerably greater problem subduing the Communists. Hence, he stockpiled troops and supplies, for example the X, Y, and Z forces later outfitted and trained at Ramgarh, India. Magruder ended his memo by citing American domestic radio broadcasts that gave him "cause for great alarm" because of their "distortions of fact." He warned that "it is highly possible that such propaganda could lead to grave effects in American war plans if our own officials are influenced by it even to the slightest extent." Magruder's views were supported by other neutral on-the-spot observers.[30]

Only two days after Magruder's message to the War Department, the minister to the Netherlands visited Undersecretary of State Sumner Welles and read a message he received from the governor general of the Netherlands East Indies (present day Indonesia). The message's main points were made rather emphatically:

1. After Britain's initial refusal of large numbers of Chinese troops for Burma's defense, the imminent fall of Rangoon forced London to change its policy. Chiang was notified that more of his troops would be accepted but did not live up to his promise to provide them.
2. Even though the British were now willing to accept additional Chinese troops, the Chinese were not providing them.
3. Chinese inaction allowed the Japanese to remove five divisions of troops from China.
4. China apparently "has no idea of undertaking any large offensive before the Allied Governments undertake a major offensive."
5. In the minister's judgment, China had more than sufficient means to undertake an offensive but wished to wait until the end of the war, probably for political reasons.[31]

These observations although not intended to support Magruder, certainly reinforced his assessment of Chinese failures.

Of course, Magruder was castigated by State Department officials. The Chief of the Division of Far Eastern Affairs was Maxwell Hamilton. He said Magruder was "too close to unpleasant detail and ... [had] forgotten or overlooked broader aspects." But Hamilton, while acknowledging Chinese "incompetence," "inefficiency," and "confusion," cited no specific data to support opposition to Magruder's views.[32]

Stanley Hornbeck, the department's advisor on political relations, long a Magruder critic and dedicated supporter of Chiang, agreed with Hamilton that China was war weary and had been only meagerly supported prior to Pearl Harbor. Chiang was justifiably playing "national interest politics." He criticized those who had denigrated Chinese victories as less significant than they were reported, even while acknowledging it was actually happening, and claimed that allied "councils" had not provided encouragement to China. His reasoning: why should Chiang launch an attack for which he was not prepared, when the Allies were doing nothing? Hornbeck reacted to the Dutch minister's communication by linking it to Magruder's memo, which he unfairly characterized as "damning Chinese mentality and deeds."[33]

Hamilton and Hornbeck were full-bodied Sinophiles. But they were short on reality and long on emotion; China's sacrifices and standing alone against Japan for over four years were the paramount factors in their view, not the facts related in Magruder's criticisms. The Dean of American China scholars, John K. Fairbank, who worked with Hornbeck and knew him well, commented, "Dr. Hornbeck was a very vigorous and assertive, also canny person, and he worked the racket that all China hands have jumped or been pushed into — having esoteric knowledge denied to ordinary mortals. He had taught Chinese history in China but perhaps reflected a personal lack of self-confidence. "This successful experience had given him intellectual self-confidence on a very frail basis of knowledge and understanding.... His chief trait was a remarkable righteousness." Fairbank characterized Hamilton as a "rather colorless individual who followed Hornbeck's lead." Of peripheral import is that there was a near insurrection in the State Department over Hornbeck's "withholding vital information from [Secretary of State] Hull." This led to Hornbeck's finishing his career as ambassador to the Netherlands.[34]

Ambassador Gauss' opinion was solicited by Secretary of State Hull. Gauss acknowledged China was not physically or mentally prepared to operate in a major fashion in the war. He said China had made "extravagant requests" for Lend-Lease materials, and admitted China could do more in harassing attacks on lines of supply and communication.[35] Because Chiang was "irrevocably committed" to opposing Japan, he would not be supplanted. But "he seems in a measure to have lost his direct and active interest in military affairs in recent years and to have acquired a touch of unreality derived from a somewhat grandiose or 'ivory tower' conception of his and China's role in World affairs." Gauss supported Magruder when he affirmed "the American press has widely accepted and exaggerated Chinese propaganda reports ... which had little foundation in fact.... I agree that all this fulsome praise of China's war effort may have the effect not only of intoxicating the Chinese with ideas of their own prowess ... but also of inducing a greater complacency as to any vital need for real military effort on China's part at this time." In addition, he said the Chinese "have made extravagant requests under the Lend-Lease program and that they have exploited the existing situation in their recent request for a huge loan. It is also true that China is not making any all-out war effort on the military front...."[36]

Gauss was a thirty-four-year veteran of the diplomatic corps and chary of being left out of the communication loop. His first secretary was John Carter Vincent. Vincent's biographer, Gary May, states: "He [Gauss] was sharply critical of the way American economic and military planners bypassed his office in their dealings with the Chinese.... Gauss found it especially troublesome working with General Magruder and Colonel James McHugh, the Naval Attaché 'who had come to be regarded as the Assistant Ambassador' when he served under Nelson Johnson [Gauss's predecessor]. Both men were highly respected by the Chinese who often turned to them for assistance instead of to Ambassador Gauss."[37]

But in his response to Hull, Gauss empathized with the Chinese people's years-long opposition to the Japanese and said that China had to be accepted as it was even with all its "faults and shortcomings."[38] His final response came weeks later when, in a memo to Hull, Gauss estimated: "China is to us a minor asset at this time. Our task is to prevent her becoming a liability...."[39]

Less than a month after Gauss's report, the naval attaché in Chungking referred in a scathing manner to U.S. Senator Warren Austin's statement that "redoubling efforts to supply China" was the "quickest means of striking Axis." Or as the naval attaché put it, "Frequent public utterances similar to this uttered by prominent individuals lately suggests widespread belief in potentiality of China as an active military factor in defeating Japan. If such conception is seriously held by those controlling high strategy it is fatally defective. It is highly desirable to continue to encourage China to maintain morale but there should be no illusions as to practical aspects as to actual situation. Lack of China's offensive spirit, physical and political difficulties or transportation were continuously reported before the fall of Rangoon. The present situation is far worse."[40] Magruder's assessments, supported so emphatically by the ultimate truth-tellers, the men on the ground, were correct. Unfortunately, Marshall remembered China as it had been when he served there decades previously, and his support of Stilwell, who had been a star subordinate during that time, blinded Marshall to Stilwell's caustic nature, which caused his ultimate recall. Nevertheless, the advent of the Stilwell Mission

12. The Culmination of AMMISCA

was so imminent by the time of this controversy that Magruder and AMMISCA were has-beens.

Throughout his tour of duty as AMMISCA's commander, Magruder was under tremendous physical and mental strain. Colonel MacMorland described it in his diary: "Never have I seen so much authority [responsibility] dished out to an officer in the field.... They [the Chinese] are almost children at times and I am much concerned about the ability of Gen. Magruder to stand the pace. He seems much harassed by the tossing of babies in his lap from all directions and the distraction of attempting to act as mediator in the squabbles between the Chinese and the British.... There are so many of these things it is difficult to do any real military planning. More like political maneuvering."[41] Magruder was not unique. Clarence Gauss, as the newly minted ambassador to China, complained in July 1941, "I submit that no Ambassador to China can function intelligently and efficiently under present conditions without some background on what is transpiring through other than the usual diplomatic channels. For example, we are in almost complete ignorance of what is being done by way of aid to China under the Lend-Lease Act." This a reference to China and Burma being at the bottom of all priority lists.[42]

Magruder was forced to act as an arbiter between the Chinese, Americans, and British many times, and on more than one occasion he had to defend himself against false charges from General Brett, Gauss, and the State Department.[43] In addition, as noted throughout, there was a great deal of backdoor communication concerning Lend-Lease, the AVG, and other AMMISCA-related matters that were in place before Magruder arrived in China. The backdoor communication increased after his arrival. We should note, for example, Gauss' inference in November 1941 that Magruder was responsible for the misuse of Lend-Lease supplies at Rangoon in the days prior to the city's fall.

Magruder traveled frequently and spent long hours performing administrative and ceremonial duties. Disregarding career ramifications, he constantly badgered the War Department for critical personnel and supplies for the AVG, further aggravating Marshall. A bronchial condition he contracted almost immediately upon his arrival in Chungking was a constant distraction. The War Department's habit of ignoring his on-the-spot, and almost always accurate, situation reports, and the pressure of being at the eye of "storms" spawned by international forces he was powerless to control or influence, all contributed to his discouragement and occasional negative attitude.[44] There was also the matter of guidance from the top leadership. "Roosevelt so kept his plans and policies to himself that ... neither Army Chief of Staff, General George C. Marshall nor his military representative and theater commander in China, Burma, and India, Lt Gen. Joseph W. Stilwell [like Magruder] ever received a policy statement."[45] Perhaps worst of all — at least as far as Magruder was concerned — he was still a brigadier general even though the question of promotion had arisen on at least two occasions.

An unrelated event finished Magruder's tenure in China. In late spring, Magruder's doctor warned him that his bronchial condition was worse and could soon be severe. On May 17 Magruder notified Marshall that his surgeon recommended his immediate return to America for observation and treatment at Walter Reed Hospital in order to avoid a possible permanent disability. Magruder was undoubtedly worn out. As early as December 4, even before Pearl Harbor, MacMorland noted, "The General is getting quite fatigued with the daily grind. Visitors all have problems they want to shove off on him." Marshall approved Magruder's return the same day.[46]

Magruder did not advise Stilwell that he was leaving, because Stilwell was "unavailable" in India.[47] On May 18 Magruder did send a last message to Stilwell and left for the United States. Magruder noted that the original activities — for example the Burma Road — to which most of the mission personnel were assigned had been overrun by the Japanese. He felt that the retention of only a small planning staff was now necessary.[48]

Colonel MacMorland's diary notes, "General Magruder went through to Calcutta today en route to the U.S. to Walter Reed hospital.... Coudray [an AMMISCA officer] said he looked very sick."[49] Stilwell instead queried Marshall regarding the details surrounding Magruder's departure. Marshall advised Stilwell that Magruder had been unable to contact him and, thus, advised the chief of Staff. No personal assessments were included.[50]

Epilogue

From the beginning of our wartime alliance, American officials found themselves dealing with an ineffective administration too debilitated by its domestic problems to respond to foreign stimuli. Trying to aid it, we became entangled in its decline and fall.
— John K. Fairbank, *The United States and China*

During a short life, the Magruder Mission appeared to have succeeded admirably as a diplomatic mission. It established cordial relations with the Generalissimo and Madame Chiang Kai-shek, and its reports on the conditions in the Chinese Army proved illuminating to the War Department. However, the rapidly deteriorating situation soon brought into focus the necessity for a more direct and forceful approach to the problem of aiding China.
— Riley Sunderland and Charles Romanus, editors, *Stilwell's Personal File: China — Burma — India 1942–1944*

Confusion, politics, and greed: these were the major challenges facing AMMISCA during the period of operations in China and Burma. More than the physical challenges of unloading in Rangoon, more than the difficulties of trucking goods along the Burma Road, more even than evacuating Lend-Lease goods from a soon-to-be overrun city, it was the plethora of problems in dealing with the people — in Burma, China, and distant national capitals — that made the work of the mission unusually challenging. Further, AMMISCA was a pioneering effort, the first U.S. venture into military aid. There were no precedents to follow, no previous experience to provide practical guidance in the field or from the War Department, the White House, or others involved at a policy level. Further, military and political priorities placed little emphasis on the war in the China-Burma-India theater; it was a "Germany first" outlook in Washington and London; little serious attention was paid to AMMISCA's day to day activities. Planning and coordination of policy were lacking. Responses to problems in the field were often conflicting or unrealistic.

From the time it arrived in China, AMMISCA concentrated its attention on speeding up, increasing quantities, and properly employing Lend-Lease consignments. The mission was encumbered by politics, especially national goals, and bureaucratic ignorance in Washington, London, and Chungking. But it cannot be denied that Magruder and his unit made positive contributions to several significant projects. They worked to improve and expand the Burma Road's carrying capacity, mitigate disputes and congestion at Rangoon, construct the Yunnan-Burma Railroad, build an oil pipeline, build maintenance facilities on the Burma Road, and establish several alternate supply routes, such as the air and road routes from India and Iran. AMMISCA was instrumental in the sustenance of the AVG and its induction into the American military. The transportation system from Rangoon to Lashio and on to Kunming was expanded and improved through AMMISCA's efforts. The mission was also involved in the initial establishment of an air supply route from India. Regrettably, conditions well beyond AMMISCA's influence prevented the successful completion of some of these projects.

As early as the weeks following Pearl Harbor, the United States and China began to drift apart. This rift expanded significantly in the summer of 1942 when America could not or, as Chiang believed, would not supply China with the quantities of Lend-Lease supplies that the Chinese demanded and, in many cases, had been promised. In truth, Chiang and Soong's requests often bordered on the ridiculous. But in fairness to Chiang, he was promised much that was not delivered.

Up to a point one has to sympathize with Chiang. Americans bristle when commitments are broken, yet almost every promise made to Chiang by Roosevelt regarding date and quantity of supplies went unfulfilled.[1] The same was true in the realm of policy. As was demonstrated in the chapter on Rangoon, Chiang was told that all goods consigned to China Defense Supplies were owned by China the moment they were put aboard ship at an American port. But in the spring of 1942 promised airplanes were not delivered, promised supplies were cut drastically, and airplanes en route to China, and thus theoretically owned by China, were diverted to other theaters.

In the spring of 1942, Stilwell, as chief of staff, was ordered by Washington to allocate Lend-Lease goods, if he chose, to other areas without consulting Chiang, his immediate superior, who was convinced that the supplies belonged to him. During Stilwell's tenure, Washington imposed the "quid-pro-quo" policy forcing China to conform more closely to American wishes as to how the "made in America" materials were utilized once they reached China. As of 1 March 1942, requisitions from China Defense Supplies no longer proceeded to the Lend-Lease administration, but went directly to the

War Department.² The United States adopted a new Lend-Lease strategy for China based on recommendations initially proposed by Magruder. Simply stated, the policy became "If it's not paid for, it belongs to America."³ Marshall stated that Chiang be consulted for reasons of political expediency, but Stilwell wielded the major influence and informed Chiang that the supplies belonged to America until Stilwell allocated them.⁴ This was one of the causes in 1944 of Chiang's demand that Stilwell be recalled.

Chiang Kai-shek was a man easily disliked. His road to power was strewn with bodies of political competitors and opponents; few World War II historians outside of Taiwan praise him. The Kungs, Soongs, and other close associates, including secret police leader Tai Li, employed appalling methods to assure Chiang's position and power base remained secure. But for thousands of years prior to Japan's invasion in 1937 actions and policies employed by Chiang were customary methods of governing in China; to him it was reasonable and proper that the overall procedure continue.⁵ He came from a vastly different tradition where democracy was almost unknown and warlord methods carried more weight than votes. Therefore, the interests and goals of the Chinese and Americans often did not mesh.

From an American point of view, Chiang's requests were often exorbitant and ill-conceived, yet those who made this judgment assumed that Chiang's long-range goals were the same as America's, which they definitely were not. After Pearl Harbor, when China and the United States became "allies" overnight, all the attendant problems that coalitions based on political expediency inevitably produce came to the fore, not to mention the clashes resulting from traditional cultural differences. On several occasions only Magruder's unshakable concentration on AMMISCA's true role in China was instrumental in preventing a severe rupture in Sino-American or Sino-British relations.

This book focuses on the AMMISCA experience, particularly the points of view and perceptions of AMMISCA personnel (with the exception of Magruder) who saw the war through the unique prism of their own cultural realities and experiences. They reported and made recommendations that were heavily influenced by their own value systems and personal relationships with their British, Chinese, and Burmese counterparts. They were products of Western civilization and when international sides were drawn, for example in the *Tulsa* crisis, it was natural for race and common cultures to align.

The American Military Mission to China was a unique event in American history and a true pioneering effort. Although America and Britain discussed possible unified actions in the event of war with Japan, America and China never held such meetings. Thus, no appropriate prior planning took place and the mission was not prepared for the constant state of flux of the China-

Burma campaign. Magruder went to China under restrictive directives and with little flexibility. Worse, AMMISCA's efforts were beset by almost constant interference via back channel communications employed by policy makers, bureaucrats, and special interest groups.

AMMISCA was able to quickly establish a presence in Chungking, and Chiang came to trust Magruder as much as any other American member of the military except Chennault. Consequently, AMMISCA opened a Far Eastern listening and reporting post that also served as a valuable liaison center for discussions with Asian allies. Through Magruder's reports, Marshall was convinced of his own inclination to establish a quid pro quo policy to convince the Chinese that the day of the blank check was over. If China expected further Lend-Lease support, it must adhere to proper ordering and implementation as prescribed by Washington.

The mission began as an effort to aid China, through Lend-Lease. It was confronted immediately with many unanticipated severe challenges and understandably suffered several setbacks. Nevertheless, AMMISCA performed valuable services. Magruder's situation reports to the war Department were essentially accurate and described events and situations comprehensively. They conveyed information regarding British and Chinese attitudes and actions that was frequently missing or was reported from a different interpretative bias by State Department personnel, Currie, or the Chiangs.

The mission was necessarily divided into several small units stationed in three countries. By today's standards, their communications and transportation capabilities were primitive. Many historians refer to the China-Burma operations area as World War II's "Asian backwater." It was never an area where high-level, time-consuming, detailed coordination was considered essential by officials in London and Washington. Another reason allied cooperation was less than perfect was the extended Roosevelt-Churchill disagreement on the role of China after the war. Churchill hoped to maintain its sovereignty over parts of Asia, but Roosevelt had no such thoughts. The Allied leaders were all consummate politicians with unique personalities and deeply ingrained personal and national goals. Numerous Anglo-Sino-American projects were impacted and often hindered by this "we'll do it our own way" attitude.

Magruder was able to maintain positive Sino-American relations through several tense situations. He calmed several anti–British tirades as well as the generalissimo's anger at Twitty's pro–British actions. Magruder's positive relationship with Chiang, especially as an intermediary in Sino-British disputes, was of incalculable assistance to America. AMMISCA overcame the inertia at the General Motor's plant in Rangoon and increased production.

The unit's involvement in the evacuation of Rangoon helped salvage a large quantity of materials, a poignant reminder of what might have been if there had been less red tape and more allied cooperation. His influence with Chiang led to some realigning of the AVG supply needs. Adherence to proper ordering and employment of Lend-Lease materials and his persistence regarding integration of the AVG were definite accomplishments.

Upon his return to Washington, Magruder was assigned to Army Group, Washington, D.C., for duty at headquarters, Army Service Forces. He served there, officially, until October 1943 when he was attached, officially, to the Office of Strategic Services (OSS) in Washington. Actually, he became OSS Director William Donovan's "deputy" early in August 1942.[6] Several expert sources state that although he was not the founder, he was deeply involved in the formulation of the OSS. He later served as a primary figure on the transition of the OSS into the Central Intelligence Agency after President Truman declared there would be no "Gestapo" in his administration.[7]

In an 18 September 1945 letter to Marshall, Donovan described Magruder as having "made in the intelligence field an important and valuable contribution to this war." Marshall's response, through a subordinate, was vapid and uncaring.[8] Nevertheless, Magruder did play a notable role in the project transitioning the OSS into the CIA and was prominent in the agency as head of the Strategic Services Unit.[9] He retired as a brigadier general, the same rank he held when he took command of AMMISCA in mid–1941.[10]

The palpable lack of Washington concern for the China-Burma "backwater" extended beyond AMMISCA. Ambassador Clarence Gauss not only felt it; he reacted. Even before the chaos resulting from Pearl Harbor, Gauss told Secretary of State Hull that in all earnestness he felt he "could not function [with] present conditions" without more knowledge of what was transpiring through other than "diplomatic channels."[11]

In Churchill's opinion, Burma was one of the most horrible places in the world to conduct any kind of military operations or construct road, railroad, or airline systems; AMMISCA was involved in all these activities. The monsoon rains fell five months a year, tropical diseases were common, food quality and quantity were often inferior, and many non–Burmese were afflicted by what medical reports defined as "f.u.o." ("fever of unknown origin").

After the Great War ended in 1918, America devised a series of war plans, steps to be taken if war with a particular nation came about. AMMISCA's experience vividly demonstrates the inadequacy and need to expand that system. No plan is viable that does not consider alignment with probable allies. A familiarity with the anticipated cultures and geography of the area of operations is critical. Military officers cannot go to war with "how to" pamphlets in their pockets and be successful.

It is essential to assign a commander with authority to deal from a position of strength and prestige with his international counterparts but also with those above him in the military chain of command and those allegedly sharing a common cause such as the State Department.

The mission's experience highlighted the criticality of commanders and subordinates having a broad knowledge of the history and culture of the nation to which they are assigned. The author taught seminars on this subject at the Marine Corps Command and Staff College in a program that included international students. The seminar thesis——the need for familiarity with other cultures——was often questioned initially as to its value for military personnel (whose role, after all, is essentially to "break things and kill people"). The course included some incidents covered in this book, and by class completion there was almost universal agreement of the value of the material. The field grade officer students, most with master's degrees, came to realize that "other cultures" include likely allies as well as enemies, and that "ally" does not automatically connote "friend," "loyalty," or "obedience," or even "agreement."

Without AMMISCA preceding him, General Stilwell, although well acquainted with China's language, customs, and leaders' personalities, would not have been aware of many contemporary issues, including current Sino-Anglo-American matters, the numerous allied projects underway, and the forces of nationalism at work in China and Burma. Before he left for China, Stilwell spent hours studying Magruder's reports and recommendations. In going through these documents, Stilwell became receptive to urging the War Department to adopt a quid pro quo policy towards China. There is no way of knowing the individual impact of Magruder's documents on Stilwell, but it is quite appropriate to say that Stilwell's tenure would have been much more turbulent and less productive without the information provided by AMMISCA.

Chapter Notes

Introduction

1. Arthur Young, *China and the Helping Hand, 1937–1945* (Cambridge: Harvard University Press, 1963), 115.
2. Chiang Kai-shek to T. V. Soong, memo, 12 April 1942, *Papers Relating to the Foreign Relations of the United States* (hereafter cited as FRUS) *1942, China* (Washington, D.C.: U.S. Government Printing Office, 1956), 33.
3. Charles F. Romanus and Riley Sunderland, *Stilwell's Mission to China* (Washington, D.C.: Office of the Chief of Military History, Department of the Army, 1953), 7.
4. Romanus and Sunderland, *Stilwell's Mission*, 28.
5. Ibid.
6. Dorothy Borg, *The United States and the Far Eastern Crisis of 1933–1938* (Cambridge: Harvard University Press, 1964), passim. For additional information regarding the American public's concern over the depredations wrought by the Great Depression see William S. Leuchtenburg, *Franklin D. Roosevelt and the New Deal* (New York: Harper and Row, 1963), 18–14.
For additional information regarding contemporary (late 1930s–early 1940s) American concern over Japanese expansion and Asian economics see Warren I. Cohen, *America's Response to China* (New York: John Wiley, 1971), 125–136; Stanley Hornbeck, Chief of the State Department's Division of Far Eastern Affairs, memo, 9 May 1933, "Manchurian Situation," President's Secretary's File: 1933–36 China, Franklin D. Roosevelt Library, Hyde Park, New York (hereafter cited as PSF China FDR Library), 8–10; John R. Stewart, "Another Blow to the Open Door in Manchuria," *Far Eastern Survey* 7 (5 January 1938): 8–9; John W. Masland, "Commercial Influence upon American Far Eastern Policy, 1937–1941," *Pacific Historical Review* 11 (September 1942): 285; "The Fortune Survey," *Fortune* 23 (September 1940): 73; FRUS: Japan 1931–1941, I: 231; FRUS 1934, III: 163.

7. Herbert Feis, *The China Tangle* (New York: Atheneum, 1967), 42. John K. Fairbank notes that China was never more than a "low-priority sideshow" in the Pacific and "the American aim [was] merely to keep free China in the war" (John K. Fairbank, *The United States and China* [New York: Viking, 1966], 263). According to Cohen (*America's Response*, 153), "China was allotted the role of keeping Japan busy until the major task was completed in Europe." In January 1941, Roosevelt advised his military leaders that Europe would be the primary theater of interest if America entered the war. The United States would adopt a policy of defense, a holding action, in the Pacific (James M. Burns, *Roosevelt, The Soldier of Freedom 1940–1945* [New York: Harcourt Brace Jovanovich, Inc., 1970], 86, 87, 378–381; Cohen, *America's Response*, 153; Barbara Tuchman, *Stilwell and the American Experience in China 1911–1945* [New York: Macmillan, 1971], 214–215; Forrest C. Pogue, *George C. Marshall: Ordeal and Hope: 1939–1942* [New York: Viking, 1965], 354). See also Romanus and Sunderland, *Stilwell's Mission*, interview, 6 July 1949, with Chief of Staff George C. Marshall: "Asked in so many words, 'what was the President's policy toward China? Did he ever explain it to you?' General Marshall replied after some reflection that the policy was to treat China as a great power." See also President Roosevelt to Chiang Kai-shek, memo, 9 February 1942, FRUS 1942 China. See also Hornbeck, Division of Far Eastern Affairs, memo, 29 May 1941, FRUS, 651–656. See also Hornbeck to Hull, memo, stating that Britain received "98 to 100 units of Lend-Lease materials for every unit received by China" (FRUS V: 660–61).

Chapter 1

1. Memo, 30 June 1941, War Department Military Intelligence Division files, RG165, National Records Center (hereafter cited as NRC).

2. Sterling Seagrave, *Soong Dynasty* (New York: Harper and Row, 1986), 404.
3. Stanley K. Hornbeck, advisor on political relations, memo prepared at "Hornbeck's suggestion ... as comment on certain statements contained in a letter of May 8 from the Office of Production Management to the Treasury Department (not printed) and which went 'all over the Lease Lend organization,'" 29 May 1941, FRUS 1941, V: 656.
4. Burns, *Roosevelt*, 375.
5. Ibid., 83–87, 242, 248.
6. See Akira Iriye, *Across the Pacific* (New York: Harcourt, Brace and World, 1967), 243; Riley Sunderland, "General Joseph W. Stilwell," in *The War Lords*, ed. Sir Michael Carver (Boston: Little, Brown, 1976), 342–56; also see, for example, telegram, Chiang to Roosevelt, 19 April 1942, FRUS 1942, 33–34.
7. Burns, *Roosevelt*, 248.
8. Sunderland, "General Joseph W. Stilwell," 349.
9. Chinese Ambassador Hu Shih to Hull, memo, 2 May 1941, FRUS 1941, V: 640; Hu Shih to Hull, memo, 24 May 1941, FRUS 1941, V: 648–49; see also Charles W. Yost, acting chief, Division of Controls, Department of State, to All Collectors of Customs, memo, 28 August 1941, FRUS 1941, V: 717. Yost's memo notified the customs collectors that China Defense Supplies had been issued an unlimited (except regarding munitions) export license. For a complete list of Soong's early requests see Romanus and Sunderland, *Stilwell's Mission*, 16–17.
10. Romanus and Sunderland, *Stilwell's Mission*, 14.
11. John King Fairbank, *Chinabound: A Fifty Year Memoir* (New York: Harper and Row, 1982), 319.
12. Romanus and Sunderland, *Stilwell's Mission*, 26.
13. Ibid., 27.
14. Ibid., 15, 28.
15. War Department Adjutant General files (hereafter cited as War Department AG), AG400.3295 (4-14-41) Sec. 1A, NRC; Currie to Hopkins, memo, 25 April 1941, Hopkins Papers, China, Pre-Pearl Harbor, Box 305, FDR Library.
16. Eliot Janeway, "Roosevelt vs. Hitler," *Life*, 5 May 1941, 101–2.
17. John P. Davies, *Dragon by the Tail* (New York: W. W. Norton, 1972), 212.
18. Michael Schaller, *The U.S. Crusade in China, 1938–1945* (New York: Columbia University Press, 1979), 50.
19. Currie to Roosevelt, memo, 13 September 1941, Currie Papers, PSF China, 1941, FDR Library.
20. Lauchlin Currie, "Confidential Report to the President on Some Aspects of the Current Political, Economic and Military Situation in China," 15 March 1941, PSF China 1941, FDR Library; Leighton and Coakley, *Global Logistics and Strategy*, 85–88.
21. Currie, "Confidential Report to the President," 31.
22. Richard M. Leighton and Robert W. Coakley, *Global Logistics and Strategy: 1940–1943* (Washington, D.C.: Office of the Chief of Military History, Department of the Army, 1955), 85.
23. Currie to Hull, memo, 14 April 1941, PSF China 1941, FDR Library; Lieutenant General H. H. Arnold, Senior Member, Joint Aircraft Committee, to Secretary of War Stimson, memo, 10 May 1941, Joint Board memo No. 355, War Department ASF, Record Group (hereafter cited as RG) 160, NRC; Roosevelt to Currie, memo, 15 May 1941, PSF China 1941, FDR Library; Currie to Roosevelt, memo, 9 May 1941, PSF China 1941, FDR Library; Chiang to Roosevelt, telegram, 31 May 1941, PSF China 1941, FDR Library.
24. Currie to Roosevelt, memo, 10 May 1941, PSF China 1941, FDR Library.
25. Brigadier General Eugene Reybold to Chief of Staff War Department Supply Division, memo, 16 June 1941, WD-MID RG165, NRC.
26. See Leighton and Coakley, *Global Logistics and Strategy*, 85, 86; Arnold to Stimson, 10 May 1941, Lieutenant Colonel E. E. MacMorland, Defense Aid Division, to the Assistant Chief of Staff, memo, 20 June 1941, War Department War Plans Division (hereafter cited as WPD) 4389-7, NRC.
27. Major Edwin N. Clark to Lieutenant Colonel E. E. MacMorland, Chief of the Defense Aid Division for Lend-Lease, memo, 16 June 1941, War Department WPD files 4389-7, RG165, NRC.
28. Clark to MacMorland, memo, 16 June 1941. It must be understood that Currie, Reybold, and Clark all emphasized the necessity of keeping China actively engaged against Japan. Memo, "Chinese Aircraft Program," Currie to Roosevelt, 10 May 1941, PSF China 1941, FDR Library; Reybold to Chief of Staff, War Department Supply Division, memo, 16 June 1941, MID files, RG165, NRC; Clark to MacMorland, memo, 16 June 1941, War Department WPD files 4389-7, RG165, NRC; see also Currie to Roosevelt, memo, 3 August 1941, FRUS 1941, V: 361; Willys R. Peck, Division of Far Eastern Affairs, memo, 2 July 1941, FRUS 1941, V: 288–89.
29. Assistant Secretary of State Sumner Welles to Harry L. Hopkins, memo, 7 July 1941, War Department War Planning Division, 4389-7, RG165, NRC; Currie to Roosevelt, memo, 19 July 1941, PSF China 1941, FDR Library.
30. Brigadier General Wade H. Haslip, Assistant Chief of Staff, G-1, to Reybold, memo, 24 June 1941, War Department MID files, RG165, NRC; Brigadier General Sherman Miles, Acting

Assistant Chief of Staff, G-2, to Reybold, memo, 30 June 1941, War Department MID files, RG165, NRC. Both Haslip and Miles referred to the scarcity of China-trained regular army officers, noting that reserve officers would have to be found to fill the several billets.

31. Reybold to Chief of Staff, War Department Supply Division, memo, 9 July 1941, War Department MID files, RG165, NRC.

32. Ibid.

33. Lieutenant Colonel William Mayer to the Assistant Chief of Staff, G-2, memo, 28 October 1941, War Department WPD files, 4389-36, RG165, NRC; Gauss to Hull, memo, 24 June 1941, War Department RG338, NRC; Major J. M. McHugh USMC, Naval Attaché, Chungking, to Ambassador Gauss, memo, 24 June 1941, War Department RG338, NRC.

34. Mayer to Adjutant General, War Department, memo, 8 July 1941, War Department WPD files, 4389-11, RGl65, NRC; Gauss to Hull, memo, 24 June 1941, War Department RG338, NRC; Lieutenant Colonel F. W. Vogel, British Military Mission, Washington, to Brigadier General L. T. Gerow, WPD, memo, 19 November 1941, War Department WPD files, 4389-35, RG165, NRC.

35. In December 1941 at Rangoon the British seized large quantities of Lend-Lease goods invoiced to the Chinese. This is covered in the chapter on Rangoon.

36. Assistant Secretary of State Sumner Welles to Hopkins, memo, 7 July 1941, cited in Romanus and Sunderland, *Stilwell's Mission*, 28.

37. War Department's Joint Planning Committee to War Department's Joint Board, memo, 9 July 1941, J. B. No. 355, Serial 691, Records of War Department's ASF, RG160, NRC; Romanus and Sunderland, *Stilwell's Mission*, 29. For an opinion of how the mission fitted into the War Department's overall strategy vis-à-vis China, see Romanus and Sunderland, *Stilwell's Mission*, 30.

38. Letter, 11 July 1941, U.S. Army AMMISCA File, "The Magruder Mission to China," Office of the Chief of Military History, General Reference Branch, Forrestal Building, Washington, D.C.

39. Roosevelt to Soong, letter, 20 August 1941, Currie papers, PSF China, FDR Library; T. V. Soong to Roosevelt, letter, 7 August 1941, War Department AG file 334.8, RG407, NRC; Stimson to Chiang, letter, 15 September 1941, AMMISCA File, "The Magruder Mission to China," Office of the Chief of Military History, General Reference Branch, Washington, D.C. (hereafter cited as AF-MMC).

40. Currie to Roosevelt, memo, 27 August 1941, Currie Papers, PSF China 1941, FDR Library; Madame Chiang to Currie, radio, 30 October 1941, FRUS 1941, IV: 741.

41. Miles to Magruder, letter, 11 July 1941, AF-MMC, Washington, D.C.

42. Ibid.; Romanus and Sunderland, *Stilwell's Mission*, 70.

43. Gerow to General Marshall, memo, 3 September 1941, War Department WPD files 4389-17, RG165, NRC; see also Gerow to Rear Admiral R. K. Turner, Director, War Plans Division, memo, 28 August 1941, War Department WPD files 4389-17, RG165, NRC; Turner to the Chief of Naval Operations, memo, 3 September 1941, War Department WPD files 4389-17, RG165, NRC.

44. Biographical information on General Magruder is from the files of the Office of the Chief of Military History, Forrestal Building, Washington, D.C. His tour in intelligence and the contacts he established there paved the way for his post-AMMISCA career at the Office of Strategic Services and the Central Intelligence Agency.

45. John M. Magruder, "The Chinese as a Fighting Man," *Foreign Affairs*, April 1931, 468-476.

46. Magruder, "The Chinese as a Fighting Man," 468-476.

47. Magruder to Hornbeck, letter, 20 November 1931, Hornbeck Papers, Hoover Institution, Stanford, CA.

48. Major Nevin Wetzel, 7 December 1977; letter to author written by Mrs. Lucy M. MacMorland as she sat by her husband's deathbed (he was a stroke victim) in the hospital, 8 November 1977.

49. Letter to author, Lucy M. MacMorland.

50. Davies, *Dragon by the Tail*, 216.

51. Acting Secretary of State Welles to Secretary of War Stimson, memo, 8 August 1941, FRUS 1941, V: 696-698; Robert P. Patterson, Acting Secretary of War, to Magruder, memo, 27 August 1941, War Department ASF files 334.8, RG160, NRC.

52. AMMISCA 40, radio, to Chungking, 15 November 1941, WPD 4389-30, cited in Romanus and Sunderland, *Stilwell's Mission*, 29.

53. AG (AMMISCA), 210, cited in Romanus and Sunderland, *Stilwell's Mission*, 31.

54. Under Secretary of State Welles to Secretary of War Stimson, 8 August 1941.

55. Joint Planning Committee to the Joint Board, memo, 15 September 1941, War Department WPD files 4389-17, RG165, NRC.

56. Wetzel, letters to author; MacMorland, letters to the author.

57. Romanus and Sunderland, *Stilwell's Mission*, 32.

58. Ibid., 90-92.

59. Romanus and Sunderland, *Stilwell's Mission*, 43, citing HIS 330.14 *CBI* 1950; for specifics see Sliney to Magruder, radio, 10 December 41, AMMISCA Folder 4, NRC.

60. Romanus and Sunderland, *Stilwell's Mission*, 43-44.

Chapter 2

1. Maurice Matloff and Edwin M. Snell, *Strategic Planning for Coalition Warfare 1941–1942* (Washington, D.C.: Office of the Chief of Military History, Department of the Army, 1953), 410.
2. Matloff and Snell, *Strategic Planning*, 411.
3. Burns, *Roosevelt*, 133–134.
4. Matloff and Snell, *Strategic Planning*, 435.
5. Ibid., 436, 438.
6. Ibid., 435.
7. Burns, *Roosevelt*, 247. For a more detailed account of the Anglo-American view of China's becoming a member of a three-nation version of the CCS, see Romanus and Sunderland, *Stilwell's Mission*, 61–62, 158, 159, 160, 161.
8. Matloff and Snell, *Strategic Planning*, 428.
9. Ibid., 429.
10. Leighton and Coakley's *Global Logistics and Strategy 1940–1943* provides a comprehensive background to the evolution of the national and international need for great quantities of almost every category of weapons, munitions and all support materials.
11. Leighton and Coakley, *Global Logistics and Strategy*, 43.
12. Ibid., 44–45.
13. Marcus R. Erlanson, "Lend-Lease: An Assessment of a Government Bureaucracy," in *The Big L: American Logistics in World War II*, ed. Allen Gropman (Washington, D.C.: National Defense University Press, 1997), 265.
14. Erlanson, "Lend-Lease," 265.
15. Immanuel C. Y. Hsu, *The Rise of Modern China* (New York: Oxford University Press, 1970), 697.
16. Erlanson, "Lend-Lease," 273–276.
17. Ibid., 283; Leighton and Coakley, *Global Logistics and Strategy*, 251–54; Hannah Pakula, *The Last Empress: Madame Chiang Kai-shek and the Birth of Modern China* (New York: Simon and Schuster, 2009), 362.
18. Leighton and Coakley, *Global Logistics and Strategy*, 85.
19. Schaller, *U.S. Crusade*, 76.
20. Romanus and Sunderland, *Stilwell's Mission*, 13.
21. Edward R. Stettinius, *Lend-Lease: Weapon for Victory* (New York: Macmillan, 1944) 73; Matloff and Snell, *Strategic Planning*, 56.
22. Matloff and Snell, *Strategic Planning*, 75. See also Romanus and Sunderland, *Stilwell's Mission*, 40–41.
23. Matloff and Snell, *Strategic Planning*, 75.

Chapter 3

1. Burns, *Roosevelt*, 552.
2. Ibid., 551–52.
3. Joseph Persico, *Roosevelt's Secret War: FDR and World War II Espionage* (Toronto: Random House of Canada, 2001), 411.
4. Warren F. Kimball, *The Juggler: Franklin Roosevelt as War Time Statesman* (Princeton, NJ: Princeton University Press, 1991), 8.
5. Kimball, *Juggler*, 9.
6. Ibid., 10–14.
7. Ibid., 14–16.
8. Pogue, *George C. Marshall*, passim; Kimball, *Juggler*, 16.
9. Burns, *Roosevelt*, 84.
10. Ibid., 84.
11. Kent R. Greenfield, *American Strategy in World War II: A Reconsideration* (Melbourne Florida: Krieger, 1963), 49; see also pp. 51–55 for insights on other historians' opinions regarding how deeply President Roosevelt involved himself in military planning and strategy.
12. Greenfield, *American Strategy*, 51, 52.
13. Burns, *Roosevelt*, 79.
14. Edgar Snow, *Journey to the Beginning* (New York: Random House, 1958), 347.
15. Snow, *Journey*, 347.
16. Pogue, *George C. Marshall*, 157.
17. Burns, *Roosevelt*, 85.
18. Eric Larrabee, *Commander in Chief: Franklin Delano Roosevelt, His Lieutenants and Their War* (New York: Harper and Row, 1987), 511.
19. Larrabee, *Commander in Chief*, 511.
20. Schaller, *U.S. Crusade*, 94.
21. Thomas Hachey, ed., *Confidential Dispatches: Analysis of America by the British Ambassador 1939–1945* (Evanston, IL: New University Press, 1973), xvii.
22. Peter Calvocoressi, Guy Wint, and John Pritchard, *The Penguin History of the Second World War* (London: Penguin, 1999), 125–126.
23. Gordon A. Craig, "The Political Leader as Strategist," in *Makers of Modern Strategy: From Machiavelli to the Nuclear Age*, ed. Peter Paret, (Princeton, NJ: Princeton University Press 1986), 498; Ronald Lewin, *Churchill as Warlord* (London: Batsfords, 1973), 32.
24. Schaller, *U.S. Crusade*, 91.
25. Kimball, *Juggler*, 49.
26. Davies, *Dragon by the Tail*, 268.
27. Ibid., 268.
28. Mary Soames, ed., *Winston and Clementine: The Personal Letters of the Churchills* (Boston: Houghton Mifflin, 1998), 501.
29. Julian Thompson, *The Imperial War Museum Book of the War in Burma, 1942–1945* (London: Pan, 2003), 2.
30. Jonathon Fenby, *Chiang Kai-shek: China's Generalissimo and the Nation He Lost* (New York: Carroll and Graf, 2004), 238–239.
31. Hsu, *Rise of Modern China*, 672.
32. Charles Wertenbaker, "The China Lobby: The Legacy of T. V. S. Soong," *The Reporter* 6.8 (15 April 1952): 5.
33. Wertenbaker, "The China Lobby."

34. Ibid., 5.
35. Ibid., 6.
36. Schaller, *U.S. Crusade*, 55.
37. Pakula, *Last Empress*, 235.
38. Romanus and Sunderland, *Stilwell's Mission*, 34.
39. Ibid., 34.
40. Ibid., 33.
41. Theodore H. White and Annalee Jacoby, *Thunder Out of China* (New York: William Sloan, 1946), 117.

Chapter 4

1. John King Fairbank, *China: A New History* (Cambridge: Harvard University Press, 1992), 3.
2. Fairbank, *New History*, 3.
3. Ibid., 3.
4. Davies, *Dragon by the Tail*, 37.
5. Ibid., 37–38.
6. Ibid., 39.
7. Ibid., 42.
8. Wolfgang Franke, *China and the West: The Cultural Encounter, 13th to 20th Centuries* (New York: Harper and Row, 1967), 4.
9. Franke, *China and the West*, 22.
10. Dennis Bloodworth and Ching Ping Bloodworth, *The Chinese Machiavelli* (New York: Dell, 1977), 275.
11. Bloodworth and Bloodworth, *Chinese Machiavelli*, 275.
12. John Fairbank, Edwin Reischauer, and Albert Craig, *East Asia: Tradition and Transformation* (Boston: Houghton Mifflin, 1973), 179.
13. Fairbank, Reischauer, and Craig, *East Asia*, 195; John K. Fairbank, "Tributary Trade and China's Relations with the West," *Far Eastern Quarterly* 1.2 (1942): 129–35.
14. Fairbank, Reischauer, and Craig, *East Asia*, 198.
15. Ibid., 198.
16. Ibid., 199.
17. Ibid., 178.
18. Jonathan Spence, *To Change China: Western Advisors in China 1620–1960* (Boston, Little, Brown, 1969), 4.
19. Spence, *To Change China*, 5.
20. Hsu, *Rise of Modern China*, 217.
21. For a brief summary of the sequence of these events and the acrimonious outcomes, see Hsu, *Rise of Modern China*, 263–69.
22. Jonathan Spence, *Search for Modern China* (New York: W. W. Norton, 1999), 173.
23. Fairbank, *New History*, 208.
24. Hallett Edward Abend, *The God from the West: A Biography of Frederick Towns Ward* (Garden City, New York: Doubleday, 1947), passim.
25. Hsu, *Rise of Modern China*, 11.
26. Spence, *Search for Modern China*, 281.
27. Hsu, *Rise of Modern China*, 594.
28. Ibid., 595; for a description of the various philosophies and "isms," and "the new Cultural movement" that percolated for years in urban China, see pp. 595–602. See also Spence, *Search for Modern China*, 300, 302, 307.
29. In Russia, Joseph Stalin and Leon Trotsky were engaged in an intense competition to replace the ailing Vladimir Lenin. Each tried to manipulate the growth, political ideology and support of the Chinese Communists.
30. Fairbank, Reischauer, and Craig, *East Asia*, 700.

Chapter 5

1. F. S. V. Donnison, *Burma* (New York: Praeger, 1970), 75; Donnison, *Burma*, 58, 59, 60, and 63.
2. Hsu, *Rise of Modern China*, 365.
3. Ibid., 367.
4. For a detailed account of the confusion and corruption in trade system that evolved in Burma, see John L. Christian, *Modern Burma: A Survey of Political and Economic Development* (Berkeley: University of California Press, 1942), 226–38; Donnison, *Burma*, passim.
5. Donnison, *Burma*, 63.
6. Calvocoressi, Wint, and Pritchard, *Penguin History*, 999.
7. G. E. Harvey, *British Rule in Burma 1824–1942* (London: Faber and Faber, 1946), 82.
8. Donnison, *Burma*, 116.
9. Ibid., 116.
10. Romanus and Sunderland, *Stilwell's Mission*, 46.
11. Ibid., 46.
12. Fenby, *Chiang Kai-shek*, 209–10.
13. Memo, James McHugh Papers, Carl A. Kroch Library, Cornell University.
14. Christian, *Modern Burma*, 3.
15. McHugh to Ambassador Nelson Johnson, memo, 31 December 1938.
16. Hugh Deane in the *China Weekly Review*, cited in *Review of the Foreign Press* (Oxford: Foreign Research and Press Service Balliol College, 27 February 1941), 73; see also Joseph W. Alsop, *I've Seen the Best of It* (New York: W. W. Norton, 1992), 168–69; G. E. Stockley, British Consul at Tungyueh, China, to Sir Archibald Clark Kerr at the British Embassy, Shanghai, memo, 18 March 1939, War Office File 208/278, British Public Records Office, Kew, London.
17. Catherine E. Baxter, "Britain and the War in China, 1937–1945" (Doctoral thesis, University of Wales, Penglais Campus, Hugh Owen Library, 1994), 140.
18. Major John Russell, AMMISCA, Report on "Lease-Lend Supply and Transportation in Burma," 12 November 1941, POR 332, 970.
19. Mr. K. Selby-Walker of Reuters, 9 to 18

February 1941; extract from "Notes on a visit to Chunking, Kunming, and the Burma Road," War Office 208/298A, British National Archives (hereafter cited as BNA), Kew, London.
20. Ibid.
21. Ashley Clark Kerr, memo, 1 October 1941, Foreign Office Document FO 371/27657, BNA, Kew, London.
22. Seagrave, *Soong Dynasty,* 161; Young, *China and the Helping Hand,* 110.
23. Christopher Bayly and Tim Harper, *Forgotten Armies: The Fall of British Asia 1941–1945* (Cambridge: Belknap, 2004), 8.
24. Bayly and Harper, *Forgotten Armies,* 9.
25. Ibid., 29.
26. Ibid., 102, 103.
27. Sir Reginald Dorman-Smith, Governor of Burma, to Secretary of State for Burma, memo, 22 July 1940, British War Office WO 106/3540 NO 116813, BNA, Kew, London.
28. Dorman-Smith to Secretary of State for Burma, telegram, 21 July 1940, War Office 106/3540, 116813, BNA, Kew, London.
29. Calvocoressi, Wint, and Pritchard, *Penguin History,* 908; the reopening date was 10 October, China's equivalent of the Fourth of July. For an account of the views of Robert Craigie, British ambassador to Japan, to former prime minister Neville Chamberlain and the American State Department, see Peter Lowe, *Great Britain and the Origins of the Pacific War: A Study of British Policy in East Asia 1937–1941* (Oxford: Clarendon, 1977), 139, 141, 151, and passim.
30. Young, *China and the Helping Hand,* 115.
31. http://homepages.force9.net/rothwell/burmaweb/preparat.html.
32. Bayly and Harper, *Forgotten Armies,* 82.
33. Winston S. Churchill, *The Hinge of Fate* (Boston: Houghton Mifflin, 1950), 155–171, passim.
34. Australian Prime Minister Curtin to Prime Minister Churchill, message, 21 February 1942, Operations Division, ABDA Message File. Cited in Matloff and Snell, *Strategic Planning,* 130.
35. Rothwell, http://www.rothwell.force9.co.uk/burmaweb/BurmaArmy.htm.
36. Bayly and Harper, *Forgotten Armies,* 86.

Chapter 6

1. Memo, FRUS V 1941, 715.
2. Young, *China and the Helping Hand,* 110.
3. Ibid., 110, 111.
4. Ibid., 111.
5. Ibid.
6. Daniel G. Arnstein, et al., to Chiang Kai-shek, memo, 9 August 1941, Adjutant General file (AMMISCA), RG231.5, NRC.
7. Ibid.
8. Ibid., 4.
9. Ambassador Johnson to Hull, memo, 24 February 1941, FRUS 1941, V: 602; Hornbeck, Advisor on Political Relations, Department of State, to Currie, memo, 29 May 1941, FRUS 1941, V: 653.
10. M. E. Lloyd, Standard-Vacuum Oil Company, Kunming, to General Manager Standard-Vacuum Oil Company Manager for India (unnamed), Calcutta, memo, postmarked 1 September 1941, intercepted 20 September 1941, War Office W 208/311 114853, BNA, Kew, London.
11. Hornbeck to Currie, memo, 29 May 1941, FRUS 1941, V: 654.
12. Dorman-Smith to Secretary of State Craw for Burma, memo, 8 August 1941.
13. Young, *China and the Helping Hand,* 120.
14. Ibid, 121.
15. Gauss to Hull, memo, 15 August 1941, Harry Hopkins Papers, China, PPH, Box 305, FDR Library; Young, *China and the Helping Hand,* 120.
16. Currie to Hopkins, memo, 20 August 1941, Currie Papers, PSF China, FDR Library; Hull (Currie) to Gauss, memo, 21 August 1941, FRUS 1941, V: 710; memo by Yu Fei-peng, 11 August 1941, Harry Hopkins Papers, China, PPH, Box 305, FDR Library.
17. Gauss to Hull, memo, 24 August 1941, FRUS 1941, V: 715; Gauss (Arnstein) to Hull (Currie), memo, 21 August 1941, FRUS 1941, V: 710. Gauss to Hull, memo, 15 August 1941, Harry Hopkins Papers, China, PPH, Box 305, FDR Library; Gauss to Hull, memo, 24 August 1941, FRUS 1941, V: 715; Gauss to Hull, memo, 10 August 1941, FRUS 1941, V: 700.
18. Hull (Currie) to Gauss, memo, 26 August 1941, FRUS 1941, V: 716–17; Currie to Chiang, memo, 8 January 1941, Currie Papers, PSF China, FDR Library.
19. Hull (Currie to Gauss), memo, 26 August 1941.
20. Gauss to Hull, memo, 30 August 1941, FRUS 1941, V: 720.
21. Army Service Forces, Defense Aid Division, International Division (hereafter cited as ASF [DAD] Int. Div.), "China Lend-Lease," RG160, NRC.
22. Hull (Currie to Gauss), memo, 28 August 1941.
23. Governor of Burma to Secretary of State of Burma, 10 October 1941, memo, WO 208/311, 114853 BNA, Kew, London.
24. Hull (Currie to Gauss), memo, 28 August 1941.
25. Craw, memo, 10 October 1941, War Office 208/311 114853, BNA, Kew, London.

Chapter 7

1. Box 331: 9, 17, 15 August 1941, FDR Library.
2. Magruder to Adams, radio, 21 October 1941, WD-IDM-1941, RG160, NRC.

3. Magruder to Adams, radio, 22 October 1941, WD-IDM-1941, RG160, NRC.
4. Ibid; Magruder to Eglin, radio, 24 October 1941, WD-IDM-1941, RG160, NRC; Eglin to Magruder, radio, 7 November 1941, WD-IDM-1941, RG160, NRC. Tragically, Wilson did not survive the war; he was killed in an air raid on Mandalay on 26 April 1941. Radio, Magruder to Adams, 19 February 1941, WD-IDM-1941, RG160, NRC; Stilwell to Adams, radio, 19 May 1942, WD-IDM-1942, RG160, NRC.
5. Wilson, report, 28 October 1941, ASF (DAD) Int. Div., Country File, "China Requirements," RG160, NRC.
6. Ibid.; Magruder to Eglin, radio, 5 November 1941, WD-IDM-1941, RG160, NRC.
7. Wilson to Magruder, radio, 29 November 1941, WD-IDM-1941, RG160, NRC; Wilson to Magruder, memo, 13 January 1942, ASF (DAD) Int. Div., Missions Branch Project Decimal File 319.1, "Weekly Reports From China," RG160, NA.
8. Eglin to Magruder, radio, 4 December 1941, WD-IDM-1941, RG160, NRC.
9. Magruder to Eglin, radio, 15 November 1941, WD-IDM-1941, RG160, NRC.
10. Eglin to Magruder, radio, 19 January 1942, WD-IDM-1942, RG160, NRC.
11. Magruder to Eglin, radio, 6 December 1941, WD-IDM-1941, RG160, NRC.
12. Wilson to Magruder, memo, 13 January 1942, ASF (DAD) Int. Div., Missions Branch Project Decimal File 319.1, "Weekly Reports from China," RG160, NRC.
13. Ibid.
14. William S. Youngman, Jr., Executive Vice-President, China Defense Supplies, to Lieutenant Colonel John B. Franks, Chief, Defense Aid Division, memo, 11 February 1942, ASF (DAD) Int. Div., China Correspondence "Lend Lease," RG160, NRC; Magruder to Eglin, radio, 4 December 1941, WD-IDM-1941, RG160, NRC; Eglin to Magruder, radio, 1 January 1942, WD-IDM-1942, RG160, NRC.
15. Major Edward S. Hemphill, AMMISCA Washington Detail, memo, 21 February 1942, ASF (DAD) Int. Div., China Correspondence "Lend Lease," RG160, NRC.
16. Ibid.

Chapter 8

1. Radio, 2 January 1942, AVG file, RG332, NRC.
2. Russell Whelan, *The Flying Tigers* (New York: Viking, 1943), 47.
3. Chiang to Currie, memo, 4 January 1942, Currie Papers, PSF China, FDR Library.
4. Schaller, *U.S. Crusade*, 57.
5. Chiang to Currie, radio, 15 January 1942, Currie Papers, PSF China, FDR Library; Chiang to Currie, radio, 16 January 1942, Currie Papers, PSF China, FDR Library.
6. Pogue, *George C. Marshall*, 355.
7. Brigadier General L. T. Gerow to the Adjutant General, memo, 27 January 1942, War Department WPD 4626-7, RG165, NRC.
8. Magruder to Wing Commander J. Warburton, British Military Mission, Chungking, memo, 30 January 1942, WD-IDM-1942, RG160, NRC.
9. Air Marshal A. T. Harris to Arnold, memo, 31 January 1942, War Department WPD 4626-7, RG160, NRC.
10. Arnold to the Assistant Chief of Staff, memo, 2 February 1942, War Department WPD 4626-7, RG165, NRC.
11. Arnold to Roosevelt, memo, 4 February 1942, Currie Papers, PSF China, FDR Library.
12. Magruder to Adams, radio, 4 February 1942, WD-IDM-1942, RG160, NRC.
13. See letters from Joseph Alsop to Harry Hopkins, 1 September 1942, 10 December 1942, 22 December 1942, and 28 December 1942, Harry Hopkins Papers, "Chinese Affairs 1942," Box 331, FDR Library; Romanus and Sunderland, *Stilwell's Mission*, 252, 265, 323.
14. Claire Lee Chennault, *Way of a Fighter, the Memoirs of Claire Lee Chennault* (New York: G. P Putnam's Sons, 1949), 152-53; Madame Chiang to Currie, radio, 19 April 1942, Currie Papers, PSF China, FDR Library; Romanus and Sunderland (*Stilwell's Mission*, 112) state that twenty-six planes reached China, not twenty as Chennault claimed.
15. Chennault, *Way of a Fighter*, 152-153; Madame Chiang to Currie, radio, 19 April 1942, Currie Papers, PSF China, FDR Library.
16. Romanus and Sunderland, *Stilwell's Mission*, 113; Chennault, *Way of a Fighter*, 155-56; Stilwell to Adams, memo, 3 April 1942, WD-IDM-1942, RG160, NRC.
17. Romanus and Sunderland, *Stilwell's Mission*, 199-200; see also 14th Air Force History, Vandenberg AFB, http://www.vandenberg.af.mil/library/factsheets.
18. Romanus and Sunderland, *Stilwell's Mission*, 32-41, 152-57, 173-77; Pogue, *George C. Marshall*, 354.
19. In terms of the latter, see Leighton and Coakley, *Global Logistics and Strategy*, 526-42.
20. Memo, 12 November 1941, Port of Rangoon file, RG332, National Records Center, Suitland, Maryland.
21. Consul Austin C. Brady, memo, 23 June 1941, WD-IDM-1941, NRC; Brady to Hull, memo, 19 July 1941, POR, RG332, NRC.
22. Brady to Hull, memo, 14 June 1941, POR, RG332, NRC.
23. Brady, memo, 27 August 1941, POR, RG332, NRC; Winant to Hull; memo, 7 September 1941, POR, RG332, NRC; see also

"China: Burma Roadster," *Time*, 1 September 1941.

24. Brady to Hull, memo, 14 June 1941, POR, RG332, NRC.

25. Russell to Magruder, memo, 20 October 1941, POR, RG332, NRC.

26. Ibid.

27. Ibid.

28. Magruder to Eglin, memo, 22 November 1941, WD-IDM-1941, RG160, NRC; Eglin to Magruder, memo, 24 November 1941, ASF (DAD) Int. Div. Mission Branch Project, Decimal File 311.5–319.1, "China," RG160, NRC; Eglin to Magruder, radio, 25 November 1941, WD-IDM-1941, RG160, NRC.

29. "Customs Officers in Burma," Major John E. Ausland, undated unpublished article, used through the courtesy of Mrs. John E. Ausland, Palo Alto, California.

30. Aldrich to Magruder, memo, 2 November 1941, AF-MMC, NRC.

31. Russell, memo, 12 November 1941, POR, RG332, NRC.

32. Ibid.; Magruder to Eglin, radio, 22 November 1941, WD-IDM-1941, RG165, NRC.

33. Leland Stowe, *Washington Evening Star*, 31 December 1941, ASF (DAD) Int. Div. Mission Branch Project Decimal File 611, "Burma Road," RG160, NRC; see also Thomas B. McCabe, CEO, Scott Paper Company, Executive Assistant to Undersecretary of State Edward Stettinius, and deputy Lend Lease Administrator, to Roosevelt, letter, 13 May 1942, Harry Hopkins Papers, FDR library.

34. Brigadier General Sherman Miles, Acting Chief of Staff, Intelligence, to Magruder, radio, 26 December 1941, WD-IDM-1941, RG160, NRC.

35. Twitty, memo, circa 31 December 1941, POR, RG332, NRC; Twitty to Stimson, radio, 12 December 1941, POR, RG332, NRC.

36. Twitty to Magruder, memo, 16 December 1941, POR, RG332, NRC; Twitty to Hull, radio, 12 December 1941, POR, RG332, NRC.

37. Twitty to Magruder, memo, 16 December 1941, POR, RG332, NRC; Twitty to Stimson, radio, 12 December 1941, POR, RG332, NRC.

38. Hull to Twitty, radio, 17 December 1941, POR, RG332, NRC; Brigadier General L. T. Gerow, Acting Assistant Chief of Staff, WPD, radio, 14 December 1941, War Department WPD 4389–47, RG165, NRC.

39. Magruder to Twitty, radio, 15 December 1941, AF-MMC, NRC, Washington, D.C.

40. Twitty to Magruder, radio, 17 December 1941, WD-IDM-1941, RG165, NRC.

41. Magruder to Twitty, radio, 17 December 1941, WD-IDM-1941, RG165, NRC.

42. Wetzel, letter to author, 20 April 1977.

43. Brett's sympathies were clearly with the British — he was "appalled" by Chinese military methods (Tuchman, *Stilwell and the American Experience in China 1911–45*, 236–237).

44. Twitty, memo, circa 31 December 1941, POR, RG332, NRC.

45. On December 19 Brett radioed Washington that he had "advised" Twitty to "take immediate action to control and safeguard [Lend-Lease] material until definite plans for its use is decided upon" (Brett to Arnold, radio, 19 December 1941, POR, RG332, NRC).

46. Twitty, memo, circa 31 December 1941, POR, RG332, NRC.

47. Russell to Twitty, memo, 19 December 1941, POR, RG332, NRC.

48. Ibid.; Romanus and Sunderland, *Stilwell's Mission*, 60.

49. Magruder to Twitty, memo, 19 December 1941, POR, RG332, NRC.

50. Magruder, memo, 21 December 1941, POR, RG332, NRC.

51. Magruder to Twitty, radio, 21 December 1941, POR, RG332, NRC.

52. Magruder, radio, 21 December 1941, POR, RG332, NRC.

53. Romanus and Sunderland, *Stilwell's Mission*, 56.

54. Major General E. E. MacMorland, personal diary (in possession of Mrs. E. E. MacMorland, Wallingford, Pennsylvania), 21 January 1942.

55. Romanus and Sunderland, *Stilwell's Mission*, 55.

56. Magruder to Twitty, memo, 23 December 1941, POR, RG332, NRC. MacMorland's diary says Magruder and MacMorland met with Chiang at "5:00 P.M." on December 26 (MacMorland diary, 26 December 1941).

57. Memo of the first meeting of the Committee for Survey, POR RG332, NRC.

58. R. C. Chen, Officiating Manager, Southwest Transportation Company, to Twitty, letter, 21 December 1941, POR, RG332, NRC.

59. Ibid.

60. Minutes of the second meeting of the Committee for Survey of Chinese Government Supplies in Burma, 22 December 1941, POR, RG332, NRC.

61. Major Merrill and General Yu P'ei-feng, minutes of a conference, 22 December 1941, POR, RG332, NRC.

62. Ibid.

63. Brett to Stimson, radio, 22 December 1941, POR, RG332, NRC.

64. Magruder to Lieutenant Colonel Arcadi Gluckman, AMMISCA Detail, Chungking, memo, 25 December 1941, POR, RG332, NRC.

65. Ibid.

66. Magruder, memo, 21 December 1941, POR, RG332, NRC; Brett, memo, 27 December 1941, War Department WPD 4389–58, RG165, NRC; Magruder to Twitty, radio, 21 December

1941, POR, RG332, NRC; Brett to Magruder, radio, 21 December 1941, POR, RG332, NRC.
67. Magruder to Eglin, radio, 27 December 1941, WD-IDM-1941, RG160, NRC.
68. Ibid.
69. Magruder to Adjutant General, radio, 4 January 1942, WD-IDM Message File 1941–46, RG160, NRC; Secretary of State Hull to Consul General Brady at Rangoon, memo, 30 December 1941, FRUS 1941, V: 769; Ambassador to China Gauss to Secretary of State Hull, 30 December 1941, POR, RG332, NRC; Magruder, Memorandum for the Files, 21 December 1941, POR, RG332, P970 NRC.
70. Hull to Brady, radio, 30 December 1941, FRUS 1941, V: 769–770.
71. Hull to Gauss, radio, 31 December 1941, FRUS 1941, V: 772–73.
72. Marshall to Magruder, radio, 10 January 1942, WD-IDM-1942, RG160, NRC; Marshall to St. John, radio, 10 January 1942, ASF (DAD) Int. Div., Mission Branch Project, Decimal File 322.92, "Port Rangoon," RG160, NRC.
73. Magruder to Eglin, radio, 4 January 1942, WD-IDM-1942, RG160, NRC.
74. Magruder to St. John, radio, 27 January 1942, WD-IDM-1942, RG160, NRC.
75. Magruder to Eglin; British Military Mission, Chungking, to Magruder, memo, 31 December 1941, POR, RG332, NRC; General Dennys to the British Ambassador to China, memo, 9 January 1942, WD-IDM-1942, RG160, NRC; Anthony Eden, British Foreign Secretary, to Lord Halifax, British Ambassador to America, memo, 12 January 1942, ASF (DAD) Int. Div., Mission Branch Project, Decimal File 322.92, RG160, NRC.
76. MacMorland diary, 20 and 21 January 1942.
77. Twitty, memo, circa 31 December 1941, POR 332, 970 NRC.
78. St. John to Magruder, radio, 6 January 1942, WD-IDM-1942, RG160, NRC.
79. Adams to Magruder, radio, 11 January 1942, WD-IDM-1942, RG160, NRC.
80. Magruder to St. John, radio, 10 January 1942, WD-IDM-1942 RG160, NRC; Adams to Magruder, radio, 28 January 1942, WD-IDM-1942, RG160, NRC.
81. Brett to Stimson, radio, 28 December 1941, POR, RG332, NRC.
82. Magruder to St. John, radio, 12 January 1942, WD-IDM-1942, RG160, NRC.
83. MacMorland diary, 6 February 1942.
84. For a description of the British Order of Battle in Burma (assets and personnel) see British historian Steve Rothwell's "Preparations for War" (http://www.rothwell.force9.co.uk/burmaweb/preparat.htm) and "Burma Army 1937–1942" (http://www.rothwell.force9.co.uk/burmaweb/BurmaArmy.htm).

85. Lieutenant General H. C. B. Wemyss, Head, British Military Mission to Washington, memo, 2 January 1942, War Department WPD 4389-57, RG165, NRC.
86. St. John to Magruder, radio, 24 January 1942, WD-IDM-1942, RG160, NRC.
87. Magruder to St. John, radio, 27 January 1942, WD-IDM-1942, RG160, NRC.
88. St. John to Magruder, radio, 30 January 1942, WD-IDM-1942, RG160, NRC.
89. Magruder to Major Paul L. Freeman, Jr., letter, 5 February 1942, WD-IDM-1942, RG160, NRC.
90. Dennys to General Ho Ying-chin, Minister for War, memo, 19 January 1942, POR, RG332, NRC; Dennys to Ho, memo, 22 January 1942, POR, RG332, NRC; Dennys to General Shang Chen, memo, 31 January 1942, POR, RG332, NRC; Dennys to General Shang Chen, memo, 5 February 1942, POR, RG332, NRC; Dennys to Ho, memo, 10 February 1942, POR, RG332, NRC.
91. Dennys to General Ho, memo, 19 January 1942, POR, RG332, NRC; Dennys to General Shang Chen, memo, 31 January 1942, POR, RG332, NRC; General Ho to Magruder, memo, 14 February 1942, WD-IDM-1942, RG160, NRC.
92. General Ho to Magruder, memo, 14 February 1942, WD-IDM-1942, RG160, NRC; General Ho to Magruder, memo, 21 February 1942, POR, RG332, NRC.
93. Brett, memo, 27 December 1941, WD-IDM-1941, RG160, NRC.
94. St. John to Magruder, radio, 24 January 1942, WD-IDM-1942, RG160, NRC. For a description of the difficulties encountered by Major Paul Freeman in establishing and administrating the AMMISCA office in Calcutta, see Major Paul L. Freeman, Jr., to Magruder, letters, 21, 24, and 26 January 1942, POR, RG332, NRC.
95. Magruder to St. John, radio, 25 January 1942, WD-IDM-1942, RG160, NRC.
96. Magruder to Eglin, radio, 26 January 1942, WD-IDM-1942, RG160, NRC. For a detailed account of the Malay and Burma campaigns see B. H. Liddell Hart, *History of the Second World War* (New York: G. P. Putnam, 1970), 226–229, 234–236.
97. Magruder to Eglin, radio, 27 January 1942, WD-IDM-1942, RG160, NRC.
98. St. John to Magruder, radio, 30 January 1942, WD-IDM-1942, RG160, NRC; St. John to Eglin, radio, 29 January 1942, ASF (DAD) Int. Div. Mission Branch Project, Decimal File 322.92, NRC.
99. St. John to Eglin, radio, 29 January 1942, ASF (DAD) Int. Div. Mission Branch Project, Decimal File 322.92, NA; St. John to Magruder, memo, 12 April 1942, WD-IDM-1942, RG160, NRC; Wilson to Magruder, memo, 10 February 1942, POR, RG332, NRC.

100. For an additional account into AMMISCA's participation in the evacuation of Rangoon, see Daniel Ford, *Flying Tigers: Claire Chennault and the American Volunteer Group* (Washington, D.C.: Smithsonian Institute Press, 1991), 231.
101. Wilson to Magruder, memo, 10 February 1942, POR, RG332, NRC.
102. Ibid.; Magruder to Adams, radio, 19 February 1942, ASF (DAD) Int. Div. Mission Branch Project, Decimal File 322.92, RG160, NRC.
103. Magruder to Eglin, radio, 31 January 1942, WD-IDM-1942, RG160, NRC.
104. St. John to Adams, radio, 14 February 1942, ASF (DAD) Int. Div. Country File, "China Correspondence," "Lend-Lease," RGl65, NRC.
105. Brigadier General II. S. Aurand, Defense Aid Director, memo, 19 February 1942, ASF (DAD) Int. Div. Country File, "China Correspondence," "Lend-Lease," RG165, NRC.
106. Madame Chiang to Currie, cable, 25 April 1942, Currie Papers, FDR Library.
107. Soong to McCloy, memo, 12 February 1942, ASF (DAD) Int. Div. Country File, "China Correspondence" "Lend-Lease," RG160, NRC.
108. Magruder to Adams, radio, 12 February 1942, War Department G-2 file, Box 62, China/Chungking, RG319, NRC; Liddell Hart, *History*, 234–35.
109. St. John to Magruder, memo, 12 April 1942, WD-IDM-1942, RG160, NRC.
110. Nevin Wetzel, letter to author, 27 March 1977.
111. Gerald Astor, *The Jungle War: Mavericks, Marauders, and Madmen in the China-Burma-India Theater of World War II* (New York: John: Wiley, 2004), 64.
112. Bayly and Harper, *Forgotten Armies*, 166.
113. Magruder to Adams, radio, 6 March 1942, WD-IDM-1942, RG160, NRC.
114. Stilwell, Commanding General American Forces in China, Burma and India from Colonel Adrian St. John, CO Rangoon Unit American Military Mission, memo, 12 April 1942, POR, AMMISCA file.

Chapter 9

1. Letter, 9 October 1941, Harry Hopkins Papers, China, Box 305, FDR Library.
2. Stettinius, *Lend-Lease*, 113.
3. J. P. Sanger, Assistant Director of Purchases, Office of Production Management, to Clifton E. Mack, Director of Procurement, Department of the Treasury, memo, 8 May 1941, Harry Hopkins Papers, PPH, Box 305, FDR Library; see also "Burma Road Bottleneck," *Far Eastern Survey*, April 1941, 63; "Far Eastern Press Notes," *Far Eastern Survey*, 5 May 1941, 95; Reybold memo, 16 June 1941, War Department MID files, Tab A, RG165, NRC; report to Chiang Kai-shek by Daniel G. Arnstein, et al., 9 August 1941, Harry Hopkins Papers, "Chinese Affairs," 1941–1942, Box 331, FDR Library; see also Pei-ying Tan, *The Building of the Burma Road* (New York: McGraw Hill, 1945), 15–17, 124, 157, 158.
4. American Embassy, Office of the Military Attaché, to the Assistant Chief of Staff, G-2 War Department, memo, 31 May 1941, MID files, RG165, NRC.
5. Ibid.
6. American Embassy, Office of the Military Attaché, to the Assistant Chief of Staff, G-2, War Department, memo, 6 April 1941; War Department ID files, RG165, NRC; see also memo, American Embassy, Office of the Military Attaché, to the Assistant Chief of Staff, G-2, War Department, 7 March 1941, War Department MID files, RG165, NRC.
7. Memo, 31 October 1941, ASF (DAD) Int. Div., Missions Branch Project, Decimal File 311.5–319.1 China, "Weekly Reports from China," RG160, NRC.
8. Eglin to Magruder, radio, 16 October 1941, WD-IDM-1941, RG160, NRC; Magruder to Eglin, radio, 21 October 1941, WD-IDM-1941, RG160, NRC; Eglin to Magruder, radio, 28 October 1941, WD-IDM-1941, RG160, NRC; Eglin to Magruder, radio, 23 November 1941, WD-IDM-1941, RG160, NRC.
9. Magruder to Eglin, radio, 13 February 1941, WD-IDM-1941, RG160, NRC; Stilwell to Adams, radio, 4 April 1942, WD-IDM-1942, RG160, NRC; Lieutenant Colonel Brehon B. Somervell, Chungking Detail, to Stilwell, radio, 14 April 1941, WD-IDM-1941, RG160, NRC; Lieutenant Colonel Paul I. Robinson, Assistant Surgeon General, to Washington detail, memo, 13 April 1941, WD-IDM-1941, RG160, NRC.
10. Eglin to Magruder, radio, 8 October 1941, WD-IDM-1941, RGl60, NRC.
11. Eglin to Magruder, radio, 31 October 1941, WD-IDM-1941, RG160, NRC; Wetzel, letter to author; American Consul at Rangoon, radio, 27 August 1941, WD-IDM-1941, RG160, NRC.
12. Eglin to Magruder, radio, 31 October 1941, WD-IDM-1941, NRC; Eglin to Magruder, radio, 4 November 1941, WD-IDM-1941, NRC.
13. Magruder to Eglin, radio, 20 November 1941, WD-IDM-1941, RG160, NRC; see also Eglin to Magruder, radio, 4 November 1941, WD-IDM-1941, RG160, NRC; Eglin to Colonel E. Santschi, Office of the Quartermaster General, memo, 25 November 1941, ASF (DAD) Int. Div., Country File, "China Correspondence" "Lend Lease," RG160, NRC.
14. Eglin to Magruder, radio, 27 November 1941, WD-IDM-RG160, NRC.
15. Magruder to Eglin, radio, 4 December

941, WD-IDM-1941, RG160, NRC, 1942, ASF (DAD) Int. Div., Missions Branch Project, Decimal File 319.1, "Weekly Reports from China," RG160, NA; St. John to Adams, radio, 12 February 1942, ASF (DAD) Int. Div., Mission Branch Project, Decimal File 322.92, RG160, NA; Adams to Magruder, radio, 16 February 1942, WD-IDM-1942, RG160, NRC.

16. From an unsigned memo, probably written by Magruder or Major Wilson, attached to the China Detail's copy of a radio message from Eglin to Magruder, 27 November 1941 (WD-IDM-1941, RG160, NRC).

17. Magruder to Eglin, radio, 11 January 1941, WD-IDM-1941 RG160, NRC; "Doubling Burma Road Load," *New York Times*, 18 January 1942, 8; Colonel E. Santschi, Jr., Assistant Quartermaster General, to the Quartermaster General, memo, 2 January 1941, ASF (DAD) Int. Div., Country File "China-Correspondence," RG160, NRC.

18. Covered in detail in a previous chapter.

19. Magruder to Eglin, radio, 11 January 1942, WD-IDM-1942, RG160, NRC; Eglin to Magruder, radio, 11 January 1942, WD-IDM-1942, RG160, NRC.

20. Author's conversations with Charles Romanus, April 1978.

21. For a detailed account of the tactics and events of the early phase of the Japanese invasion of Burma, see Major-General S. Woodlawn Kirby, *The War Against Japan*, vol. 2 (Uckfield, East Sussex, UK: Naval and Military Press, 2004), 1–46, 59–104; see also Bayly and Harper, *Forgotten Armies*, passim.

22. Eglin to Magruder, radio, 25 January 1942, WD-IDM-1942, RG160, NRC; Eglin to Magruder, radio, 29 January 1942, WD-IDM-1942, RG160, NRC.

23. Marshall to Magruder, radio, 7 February 1942, WD-IDM-1942, RG160, NRC.

24. Magruder to Eglin, radio, 10 February 1942, WD-IDM-1942, RG160, NRC.

25. Magruder to Adams, radio, 19 February 1942, WD-IDM-1942, RG160, NRC.

26. Magruder to Adams, radio, 12 February 1942, WD-IDM-1942, RG160, NRC; MacMorland to Adams, radio, 23 February 1942, WD-IDM-1942, RG160, NRC.

27. Adams to Magruder, radio, 25 February 1942, WD-IDM-1942, RG160, NRC; Adams to Magruder, radio, 27 February 1942, WD-IDM-1942, RGl60, NRC.

28. MacMorland to Adams, radio, 3 March 1942, WD-IDM-1942, RG160, NRC.

29. Magruder to Quartermaster General, memo, 7 March 1942, WD-IDM-1942, RG160, NRC.

30. Baxter, "Britain and the War in China," 274, Citing Foreign Office memo, circa February 1938, FO 371.23513.

31. For a detailed account of the discussions at and within the War and Foreign offices, see Baxter, "Britain and the War in China," 273–76, 319.

32. Romanus and Sunderland, *Stilwell's Mission*, 46–47.

33. Memo, 21 December 194, War Office, British Archives, Kew, 106/3540, 11613.

34. Romanus and Sunderland, *Stilwell's Mission*, 15.

35. Department of State to the British Embassy, Aide-memoire, 28 February 1941, FRUS 1941, V: 603.

36. Welles to Hull, memo, 28 February 1941, FRUS 1941, V: 604–5.

37. Legal Advisor Hackworth to Hamilton, Chief of the Division of Far Eastern Affairs, memo, 25 March 1941, FRUS 1941, V: 615–16.

38. Johnson to Hull, memo, 26 March 1941, FRUS 1941, V: 617.

39. George P. Jan, "Public Opinion and American Policy toward the Sino-Japanese War, 1937–1945," paper presented at the 18th annual meeting of the American Association for Chinese Studies, St. Louis, MO, 5 November 1976.

40. Major L. T. Ross, Chief, Railway Section, Corps of Engineers, to Assistant Secretary of War Patterson, memo, 25 April 1941, ASF (DAD) Int. Div., Country File, "China Lend-Lease Railroad Requirements," RG160, NRC; memo, Morgenthau to Welles, 25 April 1941, FRUS 1941, V: 634.

41. Major General Haydon Boatner, USA (Ret.), letters to the author, April 1977.

42. Ibid.

43. Ibid.

44. Ibid.

45. Ross to Patterson, memo, 25 April 1941, ASF (DAD) Int. Div., Country File, "China Lend-Lease Railroad Requirements," RG160, NRC.

46. Tseng also allegedly knew how to take care of himself. He "formed a corporation to control all mineral rights within 50 miles of the railroad upon its completion" (Nevin Wetzel, "The Old Gray Major," *Ex-CBI Roundup* 30 (November 1975): 10; the author of this article, Wetzel, was the only American assistant to Major John Ausland, the chief AMMISCA advisor to the Burma-Yunnan Railroad project).

47. Wetzel, "The Old Gray Major."

48. Major John S. Ausland, "South of the Clouds," *Ex-CBI Roundup* 28 (July 1973): 22. William E. Jellison, an entomologist, served with the medical teams sent out by the American Public Health Service. In a letter to the author, April 1977, he noted that, to his knowledge, workers on the middle section of the railroad were supplied with food by their home villages and never received any pay from the federal government during the several months he spent with them in the spring of 1942.

49. William L. Jellison, "Malaria Was an Enemy," *Ex-CBI Roundup* 30 (March 1976): 8.

50. Jellison, "Malaria Was an Enemy," 9.
51. Ausland, "The Details ... Are Left to You," *Ex-CBI Roundup* 26 (January 1971): 18–19; letter from *Life* magazine reporter George Rodger to his editor, 1 March 1942, ASF (DAD) Int. Div., Country File, "China Correspondence," RG160, NRC. See also Tan, *Building of the Burma Road*, 72–80.
52. George Rodger, letter to *Life*, [DATE], 2.
53. Ausland, "The Details ... Are Left to You," 19. Magruder put the figure at 1,150 (report by Magruder to Major L. T. Ross, 8 April 1942, ASF [DAD] Int. Div., Decimal File 453, "Yunnan and Burma Railroad, RG160, NRC).
54. Major John E. Ausland, "South of the Clouds," 21.
55. Dr. Victor H. Haas, Federal Security Agency, U.S. Public Health Service, National Institute of Health, to Dr. Dyer, Director of National Institute of Health, U.S. Public Health Service, memo, 25 July 1942 (memo provided to author 21 April 1977 by Dr. William Jellison, a staff member of the Haas group who became an AMMISCA officer and served in China for three years).
56. Lieutenant Nevin Wetzel (Major Ausland's assistant), personal diary and notes, Salt Lake City, Utah; see also memorandum by Acheson, Assistant Chief of the Division of Far Eastern Affairs, of a conversation whose participants included Acheson, Dr. Paul M. Stewart, Assistant Surgeon General, U.S. Public Health Service, and Dr. Victor H. Haas, U.S. Public Health Service, FRUS 1941, V: 678–79.
57. Rodger, letter to *Life*, 2.
58. Ausland, "The Details ... Are Left to You," 21.
59. Eglin to Magruder, radio, 19 November 1941, WD-IDM-1941, RG160, NRC.
60. Magruder to Eglin, radio, 3 December 1941, WD-IDM-1941, RG160, NRC.
61. Letter to author from Nevin Wetzel, April 1977.
62. Ausland, "The Details ... Are Left to You," 11.
63. Romanus and Sunderland, *Stilwell's Mission*, 47.
64. Ausland, "South of the Clouds," 18.
65. Eglin to Magruder, radio, 8 October 1941, WD-IDM-1941, RG160, NRC.
66. Eglin to Magruder, radio, 29 November 1941, WD-IDM-1941, RG160, NRC.
67. Ausland, "South of the Clouds," 20.
68. Ross to Patterson, memo, 25 April 1941, ASF (DAD) Int. Div., Country File, "China Lend-Lease Railroad Requirements," RG160, NRC.
69. For an in-depth description of the structure and function of the Munitions Assignment Board, see Leighton and Coakley, *Global Logistics and Strategy*, chapters 10 and 11, 247–91.

70. Lieutenant Colonel John B. Franks, Quartermaster Corps, Defense Aid Division, to Captain E. B. White, Priorities Committee, War Department Army and Navy Munitions Board, memo, 23 August 1941 ASF (DAD) Int. Div., Country File, "China Lend-Lease," RG160, NRC.
71. Lieutenant Colonel J. L. Philips, Member, Priorities Committee, to Lieutenant A. C. Pierson, Office of the Chief of Engineers, memo, 10 September 1941, ASF (DAD) Int. Div., Country File, "China Lend-Lease," RG160, NRC.
72. Philips to Pierson, memo, 10 September 1941.
73. See, for example, the following memoranda that relate to railway track and cars: memo, Lieutenant Colonel L. T. Ross, Chief, Railway Section, Corps of Engineers, to Lieutenant Colonel E. E. MacMorland, Chief of Staff, AMMISCA, 23 September 1941, ASF (DAD) Int. Div., Country File, "China Lend-Lease," RG160, NRC; memo, Lieutenant Colonel John B. Franks, Quartermaster Corps, Defense Aid Division, to Captain E. B. White, Priorities Committee, War Department Army and Navy Munitions Board, 26 September 1941, ASF (DAD) Int. Div., Country File, "China Lend-Lease," RG160, NRC. See the following memoranda, which relate to problems of medical equipment (medical equipment was of particular importance in the malarial areas of the railway route): Lieutenant Colonel Park Holland, Army Air Corps, to Brigadier General J. W. N. Schulz, Medical Department, memo, 26 September 1941, ASF (DAD) Int. Div., Country File, "China Lend-Lease," RG160, NRC; memo, Colonel H. W. Eglin, Chief of AMMISCA's Washington Detail, to Currie, 27 October 1941, ASF (DAD) Int. Div., Country File, "China Lend-Lease," RG160, NRC.
74. Ausland, "South of the Clouds," 21.
75. Magruder to Eglin, radio, 17 October 1941, ASF (DAD) Int. Div., Missions Branch Project Decimal File 312.2, "Numbered Letters from Chungking, China," RG160, NRC.
76. Stanley Hornbeck, State Department Advisor on Political Relations, memo of conversation with Noel Hall, British Minister to the United States, 17 July 1941, FRUS 1941, V: 676.
77. Hornbeck, FRUS, 1941, V: 676–77.
78. MacMorland diary, 9 February 1942.
79. Ausland diary, 21 March 1941, from the private papers of Nevin Wetzel, Salt Lake City, Utah, provided to the author April 1977 by Nevin Wetzel.
80. Ausland diary, 21 March 1941.
81. Ausland diary, 29 September 1941.
82. Major General Dennys to Brigadier General Magruder, memo, 22 October 1941; Magruder to Dennys, memo, 25 October 1941, unattributed AMMISCA file.

83. Magruder to Ausland, radio, 20 October 1941, unattributed AMMISCA file.
84. Ausland diary, 21 March 1941.
85. Ibid.
86. Ibid. American mistrust of British performance was not a new phenomenon; see letter from Naval Attaché Major James McHugh to Ambassador Nelson T. Johnson, 31 January 1939, James McHugh Papers, Rare and Manuscript Collections, Carl A. Kroch Library, Cornell University, Ithaca, NY.
87. Lieutenant Colonel J. E. MacCammon, Chief, Missions Branch, War Department Defense Aid Division, to Major General Joseph Stilwell, letter, 23 January 1942, ASF (DAD) Int. Div., Decimal File 453, "Yunnan and Burma Railroad," RG160, NRC; radio, Magruder to Eglin, 17 October 1941, ASF (DAD) Int. Div., Missions Branch Project Decimal File 312.2, "Numbered Letters From Chungking, China," RG160, NRC. The British were still very chary of substantial numbers of Chinese entering Burma; best exemplified by the previous reference to General Wavell's refusal to employ Chinese divisions in defense of Burma—for which he was severely criticized after Burma fell. See memo from Perkins, the Consul at Kunming, to the Secretary of State, 15 February 1941, FRUS, V: 486; personal letter, Army Chief of Staff General George C. Marshall to General Wavell, Commander British and Commonwealth Forces in Burma, 22 January 1942, FDR Library, PSF; see also memo, Lauchlin Currie to President Roosevelt, 24 January 1942, FDR Library, PSF.
88. Letter to author from Nevin Wetzel. In the section from Kunming to Kweiyang the Chinese were using rails that had been torn up and hand-carried from east China.
89. Letter to author from Nevin Wetzel; War Office Report WO1056.3540, "Support to China, November 1941–January 1942" (undated; possible March 1941), cited in Baxter, "Britain and the War in China," 292, 325.
90. McHugh to U.S. Ambassador Nelson T. Johnson, 31 January 1939, memo, McHugh Papers, File 2770, Box 1, Rare and Manuscript Collections, Carl A. Kroch Library, Cornell University, Ithaca, NY.
91. Baxter, "Britain and the War in China," citing War Office report, 106.3540, 11 July 1941, 292.
92. Ibid., 294.
93. Ibid., 295.
94. Ibid.
95. Brigadier General L. T. Gerow, Assistant Chief of Staff, War Plans Div., to Marshall, memo, 11 February 1941, ASF (DAD) Int. Div., Decimal File 160, "Alternate Routes to India," RG160, NRC.
96. Magruder to Eglin, radio, 18 February 1942, WD-IDM-1942, NRC.

97. Currie to Roosevelt, memo, 16 March 1941, PDF China, FDR Library.
98. Magruder to Ross, Report, 8 April 1942, ASF (DAD) Int. Div., Decimal File 453, "Yunnan and Burma Railroad," RG160, NRC.
99. Ausland, "South of the Clouds," 25.
100. Letter to author from Nevin Wetzel; see also Lieutenant Colonel J. E. MacCammon to the Assistant Chief of Staff, memo, 15 May 1942, ASF (DAD) Int. Div., "China Correspondence," RG160, NRC, 2.
101. Magruder to the Chief of Engineers, memo, 18 September 1941, ASF (DAD) Int. Div., Missions Branch Project, Decimal File 311.5–319.1, China, "Weekly Reports from China," RG160, NRC.
102. Magruder to Eglin, radio, 21 October 1941, WD-IDM-1941, RG160, NRC.
103. Eglin to Magruder, radio, 28 October 1941, WD-IDM-1941, RG160, NRC. This radio also advised that the War Department was under no obligation to accept Hall's recommendations.
104. Lieutenant Colonel R. G. Adams (Colonel Eglin's replacement at the Adjutant General's desk in Washington) to Magruder, radio, 13 January 1942, WD-IDM-1942, RG160, NRC; radio, Magruder to Adams, 21 January 1942, WD-IDM-1942, RG160, NRC; radio, Magruder to Adams, 23 January 1942, WD-IDM-1942, RG160, NRC; radio, Magruder to Adams, 2 February 1942, WD-IDM-1942, RG160, NRC; letter, Brigadier General H. S. Aurand, Defense Aid Director, to T. V. Soong, 9 February 1942, ASF (DAD) Int. Div., Missions Branch Project, China, RG160, NRC.
105. Adams to Magruder, radio, 25 February 1942, WD-IDM-1942, RG160, NRC.
106. Lieutenant Colonel J. E. MacCammon, memo, 10 March 1942, ASP (DAD) Int. Div., Missions Branch Project Decimal File 679, "Pipelines For China," RG160, NRC. See also memo from Colonel S. G. Brown, Chief of the AMMISCA Washington Detail, to the Defense Aid Director, 20 March 1942, ASF (DAD) Int. Div., Missions Branch Project Decimal File 679, "Pipelines For China," RG160, NRC; radio, MacMorland to Adams, 4 March 1942, WD-IDM-1942, RG160, NRC.
107. Colonel S. G. Brown, memo, 20 March 1942, ASF (DAD) Int. Div., Missions Branch Project Decimal File 679, "Pipelines For China," RG160, NRC.
108. Colonel John B. Franks, General Staff Corps, to Colonel S. G. Brown, memo, 13 March 1942, ASF (DAD) Int. Div., Missions Branch Project Decimal File 679, "Pipelines For China," RG160, NA.
109. Colonel S. G. Brown, memo, 25 April 1942, ASF (DAD) Int. Div., Missions Branch Project Decimal File 679, "Pipelines for China," RG160, NA.

110. Stillwell to Adams, radio, 29 March 1942, WD-IDM-1942, RG160. NRC.
111. Stilwell to Adams, radio, 15 November 1942, WD-IDM-1942, RG160, NRC.
112. Romanus and Sunderland, *Stilwell's Mission*, 290.
113. William B. Sinclair, *Confusion Beyond Imagination* (Coeur d'Alene, Idaho: Joe F. Whitley, 1986), vols. 3, 4.
114. Telegram, 9 May 1942, FRUS 1942 (China), 592.
115. William S. Youngman to Edward R. Stettinius, Jr., memo, 1 January 1942, ASF (DAD) Int. Div., "China Correspondence," RG160, NRC.
116. Adams to Magruder, radio, 11 January 1942, WD-IDM-1942, RG160, NRC.
117. Magruder to Adams, radio, 19 January 1942, WD-IDM-1942, RG160, NRC.
118. Ibid.
119. Currie, presumably at Soong's instance, also became involved in the search for supply routes (Currie to Magruder, radio, 5 February 1942, WD-IDM-1942, RG160, NRC).
120. Magruder to Adams, radio, 28 January 1942, WD-IDM-1942, RG160, NRC. The airline was owned jointly by the Nationalist government and private American firms.
121. T. V. Soong, memo, 29 January 1942, War Department WPD 4389-89, NRC.
122. Soong to Roosevelt, memo, 30 January 1942, War Department WPD 4389-90, NRC.
123. Soong to McCloy, memo, 31 January 1942, War Department WPD 4389-90, NRC.
124. Gerow to Marshall, memo, 2 February 1942, War Department WPD 4389-85, NRC.
125. Gerow to Lieutenant General H. C. B. Wemyss, British Army Delegation, British Embassy, memo, 3 February 1942, War Department WPD 4389-85, NRC.
126. Lieutenant Colonel W. G. Pike, Assistant to General Wemyss, to Gerow, memo, 11 February 1942, War Department WPD 4389-85, NRC; Magruder to Adams, radio, 11 February 1942, WD-IDM-1942, RG160, NRC; Adams to Magruder, radio, 23 February 1942, WD-IDM-1942, RG160, NRC. The February 11 radio from Magruder also advised Washington that the Chinese had officially abandoned their Sichang-Sadiya plans in favor of the Ledo-Lungling route. See also Gerow to Marshall, memo, 11 February 1942, ASF (DAD) Int. Div., Decimal File 160, "Alternate Routes to India," RG160, NRC.
127. Magruder to Adams, radio, 7 February 1942, WD-IDM-1942, RG160, NRC; Marshall to Wemyss, memo, 12 February 1942, War Department WPD 4389-92, NRC; Brigadier General Eisenhower to Lieutenant Colonel Pike, memo, 18 February 1942, War Department WPD 4389-85, NRC; Eisenhower to Pike, memo, 19 February 1942, War Department WED 4389-85, NRC; Chiang Kai-shek to T. V. Soong, telegram, 2 March 1942, ASF (DAD) Int. Div., "China Correspondence," "Lend-Lease," RG160, NRC.
128. Eisenhower to Magruder, radio, 22 February 1942, War Department WPD 4389-92, NRC. There was no problem convincing the Chinese, who were already diverting materials and workers from the Burma Road and Burma-Yunnan railway to the Ledo project. C. S. Liu, China Defense Supplies, to Lieutenant Colonel John E. McCammon, AMMISCA Washington Detail, memo, 14 February 1942, ASF (DAD) Int. Div., Decimal File 160, "Alternate Routes to India," RG160, NRC.
129. Major John Russell, China Detail, to Stilwell, memo, 25 March 1942, ASF (DAD) Int. Div., Decimal File 451.2, "Trucks for China," RG160, NRC.
130. Stilwell to Adams, radio, 10 March 1942, WD-IDM-1942, RG160, NRC.
131. Ibid.; S. Liu to McCammon, memo, 17 March 1942, ASF (DAD) Int. Div., Decimal File 451.2, "Trucks for China," RG160, NRC.
132. Ibid.
133. J. A. Ulio, Washington AMMISCA Detail, to Stilwell, radio, 27 March 1942, WD-IDM-1942, RG160, NRC.
134. Stilwell to Adams, radio, 15 April 1942, WD-IDM-1942, RG160, NRC.
135. Russell, China Detail, to Magruder, report, 26 April 1942, ASF (DAD) Int. Div., Decimal File 451.2, "Trucks for China," RG160, NRC.
136. On April 13 Chiang attempted to obtain a total of six thousand trucks to be divided evenly between the Imphal and Ledo roads. Chiang asked Stilwell for his support for one thousand road construction trucks and two thousand transportation trucks for each route (Russell to Magruder, 26 April 1942; see also Colonel S. G. Brown, Washington Detail, to Defense Aid Director, memo, 7 April 1942, WD-IDM-1942, RG160, NRC).
137. Russell to Magruder, 26 April 1942.
138. Romanus and Sunderland, *Stilwell's Mission*, 140-141.
139. Telegram, 13 February 1942, War Department AG files 580.81, 2-13-42, RG407, NRC.
140. Romanus and Sunderland, *Stilwell's Mission*, 78, 79. Magruder and an official of the Chinese National Airlines Corporation supported this figure. On January 29 Magruder asked for "one hundred DC-3's or fewer number new Curtiss transports [four engine as opposed to the DC-3's two]." Magruder could accommodate them in "monthly increments of five to ten" (Magruder to Adams, radio, 29 January 1942, WD-IDM-1942, RG160, NRC).
141. Romanus and Sunderland, *Stilwell's Mission*, 78, 79.

142. President Roosevelt to Chiang Kai-shek, message "transmitted through unidentified channels," 9 February 1942, FRUS 1942 China: 13. An excellent account of the rigors of flying the "hump" is *The Aluminum Trail* by Chic Marrs Quinn, the widow of a pilot killed flying the hump route. The book documents every hump mission in which there was a fatality. Marrs Quinn self-published the book in 1989.
143. Arnold to Magruder, radio, 12 February 1942, WD-IDM-1942, RG160, NRC.
144. Jeff Ethel and Ron Downie, *Flying the Hump* (St. Paul, MN: Notebooks International, 2004), 11.
145. "Keeping China Alive: Tales of Flying the Hump by Charles R. "Bob" Pitzer, who flew C-46 and C-54 aircraft from India to Kunming, China (http//www.Kilroywashere.org).
146. MacMorland to Adams, radio, 25 February 1942, ASF (DAD) Int. Div. Decimal File 160, "Alternate Routes to India," RG160, NRC.
147. Adams to Magruder, radio, 24 February 1942, WD-IDM-1942, RG160, NRC.
148. Stilwell to Adams, radio, 11 March 1942, WD-IDM-1942, RG160, NRC; Adams to Magruder, radio, 9 February 1942, WD-IDM-1942, RG160, NRC.
149. Adams to Magruder, radio, 9 February 1942, WD-IDM-1942, RG160, NRC.
150. Leighton and Coakley, *Global Logistics and Strategy*, 528, 530; Roosevelt to Chiang, memo, 9 February 1942, FRUS 1942, China: 13.
151. Leighton and Coakley, *Global Logistics and Strategy*, 523, 530.
152. Magruder to Adams, radio, 11 February 1942, WD-IDM-1942, RG160, NRC. Chinese National Airlines Corporation's staff was badly in need of augmentation. Magruder to Adams, radio, 12 February 1942, WD-IDM-1942, RG160, NRC. This radio also outlined the national airline's extensive personnel shortages, as did Magruder to Adams, radio, 13 February 1942, WD-IDM-1942, RG160, NRC.
153. Adams to Magruder, radio, 14 February 1942, WD-IDM-1942, RG160, NRC.
154. Magruder to Adams, radio, 16 February 1942, WD-IDM-1942, RG160, NRC.
155. Adams to Magruder, radio, 19 February 1942, WD-IDM-1942, RG160, NRC.
156. Arnold to Magruder, radio, 21 February 1942, WD-IDM-1942, RG160, NRC.
157. Stilwell to Adams, radio, 17 March 1942, WD-IDM-1942, RG160, NRC.
158. Stilwell to Adams, radio, 22 March 1942, WD-IDM-1942, RG160, NRC.
159. Ibid.; Stilwell to Adams, radio, 2 May 1942, WD-IDM-1942, RG160, NRC.
160. Leighton and Coakley, *Global Logistics and Strategy*, 530–31.
161. Brigadier General S. Aurand, Director, International Division of Defense Aid, memo, 15 May 1942, ASF (DAD) Int. Div., "China Correspondence," RG160, NRC.
162. Romanus and Sunderland, *Stilwell's Mission*, 158.
163. Ibid., 164.
164. Stilwell to Adams, radio, 21 May 1942, WD-IDM-1942, RG160, NRC.
165. Chiang Kai-shek to Roosevelt, telegram, 1 June 1942, PSF China, FDR Library.
166. Arnold to Roosevelt, memo, 16 June 1942, PSF China, FDR Library; see also Romanus and Sunderland, *Stilwell's Mission*, 78–79.
167. Roosevelt to Arnold, memo, 15 June 1942, PSF China, FDR Library.
168. Arnold to Roosevelt, memo, 20 June 1942, PSF China, FDR Library. In June there was only one airfield in Assam used by the transport command — Dinjan (Romanus and Sunderland, *Stilwell's Mission*, 165).
169. Romanus and Sunderland, *Stilwell's Mission*, 115; Stilwell to Adams, memo, 29 April 1942, WD-IDM-1942, RG160, NRC; Madame Chiang to Currie, memo, 19 April 1942, Currie Papers, PSF China, FDR Library; Magruder to Adams, radio, 8 February 1942, WD-IDM-1942, RG160, NRC.
170. Stilwell to Adams, radio, 14 June 1942, WD-IDM-1942, RG160, NRC.
171. Romanus and Sunderland, *Stilwell's Mission*, 169.
172. Chiang to Roosevelt, memo, 5 July 1942, War Department Operations Division Executive File #10, cited in Romanus and Sunderland, *Stilwell's Mission*, 174; Madame Chiang to Currie, memo, 19 April 1942, FRUS 1942, China: 578–579. Romanus and Sunderland, *Stilwell's Mission*, 168; Calvin H. Oakes, Division of Near Eastern Affairs, Department of State, memo, 26 May 1942, FRUS 1942, China: 56–67; Gauss, memo, 26 May 1942, FRUS 1942, China: 64–67.
173. Stilwell to Adams, radio, 16 June 1942, WD-IDM-1942, RG160, NRC; Gauss to Hull, memo, 26 March 1942, FRUS 1942, China: 673.
174. Stilwell to Adams, radio, 18 June 1942, WD-IDM-1942, RG160, NRC; Marshall to Stilwell, radio, 16 June 1942, WD-IDM-1942, RG160, NRC; Marshall to Stilwell, radio, 23 June 1942, WD-IDM-1942, RG160, NRC; Stilwell to Adams, radio, 2 July 1942, WD-IDM-1942, RG160, NRC; Stilwell to Adams, radio, 19 July 1942, WD-IDM-1942, RG160, NRC; Stilwell to Adams, radio, 1 August 1942, WD-IDM-1942, RG160, NRC.
175. Romanus and Sunderland, *Stilwell's Mission*, 167; Stilwell to Marshall, radio, 16 June 1942, WD-IDM-1942, RG160, NRC; Brigadier General Thomas T. Handy, Assistant Chief of Staff, to the Joint Chiefs of Staff, memo, 4 July 1942, War Department AG File 4521 7-4-42, RG407, NRC.
176. Wellington Koo, Chinese Ambassador to

Britain, to Harry Hopkins, memo, 11 April 1942, Harry Hopkins Papers, "Chinese Affairs 1941–1942," Box 331, FDR Library; Admiral Standley, Ambassador to Russia, to Hull, memo, 29 May 1942, FRUS 1942, China: 596–97.

177. Stettinius to Hopkins, memo, 21 September 1942, Harry Hopkins Papers, "Chinese Affairs 1941–1942," Box 331, FDR Library; Stettinius to Hopkins, memo, 25 September 1942, Harry Hopkins Papers, "Chinese Affairs 1941–1942," Box 331, FDR Library; Soong to Hopkins, memo, 21 September 1942, Harry Hopkins Papers, "Chinese Affairs 1941–1942," Box 331, FDR Library.

178. Hull to Hopkins, memo, 24 September 1942, Harry Hopkins Papers, "Chinese Affairs 1941–1942," Box 331, FDR Library.

179. Standley to Hull, memo, 2 October 1942, FRUS 1942, China: 609.

180. Henderson, Charge in the Soviet Union, to Hull, memo, 31 October 1942, FRUS 1942, China: 612–14; unsigned memo to Hopkins, 16 December 1942, Harry Hopkins Papers, "Chinese Affairs 1941–1942," Box 331, FDR Library.

181. MacMorland, letter to author, 25 March 1977; Wetzel, letter to author, 27 March 1977.

Chapter 10

1. Schaller, *U.S. Crusade*, 77.
2. Ford, *Flying Tigers*, 50–51; for information on the trademark shark tooth caricature painted on the airplanes' noses see p. 81.
3. Martha Byrd, *Chennault: Giving Wings to the Tiger* (Tuscaloosa, Alabama: University of Alabama Press, 1987), 132.
4. Magruder to Eglin, radio, 24 October 1941, WD-IDM-1941, RG160, NRC; Magruder to Eglin, radio, 25 October 1941, WD-IDM-1941, RG160, NRC.
5. Magruder to Eglin, radio, 26 October 1941, WD-IDM-RG160, NRC.
6. Magruder to Eglin, radio, 2 November 1941, WD-IDM-RG160, NRC.
7. Ibid.
8. Ibid.
9. Magruder to Stimson and Marshall, radio, 6 November 1941, WD-IDM-1941, RG160, NRC.
10. Magruder to Eglin, radio, 2 November 1941. Magruder noted that this assessment was not a reflection on Chennault.
11. Magruder to Eglin, radio, 21 November 1941, WD-IDM-1941, RG160, NRC.
12. Magruder to Eglin, radio, 22 November 1941, WD-IDM-1941, RG160, NRC.
13. Eglin to Magruder, radio, 28 November 1941, WD-IDM-1941, RG160, NRC.
14. Colonel Ross G. Hoyt, China Detail, to Magruder, memo, 4 December 1941, ASF (DAD) Int. Div., "Weekly Reports from China," RG160, NA.

15. Byrd, *Chennault*, 117.
16. Memo, 17 December 1941, War Department WPD 4626, RG165, NRC.
17. Currie to Roosevelt, memo, 8 December 1941, Currie Papers, PSF China, FDR Library.
18. Magruder to Chennault, memo, 12 December 1941, WD-IDM-1941, RG160, NRC.
19. Romanus and Sunderland, *Stilwell's Mission*, 91.
20. Gerow to Marshall, memo, 17 December 1941, War Department WPD 4626, RG165, NRC: Gerow to Marshall, memo, 18 December 1941, War Department WPD 4626, RG165, NRC.
21. Magruder to Eglin, radio, 29 December 1941, WD-IDM-1041, RG160, NRC.
22. Currie to Chiang, radio, 30 December 1941, Currie Papers, PSF China, FDR Library.
23. Magruder to Eglin, radio, 31 December 1941, WD-IDM-1941, RG160, NRC. For specific information on Currie's responsibility in fostering Chiang's recommendation, see Chiang to Currie, radio, 4 January 1942, Currie Papers, PSF China, FDR Library.
24. Magruder to Eglin, radio, 31 December 1941, WD-IDM-1941, RG160, NRC.
25. Ibid.
26. Brigadier General L. T. Gerow to Magruder, radio, 17 December 1941, War Department WPD 4626, RG165, NRC.
27. United States War Department to Wavell, memo, no date, WPD 4626–5, NRC. See also Chief of Staff Marshall to Chief of Naval Operations Stark, memo, 27 December 1941, confirming Magruder's new responsibilities and designating him "Commanding General of American Forces in Burma and China," WPD 4626–2, NRC.
28. Magruder to Eglin, radio, 1 January 1942, War Department WPD 4389–64, RG165, NRC.
29. Magruder to Eglin, radio, 5 January 1942, FRUS 1942, China: 769.
30. Gerow to Magruder, radio, 9 January 1942, War Department WPD 4389–64, RG165, NRC.
31. Magruder to Eglin, radio, 12 January 1942, WD-IDM-1942, RG160, NRC.
32. Colonel L. S. Gerow, Operations Division, to the Assistant Chief of Staff Eisenhower, memo, 13 January 1942, War Department WPD 4626–5, RG165, NRC; Brigadier General L. T. Gerow to the Adjutant General, memo, 24 January 1942, War Department WPD 4626–5, RG265, NRC; Brigadier General L. T. Gerow to the Adjutant General, memo, 24 January 1942, War Department WPD 4626–5, NRC.
33. Magruder to Eglin, radio, 21 January 1942, WD-IDM-1942, RG160, NRC.
34. Chennault to Magruder, memo, 27 Janu-

ary 1942, WD-IDM-1942, RG160, NRC; Magruder to Adams, radio, 25 January 1942, WD-IDM-1942, RG160, NRC; Magruder to Adams, radio, 29 January 1942, WD-IDM-1942, RG160, NRC.

35. Magruder to Adams, Washington Detail, radio, 28 January 1942, WD-IDM-1942, RG160, NRC.

36. Spence, *To Change China*, 232.

37. Magruder to Adams; Magruder's Chief of Staff Colonel E. E. MacMorland, memo, 26 January 1942, ASF (DAD) Int. Div. Decimal File 319.1, "Weekly Reports from China," RG160, NRC.

38. Magruder to Adams, radio, 28 January 1942, WD-IDM-1942, RG160, NRC.

39. Currie to Chennault (via Chiang Kai-Shek), memo, 2 February 1942, Currie Papers, PSF China, FDR Library.

40. Chennault to Currie, memo, 6 February 1942, Currie Papers, PSF China, FDR Library; Chennault, *Way of a Fighter*, 171.

41. Magruder to Adams, radio, 10 February 1942, WD-IDM-1942, RG160, NRC.

42. Currie to Chiang, memo, 9 February 1942, Currie Papers, PSF China, FDR Library.

43. Madame Chiang to Currie, cable, 13 February 1942, Currie Papers, PSF China, FDR Library.

44. Chiang to Currie, memo, 26 March 1942, Currie Papers, PSF China, FDR Library.

45. Chiang to Currie, memo, 2 March 1942, Currie Papers, PSF China, FDR Library; Currie to Chiang, memo, 31 March 1942, Currie Papers, PSF China, FDR Library.

46. Currie to Chiang, memo, 31 March 1942, Currie Papers, PSF China, FDR Library.

47. Captain Stephen Manning, "Old Leatherface's Bombers," *Ex-CBI Roundup*, July 1977, 8.

48. Romanus and Sunderland, *Stilwell's Mission*, 91–92.

49. Ibid., 93.

50. Stilwell to Stimson and Marshall, radio, 7 March 1942, WD-IDM-1942, RG160, NRC.

51. Brigadier General Dwight D. Eisenhower, Deputy Chief, War Plans Division for the Far East, to the Adjutant General, memo, 10 March 1942, WD-IDM-1942, RG160, NRC.

52. Stilwell to Arnold, radio, 24 March 1942, WD-IDM-1942, RG160, NRC.

53. Ibid.

54. Chiang to Currie, memo, 26 March 1942, Currie Papers, PSF China, FDR Library.

55. Lieutenant General Albert C. Wedemeyer to Marshall, letter, 4 November 1944, in Charles F. Romanus and Riley Sunderland, *Time Runs Out in CBI* (Washington, D.C.: Office of the Chief of Military History, Department of the Army, 1953), 54.

56. Stilwell to Adams, radio, 30 March 1942, WD-IDM-1942, RG160, NRC.

57. E. J. Harris, Lieutenant Colonel USAF (Retired), Chennault's Administration Chief, letter to author, May 1977. For an insightful view of the pilots' perspectives of induction see Major General (Ret.) USAF Charles R. Bond Jr. and Terry Anderson, *A Flying Tiger's Diary* (College Station: Texas A and M University Press, 1984), 91, 102, 109, 197–213.

58. Currie to Magruder, radio, 7 February 1942, WD-IDM-1942, RG160, NRC; see also the handwritten margin notes in the War Department copy of Currie's radio message to Magruder, 7 February 1942 (WD-IDM-1942, RG160, NRC).

59. Chiang to Currie, radio, 16 January 1942, Currie Papers, PSF China, FDR Library.

60. Magruder to Eglin, radio, 16 January 1942, WD-IDM-1942, RG160, NRC.

61. Chiang to Currie, radio, 26 January 1942, Currie Papers, PSF China, FDR Library.

62. Stilwell to Adams, radio, 5 May 1942, AVG file, RG332, NRC.

63. Ibid.

64. Romanus and Sunderland, *Stillwell's Mission*, 114, 115, 162.

65. Marshall to Stillwell, radio, 21 May 1942, WD-IDM-1942, RG160, NRC.

66. Bissell (via Stilwell) to Marshall, radio, 19 May 1942, AVG file, RG332, NRC.

67. Pogue, *George C. Marshall*, 217.

68. Stilwell to Adams, memo, 31 March 1942, WD-IDM-1942, RG160, NRC.

69. Ibid.

70. Chiang to Currie, radio, 2 April 1942, Currie Papers, PSF China, FDR Library.

71. Stilwell to Adams, radio, 2 April 1942, WD-IDM-1942, RG160, NRC.

72. Marshall to Stilwell, memo, 3 April 1942, WD-IDM-1942, RG160, NRC.

73. Stilwell to Adams, memo, 4 April 1942, WD-IDM-1942, RG160, NRC.

74. Chennault, *Way of a Fighter*, 170–71.

75. Stilwell to Adams, memo, 16 April 1942, WD-IDM-1942, RG160, NRC; Stilwell to Chennault, memo, 29 April 1942, WD-IDM-1942, RG160, NRC.

76. Brigadier General J. A. Ulio, Adjutant General, to Stilwell, radio, 10 April 1942, War Department American Volunteer Group File (hereafter cited as AVG File), RG332, NRC.

77. Secretary of the Navy to the Naval Attaché, radio, 2 February 1942, AVG file, RG332, NRC; Adams to Stilwell, memo, 16 February 1942, AVG file, RG332, NRC.

78. Stilwell to Adams, radio, 16 April 1942, AVG file, RG332, NRC.

79. Arnold to Stilwell, radio, 28 May 1942, AVG file, RG332, NRC.

80. Ulio to Stilwell, radio, 10 April 1942, WD-IDM-1942, RG160, NRC; Stilwell to Adams, radio, 11 April 1942, AVG file, RG332, NRC; Naval Attaché McHugh to Secretary of the Navy, radio, 11 April 1942, AVG file, RG332, NRC.

81. Stilwell to Adams, memo, 20 April 1942, AVG file, RG332, NRC.
82. McHugh to Navy Department, memo, 14 May 1942, AVG file, RG332, NRC.
83. Stilwell to Adams, radio, 20 April 1942, AVG file, RG332, NRC.
84. Arnold to Stilwell, radio, 22 April 1942, AVG file, RG332, NRC.
85. Stilwell to Chennault, memo, 25 April 1942, AVG file, RG332, NRC; Marshall to Stilwell, memo, circa last week of April 1942, AVG file, RG332, NRC.
86. Stilwell to Chennault, memo, 28 April 1942, AVG file, RG332, NRC.
87. Stilwell to Chennault, memo, 28 April 1942, AVG file, RG332, NRC; Stilwell to Adams, radio, 28 April 1942, AVG file, RG332, NRC; Stilwell to Chennault, memo, 9 May 1942, AVG file, RG332, NRC; Stilwell to Adams, radio, 14 May 1942, AVG file, RG332, NRC; Marshall to Stilwell, radio, 19 May 1942, AVG file, RG332, NRC; Marshall to Stilwell, radio, 20 May 1942, AVG file, RG332, NRC; Stilwell to Adams, radio, 19 May 1942, AVG file, RG332, NRC; Naval Attaché to the Navy Department, memo, 26 May 1942, AVG file, RG332, NRC; Stilwell to Adams, radio, 21 June 1942, AVG file, RG332, NRC; Brigadier General Robert H. Dunlop, Acting Adjutant General to the Assistant Chief of Staff, G-2, memo, 27 May 1945, Adjutant General decimal file 320.2 5–13–45, RG407–07, NRC.
88. Stilwell to Adams, radio, G-2 file, Intelligence, China/AMMISCA, RG319, NRC.
89. Marshall to Stilwell, radio, 1 June 1942, AVG file, RG332, NRC.
90. Stilwell to Adams, radio, 28 May 1942, G-2 file, Intelligence, China/AMMISCA, RG319, NRC.
91. Stilwell to Adams, radio, 7 June 1942, G-2 file, Intelligence, China/AMMISCA, RG319, NRC.
92. Stilwell to Adams, radio, 15 July 1942, G-2 file, Intelligence, China/AMMISCA, RG319, NRC.
93. Stilwell to Adams, memo, 26 June 1942, G-2 file, Intelligence, China/AMMISCA, RG319, NRC.
94. Chennault, *Way of a Fighter*, 172; Keith Ayling, *Old Leatherface of the Flying Tigers* (Indianapolis: Bobbs-Merrill, 1945), 191–98.
95. Paul Frillman (AVG Chaplain) and Graham Peck, *China: The Remembered Life* (Boston: Houghton Mifflin, 1968), 162.
96. Frillman and Peck, *China*, 162.
97. E. J. Harris, letter to author, 24 April 1977.

Chapter 11

1. Memo, 22 August 1941, AF-MMC, Washington, D.C.
2. Acheson was assistant secretary of state from 1945 to 1947, and secretary of state from 1949 to 1953.
3. Romanus and Sunderland, *Stilwell's Mission*, 39.
4. Ibid., 30, 51.
5. Ibid., 29.
6. Ibid., 38.
7. Mayer to Marshall, radio, 31 December 1941, WD-ID-1941, RG160, NRC.
8. J. E. McCammon, War Department, memo for the record, 16 May 1942, WD-IDM-1942, RG160 NRC.
9. FRUS 1941, V: 758–59.
10. Magruder to Marshall and Stimson, radio, 28 October 1941, WD-IDM-l941, RG160, NRC.
11. Currie to Hornbeck, memo, 1 November 1941, FRUS 1941, V: 737–39; Madame Chiang to Currie, radio, 30 October 1941, Currie Papers, PSF China, FDR Library; Magruder to Marshall and Stimson, radio, 28 October 1941, WD-IDM-1941, RG160, NRC.
12. Magruder to Marshall and Stimson, radio, 28 October 1941, WD-IDM-l941, RG160, NRC.
13. Romanus and Sunderland, *Stilwell's Mission*, 37.
14. Ibid., 38.
15. Ibid., 40–41.
16. Romanus and Sunderland citing RAD AMMISCA 32, Magruder to Marshall and Stimson, 31 October 1941, Book A (1941), OPD, Exec. 8, page 38.
17. Currie to Hornbeck, memo, 1 November 1941, FRUS 1941, V: 742–44.
18. Lattimore was one of those later accused by Senator McCarthy of being pro-communist.
19. Lattimore to Currie, radio, 2 November 1941, Currie Papers, PSF China, FDR Library.
20. British Ambassador to China Clark Kerr to the Foreign Office, memo, 31 October 1941, British National Archives, Kew, WO208/3536.
21. Colonel C. W. Bundy, memo, 1 November 1941, War Department WPD 4389–27, RG165, NRC.
22. Ibid.
23. Admiral Stark and General Marshall to Roosevelt, memo, 5 November 1941, War Department WPD 4389–29, RG165, NRC.
24. Bundy, memo, 2 November 1941, War Department WPD 4389–27, RGl65, NRC.
25. Brigadier General L. T. Gerow, Acting Assistant Chief of Staff, to Marshall, memo, 3 November 1941, War Department WPD 4389–29, RG165, NRC; Captain R. E. Schurmann, Navy Department, to Hull, memo, 31 October 1941, FRUS 1941, V: 742.
26. Brigadier General L. T. Gerow to Marshall, memo, 3 November 1941, War Department WPD 4389–29, RG165, NRC.
27. Ibid.
28. General Marshall and Admiral Stark to

Roosevelt and Hull, memo, 5 November 1941, War Department WPD 4389-29, RG165, NRC.

29. Romanus and Sunderland, citing Marshall and Stark to Roosevelt, memo, 4 November 1941, subject: Far Eastern Situation, Bk. A (1941), OPD Exec 8; memo for record, Bundy, 2 November 1941, subject: Notes on Conference with Mr. Currie at State Department 1245, 1 November 1941, Bk. A (1941), OPD Exec 8, 40.

30. Roosevelt to Hull, memo, 11 November 1941, PSF China, FDR Library; Roosevelt to Chiang, radio, 14 November 1941, FRUS 1941, V: 758-60; Lattimore to Currie, radio, 25 November 1941, Currie Papers, PSF China, FDR Library; Lattimore to Currie, radio, 27 November 1941, Currie Papers, PSF China, FDR Library.

31. Lattimore to Currie, radio, 2 November 1941, Currie Papers, PSF China, FDR Library.

32. Hull to Gauss, radio, 10 November 1941, FRUS 1941, V: 757; Gauss to Hull, radio, 18 November 1941, WD-IDM-1941, RG160, NRC; MacMorland to Gauss, memo, 21 November 1941, AF-MMC, Washington, D.C.; Gauss to Hull, radio, 25 November 1941, FRUS 1941, V: 764.

33. Hull to Gauss, memo, 3 November 1942, FRUS 1941, V: 753.

34. Gauss to Hull, radio, 18 November 1941, WD-IDM-1941, RG160, NRC; MacMorland to Gauss, memo, 21 November 1941, AF-MMC, Washington, D.C.; Gauss to Hull, radio, 25 November 1941, FRUS 1941, V: 764.

35. Gerow to the Secretary, Army General Staff, memo, 15 November 1941, War Department WPD 4 389-30, RG165, NRC; Gerow to the Adjutant General, memo, 15 November 1941, War Department WPD 4389-30, RG165, NRC.

36. Radio, 15 March 1942, WD-IDM-1942, RG160.

37. Magruder to Marshall, radio, 9 December 1941, WD-IDM-1941, RG160, NRC; Burns, *Roosevelt*, 381.

38. Theodore White, ed., *The Stilwell Papers* (New York: Macfadden, 1962), 53; MacMorland diary, 9 March 1942, both in Romanus and Sunderland, *Stilwell's Mission*, 95.

39. MacMorland, memo, 10 December 1941, AF-MMC, Washington, D.C.

40. Magruder to Marshall and Stimson, radio, 10 December 1941, WD-IDM-1941, RG160, NRC.

41. Roosevelt to Chiang, memo, 14 December 1941, Chiang Kai-shek file, PSF Safe File, FDR Library.

42. MacMorland, memo, 17 December 1941, AF-MMC, NRC.

43. Magruder to Marshall and Stimson, radio, 16 December 1941, WD-IDM-1941, RG160, NRC; Field Marshall the Viscount Slim, *Defeat into Victory* (New York: David McKay, 1961), 8-9, 20-23.

44. MacMorland, memo, 18 December 1941, WD-IDM-1941, RG160, NRC.

45. MacMorland, memo, 20 December 1941, WD-IDM-1941, RG160, NRC.

46. MacMorland, memo, 23 December 1941, WD-IDM-1941, RG160, NRC.

47. Romanus and Sunderland, *Stilwell's Mission to China*, 13.

48. White, *Stilwell Papers*, 60. Stilwell's anti-British bias is well known. However, the documents and interviews that form the basis of this book are replete with references to British unpreparedness, apathy, racism, and attitudes of superiority. See, for example, the Ausland diary; White's *The Stilwell Papers*; the author's correspondence with American Burma veterans; the Currie Papers; Romanus and Sunderland's *Stilwell's Mission to China*; Slim's *Defeat into Victory*; Bayly and Harper's *Forgotten Armies*; Calvocaressi, Wint, and Pritchard's *The Penguin History of the Second World War*; and especially Julian Thompson's *The Imperial War Museum*.

49. Major Harry S. Aldrich, memo, 24 December 1941, WD-IDM-1941, RG160, NRC.

50. Aldrich, memo, 23 December 1941, WD-IDM-1941, RG160, NRC.

51. Magruder to Stimson, radio, 28 December 1941, WD-IDM-1941, RG160, NRC; Currie to Roosevelt, memo, 2 January 1942, Currie Papers, PSF China, FDR Library; Lattimore to Currie, radio, 4 January 1942, Currie Papers, PSF China, FDR Library; Madame Chiang to Currie, radio, 2 February 1942, Currie Papers, PSF China, FDR Library; Madame Chiang to Currie, radio, 20 March 1942, Currie Papers, PSF China, FDR Library; Stilwell to Marshall, radio, 6 June 1942, War Department, Operation Planning Division (hereafter cited as OPD) file, RG319, NRC.

52. MacMorland, memo, 25 December 1941, WD-IDM-1941, RG160, NRC.

53. MacMorland, memo prepared by the Joint Military Council (Brett), 23 December 1941, WD-IDM-1941, RG160, NRC.

54. Chiang to Roosevelt, radio, 24 December 1941, FRUS 1941, V: 762.

55. Magruder, memo, 21 December 1941, POR, RG332, NRC; Magruder to Roosevelt, radio, 25 December 1941, WD-IDM-1941, RG160, NRC.

56. MacMorland, memo, 27 December 1941, WD-IDM-1941, RG160, NRC.

57. Ibid.

58. Radio, 8 February 1942, WD-IDM-1942, RG160, NRC.

59. The following documents contain references to Magruder's belief that Lend-Lease supplies would not be a factor in the war except politically: Magruder to Marshall, radio, 22 October 1941, WD-IDM-1941, RG160, NRC; Major Hemphill, memo, 29 January 1942, WD-IDM-1942, RG160, NRC; Magruder to Adjutant General, radio, 3 February 1942, WD-IDM-1942, NRC. See also Magruder to Brett,

memo, 17 December 1941, WD-IDM-1941, RG160, NRC; Magruder to Adams, radio, 7 January 1942, WD-IDM-1942, RG160, NRC; Magruder to Adjutant General, radio, 2 February 1942, WD-IDM-1942, RG160, NRC; Magruder to Marshall, radio, 10 February 1942, FRUS 1942, China: 13–16; Magruder to Marshall, radio, 2 May 1942, WD-IDM-1942, RG160, NRC.

60. Major Edward S. Hemphill, memo, 29 January 1942, War Department ASF (DAD) Int. Div., File 337, "Reports on Conferences on Lend-Lease," RG165, NRC.

61. Magruder to Marshall, radio, 8 February 1942, WD-IDM-1942, RG160, NRC.

62. Gauss to Hull, radio, 21 February 1942, FRUS 1942, China: 24–25.

63. See, for example, radio, Magruder to Marshall, 8 February 1942, WD-IDM-1942, RG160, NRC.

64. Romanus and Sunderland, *Stilwell's Mission*, 41.

65. Marshall to Magruder, radio, 14 February 1942, War Department WPD 4389–96, NRC; Romanus and Sunderland, *Stilwell's Mission*, 173, 175.

66. Romanus and Sunderland, *Stilwell's Mission*, 41, 160, 161, 223, 278. In early 1943, however, Roosevelt, in one his Machiavellian changes of mind, reversed his previous support of this policy, albeit without causing significant changes by Stilwell (277–79).

67. Marshall to Magruder, radio, 14 February 1942, War Department WPD 4389–96, NA.

68. Marshall to Magruder and Stilwell, radio, 15 March 1942, WD-IDM-1942, RG160, NRC; Marshall to Stilwell, radio, 26 March 1942, WD-IDM-1942, RG160, NRC.

69. Stilwell to Marshall and Stimson, radio, 1 April 1942, WD-IDM-1942, RG160, NRC.

70. For a detailed account of additional restrictions and cutbacks on materials already stockpiled or requested by the Chinese, especially actions taken by the Munitions Assignments Board, see Romanus and Sunderland, *Stilwell's Mission*, 160–161. Romanus and Sunderland assign a great deal of blame for the cutbacks to the Chinese for their "failure to grapple realistically with the transportation of lend-lease material and their preoccupation with simply staking out a claim to large portions of American production both military and commercial, and then defending it tooth and nail" (161).

71. Stilwell to Marshall, radio, 4 April 1942, WD-IDM-1942, RG160, NRC.

72. Romanus and Sunderland, *Stilwell's Mission*, 160.

73. Magruder to Marshall, radio, 2 May 1942, WD-IDM-1942, RG160, NRC. The memorandum was sent through Stilwell's message center and its contents must have been approved by Stilwell.

74. Soong to Hopkins, letter with memo, 20 June 1942, in Romanus and Sunderland, *Stilwell's Mission*, 168. Soong had somehow learned before the Munitions Assignment Committee announced its stance what its decision would be.

75. Stilwell to Marshall, radio, 26 June 1942, War Department G-2 files, RG319, NRC; Robert E. Sherwood, *Roosevelt and Hopkins* (New York: Harper, 1948), 599.

76. Chiang to Roosevelt, radio, 28 June 1942, Romanus and Sunderland, *Stilwell's Mission*, 172.

77. Leighton and Coakley, *Global Logistics and Strategy*, 105.

78. Currie to Roosevelt, memo, 26 June 1942, FRUS 1942, China: 88–89; Romanus and Sunderland, *Stilwell's Mission to China*, 168–69.

79. Roosevelt to Chiang, memo, 4 July 1942, FRUS 1942, China: 95–96.

80. Roosevelt to Currie, memo, circa late June, 1942, Currie Papers, PSF Executive Office file, FDR Library.

81. Currie to Roosevelt, memo, 26 June 1942, Currie Papers, PSF, FDR Library.

82. Romanus and Sunderland, *Stilwell's Mission*, 174–75.

83. Marshall to Stilwell, radio, 18 July 1942, War Department G-2 files, RG319, NRC.

84. Memo by Davies, the Second Secretary of Embassy in China, included in a memo from Gauss to Hull, 12 August 1942, FRUS 1942, China: 129.

85. Gauss to Hull, memo, 12 August 1942, FRUS 1942, China: 126–28.

86. Marshall to Stilwell, radio, 28 July 1942, War Department AG381 files, RG165, NRC.

87. Roosevelt to Chiang, radio, 10 October 1942, War Department G-2 files, RG319, NRC.

88. Chiang to Roosevelt, memo, 14 November 1942, War Department OPD 381 CTO, RG165, NRC.

89. Tang Tsou, *America's Failure in China, 1941–1950*, vol. 1 (Chicago: University of Chicago Press, 1969), 91.

Chapter 12

1. War Department WPD 4389–79, RG165, NRC.

2. Romanus and Sunderland, *Stilwell's Mission*, 63.

3. Pogue, *George C. Marshall*, 354.

4. Lieutenant Colonel W. G. Wyman, memo, 29 December 1941, War Department WPD 4389–61, RG165, NRC; memo of a conference held at the War Plans Division on 20 January 1942, War Department WPD 4389–79, RG165, NRC; Brigadier General Sherman Miles to Magruder, letter, 11 July 1941, AF-MMC, NRC.

5. Romanus and Sunderland, *Stilwell's Mission*, 61.

6. Wavell to Dennys, radio, 31 December 1941, WD-IDM-1941, RG160, NRC.

7. Wavell to Dennys, radio, 31 December 1941; memo prepared for Brigadier General L. T. Gerow, 28 December 1941, War Department WPD 4389-61, RG165, NRC; Lieutenant Colonel W. G. Wyman, memo, 29 December 1941, War Department WPD 4389-61, RG165, NRC. For an overview of the Marshall-Stilwell relationship, see Pogue, *George C. Marshall*, 355-356, and Romanus and Sunderland, *Stilwell's Mission*, 70-71.

8. Romanus and Sunderland, *Stilwell's Mission*, 70.

9. Ibid.

10. Marshall to Stilwell, letter, 2 February 1942, Romanus and Sunderland, *Stilwell's Mission*, 74.

11. Soong to Stimson, letter, 30 January 1942, U.S. Department of State, *United States Relations with China: With Special Reference to the Period 1944-1949*; Romanus and Sunderland, *Stilwell's Mission*, 73.

12. Romanus and Sunderland, *Stilwell's Mission*, 73.

13. Ibid., 75.

14. Ibid., 118.

15. Magruder to Marshall and Stimson, radio, 1 January 1942, WD-IDM-1942, RG160, NRC.

16. Adams to Magruder, radio, 4 January 1942, WD-IDM-1942, RG160, NRC; Magruder to Marshall and Stimson, radio, 7 January 1942, WD-IDM-1942, RG160, NRC.

17. Pogue, *George C. Marshall*, 357-60; see also Romanus and Sunderland, *Stilwell's Mission to China*, 63-70.

18. Magruder to Marshall, radio, 15 January 1942, WD-IDM-1942, RG160, NRC.

19. MacMorland, memo, 27 January 1942, ASF (Int. Div.) Missions Branch Project, Decimal File 319.1, RG160, NRC.

20. Romanus and Sunderland, *Stilwell's Mission*, 93.

21. Magruder to Marshall and Stimson, radio, 3 February 1942, WD-IDM-1942, RG160, NRC.

22. Marshall to Magruder, radio, 5 February 1942, WD-IDM-1942, RG160, NRC.

23. Adams to Magruder, radio, 4 February 1942, WD-IDM-1942, RG160, NRC.

24. Magruder to Marshall, radio, 11 March 1942, WD-IDM-1942, RG160, NRC.

25. Marshall to Stilwell, radio, 9 April 1942, WD-IDM-1942, RG160, NRC; Major General J. A. Ulio, Adjutant General, to Stilwell, radio, 22 June 1942, MD-IDM-1942, RG160, NRC.

26. Adams to Magruder, radio, 4 January 1942, WD-IDM-1942, RG160, NRC.

27. Stilwell clearly did not like Magruder. White, *Stilwell Papers*, 51; Colonel Bundy, memo, 1 November 1942, War Department WPD 4389-27, RG165, NRC; Magruder to Major Paul L. Freeman, Jr., letter, 17 April 1942, AMMISCA File 312.1, RG332, NRC.

28. Magruder to Marshall, radio, 2 May 1942, WD-IDM-1942, RG160, NRC; Davies, *Dragon by the Tail*, 233; Gauss to Hull, memo, 8 May 1942, FRUS 1942, China: 42; Gauss to Hull, memo, 8 May 1942, FRUS 1942, China NRC: 43-44; Hull to Marshall, memo, 9 May 1942, FRUS 1942, China NRC: 44-45; Marshall to Magruder, memo, 9 May 1942, FRUS 1942, China NRC: 46; Hornbeck, memo, 4 March 1942, Hornbeck Papers, Hoover Institute.

29. Magruder to War Department, memo, 10 February 1942, FRUS 1942: 20-21; see also Leighton and Coakley, *Global Logistics and Strategy*, 527. They refer to Magruder's message as a "classic." Magruder's comments were supported by other on-the-spot observers. See, for example, Military Attaché Mayer's memo to Marshall, 8 July 1942, G-2 File Box 62, China/Chungking, NRC.

30. Magruder to War Department, memo, 10 February 1942, FRUS 1942: 20-21; see also Leighton and Coakley, *Global Logistics and Strategy*, 527.

31. Undersecretary of State Welles, memo for the record, 12 February 1942, FRUS 1942, 16-17.

32. Hamilton, memo, 16 February 1942, FRUS 1942, China, 19.

33. Hornbeck to Welles, memo, 16 February 1942, FRUS 1942, 20-21.

34. Fairbank, *Chinabound*, 178.

35. Gauss to Hull, memo, 21 February 1942, FRUS 1942, 24-25.

36. Ibid.

37. Gary May, *China Scapegoat: The Diplomatic Ordeal of John Carter Vincent* (Washington, D.C.: New Republic, 1979), 65.

38. Gauss to Hull, memo, 21 February 1942, FRUS 1942, 24-25.

39. Gauss to Hull, 7 March 1942, FRUS 1942, 27.

40. Captain R. E. Schurmann, USN memo to State Department, 16 April 1942, in a summary of a message from Naval Attaché at Chungking, Major James McHugh, FRUS 1942, 31. Nevertheless, Hornbeck continued his efforts to degrade Magruder's status at the War Department. Advisor on Political Relations Hornbeck to Undersecretary of State Welles, memo, FRUS 1942, footnote 20.

41. MacMorland diary, 1 January 1942.

42. Gauss to Hull, memo, 24 July 1941, FRUS 1941, V: 684.

43. Gauss to Hull, memo, 17 November 1941, FRUS 1942, China, 588-90. See also MacMorland's diary entry of 8 November 1941, wherein he says that Gauss "was never interested in helping the mission."

44. Mayer to Military Intelligence Division, radio, 31 December 1941, G-2 files, RG319, NRC;

Colonel J. E. McCammon., memo, 16 May 1942, G-2 files, RG319, NRC; Magruder to Marshall, radio, 17 May 1942, G-2 files, RG319, NRC; Personal Diary of Major General E. E. MacMorland, 4 December 1941, February 6, 18, 19, 19 May 1942, cited through courtesy of Mrs. E. E. MacMorland, Wallingford, Pennsylvania.

45. Riley Sunderland, commentary on George F. Elsey's *Roosevelt and China: "The President and U.S. Aid to China—1944"* (Wilmington, Delaware: Michael Glazier, 1979). Sunderland emphasizes Roosevelt's tendencies to be a pragmatist, but too frequently keep his policy revisions to himself until they were made public; to reverse his own policies; and his unconcern regarding the ramifications of his unilateralism.

46. Marshall to Magruder, radio, 17 May 1942, WD-IDM-1942, RG160, NRC.

47. Magruder to Marshall, radio, 17 May 1942, G-2 files, RG319, NRC.

48. Magruder to Stilwell, memo, 18 May 1942, AF-MMC, NRC; MacMorland diary, 4 December 1941.

49. MacMorland diary, 19 May 1942, 79.

50. Marshall to Stilwell, radio, 25 May 1942, War Department, OPD 201, Magruder, John F., RG165, NRC.

Epilogue

1. Leighton and Coakley, *Global Logistics and Strategy*, 526–32.

2. Major Edward S. Hemphill, Washington Detail, memo, 11 March 1942, ASF (DAD) Int. Div., "China Correspondence," RG160, NRC.

3. Romanus and Sunderland, *Stilwell's Mission*, 160–61, 223, 282–83, 388.

4. Marshall to Stilwell, radio, 20 August 1942, WD-IDM-1942, RG160, NRC; Sir Michael Carver, ed., *The War Lords* (Boston: Little, Brown & Company, 1976), 343–56.

5. Romanus and Sunderland, *Stilwell's Mission to China*, 152; Hornbeck, memo, 20 May 1942, FRUS 1942, China: 49–51.

6. David F. Rudgers, *Creating the Secret State: The Origins of the Central Intelligence Agency, 1943–1947* (Lawrence: University of Kansas Press, 2000), 11.

7. Letter to author from Charles Romanus, 10 April 1972; letter to author from Major General Haydon Boatner, 26 May 1972. See also Magruder obituary, *Washington Post*, 1 May 1958.

8. Rudgers, *Creating the Secret State*, 42–43.

9. Ibid., 23, 24, 35, 67, 68, 116, 118.

10. "List of Papers," War Department OPD 201, Magruder, John F., RG165, NRC. The American military has a unique system of evaluating its officer personnel. Evaluations known as "fitness" and "efficiency" reports are written periodically by commanding officers on all officers under their direct command. A relatively small number of negative reports, or even one, if bad enough, will have a significant impact on an officer's future in the military. As noted, Magruder's call for United States opposition to a perceived Japanese offensive against Kunming was critically rejected by Marshall. Thus, as early as fall 1941 Marshall may have determined that Magruder should rise no further than brigadier general.

11. Gauss to Hull, memo, 24 July 1941, FRUS 1941, V: 684.

Bibliography

United States Government Documents

AMMISCA file: The Magruder Mission to China. War Department Office of the Chief of Military History. General Reference Branch, Forrestal Building, Washington, D.C.

Biographical files: Brigadier General John M. Magruder. War Department Office of the Chief of Military History. Washington, D.C.

Congressional Record. Vol. 87, Part 1 and Part 2, 77th Congress, 3 January 1941 to 18 February 1941. Washington, D.C.: United States Government Printing Office, 1941.

G-2 (Intelligence) file China/AMMISCA. Record Group 319. NRC. Suitland, MD.

International Division files. Record Group 160, NRC. Washington, D.C.

Papers Relating to the Foreign Relations of the United States: China 1942. Washington, D.C.: United States Government Printing Office, 1956.

Papers Relating to the Foreign Relations of the United States: The Far East 1931. Vol. 3. Washington, D.C.: United States Government Printing Office, 1946.

Papers Relating to the Foreign Relations of the United States: The Far East 1932. Vols. 3 and 4. Washington, D.C.: United States Government Printing Office, 1948.

Papers Relating to the Foreign Relations of the United States: The Far East 1933. Vol. 3. Washington, D.C.: United States Government Printing Office, 1949.

Papers Relating to the Foreign Relations of the United States: The Far East 1933. Vol. 4. Washington, D.C.: United States Government Printing Office, 1955.

Papers Relating to the Foreign Relations of the United States: The Far East 1934. Vol. 3. Washington, D.C.: United States Government Printing Office, 1950.

Papers Relating to the Foreign Relations of the United States: The Far East 1935. Vol. 3. Washington, D.C.: United States Government Printing Office, 1953.

Papers Relating to the Foreign Relations of the United States: The Far East 1936. Vol. 4. Washington, D.C.: United States Government Printing Office, 1954.

Papers Relating to the Foreign Relations of the United States: The Far East 1937. Vols. 3 and 4. Washington, D.C.: United States Government Printing Office, 1954.

Papers Relating to the Foreign Relations of the United States: The Far East 1938. Vol. 3. Washington, D.C.: United States Government Printing Office, 1954.

Papers Relating to the Foreign Relations of the United States: The Far East 1939. Vols. 3 and 4. Washington, D.C.: United States Government Printing Office, 1955.

Papers Relating to the Foreign Relations of the United States: The Far East 1940. Vol. 4. Washington, D.C.: United States Government Printing Office, 1955.

Papers Relating to the Foreign Relations of the United States: The Far East 1941. Vols. 4 and 5. Washington, D.C.: United States Government Printing Office, 1956.

Papers Relating to the Foreign Relations of the United States: The Far East 1942. Vol. 1. Washington, D.C.: United States Government Printing Office, 1960.

Papers Relating to the Foreign Relations of the

United States: Japan 1931–1941. Vols. 1 and 2. Washington, D.C.: United States Government Printing Office, 1943.

War Department Adjutant General files. AG400.3295 (4-14-41). NRC. Washington, D.C.

War Department Adjutant General files. Record Group 407. NRC. Washington, D.C.

War Department American Volunteer Group file. Record Group 332. NRC. Suitland, MD.

War Department AMMISCA file 312.1. Record Group 332. NRC. Suitland, MD.

War Department Army Service Forces files. Record Group 160. NRC. Washington, D.C.

War Department Combined Chiefs of Staff (Joint Chiefs of Staff) files. "China," 091.711 1-2-42. NRC. Washington, D.C.

War Department General and Special Staff files. Record Group 165. NRC. Washington, D.C.

War Department International Division message files, 1941, 1942. Record Groups 160, 165. NRC. Suitland, MD.

War Department Joint Planning Committee Development file. Series 573. NRC. Washington, D.C.

War Department Military Intelligence Division files. Record Group 165. NRC. Washington, D.C.

War Department Operation Planning Division files. Record Group 319. NRC. Washington, D.C.

War Department Port of Rangoon file. Record Group 332. NRC. Suitland, MD.

War Department Records of the Assistant Secretary of War for Air. Record Group 107, NRC. Washington, D.C.

War Department War Plans Division files. Record Groups 164, 165, 338. NRC. Washington, D.C.

British Government Documents

Dorman-Smith, Reginald. Memorandum, 22 July 1940. British War Office WO 106/3540 NO 116813 British Archives, Kew, London.

_____. Telegram to Secretary of State/Burma. 21 July 1940, British War Office 106/3540, 116813. British NRC, Kew, London.

_____. Memorandum to Secretary of State/Burma, 22 July 1940, Repeating Letter from Japanese Consul at Rangoon. British War Office WO 106/3540 NO 116813. British NRC: Kew, London.

_____. Memorandum to Secretary of State/Burma, 10 September 1941, Memo, WO 208/311, 114853 British NRC, Kew, London.

Kerr, Ashley Clark, British Ambassador to China [Clark Kerr] to the Foreign Office. Memo, 31 October 1941. War Office File 208/3536. British NRC, Kew, London.

_____. Memorandum, 1 October 1941. Foreign Office Document FO 371/27657. British NRC, Kew, London.

Lloyd, M. E. Memorandum postmarked 1 September 1941, intercepted 20 September 194. Standard-Vacuum Oil Company, Kunming, to General Manager Standard-Vacuum Oil Company Manager for India (Unnamed), Calcutta, Memo. War Office File 208/311 114853. British NRC, Kew, London.

Stockley, G. E. Memorandum, 18 March 1939. War Office File 208/278. British NRC, Kew, London.

Walker, K. Selby. Walker of Reuters. 9 to 18 February, 1941. Extract from "Notes on a visit to Chunking, Kunming, and the Burma Road." War Office 208/298A. British NRC, Kew, London.

Yu, General Fei-peng. Memorandum for the regulation of traffic on the Yunnan-Burma highway. 10 October 1941, War Office 208/311. British NRC, Kew. London.

Articles

Abend, Hallett. "Doubling Burma Road Load." *New York Times,* 18 January 1942, 17.

_____. "Our Loan to China Is Disappointing." *New York Times,* 27 May 1934, 2E.

Arnstein, Daniel G. "An Ex-Taxi Driver Checks Up on the Burma Road." *Life,* 6 October 1941, [PAGE].

Ausland, Major John E. "The Details ... Are Left to You." *Ex-CBI Roundup* 26 (January 1971): 8–21.

_____. "South of the Clouds." *Ex-CBI Roundup* 28 (July 1973): 16–26.

_____. "We Are the Father." *Ex-CBI Roundup* 12 (January 1958): 10–18.

Bisson, T. A. "Japan's Economic Outlook." *Foreign Policy Reports* 15 (15 June 1939): 86–87.

Bliven, Bruce. "Burma Road Bottleneck." *Far Eastern Survey* 10 (April 1941): 63.
_____. "Currie in China." *Time* (24 March 1941): 16.
_____. "This Is Where I Came In." *New Republic* 93 (January 1938): 245-246.
DeWilde, John C. "Can Japan Be Quarantined?" *Foreign Policy Reports* 13 (1 December 1937): 218-24.
Dorfman, Ben. "Two Years of the Manchukuo Regime." *Foreign Policy Reports* 10 (12 September 1934): 170-180.
New York Times. "Doubling Burma Road Load." 18 January 1942.
Far Eastern Survey. "Far Eastern Press Notes." Vol. 10 (5 May 1941): 95.
Elliston, H. B. "Silver, East and West." *Foreign Affairs* 13 (July 1933): 666-79.
Fortune. "The Fortune Forum of Executive Opinion." Vol. 22 (September 1940): 72-73.
_____. "The Fortune Survey." Vol. 23 (September 1940).
Fairbank, John K. "Tributary Trade and China's Relations with the West." *Far Eastern Quarterly* 1.2 (1942).
Foreign Policy Bulletin. "Nanking Bows to Japan in North China." Vol. 5 (25 January 1935): 1-2.
_____. "Nanking Strengthens Its Entente with Japan." Vol. 5 (1 March 1935): 1-2.
_____. "Nanking's Rapprochement with Japan." Vol. 4 (17 August 1934): 1-2.
Greene, Fred. "The Military View of American National Policy, 1904-1940." *The American Historical Review* 66 (January 1961): 334-77.
Janeway, Eliot. "Roosevelt vs. Hitler." *Life*, 5 May 1941, 99-105.
Jellison, William L. "Malaria Was an Enemy." *Ex-CBI Roundup* 30 (March 1976): 8-12.
Leary, William M., Jr. "Wings for China: The Jouett Mission, 1932-1935." Pacific Historical Review 38 (November 1969): 451-54.
Leavens, Dickson H. "American Silver Policy and China." *Harvard Business Review* 14 (Autumn 1935): 45-53.
Lewis, Sir Willmott. "The Paramount Interests of Britain and America." *Foreign Affairs* 13 (July 1935): 574-82.
Magruder, Major John M. "The Chinese as a Fighting Man." *Foreign Affairs* (April 1931): 468-76.

Manning, Captain Stephen. "Old Leatherface's Bombers." *Ex-CBI Roundup* 32 (July 1977): 8-12.
Masland, John W. "Commercial Influence upon American Far Eastern Policy, 1937-1941." *Pacific Historical Review* 11 (September 1942): 281-99.
_____. "Missionary Influence upon American Far Eastern Policy." *Pacific Historical Review* 10 (September 1941): 279-96.
May, Ernest R. "The Development of Political-Military Consultation in the United States." *Political Science Quarterly* 70 (June 1953): 161-80.
Morton, Louis. "Army and Marines on the China Station: A Study in Military and Political Rivalry." *Pacific Historical Review* 29 (February 1960): 51-74.
_____. "National Policy and Military Strategy." *Virginia Quarterly Review* 36 (Winter 1960): 1-17.
Porter, Sylvia. "Uncle Sam's Silver Scandal." *The Baltimore Sunday Sun*, 14 April 1940, 46.
Rodger, George. Letter to his editor at *Life*. 1 March 1942.
Rogers, Lindsay. "National Defense." *Foreign Affairs* 19 (October 1940): 1-11.
Ronguillo, Remigio B. "The Administration of Law among the Chinese in Chicago." *Journal of Criminal Law* 25 (July 1934): 205-24.
_____. "Secretary of Economics." *Time*, 24 July 1939, 52.
Stewart, John R. "Another Blow to the Open Door in Manchuria." *Far Eastern Survey* 7 (5 January 1938): 8-9.
_____. "The Open Door in Manchukuo." *Far Eastern Survey* 6 (1 December 1937): 272-73.
Stowe, Leland. Article, *Washington Evening Star*, 31 December 1941, [PAGE].
Stromberg, Roland N. "American Business and the Approach of War, 1935-1941." *Journal of Economic History* 13 (Winter 1953): 58-78.
Time. "Chinea: Burma Roadster." 1 September 1941.
Vinson, J. C. "The Annulment of the Lansing-Ishii Agreement." *Pacific Historical Review* 27 (February 1958): 57-69.
Washington Post. Magruder Obituary. 1 May 1958.
Wertenbaker, Charles. "The China Lobby:

The Legacy of T. V. S. Soong." *The Reporter* (New York: Fortnightly) 6.8 (15 April 1952): [PAGE].

Wetzel, Nevin. "The Old Gray Major." *Ex-CBI Roundup* 30 (November 1975): 6–11.

Yamamoto, Tatsuro, and Sumiko Yamamoto. "The Anti-Christian Movement in China, 1922–1927." *Far Eastern Quarterly* 12 (February 1953): 133–148.

Diaries and Personal Papers

Ausland, Major John E. Personal Diary. In possession of Mrs. Sylvia Ausland, Palo Alto, CA.

MacMorland, Major General E. E. MacMorland. Personal diary. In possession of Mrs. E. E. MacMorland, Wallingford, PA.

Wetzel, Nevin. Personal Diary. In possession of Nevin Wetzel, Salt Lake City, UT.

Oral History Sources

Bolt, General Charles L. United States Army Oral History Project, National War College, Carlisle Barracks, PA. No date.

Chennault, Claire L. United States Air Force Oral History Project. No date. Wright-Patterson Air Force Base, Dayton, OH.

Gates, General Clifton B. Interview, circa 1965. United States Marine Corps Oral History Project VE, 23.2, Naval Annex, Arlington, VA.

Letters to Author

Boatner, Major General Haydon. 26 May 1972.

Harris, Lieutenant Colonel E. J. (Ret.). (General Claire L. Chennault's former Administration Chief.) 12 April 1977.

Jellison, William E. (Former Chief of American Public Health Service medical team to China, 1941.) 29 March 1977.

MacMorland, Lucy M. (Wife of former AMMISCA Chief of Staff Colonel E. E. MacMorland.) 8 November 1977.

MacMorland, Major General E. E. (Ret.). (Former Chief of Staff of AMMISCA.) 25 March 1977.

Wetzel, Nevin. (Former member of AMMISCA.) 7 December 1977, 1 March 1977, and 27 March 1977.

Unpublished Materials

Bauer, Boyd H. "General Claire Lee Chennault and China, 1937–1958: A Study of Chennault, His Relationship with China, and Selected Issues in Sino-American Relations." Ph.D. thesis, June 1973, American University, Washington, D.C.

Baxter, Catherine E. "Britain and the War in China 1937–1945." Doctoral thesis, October 1993, University College of Wales Aberystwyth, Wales.

Burke, R. L. "Franklin D. Roosevelt and the Far East: 1913–1941." Ph.D. thesis, July 1969, Michigan State University, Lansing, MI.

Chou, I-kua. "American Policy in China from 1929–1939."

Currie Papers. President's Secretary's File. Franklin D. Roosevelt Library. Hyde Park, New York.

Hopkins, Harry. Harry Hopkins Papers. Franklin D. Roosevelt Library. Hyde Park, New York.

Hornbeck, Stanley. Hornbeck Papers. Hoover Institution, Stanford, CA.

Hoyt, Frederick. "People of Privilege: Americans in China 1925–1937." Decatur, IL: Unpublished manuscript, August 1975.

Jan, George P. "Public Opinion and American Policy toward the Sino-Japanese War, 1937–1945." Paper presented at the 18th Annual Meeting of the American Association for Chinese Studies, St. Louis, MO, 5 November 1976.

McHugh, James. James McHugh Papers. Ph.D. thesis, July 1949. Fletcher School of Law and Diplomacy, Philadelphia. Carl A. Kroch Library, Cornell University, Ithaca, NY.

Payer, Cheryl A. "Western Economic Assistance to Nationalist China, 1927–1937: A Comparison with Postwar Foreign Aid Programs." Ph.D. thesis, June 1971. Harvard University, Cambridge, MA.

Pickler, Gordon K. "United States Aid to the Chinese Nationalist Air Force, 1931–1949." Ph.D. thesis, June 1971. Florida State University, Tallahassee, FL.

President's Secretary's file. Franklin D. Roosevelt Library. Hyde Park, New York.

Wang, Samuel Hsuan. "The Sino-Japanese War and the American Far Eastern Policy 1931–1941." Ph.D. thesis, September 1947. Cornell University, Ithaca, NY.

Other Secondary Sources

Abend, Hallett. *My Life in China, 1926–1941.* New York: Harcourt, Brace, 1943.

———. *The God from the West: A Biography of Frederick Towns Ward.* Garden City, NY: Doubleday, 1947.

Acheson, Dean. *Present at the Creation: My Years in the State Department.* New York: W. W. Norton, 1960.

Adler, Selig. *The Isolationist Impulse.* New York: Abelard-Schuman, 1957.

Alsop, Joseph W. *I've Seen the Best of It.* New York: W. W. Norton, 1992.

Ambrose, Stephen E. *Upton and the Army.* Baton Rouge: Louisiana State University Press, 1964.

Anders, Leslie. *The Ledo Road.* Norman: University of Oklahoma Press, 1965.

Astor, Gerald. *The Jungle War: Mavericks, Marauders, and Madmen in the China-Burma-India Theater of World War II.* New York: John Wiley, 2004.

Ayling, Keith. *Old Leather Face of the Flying Timers.* Indianapolis, IN: Bobbs-Merrill, 1945.

Bayly, Christopher, and Tim Harper. *Forgotten Armies: The Fall of British Asia, 1941–1941.* Cambridge: Belknap, 2004.

Bloodworth, Dennis, and Ching Ping Bloodworth. *The Chinese Machiavelli.* New York: Dell, 1977.

Blum, John M. *From the Morgenthau Diaries.* Vol. 2. Boston: Houghton Mifflin, 1965.

———. *Roosevelt and Morgenthau.* Boston: Houghton Mifflin, 1972.

Bond, Charles R., Jr., Major General (Ret.) USAF, and Terry Anderson. *A Flying Tiger's Diary.* College Station: Texas A&M University Press, 1984.

Borg, Dorothy. *American Policy and the Chinese Revolution 1925–1928.* New York: Macmillan, 1947.

———. *The United States and the Far Eastern Crisis of 1933–1938.* Cambridge, MA: Harvard University Press, 1964.

Brennan, John A. *Silver and the First New Deal.* Reno: University of Nevada Press, 1969.

Buell, Raymond L. *Isolated America.* New York: Alfred A. Knopf, 1940.

Buhite, Russell D. *Nelson T. Johnson and American Policy Toward China 1925–1941.* East Lansing: Michigan State University Press, 1968.

Burns, James M. *Roosevelt, the Soldier of Freedom 1940–1945.* New York: Harcourt Brace Jovanovich, 1970.

Butow, Robert C. *Tojo and the Coming of the War.* Princeton, NJ: Princeton University Press, 1961.

Byrd, Martha. *Chennault: Giving Wings to the Tiger.* Tuscaloosa: University of Alabama Press, 1987.

Calvocoressi, Peter, Guy Wint, and John Pritchard. *Penguin History of the Second World War.* London: Penguin, 1999.

Carver, Sir Michael, ed. *The War Lords.* Boston: Little, Brown & Company, 1976.

Chennault, Anna. *Chennault and the Flying Tigers.* New York: Paul Eriksson, 1963.

Chennault, Claire L. *Way of a Fighter: The Memoirs of Claire L. Chennault.* Ed. Robert Hotz. New York: G. P. Putnam, 1949.

Chou, Hsun-hsin. *The Chinese Inflation, 1937–1949.* New York: Columbia University Press, 1963.

Christian, John L., *Modern Burma: A Survey of Political and Economic Development.* Berkeley: University of California Press, 1942.

Churchill, Winston. *Their Finest Hour.* Boston: Houghton Mifflin, 1949.

———. *The Hinge of Fate.* Boston: Houghton Mifflin, 1950.

Cohen, Warren L. *America's Response to China.* New York: John Wiley, 1971.

Craig, Gordon. "The Political Leader as Strategist." In *Makers of Modern Strategy: From Machiavelli to the Nuclear Age,* ed. Peter Paret. Princeton, NJ: Princeton University Press, 1986.

Craig, Gordon A., and Felix Gilbert. *The Diplomats 1919–1939.* Vol. 2. New York: Atheneum, 1971.

Craven, Wesley F., and James L. Cate, eds. *The Army Air Forces in World War II: Plans and Early Operations January 1939 to August 1942.* Chicago: University of Chicago Press, 1948.

Culbert, David H. *News for Everyman: Radio and Foreign Affairs in Thirties America.* Westport, CT: Greenwood, 1976.

Current, Richard N. *Secretary Stimson: A Study in Statecraft.* New Brunswick, NJ: Rutgers University Press, 1954.

Danton, George H. *The Culture Contacts of the United States and China.* New York: Columbia University Press, 1931.

Davies, John P. *Dragon by the Tail.* New York: W. W. Norton, 1972.

Deane, Hugh. *Review of the Foreign Press.* Oxford: Foreign Research and Press Service Balliol College, 27 February 1941.

Delano, Amasa. *A Narrative of Voyages and Travels.* Boston: B. G. House, 1817.

Dennett, Tyler. *Americans in Eastern Asia.* New York: Macmillan, 1922.

Divine, Robert A. *American Foreign Policy.* New York: Meridian, 1960.

———. *Foreign Policy and U.S. Presidential Elections.* New York: New Viewpoints, 1974.

Donnison, F. S. V. *Burma.* New York: Praeger, 1970.

Dulles, Foster R. *China and America.* Princeton, NJ: Princeton University Press, 1946.

Elsey, George F. *Roosevelt and China.* Wilmington, DE: Michael Glazier, 1979.

———. *Roosevelt and China: The White House Story.* Wilmington, DE: Michael Glazier, 1979.

Erlanson, Marcus R. "Lend-Lease: An Assessment of a Government Bureaucracy." In *The Big L: American Logistics in World War II*, ed. Allen Gropman. Washington, D.C.: National Defense University Press, 1997.

Esherick, Joseph W., ed. *Last Chance in China: The World War II Dispatches of John S. Service.* New York: Vintage, 1974.

Ethel, Jeff, and Ron Downie. *Flying the Hump.* St. Paul, MN: Notebooks International, 2004.

Everest, Allan S. *Morgenthau, the New Deal and Silver.* New York: Columbia University Press, 1950.

Fairbank, John King. *The United States and China.* New York: Viking, 1966.

———. *Chinabound: A Fifty Year Memoir.* New York: Harper and Row, 1982.

———. *China: A New History.* Cambridge, MA: Harvard University Press, 1992.

———. *Trade and Diplomacy on the China Coast.* Stanford, CA; Stanford University Press, 1969.

Fairbank, John K., Edwin Reischauer, and Albert Craig. *East Asia: Tradition and Transformation.* Boston: Houghton Mifflin, 1973.

Feis, Herbert. *The China Tangle.* New York: Atheneum, 1967.

———. *The Diplomacy of the Dollar: First Era 1919–1932.* Baltimore, MD: Johns Hopkins Press, 1950.

———. *The Road to Pearl Harbor.* New York: Atheneum, 1967.

Fenby, Jonathon. *Chiang Kai-shek: China's Generalissimo and the Nation He Lost.* New York: Carroll and Graf, 2004.

Ferrell, Robert H., ed. *America as a World Power, 1872–1945.* New York: Harper, 1971.

———. *American Diplomacy in the Great Depression.* New Haven, CT: Yale University Press, 1957.

Finney, Charles G. *The Old China Hands.* Garden City, New York: Doubleday, 1961.

Fleisher, Wilfrid. "The Manchurian Incident." In *They Were There: The Story of World War II and How It Came About by America's Foremost Correspondents.* New York: Curt Reiss, Books for Libraries Press, Freeport 1945.

Ford, Daniel. *Flying Tigers: Claire Chennault and the American Volunteer Group.* Washington D.C.: Smithsonian Institute Press, 1991.

Franke, Wolfgang. *China and the West: The Cultural Encounter, 13th to 20th Centuries.* New York: Harper and Row, 1967.

Frillman, Paul, and Graham Peck. *China: The Remembered Life.* Boston: Houghton Mifflin, 1968.

Garrett, Shirley S. "Why They Stayed: American Church Politics and Chinese Nationalism in the Twenties." In *The Missionary Enterprise in China and America*, ed. John K. Fairbank, pp. 283–310. Cambridge, MA: Harvard University Press, 1974.

Greenfield, Kent R. *American Strategy in World War II: A Reconsideration.* Melbourne, FL: Krieger, 1963.

Greenlaw, Olga. *The Lady and the Tigers.* New York: E. P. Dutton, 1943.

Grew, Joseph. *Turbulent Era.* Boston: Houghton Mifflin, 1952.

Griswold, A. W. *The Far Eastern Policy of the United States.* New Haven, CT: Yale University Press, 1938.

Hachey, Thomas, ed. *Confidential Dispatches: Analysis of America by the British Ambassador 1939–1945.* Evanston, IL: New University Press, 1973.

Harvey, G. E. *British Rule in Burma 1824–1942.* London: Faber and Faber, 1946.

Holbrook, Silas. *Sketches by a Traveler.* Boston: Carter and Hendee, 1830.

Hsu, Immanuel C. Y. *The Rise of Modern*

China. New York: Oxford University Press, 1970.

Hull, Cordell. *The Memoirs of Cordell Hull*. 2 vols. New York: Macmillan, 1948.

Hunt, Michael E. "Chinese Foreign Relations in Historical Perspective." In *China's Foreign Relations in the 1980's*, ed. Harry Harding. New Haven, CT: Yale University Press, 1984.

Hutchmacher, J. J. *Trial by War and Depression: 1917–1941*. Boston: Allyn and Bacon, 1973.

Iriye, Akira. *Across the Pacific*. New York: Harcourt, Brace and World, 1967.

Isaacs, Harold R. *Scratches on Our Minds: American Images of China and India*. New York: J. Day, 1953.

Johnson, Walter. *The Battle Against Isolation*. New York: Da Capo, 1973.

Kahn, E. J. *The China Hands*. New York: Viking, 1975.

Kao, Ping-shu. *Foreign Loans to China*. New York: Sino-International Economic Research Center, 1946.

Kates, George N. *The Years That Were Fat: The Last of Old China*. Cambridge, MA: M.I.T. Press, 1967.

Keller, Morton, ed. *The New Deal, What Was It?* New York: Holt, Rinehart and Winston, 1964.

Kennan, George F. *American Diplomacy, 1900–1950*. Chicago: University of Chicago Press, 1951.

Kimble, Warren F., ed. "F.D.R.—The Dilemma of Democracy and Foreign Policy." In *Franklin D. Roosevelt and the World Crisis, 1937–1945*. Lexington, MA: D. C. Heath, 1973.

———. *The Juggler: Franklin Roosevelt as War Time Statesman*. Princeton, NJ: Princeton University Press, 1991.

Kirby, General S. Woodlawn. *The War Against Japan*. Vol. 2. Uckfield, East Sussex, UK: Naval and Military Press, 2004.

Koen, Ross Y. *The China Lobby in American Politics*. New York: Harper and Row, 1974.

Korb, Lawrence J. *The Joint Chiefs of Staff: The First Twenty Five Years*. Bloomington: Indiana University Press, 1976.

Larrabee, Eric. *Commander in Chief: Franklin Delano Roosevelt, His Lieutenants and Their War*. New York: Harper and Row, 1987.

Latourette, Kenneth S. *The American Record in the Far East, 1945–1951*. New York: Macmillan, 1962.

———. *A History of Christian Missions in China*. New York: Russell and Russell, 1967.

Lawson, Robert. *At That Time*. New York: Viking, 1947.

Leighton, Richard M., and Robert W. Coakley. *Global Logistics and Strategy: 1940–1943*. Washington, D.C.: Office of the Chief of Military History, Department of the Army, 1955.

Leuchtenberg, William E. *Franklin D. Roosevelt and the New Deal 1932–1940*. New York: Harper and Row, 1963.

———. *The New Deal*. New York: Harper and Row, 1968.

Lewin, Ronald. *Churchill as Warlord*. London: Batsfords, 1973.

Liang, Chih-tung. *General Stilwell in China 1941–1944*. Jamaica, NY: St. John's University Press, 1972.

Liddell Hart, B. H. *History of the Second World War*. New York: G. P. Putnam, 1970.

Lin, W. Y. *China Under Depreciated Silver 1926–1931*. Shanghai: Commercial Press, 1935.

———. *The New Monetary System of China*. Chicago: University of Chicago Press, 1936.

Linebarger, Paul M. A. *Government in Republican China*. New York: McGraw-Hill, 1938.

Liu, Frederick F. *A Military History of Modern China, 1924–1949*. Port Washington, NY: Kennikat, 1972.

Louis, William R. *British Strategy in the Far East, 1919–1939*. Oxford: Clarendon, 1971.

Lyman, Stanford. *The Asian in the West*. Reno: University of Nevada Press, 1970.

Matloff, Maurice, and Edwin M. Snell. *Strategic Planning for Coalition Warfare 1941–1942*. Washington, D.C.: Office of the Chief of Military History, Department of the Army, 1953.

———. *American Military History*. Washington, D.C.: United States Army, Office of the Chief of Military History, 1969.

May, Gary. *China Scapegoat: The Diplomatic Ordeal of John Carter Vincent*. Washington, D.C.: New Republic, 1979.

Michie, Peter S. *The Life and Letters of Emory Upton*. New York: D. Appleton, 1885.

Miller, Stuart C. *The Unwelcome Immigrant:*

The American Image of the Chinese, 1785–1882. Berkeley: University of California Press, 1969.

Morison, Elting E., ed. *Letters of Theodore Roosevelt.* Vol. 4. Cambridge, MA: Harvard University Press, 1954.

Morison, Samuel E. *The Rising Sun in the Pacific 1931–April 1942.* Boston: Little, Brown, 1948.

Myers, William S. *The Foreign Policies of Herbert Hoover: 1929–33.* New York: Scribners, 1940.

Offner, Arnold A., ed. *America and the Origins of World War II.* Boston: Houghton Mifflin, 1971.

Ogata, Sadako N. *Defiance in Manchuria: The Making of Japanese Foreign Policy 1931–1932.* Berkeley: University of California Press, 1964.

Persico, Joseph. *Roosevelt's Secret War: FDR and World War II Espionage.* Toronto: Random House of Canada, 2001.

Plating, John. *The Hump: America's Strategy for Keeping China in World War II.* College Station: Texas A&M, 2011.

Pogue, Forrest C. *George C. Marshall Ordeal and Hope: 1939–1942.* New York: Viking, 1966.

Powell, John B. *My Twenty-Five Years in China.* New York: Macmillan, 1945.

Quinn, Chic Marrs. *The Aluminum Trail.* Printed by author, 1989.

Rapoport, Anatol. *Carl Von Clausewitz on War.* New York: Penguin Classics, 1979.

Rappaport, Armin. *Henry L. Stimson and Japan, 1931–33.* Chicago: University of Chicago Press, 1963.

Rauch, Basil. *Roosevelt: From Munich to Pearl Harbor.* New York: Creative Age, 1950.

Reischauer, Edwin O. *The United States and Japan.* New York: Viking, 1967.

Rieselbach, Leroy N. *The Roots of Isolationism.* Indianapolis, IN: Bobbs-Merrill, 1960.

Romanus, Charles F., and Riley Sunderland. *Stilwell's Mission to China.* Washington, D.C.: Office of the Chief of Military History, Department of the Army, 1953.

_____. *Stilwell's Personal File.* Vol. 1. Wilmington, Delaware: Scholarly Resources, 1976.

_____. *Time Runs Out in CBI.* Washington, D.C.: Office of the Chief of Military History, Department of the Army, 1953.

Roosevelt, Elliott. *As He Saw It.* New York: Duell, Sloan and Pearce, 1946.

Roskill, Stephen. *Naval Policy Between the Wars.* Vol. 1. New York: Walker, 1968.

Rozwenc, Edwin C., ed. *The New Deal, Revolution or Evolution.* Boston: Heath, 1952.

Rudgers, David F. *Creating the Secret State: The Origins of the Central Intelligence Agency, 1943–1947.* Lawrence: University of Kansas Press, 2000.

Schaller, Michael. *The U.S. Crusade in China, 1938–1945.* New York: Columbia University Press, 1979.

Schurmann, Franz, and Orville Schell. *Imperial China: The Decline of the Last Dynasty and the Origins of Modern China.* New York: Random House, 1967.

Scott, Robert L. *Flying Tiger: Chennault of China.* New York: Doubleday, 1959.

Seagrave, Sterling. *Soong Dynasty.* New York: Harper and Row, 1986.

Seymour, Charles, ed. *The Intimate Papers of Colonel House.* 4 vols. Boston: Houghton Mifflin, 1926–28.

Shaw, Samuel. *The Journals of Samuel Shaw, the First American Consul at Canton with a Life of the Author by Josiah Quincy.* Boston: W. Crosby and H. P. Nichols, 1847.

Sherwood, Robert E. *Roosevelt and Hopkins.* New York: Harper, 1948.

Sinclair, William B. *Confusion Beyond Imagination.* Coeur d'Alene, ID: Joe F. Whitley, 1986.

Slim, Field Marshall the Viscount. *Defeat into Victory.* New York: David McKay, 1961.

Smith, Nicol. *Burma Road.* Indianapolis, IN: Bobbs-Merrill, 1940.

Smith, Sara R. *The Manchurian Crisis, 1931–1932.* New York: Columbia University Press, 1948.

Snow, Edgar, *Journey to the Beginning.* New York: Random House, 1958.

Soames, Mary, ed. *Winston and Clementine: The Personal Letters of the Churchill's.* London: Doubleday, 1998.

Spence, Jonathan. *The China Helpers.* London: Bodley Head, 1969.

_____. *To Change China: Western Advisors in China 1620–1960.* Boston: Little, Brown, 1969.

_____. *Search for Modern China.* New York: W. W. Norton, 1999.

Stettinius, Edward R. *Lend-Lease: Weapon for Victory.* New York: Macmillan, 1944.

Stimson, Henry L. *The Far Eastern Crisis: Recollections and Observations.* New York: Harper, 1936.

Stimson, Henry, and McGeorge Bundy. *On Active Service in Peace and War.* New York: Harper, 1948.

Storry, Richard. *The Double Patriots.* London: Chatto and Windus, 1957.

Stout, Rex, ed. *The Illustrious Dunderheads.* New York: Knopf, 1942.

Strauss, W. P. *Isolation and Involvement.* Waltham, MA: Xerox College Publishing, 1972.

Stuart, John L. *Fifty Years in China.* New York: Random House, 1954.

Sunderland, Riley. "General Joseph W. Stilwell." In *The War Lords*, ed. Sir Michael Carver. Boston: Little, Brown, 1976.

Tan, Pei-ying. *The Building of the Burma Road.* New York: McGraw-Hill, 1945.

T'ang Liang-li. "Missions, the Cultural Arm of Western Imperialism." In *Christian Missions in China: Evangelists of What?* ed. Jesse G. Lutz. Lexington, MA: D. C. Heath, 1965.

Thomason, John W. *—and a Few Marines.* New York: Charles Scribner, 1943.

Thompson, Julian. *The Imperial War Museum Book of the War in Burma, 1942–1945.* London: Pan, 2003.

Tolley, Kemp. *Yangtze Patrol.* Annapolis, MD: Naval Institute Press, 1971.

Tsou, Tang. *America's Failure in China, 1941–1950.* Vol 1. Chicago: University of Chicago Press, 1969.

Tuchman, Barbara W. *Stilwell and the American Experience in China 1911–45.* New York: Macmillan, 1971.

Tuleja, Thaddeus V. *Statesmen and Admirals.* New York: W. W. Norton, 1963.

Tupper, Eleanor, and George E. McReynolds. *Japan in American Public Opinion.* New York: Macmillan, 1937.

Van Alstyne, Richard W. *The Genesis of American Nationalism.* Waltham, MA: Blaisdell, 1970.

_____. *The United States and East Asia.* New York: W. W. Norton, 1973.

Varg, Paul A. *Missionaries, Chinese, and Diplomats: The American Protestant Missionary Movement in China, 1890–1952.* Princeton, NJ: Princeton University Press, 1958.

Vinacke, Harold M. *The United States and the Far East, 1945 to 1951.* Stanford, CA: Stanford University Press, 1952.

Wedemeyer, General Albert C. *Wedemeyer Reports.* New York: Holt, 1958.

Weigley, Russell F. *The American Way of War.* New York: Macmillan, 1973.

_____. *History of the United States Army.* New York: Macmillan, 1967.

Welles, Sumner. *Seven Decisions That Shaped History.* New York: Harper, 1951.

Whelan, Russell. *The Flying Tigers.* New York: Viking, 1943.

White, Edwin S. *Ten Thousand Tons by Christmas.* St. Petersburg, FL: Valkyrie, 1975.

White, Theodore H., ed. *The Stilwell Papers.* New York: Macfadden, 1962.

White, Theodore and Annalee Jacoby. *Thunder out of China.* New York: William Sloane, 1946.

Williams, Frederick W. *The Life and Letters of Samuel Welles Williams.* New York: G. B. Putnam, 1899.

Wiltz, John E. *From Isolation to War, 1931–1941.* New York: Crowell, 1968.

Wu, Cheng-tsu, ed. *Chink.* New York: World, 1972.

Young, Arthur K. *China and the Helping Hand 1917–1945.* Cambridge, MA: Harvard University Press, 1963.

_____. *China's Nation-Building Effort, 1927–1937.* Stanford, CA: Hoover Institute Press, 1971.

_____. *China's Wartime Finance and Inflation, 1937–1945.* Cambridge, MA: Harvard University Press, 1965.

Internet Sources

Rothwell, Steve. *The Burma Campaign.* "Burma Army 1937–1943." http://www.rothwell.force9.co.uk/burmaweb/BurmaArmy.htm.

_____. *The Burma Campaign.* "Preparations for War." http://www.rothwell.force9.co.uk/burmaweb/preparat.htm.

Pitzer, Charles R. "Bob." "Keeping China Alive: Tales of Flying the Hump." http://kilroywashere.org.

Vandenberg Air Force Base. 14th Air Force History. http://www.vandenberg.af.mil/library/factsheets.

Index

Page numbers in ***bold italics*** indicate pages with illustrations.

abbreviations 5
Aldrich, Major Harry 24, 107
Allied planners headquartered at Chungking 189
American Military Mission to China (AMMISCA): alternate routes of supplying China 145–150; American Volunteer Group and 101–104; arrival in China 52, 94–95; build up of supplies in Indian ports 148; bureaucratic ignorance 212; candidates for leadership of 20; challenges 211; Chiang not told Magruder was forbidden to engage in staff talks 179–180; concept 16–19; confusion about mission 103, 129; deployment of staff 24–25; disillusionment of staff 25; Dorman-Smith, Colonal Sir Reginald, and 87; Flying Tigers and 158–178; formation 19–25; knowledge of needed Burma Road improvements 92; Magruder restricted by his rank 180–181; Marshall, General George C., and 39; mission's tasks 127–128; need for personnel to have knowledge of history and culture of nations to which they are assigned 216; need to expand war planning 215; pioneering role of 131, 211, 213; Rangoon operations 100–101; reassignment of personnel 204; Roosevelt's micromanagement and 40–41; situation reports 179; spare parts depots 129; staff 24–25; State Department requests for 23–25; supplies piling up at Rangoon 105; *Tulsa* incident 108–121; valuable liaison center 214; view of Anglo-Burmese strategy 105; Washington-Chungking discord over Kunming 181–187; Yunnan-Burma Railroad 132–143
American Volunteer Group (Flying Tigers) 14, 17, 34, 124; airplane delivery problems 103; American air forces in China and 173–174; American policies regarding 160; AMMISCA assigned initial responsibility for 158; back-door communications and 102, 159; Chennault and induction into the army air forces 167–168; China relations and 195; choice of P-40 plane 159; difficulties inducting the AVG into the army air forces 166–167; factors against induction 178; formation of 158–159; inducements to transfer 174–178; induction into the American army air forces 163–178; internecine warfare over induction into army air forces 172–173; Magruder's standards for supplies 160; material and personnel needs 161; need for more material support 162; no provision made for material or personnel replacement 159; personnel not transferring to army air forces 174; personnel problems and morale problems 103–104; "quid-pro-quo" policy 194–200; relationship with AMMISCA 159; reputation endures 158; reinforcements from China 102; Sino-British enmity 189; transfer to the American army air forces 160; Twenty-Third Pursuit Group 168; use in Burma 188–189; war record of 161
AMMISCA *see* American Military Mission to China (AMMISCA)
Arcadia Conference 28–30
Army, U. S. 26–30
Arnold, Lieutentant General H. H. 30, ***111***, 162
Arnstein, Daniel G. 93, 129; Burma Road report and recommendations 89–95
attitudes toward Army, 1941 27
Ausland, Majolr John 106–107, 136–137, 138–139
Austin, Warren 208
Australian troops not sent to Burma 86, 87
AVG *see* American Volunteer Group (Flying Tigers)

Baker, John E. 92–93
Balfour, Dr. M. C. 136
Barrett, Major David D. 127
Baw Ma 84
Beijing, China *see* Peking, China
Bissell, Colonel Slayton L. 168, 172
Boatner, Major Hayden 134
Borodin, Michael 70
Bowley, A. J. 20
Boxer Protocol 65
Boxer Rebellion 64–65

249

Brady, Austin C. 104–105
Brereton, Major General Lewis H. 150
Brett, Major General George 110–112, 189, 190–191, 194
Britain *see* Great Britain
Burma: British in 75–76, 84–85; and British trade with China 75; complaints about customs procedures 104–105; early European explorers 74–75; evacuation of Rangoon 121; formation of British Burma 75; gasoline pipeline 143–145; geography 76; Government of Burma (India) Act of 1935 (1937) 76; Japanese ambitions in 83–84; Japanese invasion of 120–121; opposition to British rule 84; people not tied to India 76; pre–World War II history 83–85; primary overland trade route 76; railroad 77; Thakins 84; "Thirty Comrades" 84; transit tax 104–105; union with British India 75–76; water routes 76, 79–80; *see also* Rangoon, Burma
Burma Independence Army 84
Burma Road: alternate routes of supply 145–150; American civilians employed on 128–131; Arnstein report on 89–95; British assessment of problems on 81; Chinese fear of "foreign" control of 93–94; Chinese laborers forced to repair bomb damage **66**; condition of 80–81; connecting routes **22**; control by Yu Fei-peng 93; corruption at Chungkind and 82–83; early reports on 88–89; governmental agencies operating over 89–90; negative aspects of current operations 90–92; market day in Chefang, China **80**; opening 88; opening of Chinese portion 79–81; politics and 92–93; prior to arrival of AMMISCA 127–128; repair by Chinese laborers **54**; repair shop proposals 97–99; untrained Chinese truck drivers and **61**; vehicle service facilities proposal 96–97; view of switchbacks **29**; village street along **72**
Burma Road Commission 92–93

Central Aircraft Manufacturing Corporation (CAMCO) 159
Chamberlin, Neville 41–42
Chen, R. C. 114
Cheng Ho 57–58
Chennault, Lieutenant General Claire Lee 101–102, 158–160, 163–164, 167–172
Chiang, Madam (Soong May-ling) 45–46
Chiang Kai-shek 13–14, 17, 33, 38, 44–51; anti-communist position shown 71; appointed commander of KMT Army 71; assessment of Chinese air force 161–162; bemoans lack of "allied cooperation" 189; campaign against Chinese CCP stronghold 72–73; complaints about Lend-Lease supplies 198–199; creating an illusion that things were worse than they were 183; death of Sun Yat-sen and 71; discussion of seizure of *Tulsa* cargo 193–194; hard to like 213; induction of the AVG into American army air force and 163–165; inflated assessment of Magruder's influence 183; kidnapping of 73; knowledge of British reluctance to aid the Chinese 34; looking ahead to after the war 206; Northern Expedition 71; outlook after Pearl Harbor 188–189; possible ploy to get more arms 182; push for Allied planning council in Chungking 190; relationship with Stilwell 200; request for help against attack on Kunming 182; requests membership on the Combined Chiefs of Staff (CCS) 153–154; Russian visit 70; threat to seek separate peace with Japan 155; Three Demands 198
China: alternate routes of supply 145–150; air supply system 150–155; American sympathizers 16; AMMISCA mission acknowledgement 19–20; anti-foreign fervor 68; attitudes toward Japan 25; back channel lobbying 48–49; Boxer Rebellion. 64–65; Churchill's view of 42–43, 44; commerce 56–59; contact with Roosevelt 38; control of spare parts depots 129; detail for Chinese aid proposed 18; extra-territorial rights surrender 14; gaining seat on Combined Chiefs of Staff 193; gasoline pipeline 143–145; goals did not match America's 213; importation of goods 60–61; Japanese military successes 49–50; laborers sent to dig trenches for Allies 68; land supply routes from Russia and Iran 156–157; Lend-Lease and 13–14, 33; loans 48–49; loss of seacoast ports 79–80; Magruder's history and 20–21; Magruder's opinion of Chinese army 21; Manchu dynasty, end of 65–67; Marco Polo Bridge incident 49; military and economic weaknesses 49; minor player under Lend-Lease 33; missionaries in 59–60; move of capital to Chungking 49; national currency 46; need to avoid war with Japan 184–185; Northern Expedition 49; opium addiction in 60; ports severed 100; post-Pearl Harbor allied policy formulation at Chungking 188–194; potential to help defeat Japan 208; promises made to 212; reforms under Chiang 49; Sino-American relations strained 153–155; starvation in **114**; student protests and intellectual ferment 68–69; supply lines to 84–85; support for Yunnan-Burma railroad 132–133; suspicions regarding British motives 189; trade through Burma, history 74–77; war responsibilities 30; warlords 49, 70
China-Burma-India Theater 43–44, 214; allied cooperation failed to evolve 189; creation of China theater 201–202; military leaders in **111**; no planning prior to Pearl Harbor 201
China-Burma Transportation Administration proposal 96–97
China Defense Supplies (CDS) 14–15, 17–18, 33; Corcoran, David M., and 15; lack of military advisor 15

Index

Chinese air force 17, 19, 161
Chinese communists 71, 78
Chinese culture: attempts to change the status quo, late 19th century 63–64; belief in superiority of 57–58; Confucianism 53–56; history and traditions 52–53; rapid rise of scientific thinking in the West 53; stoppage of contact with outside world 58
Chongqing, China *see* Chungking, China
Chungking, China 15, 18, 49, *91*
Churchill, Winston 30, 32, 40, 41–44
Claggett, Brigadier General H. B. 162
Clark, Major Edwin N. 18
Combined Joint Chiefs of Staff (CCS) 30, 192–193
Combined Munitions Assignment Board (MAB) 30, 32
commanders: Chiang Kai-shek 44–51; Churchill, Winston 41–44; Marshall, General George C. 38–41; overview 35–36; Roosevelt, Franklin D. 36–38
commerce, China's traditional view 56–59
Communists, Chinese 50
Confucianism 53–56
Corcoran, David M. 15
Corcoran, Thomas (Tommy, "The Cork") 15, 33
corruption at Chungking 82–83
Craw, H. H. 94–95
Currie, Lauchlin 15–16, 33, 93, 102, 159, 164–165, 171, 198; support for China 16–17

Davies, John Paton 16, 199; opinion of Magruder 23
Dennys, L. E. 19, 189, 190–192
Diconti, Nicola 74
Dill, Field Marshall Sir John *111*
diplomacy and Lend-Lease 32
Dorman-Smith, Colonel Sir Reginald 84, 87, 107, 109, 110–111, 142–143
draft, first peacetime 28
Drum, Lieutenant General Hugh A. 20, 202
Dutch East Indies 79

"Europe First" policy 14
extraterritoriality 62

Fairbank, John K. 14–15, 207
flying in drums of gasoline *148*
flying the hump *see* India-China Air Supply System
Flying Tigers *see* American Volunteer Group (Flying Tigers)
14th Air Force Headquarters, Kunming, China *101*
French Indochina 78–79

gasoline 143–145, *148*
Gauss, Clarence E. 93, 207–208, 215
General Motors in Rangoon 128–129
Gerow, Brigadier General L. T. 20, 147, 187

Gluckman, Colonel Arcadi 24
Great Britain 44; actions in Burma, prewar 19; agreement with Japan to stop supplies to China via Burma Road 85; command structure in 42; efforts to expand trade 61–63; exclusion of Burmese from military service 86; future confiscations 107; high-handedness at Rangoon 193; impounded goods at Rangoon 112–118; intransigence 192; need for imperial troops in Burma 87; obstructionism on the part of officials in Burma 105–108; opium exports 60; opposition to using rails from Mandalay-Myitkyina railroad 136–137; refused offered Chinese troops 192; reluctance to aid Chinese 34; Sino-British enmity 189, 192; skepticism about China's willingness to support war effort 188–189; trade status in 1842 62; trade with China through Burma 75–76; *Tulsa* incident 108–121

Haas, Dr. Lt. Colonel Viictor H. 135–136
Hall, Allen 144
Hamilton, Maxwell 206, 207
Hitler, Adolf 41
Ho Ying-ch'in, General 191–192, 202
Hong system 60–61
Hopkins, Harry 16, 36–37
Hornbeck, Stanley K. 13–14, 49, 207
Hull, Cordell 32, 186–187
"the hump" *see* India-China Air Supply System
Hung Hsiu-ch'uan 62–63

India-China Air Supply System: British control of Tenth Air Force 154; broken supply promises to China 155; Chinese National Aviation Corporation 155; flying the hump 150–151; Indian air fields and 154; personnel for 152–153; planes for 151–152, 154–156
Irrawaddy River, commercial traffic on 100
isolationism, U.S. 26–30

Japan 27, 49–50; British agreement to stop supplies to China via Burma 85; Chinese attitudes toward 25; confused by Roosevelt 37–38; creation of Manchukuo 78; expansion into Manchuria 21–22, 71–72; invasion of Dutch East Indies 79; invasion of French Indochina 78–79; invasion of Shanghai 78; Kwantung army moved into Manchuria 77; military incidents in China 78; Pearl Harbor plans 79; pre–World War II Burma and 83–85; rise of militarists in 71; sinking of ships on Irrawaddy River 100; *see also* Sino-Japanese war
Joint Chiefs of Staff (JCS) 30

K'ang Yu-Wei 63–64
Keating, John C. 106
Kerr, Sir Archibald Clark 184
Kung, H. H. 46–*47*
Kuomintang (KMT) 45, 70–71

Ladin, C. F. 128, 130
Lattimore, Owen 16, 183–184, 186
Lend-Lease 30–34; approval and China detail 18–19; China and 15, 16–17, 95, 199–200; Chinese air force and 19; distribution of goods 13–14, 32; diversion of goods from Rangoon to Calcutta 122; diversion of some materials to British 189; evacuation of goods from Rangoon 121–126; ownership of goods 112–113; seen by Burmese as additional source of revenue 129; shipment of unneeded goods under 107; shortage of munitions and 28; supplies urgently needed by British troops in Rangoon 190–191; transfer of goods to British 112–113; under control of Stilwell 196; unlimited goods and services 33–34; War Department and 18
Lend-Lease Act 28

MacMorland, Lieutenant Colonel (later Major General) F. E. 18, 24, 130–131; opinion of Magruder 23
Magruder, Brigadier General John M. 4, 14, 20–24, 96–97, 203–204; accusations of engaging in diplomacy 186; assessment of Chinese army 195–196, 205, 208; belief that China should not control depots 130; belief that Chinese were inefficient 160; belief in need for limits on Lend-Lease goods 108; castigated by State Department officials 206–207; CIA and 215; civilian employees and 128–131; diminishing role of 165–166; explores alternate routes of supplying China 145–150; fall from grace 184–185; forced to act as an arbiter 209; given no latitude 187; health problems forced departure 210; ignored situation reports 209; Joint Military Council and 193; management system of Burma Road 94; Office of Strategic Services (OSS) 215; opinion of Chinese army 21, 205; possible manipulation by Chiang 187; pressure on 186; recommended supply base in India 131; reduction in credibility 181–182; reports regarded as accurate 195; after Stilwell 204–205; strain of AMMISCA commmand 209; *Tulsa* incident and 113–121; views on Chinese leadership 21–22
Manchukuo, creation of 78
Mao Pang-tzo, Major General 159
Mao Tse-tung 72–73
Margary, William 75
Marshall, General George C. 29–30, 32, 38–41; dislike of Chennault 204; view of Chinese requests under Lend-Lease 34
Marco Polo 74
May 4th Movement 67–69
Mayer, Lieutenant Colonel William 19
McHugh, Major J. W. 19
Mendlesohn, Dr. 24
"Merchants of Death" 27
Merrill, Major Frank D. 115–116

Miles, Brigadier General Sherman 20
Ming dynasty 57–58
missionaries in China 59–60
Morgenthau, Henry, Jr. 133–134
munitions, shortage of 28
Myanmar *see* Burma
Myers, D. F. 88

Nanking, China 49, 73
National Guard and Reserve units, 1940–1941 27
Neutrality Acts 27
New Life Movement 49
Northern Expedition 71

opium 60, 136
opium wars 62
opposition to Lend-Lease 31–32
Oxbury, H. F. 106–107

Pearl Harbor attack 28; America's China policy and 163–164; Irrawaddy River traffic and 100
Peking, China 20, 45, 49, 59, 65, 66, 68, 69, 71, 75
pipeline for gasoline 143–145

Rajchman, Ludwig 46–47
Rangoon, Burma 17, 73; AMMISCA problems in 125–126; British warnings of future confiscations 107; build up of supplies in 89, 105; "dead cargo" 105, 107; distribution of goods in disarray 120; evacuation of 121–126, 130; final hours before fall of 124–125; General Motors plant in 126; limits on transportation from 77; obstruction by British officials 106–107; *Tulsa* incident 108–121; *see also* Burma
Rape of Nanking 73
rats prepared as food **91**
Republican era in China 70
Reybold, Brigadier General Eugene 17
Roosevelt, President Franklin D. 36–38; aid allocation and 31; Churchill, Winston, and 42–43; Currie, Lauchlin, and 15–16; "Europe First" policy 14; presidential powers under Lend-Lease 33–34; strongly-worded messages to Chiang 197–199
Rowland, Sir John 138
Russell, Major John 105, 149–150; Chinese incompetence 107–108
Russia: communists and China 70–71; Lend-Lease aid for 14; visit by Chiang Kai-shek 45

St. John, Lieutenant Colonel Adrian 118, 130
Saw, U 84
Seabrave, Sterling 83
Shall, Adam 59
Shanghai, Japanese invasion of 78
Sheahan, M. E. 88–89
Shih, Hu **48**
Sino-American relations, and Magruder 214–215

Sino-Japanese war 13–14, 49–50, 73, 77–79
Sliney, Lieutenant Colonel 25
Somervell, Lieutenant General Brehon *111*
Soong, May-ling *see* Chiang, Madam (Soong May-ling)
Soong, T. L. 83
Soong, T. V. 13, 33, 46–*48*, 83, 146–147, 193
South-West Transportation Company 82–83; inability to move goods north from Rangoon 105, 106
spare parts depots, control of 129
Stark, Admiral Harold 30, 184
Stilwell, General Joseph 16, 20, *111*, 169–170, 196–197, 202–203, 212–213; recall of 213; relationship with Chiang 200
Storrs, J. K. 82–83
Stowe, Leland 108
Sun Yat-sen 45, 67, 70
Sung dynasty, and tribute system 57
Suzuki, Colonal Keiji 84

Taiping Revellion 62–63
Tojo Hideki (General) 49, 79
tribute system 56–59
Tseng Yang-fu 138–139
Ts's-hsi, Empress 65
Tulsa incident 108–121
Twenty-One Demands by Japan 68
Twitty, Lieutenant Colonel Joseph J. 109–112, 119–120

Unequal Treaties 62
Union of Soviet Socialist Republics *see* Russia
United Kingdom *see* Great Britain
United States: AMMISCA mission acknowledged 19–20; attitudes toward Europe after World War I 26–27; British frustration with American dominance of command 44; Chinese exclusion laws, repeal of 14; extra-territorial rights surrender 14; isolationism in 26–30; military unpreparedness circa 1940 26–30; popular opinions about China and Chinese people 133; reaction to Japanese invasion of Manchuria 77, 78
Universal Trading Corporation (UTC) 33

Wang, Chenting T. *47*
War Department: China Defense Supplies (CDS) and 15, 17–18; confusion in 98–99; decisions regarding Magruder and AMMISCA 185; pre-war plans 37; refusal to send army air force personnel to China 162; War Plans and Supply Divisions 30
warlord era (1916–1928) 69
Wavel, Field Marshall Sir Archibald *111*, 190–192
weapons allocation system, need for 28–29
Wells, Sumner 206
Wetzel, Major Nevin: opinion of Magruder 23
Wilson, Captain James 93, 94, 96–97, 129
Wilson, Woodrow 27
Winant, John G. 105
World War I 26–27
World War II: commanders 35–51; responsibilities among Allied nations 30

Yangon, Myanmar *see* Rangoon, Burma
Young, Arthur 7–8, 93
Yu Fei-peng 92–93, 95, 111–112
Yuan Shih-kai 66–67
Yunnan-Burma railroad: British effort to complete vital bridge 138; British opposition to using rails from Mandalay-Myitkyina railroad 136–137; construction problems 135; cost estimates 134; dissent among the leadership 139–143; growing need for 132–133; health of workers 135–136; leadership group 138–139; Lend-Lease and 133; route 134–135; war priorities and 137–138
Yunnan-to-Indochina railway, severing of 100

www.ingramcontent.com/pod-product-compliance
Ingram Content Group UK Ltd.
Pitfield, Milton Keynes, MK11 3LW, UK
UKHW041935140426
5217IPUK00014B/489